Cultural Education and History Writing

Cultural Education and History Writing

Sundry writings and occasional lectures

CALVIN G. SEERVELD

Edited by
John H. Kok

DORDT COLLEGE PRESS

Cover design by Willem Hart
Layout by Carla Goslinga

Dordt College Press   www.dordt.edu/dordt_press
498 Fourth Avenue NE
Sioux Center, Iowa, 51250
United States of America

ISBN: 978-1-940567-04-4

Printed in the United States of America

The Library of Congress Cataloguing-in-Publication Data is on file with the Library of Congress, Washington D.C.

Library of Congress Control Number: 2014934616

Cover. This beautifully embossed, heavy piece of bronze from Niger (eight pounds) is put around a young girl's ankle so that when she matures as a woman and marries, the unremovable cursed shackle makes it hard to stray from the husband's hearth. A child's schooling and a mature person's particular grasp of historical change can often act as such a dead weight on one's consciousness.

TABLE OF CONTENTS

Abbreviations used throughout this volume:

NA   Calvin G. Seerveld, *Normative Aesthetics: Sundry writings and occasional lectures*, edited by John H. Kok. Sioux Center, IA: Dordt College Press, 2014.

RA   Calvin G. Seerveld, *Redemptive Art in Society: Sundry writings and occasional lectures*, edited by John H. Kok. Sioux Center, IA: Dordt College Press, 2014.

CP   Calvin G. Seerveld, *Cultural Problems in Western Society: Sundry writings and occasional lectures*, edited by John H. Kok. Sioux Center, IA: Dordt College Press, 2014.

AH   Calvin G. Seerveld, *Art History Revisited: Sundry writings and occasional lectures*, edited by John H. Kok. Sioux Center, IA: Dordt College Press, 2014.

BSt   Calvin G. Seerveld, *Biblical Studies and Wisdom for Living: Sundry writings and occasional lectures*, edited by John H. Kok. Sioux Center, IA: Dordt College Press, 2014.

INTRODUCTION TO PART ONE

Bringing Scholarly Imaginativity to Life:
Walking wisely, with nuance

Doug Blomberg

As an undergraduate in the early '70s, I walked into the University of Sydney Bookstore to be surprised by a placard heralding a display of "Books for Thinking Christians." This collection was strange (and, one might say, strangely titled, given its implication that there are "non-thinking" or even "unthinking" Christians on a university campus). "Strange," first, in that the place in which it was housed was one of the earliest universities in the British Empire to be consciously constituted as secular; but it would have been strange also if it had been featured in one of the Christian bookstores I frequented, for it was not the usual array of theology, apologetics, Bible commentaries, church history, evangelical hagiographies, devotionals, and spiritual self-help manuals. No, these were books that addressed directly the world of the mainstream academy, and thus spoke to the concerns I had begun to have as a relatively new Christian about bringing faith to bear on my studies. And among those that caught my eye was Seerveld's *A Christian Critique of Art and Literature*. An erstwhile English major, I naturally purchased a copy, along with several others that introduced me to the "strange" yet wondrous world of reformational scholarship.

Seerveld's book was published in 1964, and the earliest of the articles in this section is from the following year; most, however, were written in the last decade or so, some in just the last few years. This span of time goes some way toward exemplifying the extent of Calvin Seerveld's contribution, but one would also have to consider his geographical reach and the diversity of his audiences, both of which are also reflected herein.

Imagination

It was that book of Seerveld's—as linguistically challenging as it was in places—that provided one of the launching pads for the research I was to pursue as a graduate student in Education. (And indeed, that I was on this path and not in theological college was because of the reformational vision of Christ's unbounded Lordship.) A problem with which Seerveld wrestled in that early work was how "imagination" might find a place in Dooyeweerd's bipartite schema of naïve experience and theoretical thought (with intuition undergirding both). He suggested that "Just as theoretical analysis evinces a peculiar node in human consciousness, so does imaginative symbolizing" (*CCAL* 71). Thus is was that my dissertation explored the hypothesis that not just these two, but each of the normative aspects could provide the *subjective* focus for knowing, and not function merely as the site of ontic (and thus, epistemic) diversity on the *objective* side.

"Imagination" gave way over time to the more active notion of "imaginativity" (another of Seerveld's hallmark neologisms), which he argues is of "fundamental importance . . . to schooling." This echoes the title of a chapter in the book I used as the text in a seminar for teachers—*Rainbows for the Fallen World*. Cal was very surprised on his extended speaking tour to Australia in 1987 that there would be such a seminar, and to be invited to lead the class. I know that there are those who, many years later, remember this (and Cal's other contributions) as a significant influence on their vision for Christian schooling—and indeed, the Christian life.

It will not surprise that I see "imaginativity" as a major thread in the present section. It is my privilege to engage with these articles as they touch on some of my fundamental concerns as an educationalist, in gratitude for the insights God has gifted us in the Seerveld treasury.

Worldview as World-and-Life Vision

In 2004, in an address to the "After Worldview" conference at Cornerstone University, Seerveld was willing to stand by a paraphrased version of the notion of worldview he had first formulated in 1960 or thereabouts:

> a worldview is a conscious, quasi-synoptic world-and-life vision of everything all together, which is imaginative and literarily suggestive in quality rather than theoretically precise, which structures and can guide one's concrete experience in God's ordered cosmos. (106)

A better known definition is that of Al Wolters in *Creation Regained*: a worldview is "the comprehensive framework of one's basic beliefs about things."[1] Yes, for Seerveld a worldview is "quasi-synoptic," but it is not this because it is a "framework of . . . beliefs" (perhaps too easily redolent of a conceptual "system"); for this reason, it is better to think of a "world-and-life *vision*," which is an "imaginative fabric" (113). It is thus not something one sets out to justify through argumentation as the most rational way of understanding the world. Already in this early definition,

---

1 Albert M. Wolters, *Creation Regained: A Transforming View of the World* (1986), 2.

Seerveld prefigures his later contention that allusivity (suggestiveness, nuancefulness, ludicity) is the identifying feature of the aesthetic mode (19, 188). More than this, he is proposing that our everyday experience, at least in part, is structured imaginatively.

But there is an immediate and initially puzzling qualification: *"not everybody has a world-and-life vision."* What in this case structures and potentially guides a person's experience? This is something even less intellectual than even Seerveld's relatively non-conceptual definition. It is "a 'way of life,' a subconscious habit of activity that is not a studied reflective view" but that is "inescapably basic, the primary outworking of one's entrusting faith orientation in God's world. . ." (107). It is only when this "reaches sustained consciousness," when the pattern of a life "gets expressed, articulated with connections and ramifications, [that] you have the network ... of a *Weltanschauung*, a world-and-life vision" (108). This sounds suspiciously like the definition of worldview that Seerveld appeared to be countering. It is perhaps not quite the philosophical conception of an examined life, but it is certainly akin to it. How are we to understand this apparent contradiction?

The examples Seerveld gives of bringing the subconscious to explicitness are highly instructive: the epics of Homer, John Bunyan's *Pilgrim's Progress*, Gustav Mahler's *Die Kindertotenlieder*. These are literary and musical artifacts birthed in imaginativity, not logically formulated treatises. A world-and-life vision is an "imaginative narrative," invigorated by *"the pulse of life"*; "worldview" has connotations that are too formulaic for Seerveld (108).

Scripture and Scholarship
Anyone who has read Seerveld will know how pervasively his intimacy with Scripture is displayed and how unapologetically his writings epitomize biblically-directed reflection. Many will also have been inspired by his evocative translations, an extended example of which we have in this section's "Song of Moses." The guidance Scripture gives is grasped intuitively, he says, inviting imaginative responses, and Seerveld exemplifies rhetorical imaginativity to overflowing. He is convinced that solid biblical study provides the "rootage to a christian philosophy" (45), not in the manner of a textbook or a compendium of theoretical theses that may be cut and pasted into a scientific manual, but as the "historical, literary, proclamational" voice of God (7). We should not read Scripture in a quest for "logical certainty," but anticipating that we will be nurtured in a spirit of supple trust (16). The Bible guides us only as we shine it into the darkness on the path ahead, the path too revealing the purposes of God as we study its contours. God revels in "creatural diversity" (133, 142) and every aspect deserves our imaginative investigation.

We may say that Scripture itself is a divinely inspired "imaginative narrative," in which "the pulse of life" of God's people gets "articulated," not merely encapsulated in statements, but expressed in a way that witnesses to how the whole of life holds together organically ("articulates") in Christ. This is neither fantasy nor emotional effluence, for "imaginative knowing" births "real objects getting seriously at real matters."[2] Seerveld helped me learn that Scripture is not "propositional revelation," but an expansive and authoritative horizon that opens one to a vision of creation touched throughout by the song of the gospel.

Dialogue

Though the significance of worldviews is now widely recognized, "worldview analysis" may too readily be employed to categorize, in order not to understand but to dismiss. If world-and-life visions are indeed "imaginative fabrics" however, the way may be opened for respectful dialogue and cooperation between those with different visions. And not only among Christians. We ought not to regard opposing, partially mistaken visions as "mortal enemies"; we should instead recognize that they are neighbors from which we and we can learn (112f.). It is thus that I take Seerveld to be upholding a crucial distinctive (though not exclusively so) of reformational scholarship: respect the fact that all people are made in God's image, upheld by God's grace, who will gain insights into aspects of creation with which they seriously engage, concretely as well as theoretically. In seeking to learn from our neighbors, communication may be better served by "winsome **imaginative** thinking" than argumentation through "the opposition of analytically certified beliefs"; Seerveld sets a beatitudinal standard in "the peace of what is true" (185). This, I believe, honors a very important pedagogical principle: students should be nurtured to listen humbly to the many voices of God's diverse image-bearers, in that suspension of (dis)belief that imaginativity requires, and that repudiation of absolute certainty unavailable to us "clay jars" (192).

Pedagogy

The critiques that Nicholas Wolterstorff, James K. A. Smith, and others have leveled against the predominance of "worldview" talk in Christian college and school circles are in important respects foreshadowed in Seerveld's early definition of "world-and-life vision."[3] But the differences in emphasis may also be instructive. Where Wolterstorff endorses active engagement and praxis-oriented scholarship and Smith emphasizes the significance of liturgical practices for the purpose of educating desire, Seerveld's focus is on what cognitive psychologist Jerome Bruner termed

---

2   Calvin Seerveld, *A Christian Critique of Art and Literature* (1968), 72.

3   See e.g., Nicholas Wolterstorff, "Teaching for Justice: On Shaping How Students Are Disposed To Act" (2004), "Teaching Justly for Justice" (2006); James. K. A. Smith, *Desiring the Kingdom* (2009).

the "narrative" (in contrast to the "paradigmatic") mode of thought.[4] Thus, as I have noted, he identifies one of the core tasks of schooling as education of the capacity for imagining (66).

There are resonances in Seerveld's formulation of "good pedagogy" (comprising "the steps of surprise, precision, formulation, and experiment") with Alfred North Whitehead's "rhythm of education" as romance, precision, and generalization. For Whitehead as for Seerveld, the aesthetic dimension is integral. Yet it is instructive that the final step for Seerveld is experimentation, the quite difficult task of encouraging students to "enter into the thought empathetically and critically" (179). In this way, despite Seerveld's qualms (of which, below), his pedagogy is also praxis-oriented and an education of the desires; "the disciplined forming of one's consciousness enabling one to make distinctions" is coupled with the capacity "to perform new actions within a certain perspective" (90).

Empathy is important in moving one to act in solidarity with one's neighbor, no matter how different that neighbor might be, and empathy is nurtured in encounter. Seerveld recounts inviting visitors to his college classroom to speak from their varying perspectives as atheists, Thomists, and Marxists; there were presumably others. These people shared their stories, but it is not always possible to meet face to face. However, "imaginative narrative" may evoke what Martha Nussbaum terms "narrative imagination," an important avenue into dialogue. Fictional accounts are obviously not theoretical treatises, even though there is a commonplace identification of books and reading with "theory" over against "practice." No, books (and other media) are part and parcel of concrete experience, ingredients of our daily lives. "Good books are congealed concentrations of human gut life"; they confront us "with **actual** temptations and the necessity to make choices in one's consciousness **now**; nodes of wisdom that are as **immediate** a reality as when you have to slam on the brakes in your moving car" (68).

History

Seerveld sees a central role in education for "understanding and developing history" (89), and rightly so, if we think of "history" not as rote rehearsal of what has transpired but as past and present events in their complex interrelation. Education is inevitably an induction into our cultural heritage, though we should conceive this ecumenically, in the spirit of loving our neighbors and their "mistaken visions" wherever and whenever they may be. But we are initiators as much as we are inductees. We are culture-makers, shapers of history.

In 1965, Seerveld expressed his concern that "modern secular education has come to value . . . exploration and problem-solving rather

---

4 Jerome S. Bruner. *Actual Minds, Possible Worlds.* (1986); *Acts of Meaning* (1990).

than retrospection. . . ." This is a "rootless education" that contributes to the "evil dehumanizing of the society. . ." (89). Some 36 years later, he challenges the promotion by Wolterstorff and Harry Fernhout of "more praxis-oriented scholarship" in Christian education.[5] He is critical of advocacy of "'the primacy of experiential knowing-in-relation' . . . rather than [of stressing] the abiding central role of **books** for christian [sic] learning by maturing students." (22).

Academic learning ought rightly be "one step removed from the streets" (22), I agree—schools are instituted as safe spaces for learning—but this does not require (and I will suggest that Seerveld fundamentally agrees) an acceptance that universal schooling be *exclusively* academic ("bookish"?). I have more than once quoted Ray Elliott to the effect that schools too often lead us to become lovers of Literary Criticism rather than literature, of the subject History rather than the historical events it seeks to interpret.[6] Seerveld's emphasis on *books* should not lead to the conclusion that he is an advocate of secondhand learning—far from it. In every subject area, he recommends working mostly with primary sources. "If one studies secondary sources all the time, your education is liable to become third-rate."[7] The "history" Seerveld has in view as the subject-matter of schooling is "actual history: the wondrous spectacle of *magnalia Dei* and the blessed unfolding of creations to their full, God-created special ordering" (89).

> History is the shining gossamer of God in which we live, move, and have our meaning. Misunderstood or disbelieved, it becomes a cobweb for death. Education that holds a false idea of history or slights this undeniable, concrete matrix of the redeeming creator God's ruling human and subhuman affairs leaves those so trained lost in a maze of abstractions. (90)

Seerveld emphasizes history—concrete experience from creation to consummation (and who is to say that history would end then?)—over against a scientist spirit that would honor theoretical insight "as a source of knowledge not relativized by history" (91). He gives continued attention to the role of history and historiography in Christian higher education, as a companion foundational discipline to systematic philosophy that "makes philosophical meaning concrete, as it were, corporeal" (47). This is part and parcel of "tak[ing] **creation** seriously as God's revelation" (20), another important touchstone of reformational scholarship.

---

5   It behooves me to acknowledge that Fernhout, in the paper cited, draws explicitly and extensively on my work.

6   R. K. Elliott. "Education, love of one's subject, and the love of truth" (1974).

7   Calvin Seerveld, "The Fundamental Importance of Imaginativity within Schooling," in *Rainbows for the Fallen World* (1980), 149.

Praxis?

It therefore seems to me that Seerveld's emphasis on history, concrete experience past and present, has an implicit intent similar to the proposals of Fernhout and the later Wolterstorff. He constantly avers that theoretical investigation must be subject to the test of ordinary experience. The latter is holistic and multi-dimensional; the former is abstractive and methodologically reductive. Yes, "**studious** thinking, imagining, speaking, writing, reading, and learning skills is **doing** something" (21), but knowing is transformed into wisdom when it is "the Spirit-filled, disciplined ability to judge what God wants done, what it is right to do, what is just (*dikaios*)" (51).

Thus, despite Seerveld's confidence that schools at all levels should be places for studied communal reflection, for addressing "virtual" rather than actual problems, one cannot but be struck by his recurring reference to John Calvin's conviction that the highest calling for a Christian is the law, for then one could become a magistrate, serving the whole community through the dispensation of justice (e.g., 49, 145). For Seerveld, this Calvinian mandate opens a broad vista: "All of life is to be faith in operation" (187), judging "what God wants done"—and, one assumes, doing it! I believe he would concur that the wisdom of artistry is nurtured best in the practice of painting, and the wise dispensation of justice through the experience of judging justly. For this is what it is both to learn from and to shape history, to act historically and not only theoretically, not only to know but to be wise.

It is because the disciplines are formed not by disembodied minds but by multi-dimensional "clay jars" acting in concrete contexts that it is vital to learn that each has a history; "the norms posited for" any discipline change with time (46). This would disabuse us of the pretension that theorizing identifies what is true at all times and in all places (and thus, in no *particular* time or place). Delving into history and the literature we have inherited gives us slices of life as it was or could have been, but *imaginatively* here and now. I think I have learned this in part from Seerveld, and my advocacy of a pedagogy of "play" (as immersion in concrete, including historical, experience) certainly owes much to his emphasis on the way in which imaginativity is woven into the fabric of daily life.

To enter into history requires imagination, which Seerveld regards not as a product of the genius invested on the incorrigibly eccentric, but as a creational given for all God's image-bearers. Imaginativity is full-bodiedly historical; as such, it is most often nurtured by perspiration. One needs "the grace to sift through countless dusty, unused books and print archives in the Bibliothèque Nationale in Paris to get the key to unlock the meaning of Watteau's subtle artwork" (an allusion to Seerveld's own, ultimately award-winning, labors) (20). Seerveld sees his calling in "theoretical aesthetics" as trying "to honor **aesthetic life** as an imaginative moment integral to our whole corporeal human existence" (19). My understanding is that honoring this educationally requires an orientation to *praxis*, our "whole corporeal" life in the world. What Seerveld helps us to affirm is that this is not only through immediate experience but also through the concrete contexts of history, literature, foreign languages, and other cultures.

Wisdom

The contingency of experience—its very historicity—perturbed many of the ancient Greek philosophers (and not a few who were their heirs). Like all of us religious beings, they were bound to commit to a source of order and meaning, and many found this in an eternal, unchanging *logos* accessed by the highest functions of reason. But it takes wisdom to know how to act here and now in accordance with God's purposes, "because the times are always changing" (51). Lawful generalities must be respected, but as they come to expression in concrete particularities. And it is here, Seerveld contends, that artistry has a significant role to play. It directs attention to that which is out of the ordinary and helps us to look anew at what we had taken for granted (53).

Seerveld is by no means alone in thinking that wisdom cannot be taught, but that it can be caught (22n). It is not a repository of information ("knowledge," in the narrow sense), but an orientation, an attitude, itself a *habitus*. It is openness to the new, and the new cannot be merely extrapolated from what has passed. Wisdom is a gift from God, but we may wait upon—and even wrestle with—God, to discover his purposes (50–51). It is not human making of meaning *ex nihilo*, but an uncovering of meaning that is responsive to its disclosure by the Lord. Wisdom also requires imaginativity (which Seerveld is loath to call "creativity"). As the *Book of Job* so starkly portrays, a fossilized tradition rests in the certainty of acquired knowledge and thus shuts down the possibility of dealing with present experience with integrity, and thereby doing "compassionate justice to the reality [we] study or administer" (44). We must find a way forward that is meet and right for a specific situation.

Conclusion

Seerveld's own career trajectory, while being doggedly scholarly, has been among the most praxically-oriented of reformational scholars. His reflections on art and the aesthetic have been willingly communicated to and enthusiastically received by artists worldwide (in Australia, a group of painters and poets he inspired met regularly as "ART – Artists for Reformational Thinking"). These insights were themselves nurtured in community with artists in Toronto's Patmos Gallery and elsewhere, and in the context of other grassroots activist organizations, such as the Christian

Labour Association of Canada. Seerveld has been and continues to be a prolific speaker and committed public intellectual, addressing college and university faculty and students, certainly, but also teachers, artists, musicians (e.g., at the Greenbelt Festival), and pastors. His devotional writings (often first presented in a chapel setting), the product certainly of multilingual erudition, are widely and enthusiastically received, and give full rein to his personal imaginativity, as indeed do his linguistically inventive and meticulously polished orations.

I trust, whatever your background, you will find much that delights, informs, and challenges you in these "strange yet wondrous" offerings.

Bibliography

Bruner, Jerome S. *Actual Minds, Possible Worlds* (Cambridge: Harvard University Press, 1986).

————. *Acts of Meaning.* (Cambridge: Harvard University Press, 1990).

Elliott, R. K. "Education, love of one's subject, and the love of truth," *Proceedings of the Philosophy of Education Society of Great Britain* 8:1 (1974): 135–53.

Seerveld, Calvin. *A Christian Critique of Art and Literature* (Toronto: Association for Reformed Scientific Studies, 1964).

————. *Rainbows for the Fallen World: Aesthetic life and artistic task* (Toronto: Toronto Tuppence Press, 1980).

————. "The Fundamental Importance of Imaginativity within Schooling," in *Rainbows for the Fallen World* (1980), 138–155.

Smith, James K. A. *Desiring the Kingdom: Worship, worldview, and cultural formation. Cultural Liturgies* (Grand Rapids: Baker, 2009).

Wolters, Albert M. *Creation Regained: A Transforming View of the World* (Leicester: Inter-Varsity Press, 1986).

Wolterstorff, Nicholas. "Teaching for Justice: On shaping how students are disposed to act," in *Educating for Shalom: Essays on Christian higher education*, edited by Clarence W. Joldersma and Gloria Goris Stronks (Grand Rapids: Eerdmans, 2004), 135–54.

————. "Teaching Justly for Justice." *Journal of Education and Christian Belief* 10:2 (2006): 23–37.

Doug Blomberg
Academic Dean
Professor of Philosophy of Education
Institute for Christian Studies, Toronto

Introduction to Part Two

Culture Making, History Keeping, and the Teaching of Philosophy

Gideon Strauss

"The best ontology is a convicting, worked out cosmology and a wise, articulate cultural theory." Calvin Seerveld, "Footprints in the snow" (274)

It has been my great privilege to have witnessed, over the past twenty-odd years, a revival of evangelical Christian seriousness about living an integral life.

As of this writing I have just enjoyed a weekend at the second Gospel and Culture Conference in Manhattan, hosted by the Center for Faith and Work of Redeemer Presbyterian Church, mere days after a catastrophic storm devastated New York City. With hundreds of New Yorkers and many from outside the city, I listened to city officials, business leaders, creative professionals, scholars and church staff recount how the gospel has been breathing new life into every area of their lives, in the midst of intense wrestling with their own brokenness and the brokenness of their communities and the world. The conference began with hundreds of us sitting in the beautiful St. Bart's Church, quietly reading through the chapters of the book of Genesis that recount the story of Jacob, reflecting on his struggle with God, and our own, while listening to a chamber choir singing a cappella – and thoroughly conscious that half of Manhattan still lacked electricity and that many homes in the city had been destroyed.

This conference was a living, breathing institutional signpost of the many lives being changed, in this generation, by a recognition that the gospel changes every aspect of our lives, and has implications for every sphere of our cultures. Just in the past few months I have seen the revitalizing effect of this recognition in the lives of artisans and executives and musicians and scholars, in work communities from architectural design studios to venture capital firms to insurance brokers to political think tanks, in local churches from Seattle to San Francisco to Phoenix to Chicago and to New York, and many places between.

This wonderful moment of recovery of the whole gospel for the whole person and the whole world, and the accompanying recovery of a sense of personal vocation and public responsibility, reaffirms the lived reality of the hope so vividly portrayed in Isaiah 60 and Revelation 21, of God's new life for God's people in God's new heavens and new earth. It is a recovery that has been surprising me day after day throughout my own working life, as I discover fresh places where the Spirit of God has been breathing new cultural life in the midst of devastation and wreckage.

People yearn for rescue from their own evil and the evil that abounds in the world around them. People yearn for hope in the face of natural catastrophe and systemic cultural brokenness. People yearn for a sense that their lives matter, that their work matters, that they have historical agency and can make a difference in their communities and the world at large.

There are many obstacles in our way as we, Christian or not, yearn and reach for hope, meaning, significance. Absent the gospel our own sinfulness brings us to despair. In cultures deeply shaped by ancient and modern idolatries, we are misguided all around the world by practices and beliefs that are deeply embedded in long traditions and powerfully enforced by existing social structures. Many Christians suffer the combined consequences of a false dichotomy of sacred and secular and a lifeboat eschatology. Many churches continue to proclaim a Sunday Christianity that undervalues the everyday vocations of most Christians because it splits reality into "spiritual" and "material" parts in which the "spiritual" really matters while the "secular" matters much less. Many Christians put their hope in the prospect of the individual soul being rescued into an ethereal heaven from an evil earth, with the church being the lifeboat – seemingly forgetting that Christians confess the resurrection of the body and that the Bible offers a vision of the renewal of the whole created cosmos as the outcome of the work of the Father, the Son, and the Spirit.

The gospel offers the hope that these obstacles can be overcome, and that in the end, they will be overcome. The Spirit of God continues to work against these obstacles, in the power of the cross and the resurrection of Christ. One significant move of the Spirit stretches from the Reformation's recovery of the gospel of the reign of God, through the profession of cultural leaders, like Abraham Kuyper a century ago, that Jesus claims and cares for every tiny little part of the cosmos, and into the scholarship of Calvin Seerveld collected in these volumes.

I cannot adequately express my own gratitude for Calvin Seerveld's lifetime of faithful study, writing, and speaking. I first bought a copy of Seerveld's *Rainbows for the Fallen World* in the mid-1980s, from a colporteur selling them out of a room in the back of his house in *apartheid*

South Africa, and I have since read three copies of *Rainbows* threadbare and to the point of falling apart. No other pages outside of the Scriptures themselves have more decisively and thoroughly shaped my understanding of God, the world, and myself than the introduction and first chapters of *Rainbows*. While in graduate school I read an essay included in Part Two of this volume, "Footprints in the Snow," that shaped my understanding of culture, history, and history-writing in a perduring manner. I can say without any doubt that *Rainbows* and "Footprints" are the most important things I have ever read, outside of the Bible itself.

I mention the importance of these writings to me personally not merely to celebrate the influence of Calvin Seerveld in my life, but to commend all of his writings to you, the reader, as a help in overcoming the obstacles that stand in the way of lives and work redolent with hope, meaning, and significance. As I re-read through the second part of this volume of essays, I reflected on their effect in my own life and work, and imagined their potential effect in the current movement of revival in evangelical Christian seriousness about the living of an integral life to which I am a witness.

Part Two of this volume opens with "Dooyeweerd's Contribution to the Historiography of Philosophy." I smiled at Seerveld's observation that Herman Dooyeweerd (the twentieth century Dutch neocalvinist philosopher who, along with is brother-in-law D.H.Th. Vollenhoven, expertedly brought Abraham Kuyper's gospel vision to bear on the scholarly practices of philosophy and historiography) "writes with the carelessness of genius" (204). Herman Dooyeweerd crafted the philosophical categories within which I do my own scholarship. I thought about a scholar of the next generation—perhaps an undergraduate currently majoring in philosophy at a small Christian liberal arts college—learning from Dooyeweerd, through this essay, that "Christian historiographic critique of philosophy is not narrow-minded . . . but evaluates a foreign philosophy from the inside out . . . in terms of its own religious motive in order to veritably understand the other's attempted and attained service toward opening up . . . creation in the ordained duration under Almighty God we call history" (208) and then going on to years of fruitful work on just such a critique, to the benefit of a generation of her students and generations of her subsequent readers.

In the next essay, on "Dooyeweerd's Idea of 'Historical Development': Christian Respect for Cultural Diversity," Seerveld writes about the need for "a honed, biblically directed analysis of historical change so that . . . two-thirds-world students . . . suffering from a secularized Western educative neocolonialism, may find a conceptual place in the present generation to breathe fresh air" (212), and posits, by means of a summary and gentle correction of Dooyeweerd's philosophical historiography, that "it is a mark of Bible-believing wisdom to show respect for cultural diversity, which Christian respect is integral to normative historical deed" (230). I breathed exactly this fresh Dooyeweerdian air in late-*apartheid* era South Africa, in the 1980s and 1990s; one result of which in my life was three years of scholarship in support of the writing of language diversity clauses for inclusion in South Africa's post-*apartheid* constitution.

For me personally the most significant of the essays in this volume is "Footprints in the Snow," in which Seerveld provides a taxonomy of major conceptions regarding tradition, an alternative working definition of the nature of tradition, biblical direction for understanding tradition here and now, observations on history and history-keeping, and suggestions toward normative traditioning. As I struggled with my own inherited legacy as a neocalvinist who grew up in apartheid South Africa, where neocalvinists were complicit in the construction of the deep injustices of that political order, and who yet believed that the neocalvinist tradition offered real help to Christians in post-colonial Africa, this essay helped me immensely. Seerveld suggests that "Traditions are human responses to God's creational call for an earlier generation to covenant with a succeeding generation in the elders' giving the younger their prized treasures" (269), and that "Traditioning an inheritance is normative if the traditioning act gentles the (reliable) wont into the inexperienced generation's hands so they do justice to its original obedience (granted it was relatively obedient) and find new avenues for its service" (271). This essay did not only inform my scholarship,[8] it helped me in my struggle with my sense of identity and responsibility as a Kuyperian out of Africa. I imagine a Korean church planter in his study, a Kenyan business founder as she flies to her factories in Uganda and Tanzania, a Brazilian political activist riding the bus to a meeting, each reading this essay and finding themselves called to fresh ways of interpreting the heritage of Christian cultural engagement that they have from their parents, their pastors, and their teachers – to the great blessing of their congregations, their employees and customers, their supporters and those with whom they contend politically.

For years one of the great delights of my life has been teaching introductory courses in philosophy to college undergraduates, and Seerveld's "The Pedagogical Strength of a Christian Methodology in Philosophical Historiography" (277–315) and "Biblical Wisdom underneath Vollenhoven's Categories for Philosophical Historiography" (see *AH*: 1–22) shaped those courses. While it is likely to be the new earth before I will have either the historical knowledge or the narrative skill to equal Seerveld's own teaching, I was helped immensely by the recognition that

8   Gideon J. Strauss and Kobus Smit, "Writing History in Postcolonial Africa," *Journal for Contemporary History* 20 (December 1995): 1–24.
     http://www.academia.edu/1355051/Strauss_G._J._1995_._Writing_history_in_postcolonial_Africa._Journal_for_Contemporary_History_20_December_1-24

"there are a number of different, recurrent conceptual neighborhoods (or if you will, 'families of ideas') that hold men and women captive, and are attractive, thoughtful ways to go to hell. That has tremendous pedagogical strength, because then teaching and learning the history of philosophy is not some pointless archive work churned out by remote specialists or like playing bridge well: it is a matter of life and death!" (314).

Calvin Seerveld, in the essays collected here and in the rest of his writings, has decisively shaped my mind, my work, and my life. His gospel-motivated vision and practice of culture making, of history keeping, and of the study and teaching of philosophy, has gentled the neocalvinist tradition into my hands, and I trust that these collected works will find their way into the hands of scholars, teachers, and leaders throughout the world, where they will discover Seerveld's original obedience and find new ways for cultural service, inspired and informed by his work and wisdom.

The day will come when everything will be made right. I dream that when that day comes, some of my years will be joyously passed in seminar with Calvin Seerveld, reading Heraclitus, Eckhart, Machiavelli, and Cassirer, considering and evaluating the legacy of geneticistic, contradictory monism, and doing fresh philosophical work among the people of the New Jerusalem. Because much of this lifetime of faithful scholarship will pass through the refining fire, and be discovered serviceable to the neighbor and delightful to God, in the age to come.

Gideon Strauss, Executive Director of the Max De Pree Center for
Leadership at Fuller Theological Seminary, Pasadena, California
(photo by his daughter Tala Azar Strauss)

Lecturing on Christian Philosophy at Juniata College,
Huntingdon, Pennsylvania, 1964

REFORMATIONAL CHRISTIAN PHILOSOPHY AND CHRISTIAN COLLEGE EDUCATION

If there were an underground booklet that profiled the Presbyterian and Reformed educational institutions that regularly hold discussions for RUNA (a Reformed University of North America[1]), like one of those stapled sheet collections put out by students at certain colleges that give you the brutal-truth lowdown in terse, humorous paragraphs on which profs to avoid and which to choose, would you be aware of how Dordt stacks up next to King's, Calvin, Trinity Christian, Redeemer, and others? They are all "Reformed," let's say. They are all sheep, no goats. But each one, because of its history, location, timing, and leadership—such as "The B.J. Haan years" at Dordt—stands on its legs a little differently as far as being "Reformed" goes. I'm not talking PR, "Best Buys," or picking favorites (although our three children are Dordt graduates). I am simply stating, to begin our discussion, that being "Reformed" shakes out a little differently in various christian colleges whose faith-thought tradition goes back to the Reformation, especially the Calvinian brand. That is to be expected.

So as not to bear false witness in advertising and because passing on and keeping alive, if not lively, a Reformation tradition in the complex matter of higher education is a difficult endeavor, it is also critically important for a college to be conscious of just what the perspective is that shapes its **educational** identity. Calvin College asked Nick Wolterstorff in 1989 to give a series of talks for new faculty on the distinctive character of Calvin College as an institution in the lived tradition of the Reformed community. Its title, *Keeping Faith*, invites new faculty to enter into a living faith-thought tradition that acknowledges that creation is good—the

---

1 Around 2001, the RUNA group re-organized and expanded its membership and became the Association of Reformed Institutions of Higher Education. In 2012 the name was changed to Association of Reformed Colleges and Universities (www.reformedcolleges.org).

This article, published in *Pro Rege* 30:3 (2002): 1–16, originated as an invited lecture for the faculty at Dordt College in October 2001.

world belongs to God—that sin deeply permeates human historical cultivation of the world, and that members of the body of Christ are called to participate in the cosmic, societal redemption afoot under the provident God and working Holy Spirit in anticipation of Jesus Christ's Rule being completed when he comes again in glory.

Wolterstorff invites new faculty who are not white Dutch-American Christian Reformed males to live into and dialogically modify but keep the promises of being "a college committed to the project of integral Christian learning" (48). Calvin College now requires new faculty to attend a series of seminars that assumes a reading list to be vigorously discussed in a serious attempt not to prescribe thought patterns but to flesh out roughly what for them as a college community "Reformed" christian education means.

When I began teaching philosophy at a brand-new Trinity Christian College in Chicago in 1959,[2] a three-semester sequence of conjoined history of philosophy (2 hours each semester) and cultural history (3 hours each semester) courses were required of all freshmen and sophomore students, so they would get a "Western Civ" knowledge from reading primary texts in "The Great Books" from Homer and Plato through Augustine, Aquinas, Descartes, and Kant to Sartre, along with the development of Greek and Roman, Medieval, and Modern European institutional history. Prior to that sequence, along with required courses in English composition and literature (3 hours each) and two courses in Reformed Doctrine (2 hours each) was an introductory philosophy course.

Philosophy 101 was conceived to give **a christian philosophical orientation**, in baby language mixed with jargon, to these high school graduates who thought they already knew everything needful to live and to die happily in suburban Chicago life, that would winsomely stretch their vision for serving Jesus Christ in any and all of their impending studies: school-teaching, law, laboratory science, nursing, artistry, medicine, or homemaking. After facing them with Bertrand Russell's tract, "Why I am not a Christian," we examined why thinking, even scientific thinking, cannot be neutral with respect to a human person's fundamental stance (*pou sto*) assumed on where the buck ultimately stops, what does everything mean anyhow, and what kind of world do we inhabit.

Collateral reading for Philosophy 101 included prolegomenal sections of John Calvin's *Institutes of the Christian Religion*, the section from Abraham Kuyper's *Encyclopedia of Sacred Theology* on "Logic impaired by sin," Oscar Cullmann's dramatic lecture on "Immortality of the Soul

---

2   See my "Autobiographical Vignettes," in *In the Fields of the Lord* (2000), 30–32.

or Resurrection of the Dead," describing why Socrates took the hemlock with poise while Jesus was afraid of death in Gethsemane and sweat blood. One of the too-hard texts for this introductory course was Herman Dooyeweerd's little book *In the Twilight of Western Thought*. Near the end of this first year Philosophy 101 first semester course (3 hours), we held "modal" seminars on how different specialized studies in mathematics, biology, psychology, sociology, economics, political science, theology, or educational theory, were shaped by different philosophies. Profs from these various fields joined in the modal seminars with their prospective majors in trying to figure out questions like these: Why there are Bayesian and non-Bayesian statistical theories? What difference does Pavlov's psychology make next to Freud's for treating neuroses? Is a Capitalistic macro-economic theory more normative than a Socialist economics? How significant is the difference between a John Dewey theory of schooling from a Thomist one? The seminar was a lot of fun because we were discovering things we didn't quite know the answers for, and knew it was important for being a follower of Jesus Christ in the world around us.

I also should mention that in the beginning we Trinity Christian College faculty held a series of weeknight lectures for our supporting constituency on how the christian faith shaped each of our conceptions in the field of our specialization—this is 1960. Those early lectures in the areas of math, biology, and psychology were not mature like Karen de Mol's essay on music and Simon du Toit's *Pro Rege* piece on theatre,[3] because some of us back then with a Ph.D. from a secular university didn't have a clue on how to show the biblical faith that was **integrally shaping** the contours of our discipline. We all knew our christian faith was not an addition to our scholarship, was not just to be parallel to our scientific reflection, or that we could not be satisfied with an earnest prayer before you neutrally examined Edgar Allen Poe's short stories; but how to have the biblical vision make a difference **in** the study of snails, learning German, examining psychosomatic trauma? Nobody was losing face because we were all searching **together**, helping each other.

As for claiming there were discernible contours for a **christian** philosophy and that a christian philosophy and a specific biblical sense of historical narrative were at the hub of a "Reformed" christian college

---

3 These originally *Pro Rege* articles, from March 1998 and June 2001 respectively, were later reprinted. See Karen deMol, *Sound Stewardship: How shall Christians think about music?* (Sioux Center: Dordt College Press, 1999/2006), and Simon du Toit's "Playing with Fire: Towards a biblical approach to theatre performance," in *Celebrating the Vision: The reformed perspective of Dordt College*, ed. John H. Kok (Sioux Center: Dordt College Press, 2004), 137–153.

of interrelated disciplines (cf., diagram): this was news in a way to Chicago. "Dooyeweerd" was also a curse word in certain circles of Reformed people at the time, unsettling. When asked what we were doing in philosophy, I said, "We're just being Reformed, biblically Reformational, you might say." That is, not "Reformed" as past tense, but as an active, ongoing Reformation of life, including thought, word, and deed, honing it all to be true to the Scriptures. I came to define it this way:

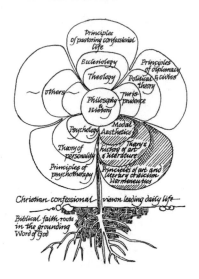

> "Reformational" identifies (1) a life that would be deeply committed to the scriptural injunction not to be conformed to patterns of this age but to be re-formed by the renewal of our consciousness so that we will be able to discern what God wills for action on earth (cf. Romans 12:1–2); and (2) an approach in history to honor the genius of the Reformation spearheaded by Luther and John Calvin in the sixteenth century, developed by Groen van Prinsterer and Abraham Kuyper in the nineteenth century, as a particular christian tradition where one could richly serve the Lord; with (3) a concern that we be communally busy reform**ing** in an ongoing way rather than standing pat in the past tense (*ecclesia reformata semper reformanda est*).[4]

I personally am deeply grateful to be "Reformed," to be a member of this "biblically Reformational" community over the centuries up to today, and I want to serve my Lord and our neighbors by being biblically Reformational in translating and reading the Bible, in experiencing artistry, in constructing policy for economic and political life, in communally (institutionally) educating a next generation, in conceiving and doing theology, and whatever. Since I think this is what Dordt College education is all about, let me lead you to consider a few perennial problems that have disturbed and probably will continue to trouble any given generation of Christ's followers who attempt to keep the promises of the historical Reformation vital in our terribly pragmaticistic, secularizing, technocratically dehumanizing age.

---

4 *Balaam's Apocalyptic Prophecies* (1980), 46; (2003), 39.

What is the Bible?

My first point, which may seem tangential to a college faculty, hits the sciatic nerve of every person who confesses Jesus Christ: What is the Bible? My Reformational answer is: we should normally sing psalms rather than gospel choruses. What do I mean?

The holy Scriptures are God-speaking literature given to us historically for our learning by faith the one true story of the Lord's Rule a-coming and the contours of what our obedient response should be. The Bible is God's Word booked, telling us the *magnalia Dei* with a Holy Spirited power that can convict us as hearers to repent of our sin, drive us to plead for adoption by the sovereign LORD into Jesus Christ's body, and teach us to carry steadfastly our neighbors' burdens (Romans 8:14–17 and 10:14–17, Galatians 6:1–3). The Bible is a Holy Spirit-packed script to be spoken that works faith in peoples' hearts and generates human life in community, a community of people who thankfully congregates to search the Scriptures together for wisdom to be obedient to God in whatever we are gifted to do on earth (2 Timothy 3:16–17, Proverbs 1:1–7, Romans 12:3–9, 1 Corinthians 12, Acts 17:10–12).

The historic European Reformation of the 1500s asked Bible readers to meet the text **fresh**. Luther and Calvin were three-language people: they spoke Greek and Hebrew as well as Latin. Augustine and Aquinas did not know the original biblical languages. So, Luther and Calvin purposefully got to the sources behind the vulgate translation of the Bible in use. Luther's moving letter thanking his professor John Staupitz in May 1518 exclaims Luther's joy when he found out that *poenitentia agere* for μετανοεῖτε in Matthew 4:17 meant not to do the penances stipulated by the clergy but to become **penitent** in your heart, **repentant**: *metanoeite* that Jesus preached asked for a fundamental turnaround, a change of heart, a pivotal conversion to your whole consciousness. Instead of a bitter word, writes Luther, *poenitentia* now became a sweetest word of the Bible.

That scholarly discovery in the Bible sparked a new-old idea of "church." Church is not the clergy, the administrative clerics, or the popes in charge because they are the only one single, true apostolic authority succeeding from Simon Peter. The "church" is the communion of ordinary, sinful saints who have repented! It is faithful **people** (ὁ λαὸς, the laity) of God, the believers sealed in the baptism of Jesus Christ and stamped, anointed by the Holy Spirit, ordained to live out and mediate the gospel to others. That's a Reformation conception of the church as **body of Christ at large.**

The *Heidelberg Catechism* (1563) in Question and Answer #32 explains what it means to be a Christian without even mentioning the (at the time often misconceived) word "church."

> Why are you called a Christian?
> Because by faith I am a member of Christ, and so I share in his anointing.
> I am anointed to confess his name,
> to present myself to him as a living sacrifice of thanks,
> to strive with a good conscience against sin and the devil in this life,
> and afterward to reign with Christ
> over all creation for all eternity.

Another key contribution of the 1500s Reformation is John Calvin's metaphorical linkage of the Bible and human knowledge of God's world. Scripture states clearly that creation, creatures, reveal God who made them (Psalm 19:2–5, Isaiah 28:23–29, Acts 14:17, Romans 1:18–25), but it takes human eyes with Scriptural vision to find the traces of the LORD God's merciful order we are to follow in cultivating God's world in our generation and in dealing with one another in society.

The Bible, says Calvin (1559), is a special gift from the LORD, like a pair of eyeglasses, spectacles that help un-confuse and bring into correct focus our coming to know the saving Creator of the universe.[5] The *Belgic Confession* of the Reformation, authored by Guido de Brés (1561–1566), reinforces Calvin's point when it says (article 2a) that creation is like a lovely book where all creatures are letters to make us ponder God's powerful, provident governance, and that the Bible, all of whose matters we believe without a doubt because the Holy Spirit testifies in our hearts that they are from God (article 5), makes God known to us more openly than creational revelation does, with its intimations of the Lord's glory and the riches of our salvation (article 2b).

The Reformation leaders understood the point Psalm 119 makes about God's law (*torah*), ordinances (*hoqqim*), Word (*dabar*), commands (*piqqud*), judgments (*mishphat*) of creational mercy to be retold, celebrated, and illuminated by the Scriptures: the Bible gives followers of Christ the wherewithal to interpret intelligibly the glossolalia of the creatural

---

5   *Institutes of the Christian Religion* (I,6,1) ". . . nempe sicuti senes, vel lippi, & quicunque oculis caligant . . . specillis autem interpositis adjuti, distincte legere incipient: ita Scriptura confusam alioqui Dei notitiam in mentibus nostris colligens, discussa caligine liquido nobis verum Deum ostendit." ("Just as old or bleary-eyed men and those with weak vision . . . with the aid of spectacles will begin to read distinctly; so Scripture, gathering up the otherwise confused knowledge of God in our minds, having dispersed our dullness, clearly shows us the true God"—Ford Lewis Battles' translation.)

voices.[6] No wonder the Reformation leaders enjoined the princes and magistrates to educate children, also girls (1528 in Wittenburg), because the whole world is declaring the wonder of God, and if education is Scripturally directed we will be able to discern God's will not only in doctrines, but also God's will for living in marriage, charging or avoiding interest in commercial life, formulating just protocols for civic life, establishing regulations for treating the sick and helplessly weak. The Reformation of the 1500s stands for sustained, on-going, intelligent redemptive work in God's world at large under the searchlight of the Bible, perceiving what disobeys the Lord too, expecting the landowner's return to review our trusteeship (Matthew 21:33–43 and 25:14–46).

And now the crux of this point on the Bible for teaching: assuming that the Bible serves as 20–20 eye-glasses, lenses, or like a focusing searchlight, then if you just stare at the glasses or the source of light, you will miss its enlightening purpose. How does one put on the armor of the view-finding, penetrating Word of God (Ephesians 6:10–17) without just coming to look bespectacled?

Christians, also those who are dedicated professionally to serve students, need, I believe, to become thoroughly at home in the Bible, honoring its historical, literary, proclamational nature. We need to become familiar with its names, times, and places that locate concretely the true story running from Genesis to the Apocalypse of Jesus Christ given to John so that, like a lover, we will know its nuanced crevices of comforting promises and fulfillments and warnings inside out. For example, by immersion one comes to understand how Genesis 50:20 connects with the *toledoth* of Genesis 2:4 to unite the diverse episodes of the whole book into a brilliant symphony of the LORD God's compassionate care for our difficult, bumbling, believing forebears, and for us, through vicissitudes of war and peace; how Exodus 20, Leviticus 19, and Deuteronomy 5–9 are not criminal statutes to club you into submission, but embraces by God to keep us out of harm's way and to norm our thankfulness; how Psalms 1 and 2 sound the keynote chord of wisdom and messy Messianic politics as the sound that reverberates through both the laments and praise of the whole collection of songs; how the accent in the book of Esther to the key verse in 4:14 is not "Who knows whether you have come to the kingdom for such a time as this," making Esther a heroine, so much as Mordecai's message, "If you keep silent now, deliverance for God's people will come from some other quarter!"

---

6   See my "Creational Revelation: God's glossolalia," in *Bearing Fresh Olive Leaves* (2000), 159–163; and "The Gospel of Creation," in *In the Fields of the Lord* (2000), 46–48.

That is, to be a teacher in the tradition of the Reformation—Luther translated the whole Bible into German; Calvin persisted until he produced a complete Psalter into sing-able French so that the illiterate people could themselves voice God's Word—you become steeped in the God-speaking literature the Bible is. So the Bible is not a source book of proof texts, but a network of connected passages coloring the Lord in a rainbow of awful glories. (That is why I think we should not neglect the habit of singing a whole psalm, which better honors the gritty complexity of the Bible than do many a repetitive Bible chorus quoting a few words.) If you are sensitive to the unfinished, enthymemic style of Mark next to the airbrushed complete gospel of John, and if you can appreciate how Matthew's account is attuned to Jewish traditionalism and catch the poignant, observed detail of Luke's gospel, you are not tempted to waste time to rationalize so-called inconsistent details in the synoptic gospels but to revel in the multifarious God-breathed truth disclosed about Jesus Christ's passionate healing ministry, resurrection, and ascension that fulfill, among others, Isaiah's striking prophecies (Isaiah 54–62). And once the book to the Hebrews grips your soul, veritably a *midrash* on Psalm 95, you get a palpable sense of the intricate mesh of the Older and Newer Testaments as God's one compelling Word to us from the LORD revealed in Jesus Christ who is the source of grace, mercy, and peace for us who have faith in the time when we need rescue (Hebrews 3–4).

Teaching is an occupation where one often needs rescue and where a chief hazard is death by millstone because of misleading a little one of the next generation (Luke 17:1–4, James 3:1). To have our teaching consciousness molded by faithful intimacy with the Scriptures—good exegetical pastoral preaching helps, reading the Bible at home in storytelling fashion to the children helps—to know conversationally the Bible's very idiom (if not its languages), so that one has been outfitted with a biblical *mentalité*, constantly surprised anew, emboldened and comforted by God's prickly, exciting Word, such that the Bible provides the a priori for searching the world we live in rather than letting the present culture set the standards and force us to take up a defensive posture, that is, making work of having the Bible so ingrained in our habit of thinking, speaking, and getting things done: all of these makes one a good heir, in my judgment, of the Reformational praxis of Martin Luther and John Calvin.

Christian historiography and philosophy in college scholarship
The second and main point is more contentious. In Abraham Kuyper's day (1837–1920) in the Netherlands, a Reformed christian school was

known as *de school met de Bijbel* (the school with the Bible). But how does the Bible operate **in** the actual schooling—in our setting, in college education, where one has numerous different fields of study? The Gideons, so to speak, have virtually put a Bible in the chemistry lab, in the Black Box theatre, and on the basketball court, but **who is academic boss at a christian college?** My Reformational answer is this: there is no papal discipline in a Reformed college curriculum (Matthew 20:20–28).

The diagram above pictures what I should like to present as a Reformational look at the problem of relating christian philosophy and historiography, christian theology, and christian teaching in any academic discipline. I will single out theology and aesthetics in my limited time because theology is especially where the rub comes for certain Reformed people and aesthetics is my field of special attention.

Note that I am not delineating what should go on at a Bible College, which has its own restricted legitimacy, to study just the Bible, plus some church music perhaps, and training in leading church youth groups. A Bible College is basically a professional school that is oriented toward practicing an honorable profession, turning out graduates who are practitioners like church workers, executive secretaries, registered nurses, and certified teachers. Also, I am not concerned here with what a seminary should be—an institution for professional training set up to produce pastors for churches who are grounded in the Scriptures, able to preach the gospel, knowledgeable of church history, committed to edifying the faithful and to reaching out to any disbelieving neighbors. The seminary undertakes this training within the definite limits of a specific confessional stand, whether it be Orthodox, Roman catholic, Reformed, Anabaptist, a liberal United Christian, or, for that matter, a Judaic or Muslim standard of belief. Seminaries are a proper source for preachers, pastors, evangelists, even though they rightly do not have a monopoly in Reformed churches on church congregational leadership: witness ruling elders and deacons, who are not usually seminary trained.

It would be a mistake, in my judgment, to think that a christian college should be a Bible college or a denominational seminary. There can be historical connections and should be on-going supportive relations between church, church seminaries, and christian colleges, yet their tasks are different, as different as between church Sunday school or catechism and a regular five-day-a-week school that teaches reading, writing, arithmetic, American literature, history-keeping, and various sciences.

So precisely how does the Bible function in carrying out the task of this kind of christian college? As I indicated in my first point, it is the calling of every believer in the Reformation tradition to become intimate with the Bible as God-speaking literature with its true story of the LORD creating the whole world, our historical fall into sin, Jesus Christ's making redemption graciously available for those who respond by faith to discipleship as we live in love, sorrow, and hope for the completion of Christ's kingdom Rule a-coming (the underground root in the diagram). In other words, **become so intimately at home with that Reformation take on the Older and Newer Testament gospel that one's consciousness subconsciously(!) assumes that heart-depth commitment in one's way-of-life and finds it shaping one's world-and-life vision of things**. This kind of intimacy corresponds, I think, with Syd Hielema's focus on wisdom[7] as the lynchpin for relating God revealed in Jesus Christ, God revealed in the Scriptures, and God revealed in creation: as the Holy Spirited Scriptures convict you of the Lord's compassionate redemptive hold on the heart of your very life and all things, you have the **beginnings**, you begin to bud in wisdom (Proverbs 1:7, 15:33).

Such an outlook and demeanor, in the variant peculiar to the Reformation strand of the christian faith, has been described as having *Gereformeerde voelhorens* (extra-strength Reformational antennae); that is, such people are like snails whose quivering antennae can detect what is subliminal; they smell it when a deed, word, or thought is wholesome, unbiblical, or off-color with what is true to the Reformation brand of the christian faith. That's the antennae uneducated Reformed people had—I know from experience—when they lived close to the Scriptures, before TV entered their homes.

This is the way, as I understand it, that the Bible enters a christian college that takes its cue from the Reformation: faculty members have *Gereformeerde voelhorens*, naturally at different stages of seasoned maturity. These faculty members willingly seek for and work toward that Bible-rooted, subterranean *consensus fidelium Reformatorum* (an underlying consensus of faithful Reformation-oriented saints). As they begin to blossom in wisdom these faculty members distinguish their christian college as a "Reformed" community from a Thomist christian college, a Shi'ite Muslim company of *mullahs* in a *madrassa*, or an American secular state undergraduate college with individual profs resting mostly on a bed of trust in scientific Reason.

Many evangelical christian colleges are content, I think, to rest the communality of their academic endeavor at the basic level of patterns

---

7   Hielema, "Reclaiming the Apex of the Triangle: Scholarship as pilgrimage" (2001), 153–155.

of life that are moral, church-going, perhaps with a few taboos against drinking wine or wearing jewelry. Reformed christian colleges may add the dimension that faculty members must subscribe to certain churchly confessional "forms of unity" or belong to a certain church denomination so that it is clear they support infant baptism as a promise of God's covenant with believers, or a common statement of world-and-life-envisioning purpose. Such subscriptions try to ensure not uniformity but at least enough conformity to the particular common objective of this christian college that concord will result—a harmony among diverse teaching faculty, administrators, and the overall assistant staff so important to the feel of a college.

A Reformational perspective would say: since college education like all human culturing happens communally, can we follow through on the unity we have in Christ, past a holy **daily lifestyle** (way of life) and an **overview** (world-and-life-vision) that we cultivate in God's world for Christ's sake, following through on those expressions of unity and wisdom into the very fabric of our vocation, namely, considered reflection on what, how, and why things mean what they do, on what has taken place, and on what should be done? **Such follow-through would mean for christian academics of the Reformation that they also find a studied way to interact across disciplines and to correlate awareness of the historical developments behind the state of each one's art or science as it now is so that we really act like a genuine thinking-imagining-talking-together community of scholarly teachers.**

If you have ever listened to an argument between, let's say, a vigorous Roman catholic and a dyed-in-the-wool Marxist on the topic of "knowledge," or tried yourself to communicate with someone across faith-thought paradigms on something important, like "normativity," you know how difficult, if not exasperating, it can be. Well, it takes almost as much patience, ingenuity, and goodwill to share knowledge across disciplinary lines in the different fields we specialize in. Can people who talk and dream isotopes and those for whom the wrench of a ninth chord speaks volumes understand one another's passion? Can those who know the crucial difference between certain herbicides and pesticides and those for whom the optative mood of a verb is critical, can they catch each other's spark? And everyone would be immeasurably more united as teachers if all grasped that 1848 and 1968, like September 11, 2001, are not just chronological dates, culturally speaking—at least if the college faculty is **a working reflective community in their teaching** the student body **together.**

Our resident American individualism militates against taking the time to go this wise second mile to mesh our diverse, often professionally technical examinations of reality. Does one with a Ph.D. still need to continue to be educated outside one's disciplinary specialty? Busy faculty can easily rest with a college unified by chapel exercises, a wholesome christian ethos on campus, and a curriculum that allocates required core courses fairly and spells out major and minor concentrations for sound graduation. Also, not every christian college for whom a faculty unified in its teaching perspective and practice is important is aware of or feels kindly toward a conceptual framework and a position taken on historical development that comes out of the Reformation; a framework that is specially geared to facilitate such encyclopedic interaction of the various disciplines along with a critical eye for what is fruitful and wasteful in the development of societal human culture through the ages.

Already Augustine in *De civitate Dei* (413–426 AD) sketched horizons where the historical struggle of the woman with child (*civitas Dei*) and the dragons of John's Apocalypse (*civitates mundi*) is seen as the only genuine war on earth. Groen van Prinsterer's *Ongeloof en Revolutie* (1847) updated Augustine's vision, contrasting the sanity of faithful constructive institution-building for humankind that honored God with the cataclysmic violence of the French Revolution in the name of the deity of Reason. And then D. H. Th. Vollenhoven's (1872–1978) method of historiography refined the same Scripturally-directed approach to history by showing how all human leaders were caught in epoch-forming dynamics and enhanced or ruined their particular inheritance from out of a typical perspective usually a-kilter to God's directives for normal creatural life. So there is in embryo a particular historiographic position focused on history-keeping that is generated by a Reformational christian approach.[8]

Moreover, there is a systematic philosophical conception on the LORD God's amazing sovereignty ordering all creatures and societal institutions that was prompted by John Calvin's *Institutes of the Christian Religion* (1536/1559), when he dropped the remark that the office of municipal judge is a highest human calling for a responsible follower of Christ to prepare for (IV, 20, 1–7). Abraham Kuyper's *Souvereiniteit in eigen kring* (1880) and attendant political, educational, and journalist leadership presented a theory of societal institutions that showed how school and government, commerce and media, as well as home and eccle-

---

8 See, e.g., my "Footprints in the Snow," *Philosophia Reformata* 56:1 (1991): 1–34; infra 235–276.

siastic communions, could serve as redemptive vehicles of God's grace. And then Herman Dooyeweerd in *A New Critique of Theoretical Thought* followed up Calvin's lead[9] and Kuyper's societology by sketching a philosophical cosmology and a refined analysis of societal structures that simply begs to be worked out by succeeding generations of scholars who specialize in various fields of study, to think-imagine-talk things through professionally **in concert** as our "reasonable service" to bring insight.

So it would be natural, it seems to me, for a christian college grateful for its debt to the Reformation for an operative (albeit fallible) christian philosophical systematics and an (unfinished) redemptive historiographic method to parlay that legacy into the blessing of strengthening and unifying a faculty member's sense of being part of and knowing how to contribute to **a genuine communion of christian academic work and teaching that will be wise.** I do not mean that there is a ready-made christian philosophy and method of historiographic narrative all set, and that once you learn the jargon, presto! we solve all our theoretical problems, and teach, talk, and think happily ever after. No, but **if a christian college makes earnest with the thrust of the Reformation that we faculty members of the body of Christ are to wash each other's educational feet with the conceptual, imaginative, verbal, and enabling gifts each has at one's disposal,[10] and if there is a philosophical systematics deepening a Reformed world-and-life-vision that can help a college teacher test the basic categories one uses in one's field, points one toward intersecting cruxes of meaning for several disciplines, provides a precise vocabulary to export the results of one's special studies, which leads to more redemptive strength in presenting one's material because you sense you are one voice within a whole reflective communal chorus of teaching saints, then imagine what such a cross-disciplinary, resonating message from different classrooms will make upon students!**

I can't say everything needful on my second point, but I can say enough to get into trouble and to suggest perhaps why the Reformational strategy for christian philosophical and historiographic mediation within and between and among what we as faculty teach is worth considering.

---

9   "Why a radical christian philosophy can only develop in the line of Calvin's religious starting-point," Herman Dooyeweerd in *De Wijsbegeerte der Wetsidee* (1935–36), translated by David Freeman and William Young, *A New Critique of Theoretical Thought* (Philadelphia: Presbyterian and Reformed, 1953), 1:515–527.

10 See my "The Fundamental Importance of Imaginativity within Schooling," in *Rainbows* (1980), 142–145.

Every discipline has a history, and every art and science sets limits to its task and draws implications from its practice. Such prolegomenal and postlegomenal decisions as well as "legomenal" narration are philosophical by nature, I dare say, because they are decisions on interrelational meaning that, in the province of theory and reflection, are meta-disciplinary, are setting categorical foundations and parameters that determine the overall contours of what gets conceived in that universe of discourse, and recognize whether that discourse's dated/located results are blessed and cursed with neighboring matters both before, presently, and a-coming, or are considered only abstractly by themselves.

Now I may think that Vollenhoven and Dooyeweerd, Sytse Zuidema, Johan Mekkes, M.C. Smit, and Klaas Popma, Johan van der Hoeven, Bob Goudzwaard, Sander Griffioen, and a host of other witnesses are good, professionally academic janitors who give precise, nuanced christian wisdom on inter-faculty matters and do not just leave connections "over-viewy" (as Ezra Pound would say). But no tribunal from the Free University of Amsterdam provides your answers. The needed philosophical and historiographic decisions have to be wormed out of the teacher who thoroughly knows the special field of study. And a faculty member can basically accept and maybe quibble with the ruling secular paradigm current in one's field, try something idiosyncratic—do it your own Sinatra way—or tap into a Reformational philosophical and historiographic habit, trying it on for size, or whatever. But faculty members as scholars and teachers are willy-nilly loaded, better yet, primed philosophically and historiographically, despite any disclaimers.

Reformed theology and reformational theology

For example, **Reformed** theology epistomized by Louis Berkhof's *Systematic Theology* adopts a traditional six loci approach: (1) the Being of God, (2) Man, (3) the God-man Jesus Christ—*Cur Deus Homo?*—(4) Redemption, (5) Church, (6) Last things. Without apology Berkhof begins by saying, "Reformed theology regards the existence of God as an entirely reasonable assumption" (21), even though one cannot demonstrate it by argumentation.[11] John Cooper states that "Standard Reformed theology . . . affirms a universally available standard for knowledge, truth, and moral order." He adds:

> In affirming general revelation and common grace, the Calvinist tradition

---

11 Berkhof almost sounds like Anselm in the *Proslogium* on *aliquid quo nihil maius cogitari potest* (c.2): since God is that than which nothing greater can be thought, God must exist. Cf. Spykman 135.

points to the existence and cognitive availability of the God-revealing cosmic order as the universal framework of meaning and condition of truth. . . . Guided by its theology, Reformed epistemology articulates what I would call a **fideistic perspectival rational realism**. . . .[12]

Karl Barth, however, was so adamantly opposed to taking over even a smidgen of the Enlightenment assumption that sound scientific (*wissenschaftliche*) knowledge must be religiously neutral in its reasoning that he conceived dogmatic theology to be simply *Kirchliche Dogmatik* (1932–1967), a churchly re-description of the church's confession of what God's Word says about (1) God's Word, (2) God, (3) Creation, (4) *Versohnung* (reconciliation through Jesus Christ's action), and (5) *Erlosung* (salvation, deliverance), which last section Barth did not live to write. Barth denies having any "philosophical" orientation to his church dogmatics: he claimed no theology but God's Word (like "no creed but Christ"). So too, the Trinity and the incarnation of Jesus Christ, a divine human, are for Barth not subject to the logic of non-contradictory reasonableness, but are nevertheless simply realities.

In contrast to Berkhof/Cooper and Karl Barth, Gordon Spykman's *Reformational Theology: A new paradigm for doing dogmatics* suggests that

> theology and philosophy form a partnership in the sense that the best prolegomena to Christian theology, more specifically to Reformed dogmatics, is a Christian philosophy. . . . Dogmatics is too important to be left to theologians who are unclear about their philosophical underpinnings.[13]

The upshot of Spykman's christian philosophical orientation is that he adopts a **confessional** focus in theology that takes **dogma** (confession officially declared binding by an ecclesial assembly) most seriously as breathing, in concentrated form, what a certain company of faithful followers of the Christ assert they **believe** (103–107, 110). Then in a christian dogmatic theology we will examine the Holy Scriptures as to their interconnected **beliefs**, and the historical development of the human race in the formation of the earlier elected Israel and **confessing church**, its nature, place, and task in fidelity and apostasy, relatively distinct from all other societal institutions as a caretaker of the faithful that God provided, Christ set up, and the Holy Spirit preserves to the end of the present age. Spykman then organizes Reformational dogmatic theology along the historical-redemptive lines of the Apostles' Creed, braided with a (*perichoretic*) Trinitarian awareness (135–137), into (1) the good creation, (2) sin

---

12 "Reformed Scholarship and the Challenge of Post-modern Pluralism" (1993), 21–22. Emphasis added.

13 Spykman (1992), 13, 107; see also, Bartholomew (2000), 33–35, 97.

and evil, (3) the Way of salvation, (4) the consummation.

Attractive to me about Spykman's **Reformational** dogmatic theology is its systematic thetical sureness on Calvinian tenets explicated with a conversational tone,[14] rather than its assuming an argumentative posture where the round creedal warmth of Reformed doctrines gets pared by Occam's razor back to the bone of "propositions" whose fixed "truth-value" can be cold-bloodedly debated in a universal logical framework and constitute the indubitable test for what is essentially Reformed orthodoxy or heresy.[15]

One difference I detect between what is "standard **Reformed** theology" and "**Reformational** dogmatic theology" is that **Reformed** dogmata seem to appear with almost *ex cathedra* finality and authority to "lead" philosophical discussion with **logical certainty**, while the **Reformational** formulation of doctrines breathes a spirit of supple, **trusting certainty** in offering to serve other fields of inquiry with its important limited contribution of constructing *regulae fide* (guidelines for expressing obedient faith). That difference depends upon the underlay of a general theistic "rational realism" for "Reformed" theology, and having "a biblically induced christian philosophy" underneath "Reformational" theology.

And it may be important in a christian college to not let **Reformed** theology (or a christian philosophy!) slip into taking the role of being "**the faith** once for all handed down to the saints" (Jude 3). Not only functional creedal testimonies but especially the systematized theological reflection on what we (churchly) confess are structurally different from, though connected to, the fundamental matter that the Bible calls faith (*pistis*), which is that existential attachment of us with certain trust at being fixed in the true God (or heart-committed to an idol) by the gift of regenerating grace in Jesus Christ (Ephesians 2:8–9).[16] **What keeps a**

---

14 G. Berkouwer's multiple volumes of *Dogmatische Studiën* (1949–1972), which deftly explicate major Reformed doctrines amid many other positions current, is very valuable, but the series seems to me to be episodic, missing a linking systematic character.

15 Mike Vanden Bosch notes the difficult role this conception of the Bible as a source book of propositions to be believed played in the troubled struggle of being "Reformed" at Dordt College during the 1968–1974 period (146–148). My own approach would be: "It makes all the difference in the world whether you take a person to be a living soul who could be x-rayed to discern the skeleton, or treat him like a skeleton with certain other accoutrements. It makes all the difference in the world whether you take Scripture as God-speaking literature narrating a true story, which can be x-rayed to get at the doctrinal skeleton, or treat it like a book of dogmatic propositions with certain other interesting features," *Rainbows* (1980), 94.

16 K.J. Popma's treatment of *De taak der theologie* (1946) explained the danger of treating confessional matters like the creeds of a church communion as if they needed to

christian college alive in the Reformation biblical faith-thought tradition, I believe, is whether the spirit at work in the Scripturally-led philosophy, theology, history-telling, and scholarly contours of all the teaching disciplines be earthily redemptive and interdisciplinarily diaconal in bearing fruit worthy of repentance.[17]

A theology of art and a christian philosophical aesthetics
One other example of the difference it makes for a christian college and christian scholarship to have a Reformational christian philosophy and historiography be the cohering disciplines or, as in many evangelical christian colleges, to have theological study be the discipline that certifies their christian cachet, is the frustrating conundrum for me of the different tack taken by a "theology of the arts" instead of "a christian philosophical aesthetics."

When "theology" is uncritically taken to mean **christian** theology (as if Jews and Muslims have no theology), and christian **theology** is loosely taken to mean "faith in Jesus Christ" (as if secular Rationalists have no *bona fide* faith in Reason), so that theo**logical** reflection is undistinguished from the Holy Spirit's existential grip on our hearts; and further, when the congregated church and its institutional task to nourish us humans as **believing** followers of Jesus Christ is confused with the kingdom Rule of God in history and the body of Jesus Christ at large who are not simply clerics or parishioners but servants of the LORD fulfilling multiple tasks in God's world: then it becomes quite a jumble to untangle, from a Reformational standpoint, so that one can try to appreciate these fellow christian attempts to give artistry a place and task in God's world, yet be troubled by what seems to be askew.

---

be theo**logicalized**. For Popma theology is specialized **theoretical analysis** of the (pre-theoretical) **faith-functioning side of human life**, how people believingly understand God's word (especially 64–71); but, Popma says, theology must not usurp the authority of primary faith and confessional life.

John Vander Stelt is wrestling too with the double meaning of *pistis/geloven*: (1) "the **gracious gift** of faith, which cannot be studied in theology" (1981:131, 128) and (2) conscious **acts of confessing** the faith worked in one's heart, which surely can be carefully scrutinized and ordered.

It would be very good for someone to delineate the family of terms used loosely with resulting confusion: saving faith, faith-commitment, the function of ultimate trust, confession of one's underlying faith, church creeds, doctrines, dogmas, biblical hermeneutics, academic dogmatic theology, catechism. . . .

17 I.e., *poenitentia*. 1 John 4:1, Romans 12–14, 1 Corinthians 12, bear fruit. ". . . a sense of organic coherence is of the essence for Reformed higher education, just as it is for a society that Christians would call good" (Bratt 1993: 38).

It is a mistaken project, in my judgment, to perform and analyze music, for example, to illustrate the (Trinitarian) nature of God. Rather than give folk music, symphonic orchestral music, improvisatory jazz, its due as a glorious creatural gift from God for us humans to laugh and weep redemptively, thankfully, or to be stolen as an idolatrous escape from the Lord, music is misconceived as *ancilla theologiae* (a handmaiden of theology). Music is then read/heard allegorically and used apologetically or evangelistically—"we should let music do some of the theological work for us."[18] Jeremy Begbie seems to go this route—"theology through the arts"—because underneath his approach is a **philosophical** position of *analogia entis* that holds "that creaturely reality participates in the rationality of God."[19] That's a problem. I respect Dr. Begbie and his ministry very much, but cannot share his adopted metaphysics, which, though time-honored, has transgressed ontologically, it seems to me, the human artist's creaturely status and has traditionally bound art to a sacred servitude. (In subsequent personal correspondence, Prof. Begbie has assured me that I misunderstood him on this matter.)

The idea that "faith" is always **Christian** faith,[20] and that *fides quaerens intellectum* is properly and singularly "theological" activity, inevitably twists theorists of physics, political science, economics, and aesthetics into contortions to be theologians if we would subject our theoretical analyses through faith into "Christian" service for God and neighbor. This is more than hassling about a term like "theology." Such a theologistic straitjacket is harmful, I think, because it is often bound up with the old idea that art, for example, can perform a kind of secular sacramental service; as though, by its great beauty for example, art could lift us up beyond the mundane world and give us a sense of transcendence, a taste of "religious life."[21]

Again, such a deep-going, concerted attempt to enlist artistry for the "christian life" is laudable, but its semi-mystical bent overrates artists as prophets, and misprizes, as I see it, ordinary aesthetic activity that can enrich human life but does not occasion epiphanies of illuminating glory. The philosophical Monarchian Aristotelian framework behind such a

---

18 Jeremy Begbie, *Theology, Music and Time* (2000), 198; see also 19–20, 125–127.

19 Ibid., 276; 255, 278. Al Wolters' inaugural address at Redeemer College gives a telling correction to the usual translation of 2 Peter 1:4, in "Partners of the Deity: A covenantal reading of 2 Peter 1:4," *Calvin Theological Journal* 25 (April, 1990): 28–44.

20 The Robert Sweetman and George Marsden 2001 exchange in *Perspectives* shows that the sleepy use of the term "faith" is very subtle and far-reaching.

21 F. B. Brown, *Good Taste, Bad Taste, and Christian Taste* (2000), 55, 58–61; see also my "Modal Aesthetic Theory," in *Rainbows* (1980), 121–125.

theological aesthetics is exemplified by Gerardus van der Leeuw's *Sacred and Profane Beauty: The holy in art* and was in full force at the University of Chicago Divinity School in the 1960s under the leadership of Nathan A. Scott, Jr.[22] Its "incarnational theology of art" position is commending itself to educated evangelical Christians nowadays who are taking more kindly to Anglican ritual or Eastern Orthodox Christian reliance on icons as an entrée to "spiritual experience."

My own theoretical aesthetics, conceived in the womb of a Reformational christian philosophical systematics, tries to honor **aesthetic life** as an imaginative moment integral to our whole corporeal human existence; as a facet of God's good creation, aesthetic activity is to be received and exercised with holy joy inside one's speaking, thinking, feeling, voting, money spending, and prayer life (modal aesthetics). As far as artistry goes (theory of art and literature) in its many splendored varieties, encapsulations, and functions—to enhance wonder, entertain, instruct, celebrate—since the crux of the aesthetic is allusivity and nuancefulness, normative art might not be beautiful but could be puzzling, tragic, even ugly, so long as the oblique artistic presentation of meaning keeps an imaginative symbolic quality defining its result or event. My appreciation of the aesthetically grotesque is a significant difference from the usual "theology of beauty" that has been for centuries a dominant traditional blight, to my thinking, on understanding art. And to upgrade the dimension of aesthetics that bridges theory with praxis (principles of art and literary criticism), claiming hermeneutics lies in the province of aesthetics, could really startle theologians. If colleges and seminaries where theology is taught would understand that biblical hermeneutics needs to consider that reading biblical text assumes you know how to read **literature, artistic texts**, with *Gereformeerde voelhorens* sharpened by an aesthetics of nuance, such trained theologians might write different kinds of sermons.

This sketchy outline of a Reformational christian theory of aesthetics I once called a "doxological aesthetics," because its whole thrust is to praise the LORD and to glory thankfully in the gift of imaginative knowledge of nuances in the world. My colleague Adrienne Dengerink-Chaplin designates such a philosophical aesthetics most insightfully, perhaps better, a "creational aesthetics." That's a defining mark of the biblically Reformational christian philosophical stance: take **creation** seriously as God's revelation, which, despite the perversions we sinners bring into history, is still

---

22 The New Orpheus collection of essays, edited by Nathan A. Scott, Jr., includes authors like Dorothy Sayers, Denis de Rougemont, Allen Tate, William F. Lynch, Walter Ong, W.K. Wimsatt, Preston T. Roberts, and Amos N. Wilder.

God's world, and is to be studied in the light of Scriptural revelation when we are a communion of saints redeemed by Jesus Christ.[23]

Higher education: apprenticeship in holy scholarship

I'll be very brief here on my third and last point (3): **What good is a college education?** My Reformational answer to both a teacher and student would be: take time to be a holy scholar.

By "scholar" I don't mean you have to cite at least two dozen chemical abstracts in your brief report, or add footnotes to your next short story, or get a major concentration in philosophy. To be a scholar means to be schooled in studying something, disciplined, thoughtfully thorough in coming to know what you are doing or are discovering. "Higher education" at college is a special opportunity for a younger generation to taste and for an older generation to show-and-tell scholarship together, to be engrossed with the musical capability of the human voice, the intricate biosphere and genetic code of weeds, or the relative power of images and words for convincing people what is important or true. During your time in higher education some reality of God's world fascinates you, and now you have the opening to spend life time in probing, examining, researching, practicing, and testing your growing **understanding** of whatever this wonder be in all its marvelous interconnected richness until you gain the beginnings, as the Dordt *Educational Task* document states (11), of "serviceable insight."

"Higher education" is substantially different from "elementary" and "secondary" schooling, I think, because pupils have made a discretionary choice (presumably) to become, for a time, **students**, to listen and watch scholar-professors—professional students—report their researched "serviceable insights" and to be led as newcomers into catching the joy of the scholarly endeavor and giving away its fruits. Scholarly research is not always cut from the same cloth but is appropriate to the subject matter. Biologist Harry Cook (The King's College, Edmonton) investigated (for years!) under microscopic laboratory conditions the pituitary gland of the snail in order to section an organism and analyze the nature of biotic growth. An art historian may need the grace to sift through countless dusty, unused books and print archives in the *Bibliothèque Nationale* in Paris to get the key to unlock the meaning of Watteau's subtle artwork so that people today might second-think the crass boy-meets-girl in back car seat or disco scene. When James Schaap spends weeks alone in a pup

---

23 Cf. my "Pertinence of the Gospel of Creation for Christian Education," in *In the Fields of the Lord*, 206–208.

tent amid the endless waste grasses of the Dakota badlands in order to recreate the setting of his next work, or when Hugh Cook (Redeemer College, Ancaster) has a two-hour coffee session every week with a retired head cop in Ontario because there is probably going to be a crime in his next novel, all that is research, to produce stories that give you pause and nuggets of wisdom.

College is the time of your life to be an apprenticed scholar, even if you do not want to be a scholar for life. And for us who teach in post-secondary education I think it is vitally christian to convey the assurance that study time has its own peculiar service to God and neighbor. Students should not be hurried, must not have to be in a pell-mell hurry to get a job to make money. That is the hypnotic crooked idea of time American culture breathes: time means money. Not, according to the Bible: time is a gift of God to be redeemed (Ephesians 5:15–20; van der Hoeven, 65).

Consecrated **studious** thinking, imagining, speaking, writing, reading, and learning skills is **doing** something, and doing something as important as a pregnancy: preparing with "serviceable insight" for the birth of "insightful service." Christian college time is seedtime; the harvest comes later. In this amazing academic crucible we know as an institution of "higher learning," mentor and novice have the busy, tiring "leisure" to build up a treasury of knowledge and understanding that will stand you in good stead when the lean years and the hard times come. Academic time allows teacher and student to meander around topics, to explore following their noses, to chew and to gnaw on books, to delve into backwater eddies of history that deserve to flow fresh in our stream of consciousness, to experiment in essay and lab and to make mistakes that become "holy" mistakes when the overview the mentor provides gives the student encouraging, forgiving, redemptive guidelines where to "do it again."

It's a good thing Moses, after his Egyptian training, could spend 40 years in the grazing land of Midian tending sheep before he had to tend twelve huge tribes of petulant people. Only four years at Dordt tending **virtual** problems is fairly short by comparison; so we should cherish this christian college time of planting and watering good seed, the precious gestation time for setting policies on counseling neuroses or for correcting miscarriages of justice **before** you have to do it in the press of actual emotional breakdowns and violent cases of racial injustice. During this seeding time, christian profs make the best manure.

I consider the emphasis on taking one's time to study to be Reformational—Luther and Calvin were scholars before they were public leaders—and I suppose that my own European educational **experience** emphasized history-keeping and learning several languages more than American education does. So I am wary of the turn in Wolterstorff, seconded by Fernhout, to promote "more praxis-oriented scholarship" (Wolterstorff 56; Fernhout 115–116 n.8). What strikes me as unwise is the pragmatist American narrowing down of **higher** education to pre-professional training, to make education more attuned to both the in-terests of government and corporate commerce, plus a determination to emphasize "the primacy of experiential knowing-in-relation" (Fernhout 125) rather than to stress the abiding central role of **books** for christian learning by maturing students.

Christian educators today certainly need a sharper awareness of non-Western world cultures, of the fact that technology is moving us into a post-literate society, and that "justice" (not the Shylock variety) and "keeping promises" (Micah 6:8) must be in the foreground of our chris-tian learning. But those concerns should not be addressed in a way that jeopardizes the norm that academic learning is to be one step removed from the streets.[24] *Credo* it is better to fight battles for the LORD in the library, where the ammunition is also live, as a soldier of Jesus Christ still being outfitted with holy armor (Ephesians 6:10–20), **before** you engage an enemy in unmediated combat, tempted to use unsanctified weapons and fight fire with fire.

Everything I have presented here is in accord, I think, with what I know about Dordt College and find in your *Educational Task* and *Educa-tional Framework* documents, albeit tweaked a little differently. My hope is not that you move "beyond" forging "serviceable insight" (Fernhout 125), but that you deepen its Reformational integrality, to use Robert Sweetman's good term (14–16). And do it with your own particular his-torical strengths that have accrued from a decided, fruitful working use

---

24 "Perhaps it would be fruitful to turn the tables, with elementary or secondary educa-tion serving as a model for post-secondary" (Fernhout, 125 n19). Such a turnabout would run the danger, it seems to me, of being patronizing toward the older students, if "modeling" (so important to this conception of education) used to form primary school children would be taken as the model for forming teenagers and college stu-dents. A reason Ken Badley's book, *Worldviews: The challenge of choice* (Toronto: Irwin Publishing, 1996), is so stimulating for high school students, I think, is that the book treats them more like college students who may have the need to jostle with others and try what is out of the ordinary in order to forge a mind of their own.

At this point I also am doubtful whether wisdom can be taught. Wisdom can only be caught, after a person comes to know and understand things.

of the biblically Reformational christian philosophy for orientation,[25] which I would prefer to call "a philosophy of God's structuring Word."[26]

One must not allow the Reformational christian philosophy (**or** *Reformed* theology) jargon ever to become mouthed shibboleths denoting kosher faculty. Instead, these should serve as winsome servants, pregnant ideas that **do** make a difference in conceiving and teaching a field of study that will contribute to everyone's joining in to be members of the lived communality as Christ's body of teachers. Only Jesus Christ deserves disciples, not Luther and John Calvin. But repossessing a faith-thought tradition once it has gone missing is almost futile. So I pray that you Dordt faculty keep the tradition of the Reformation alive, not let it become past tense, **living the faith brokered philosophically and historiographically in your disciplined field of study**, teaching congenially together by re-minting and ramifying, in the Reformational way, God-honoring "serviceable insights."

Works consulted

Bartholomew, Craig and Colin Greene and Karl Muller, eds. *Renewing Biblical Interpretation* (Grand Rapids: Zondervan, 2000).

Bavinck, Herman. "Calvin and Common Grace," also with studies by Emile Doumergue, August Lang, and Benjamin B. Warfield, in *Calvin and the Reformation* (London: Fleming H. Revell, 1909), 99–130.

Begbie, Jeremy S. *Theology, Music and Time* (Edinburgh: Cambridge University Press, 2000).

Berkhof, Louis. *Systematic Theology* [1938], 4th rev. ed. (Grand Rapids: Eerdmans, 1949).

Bratt James D. "Reformed Tradition and the Mission of Reformed Colleges," in *A Reformed University in a Secularized and Pluralized World*, the papers of a Reformed University in North America conference held on 11–12 March 1993 in Grand Rapids, Michigan. Booklet with no publisher listed, n.d., 33–47.

Bratt, James D. *Dutch Calvinism in Modern America: A history of a conservative subculture* (Grand Rapids: Eerdmans, 1984).

Brown, Frank Burch. *Good Taste, Bad Taste, and Christian Taste: Aesthetics in*

---

25 I find chapters 9 and 10 of *A Zeal for Christian Education: The Memoirs of B.J. Haan* strikingly honest and historically relevant to this very day (153-191).

    Lindbeck's comment applies here too: ". . . provided a religion stresses service rather than domination, it is likely to contribute more to the future of humanity if it preserves its own distinctiveness and integrity than if it yields to the homogenizing tendencies associated with liberal experiential-expressivism" (128).

26 Cf. "Dooyeweerd's Legacy for Aesthetics," in *The Legacy of Herman Dooyeweerd: Reflections on critical philosophy in the christian tradition*, ed. C.T. McIntire (Lanham: University Press of America, 1995), 62 {see *NA*: 71}.

religious life (Oxford University Press, 2000).

Calvin, John, *De necessitate reformandae ecclesiae* [1544], in *Tractatus Theologici Omnes*, translated J.K.S. Reid, "The Necessity of Reforming the Church," in *Theological Treatises*, Library of Christian Classics (Philadelphia: Westminster Press, 1944), 22:183–216.

Cooper, John. "Reformed Scholarship and the Challenge of Post-modern Pluralism," in *A Reformed University in a Secularized and Pluralized World*, 3–25.

de Mol, Karen. "Sound Stewardship: How shall Christians think about music?" *Pro Rege* 26:3 (1998): 1–20.

Dengerink-Chaplin, Adrienne and Hilary Brand. *Art and Soul: Signposts for Christians in the arts* (Carlisle: Solway, 1999).

du Toit, Simon. "Playing with Fire: Towards a biblical approach to theatre performance," *Pro Rege* 29:4 (2001): 1–12.

The Educational Framework of Dordt College. Sioux Center: Dordt College, 1993. 11 pp.

The Educational Task of Dordt College. Sioux Center: Dordt College, 1979. 16 pp.

Fernhout, Harry. "Serviceable Insight: Wisdom at Work," in *Marginal Resistance*, Essays dedicated to John C. Vander Stelt, ed. John H. Kok (Sioux Center: Dordt College Press, 2001), 109–127.

Frei, Hans W. *Types of Christian Theology*, eds. George Hunsinger and William C. Placher (New Haven: Yale University Press, 1992).

Goudzwaard, Bob. Conversation in Driebergen-Rijsenberg, Netherlands, on 26 August 2001.

Haan, B.J. *A Zeal for Christian Education: The memoirs of B.J. Haan* (Sioux Center: Dordt College Press, 1992).

Hielema, Sydney. "Reclaiming the Apex of the Triangle: Scholarship as pilgrimage," in *Marginal Resistance*, 153–164.

Holl, Karl. *Die Kulturbedeutung der Reformation* [1911, rev. 1919], translated by Karl and Barbara Hertz and John H. Lichtblau, *The Cultural Significance of the Reformation* (Cleveland: Meridian, 1959).

Kok, John H. "Vollenhoven and 'Scriptural philosophy,'" *Philosophia Reformata* 53:2 (1988): 101–142.

Lindbeck, George A. *The Nature of Doctrine: Religion and theology in a postliberal age* (Philadelphia: Westminster Press, 1984).

Luther, Martin. "Letter to John von Staupitz, 30.5.1518," *Werke* (Weimar: Herman Böhlau, 1883), 1:525–527, translated by Gottfried G. Krodel in *Luther's Works* (Philadelphia: Fortress Press, 1963): 48:64–70.

Marsden, George. "Reformed Strategies in Christian Scholarship: a response to Robert Sweetman," *Perspectives: A journal of reformed thought* 16:7 (2001): 20–23.

Pelikan, Jaroslav. *The Reformation of the Bible / The Bible of the Reformation* + catalog of the exhibition by Valerie R. Hotchkiss and David Price (New Haven: Yale University Press, 1996).

Philosophy in the Reformed Undergraduate Curriculum, eds. John W. Roose and George N. Pierson. Papers by William Rowe, "Philosophy and the Problem of Foundations" (1–15), Peter DeVos, "Reformed Ideal for Curriculum" (17–27), Theodore Plantinga, "Philosophy's Place in the Reformed Undergraduate Curriculum" (29–55), Gary Weaver, "Demarginalizing Philosophy" (57–76), Calvin Seerveld, "Concluding Theses" (79–89) (Palos Heights: Trinity Christian College, 1990).

Plantinga, Alvin. "Christian Philosophy at the End of the 20ᵗʰ Century," in *Christian Philosophy at the Close of the Twentieth Century: Assessment and perspective*, eds. Sander Griffioen and Bert M. Balk (Kampen: Kok, 1995), 29–53.

Popma, K.J. *De Plaats der Theologie* (Franeker: Wever, 1946).

Rookmaaker, Hans. *De Kunstenaar een Profeet?* (Kampen: Kok, 1965); "The Artist as a Prophet?" in *The Complete Works of Hans Rookmaaker*, ed. Marleen Hengelaar-Rookmaaker (Carlisle: Piquant, 2002), 5:169–187.

———. "Art Needs No Justification" (1977), in *The Complete Works of Hans Rookmaaker*, 4: 315–49.

Scott, Jr., Nathan A. ed. *The New Orpheus. Essays toward a Christian poetic* (New York: Sheed & Ward, 1964).

Seerveld, Calvin. *Balaam's Apocalyptic Prophecies: A study in reading Scripture* (1968) (Toronto: Wedge Publishing Foundation, 1980). Revised edition: *How to Read the Bible to Hear God Speak: A study in Numbers 22–24* (Sioux Center/Toronto: Dordt College Press/Tuppence Press, 2003).

———. *Rainbows for the Fallen World: Aesthetic life and artistic task* (Toronto: Tuppence Press, 1980).

———. "Footprints in the Snow," *Philosophia Reformata* 56 (1991): 1–34 {infra pp. 235–276}.

———. "Vollenhoven's Legacy for Art Historiography," *Philosophia Reformata*, 58:1 (1993): 49–79. {See *AH*: 23–60.}

———. *Bearing Fresh Olive Leaves: Alternative steps in understanding art* (Carlisle: Piquant & Toronto Tuppence Press, 2000).

———. *In the Fields of the Lord*, ed. Craig Bartholomew (Carlisle: Piquant & Toronto Tuppence Press, 2000).

———. "Why should a university exist?" Insert in *Contact*, newsletter of the International Association for the Promotion of Christian Higher Education, 12:1 (November 2000), 10 pp. {infra 29–58}.

Spykman, Gordon J. *Reformational Theology: A new paradigm for doing dogmatics* (Grand Rapids: Eerdmans, 1992).

Sweetman, Robert. "Christian Scholarship: Two Reformed perspectives," *Perspectives: A journal of reformed thought*, 16:6 (2001): 14–19.

Thompson, John Lee. *John Calvin and the Daughters of Sarah: Women in regular and exceptional roles in the exegesis of Calvin, his predecessors, and his contemporaries* (Genève: Librairie Droz, 1992).

Vanden Bosch, Mike. *A History of Dordt College: The B.J. Haan years* (Sioux

Center: Dordt College Press, 1990).

Van der Hoeven, Johan. "Christian Philosophy at the end of the 20th century," in *Christian Philosophy at the Close of the Twentieth Century: Assessment and perspective*, 55–66.

Van der Leeuw, Gerardus. *Wegen en Grenzen: De verhouding van religie en kunst* [1932, rev. 1950], translated David E. Green, *Sacred and Profane Beauty: The holy in art* (Chicago: Holt, Rinehart & Winston, 1963).

Vander Stelt, John C. "Faith and Theology: Fundamental and global issues." Workshop paper for Symposium on Cultures and Christianity, 21–25 August 2000. Hoeven, Netherlands. 14pp. typescript.

———. "Theology or Pistology?" in *Building the House: Essays on Christian Education*, eds. James A. de Jong and Louis Y. Van Dyke (Sioux Center: Dordt College Press, 1981), 115–135.

Van der Walt, B.J. *Transformed by the Renewing of your mind: Shaping a biblical worldview and a christian perspective on scholarship* (Potchefstroom: Institute for Contemporary Christianity in Africa, 2001).

Wolterstorff, Nicholas P. *Keeping Faith: Talks for new faculty at Calvin College* (Grand Rapids: Occasional papers from Calvin College [7:1] February 1989), 5–61.

Zinkand, John M. "The Use and Implications of the Phrase 'in Christ' in the Writings of Paul," in *Building the House*, 81–98.

Zuidema, S.U. "Gemene Gratie en Pro Rege bij Dr Abraham Kuyper," *Anti-Revolutionaire Staatkunde*, 24 (1954): 1–19, 49–73; translated by Harry Van Dyke, "Common Grace and Christian Action in Abraham, Kuyper," *Communication and Confrontation: A philosophical appraisal and critique of modern society and contemporary thought* (Kampen: Kok, 1972), 52–105.

I am grateful to colleague George Vandervelde for being a willing and able resource when I need to discuss hard theological questions.

Making the Most of College:
Studying Ourselves to Life or to Death?

A few suggestions for a Christian student at a secular university:

1. **Major in the best profs**, who make you think self-critically and who give solid course content in a field-area that you have gifts for or can be busy with, without noticing the passage of time.

2. **Take a double major**, if possible, to promote the ability to do interdisciplinary thinking, a kind of informal philosophy major (if the philosophy available is sophistic, skeptical or "undeep").

3. **Get in-depth knowledge** of a certain period: 5th to 4th century BC Athens, Renaissance England, Europe around the time of the French Revolution, or America during the 1920s. That is, rather than staying with survey knowledge, get close to a slice of cultural life somewhere, once upon a time, in many of its facets—a form of encyclopedia-historical study. Maybe work for a couple summers or part of a year in an African village, do volunteer work in Central America, or take a job on the south side of Chicago or in Toronto's Regent Park.

4. **Do your thesis or long paper**, if possible, on the history of the discipline you are interested in. Normative problems turn up in the decisive turns and crises an area of study undergoes, and such changes face you and your professor with the fact that the status quo did not drop out of heaven but is a response by humans driven by spirited love and philosophical commitments.

5. **Find a group of kindred spirits** with whom to read books of Christian philosophy together, any kind of communal deeper reflection on current problems, so that you exercise in community how to pin down the idolatries of our day in theory.

First posted at http://www.cardus.ca/comment/article/330 on June 23, 2006.

We need to help one another detect ideas that lead thinking programs into dead ends, or unpack concepts that foster self-righteousness.

6. **Read a novel every month** or so, to gather in the breadth and richness of the big Russian writers, the French authors like Balzac and Flaubert; get to know George Eliot, Melville, and Faulkner; read Gabriel Marquez, Chinua Achebe, Ursula le Guin, go back to the Christian Chaucer—it's all there to sift and learn from, an incredible treasury of insights and errors.

Teaching history of philosophy in the basement of
Trinity Christian College, Palos Heights, Illinois, 1959

WHY SHOULD A UNIVERSITY EXIST?

To be your guest speaker at this convocation is a great gift. But I am apprehensive: American-born, European-trained, my home is Canada; I am ignorant of your language, and know so little of Korean history and culture. What could I bring you that will not be a carefully wrapped Western, neocolonializing present? A christian Korean university does not want to duplicate a (secular) North American multiversity, does it?

I intend to respect and enjoy the wonder of our cultural differences, because we share the same humanity as a communion of scholarly saints redeemed by Jesus Christ (Romans 12:4–5). We are one in the Holy Spirit, who does not build empires but humbles peoples of the world with the common, comforting ministry of wisdom (Ephesians 1:17–23). My offering to God on this occasion is to try to lead you in a scripturally-directed reflection on what the third generation of Kosin University—your present student body—will face in God's world, if the Lord waits to come back.

Why should a university exist?
Should all of God's children become university students?
In Canada, before a small community of Dutch-immigrant christian believers of the Reformation faith-tradition (Martin Luther, John Calvin, John Knox, Abraham Kuyper) organized in the 1960s what has become the graduate Institute for Christian Studies in Toronto, where I have taught philosophical aesthetics (1971–95), there were only Bible Colleges for tertiary education in Canada, denominational seminaries, and secular universities.

Is a christian graduate-level university necessary today? What would a normative university institution and curriculum look like in our complex, differentiated, deeply troubled, globalizing society of the few liter-

Originally prepared for the March 2000 convocation at Kosin University in Busan, Korea, this text was later published as the Academic Insert in IAPCHE's newsletter *Contact*, 12:1 (2000): 1–10.

ate rich and millions of uneducated famished poor? Does the Bible speak for giving priority to a department of the arts at this stage of Kosin University's development, now that theology, a Christian education program, and medicine with nursing are well established? How can you best unfold and deepen (cf. Isaiah 54:1–3) the vision of the Presbyterian missionaries whose faith has led to what, by God's grace, is at work here today?

With Sung Soo Kim at Kosin University,
Busan, South Korea, 2000

HISTORICAL BACKGROUND ON THE CHARACTER OF UNIVERSITIES

Let me first recount a few historical events of certain significant matters that may give a context for answering such questions about university education in Canada and Korea.

Early glimmerings

Origins of institutions are usually clothed in mystery, probably so we humans cannot proudly think we could construct them as if they be makeshift, laboratory experiments. But we know Moses was trained at the Egyptian court of Pharaoh (c. 1500 BC), and King Solomon later (c. 1000 BC) could outperform internationally the learned of his day in *meschalim* (aphoristic proverbial learning) and songs (Exodus 2:1–10, Acts 7:20–22, Hebrews 11:23–28; 1 Kings 4:29–34). There was an early "seminary" for prophets at Bethel separate from King Ahaziah's court in

Israel (c. 900 BC), and it was the enlightened foreign policy of Babylonian King Nebuchadnezzar (c. 600 BC) to induct the princes of conquered peoples, like Daniel and friends, into the statecraft language and wisdom teaching of his palace school (2 Kings 2:1–18; Daniel 1). For centuries Confucius (551–470 BC), Mo Tzu (fl. 430 BC), and the editors of *Tao Te Ching* (c. 300 BC) gathered disciples around their teaching of Tao in the tradition of an oral sage dispensing life-knowledge enigmatically in poetic pieces.

At the time of ancient Athenian Pericles (died 429 BC) and Socrates (469–399 BC), orators like Gorgias (483–375 BC) and Isocrates (436–388 BC) turned teaching rhetoric into private professional schools with tuition fees, to train Greeks for leading civic affairs in the *polis*. Philosopher Plato's Academy was oriented more toward aristocrats who wanted leisure to think to the bottom of things and do mathematics, and that Academy lasted beyond Plato's death (347 BC) as a permutating school of philosophy until 529 AD—almost a millennium. Philosophical biologist Aristotle (384–322 BC), tutor of Alexander the Great: Aristotle's lecture notes cover everything from logic, natural science, and psychology to ethics, politics, poetics, and a searching analysis of "first principles," a veritable cosmic curriculum for the Aristotelian peripatetic school called Lyceum (begun 335 BC).

The educational loci of Plato, Isocrates, and Aristotle were codified by the Roman scholar Marcus Terentius Varro (116–27 BC) into nine disciplines: grammar, logic, rhetoric, arithmetic, geometry, astronomy, musical theory, medicine, and architecture. Rhetoric carried the day as the most important. The Roman emperor Vespasian funded chairs of Greek and Latin rhetoric (70 AD) to prime his imperial officials for administering the empire. Early christian leaders emphasized grammar and rhetoric too, because they wanted a literate priesthood officiating church doctrines. And gradually there came to be a tradition of seven *artes*—grammar, rhetoric, logic (*trivium*), arithmetic, geometry, astronomy, and musical theory (*quadrivium*)[1]—that one was expected to study as propaedeutic to doing scholarly work in theology, or as a course of study you needed to do first, for example, to "liberate" and prepare your mind for being a cultured official at Charlemagne's Frankish court (768–814 AD).

Meanwhile, independently about this time, around the Arabic *Qur'an* and precepts of the prophet Mohammed (507–632 AD) from

---

1 Martianus Capella, Boethius, Cassiodorus, and Isodore of Seville are all integral to forming this intellectual tradition too. Cf. A.B. Cobban, *The Medieval Universities* (1975), 12–14.

Medina edited in the Hadith, along with *fiqh* (rules for daily life behavior), there developed centers for instruction at the Muslim mosques. Early learning of *Qur'an*, *Hadith*, and *fiqh* was largely by rote recitation. Because the Muslim faith does not distinguish "sacred" and "profane" knowledge—all truth is Allah's truth—including skills necessary for *Jihad* (holy war), imams (clerics) were licensed to teach the faithful such revealed knowledge in the precinct of the mosque. When the Islamic capital was moved from Damascus to Baghdad (736 AD) during the period of the Abbasid caliphs, Arab scholars began to translate Greek philosophical manuscripts in their possession, especially Aristotle and Euclid, and to write commentaries on these documents, all housed in a *bayt al-hikmah* (house of wisdom), that is, a library. Gradually as the focus shifted from the "higher spiritual knowledge" to teaching of logic, mathematics, Arabic language, and medical texts, houses near but separate from the mosque became the centers of learning. The Al-azhal center in Cairo and the Modrasah Al-Nizamiyyah in Baghdad, like proto-universities, were meant to host all the splintering camps of Islamic theology with the other kinds of knowledge in one unified system of education.[2]

Setting the Western pattern

And that is precisely what seemed slowly to crystalize in various Western cities at this time: students from great distances congregated to follow lectures by *magistri* (masters) who wandered from city to city and spoke *ex cathedra* (with authority) on topics like philosophical mathematics and logic. The medical practitioners gathered in Salerno, however, dealt with skull fractures, pain, amputational surgery, which drugs an apothecary should mix for a fever. They and their students were not helped much by mathematics or by careful commentaries parsing what the Church Fathers had said about difficult Scriptural passages. The ancient Greek texts of Hippocrates, Aristotle, and Galen, and Arabic medical notes translated into Latin by the learned Constantine the African, who settled in Salerno c. 1077 AD, were much more pertinent for diagnosing how a human person's sickness depended upon an imbalance of humors in the body you could see in phlegm, cough, bleeding, or discolored urine.

Also about this time, in the urban travel/trade center of Bologna, there was a renewed interest in Roman law, which was taught by "glossing" the ancient texts. Canon law was added to this corpus c. 1140 AD, because the Church needed its lawyers too. The many foreign students of law who came to live in Bologna unionized to protect themselves against

---

2   Cf. Bilgrami and Ashraf, *The Concept of an Islamic University* (1985), 22–24.

profiteering townspeople on lodging and food prices, and also to control the teaching *doctores*—if the lectures were not good, the students boycotted and didn't pay the requested fees. Eventually the *magistri* formed a union or guild too (*collegium*), to set admission standards and to grant, by examination, licenses to teach jurisprudence (*licentia docendi*). The students really ran the whole operation in Bologna for a couple hundred years, until c. 1275 AD the commune salaried the teachers, and students gradually lost controlling power over appointments.

The Cathedral school of Notre Dame had the stability to let the University of Paris evolve in its neighborhood—the earliest universities had no buildings. Famed for the brilliant philosophy of Pierre Abelard (1079–1142 AD), whose *Sic et Non* (1121–22 AD) used dialectical logic to order the single intention of the only apparently differing learned church authorities, Paris attracted students internationally, also in theology, for the more mystical Victorine theology taught there. It was assumed that students spend six years studying in the seven philosophical arts before you went on to theology, law, or medicine. Whenever there was at least one magister in residence for each of the arts and also for civil and for canon law, then that collective *studium* (course of studies) was given the status of *studium generale* by some arms-length authority—pope, king, or emperor. Those who held a *studium particulare* degree could teach within the local jurisdiction of their particular school, while whoever held a degree in *studium generale* could teach at any university.[3]

A big question always was, however: Is this university conglomerate self-governing? The Paris university is outside civil municipal rules, but is it an arm of the Church? The University of Paris was formally forbidden by the papacy to teach Aristotle's "Metaphysics" and Arabic commentaries in 1210 and 1215, yet by 1254 AD Aristotle was a recognized part of the Parisian *studium*. It took a papal bull of Gregory IV (*Parens scientiarum*, 1231) to establish the authority of the university *magistri* as not being subject to the orders of the bishop of Paris and the Chancellor of Notre Dame cathedral. Skirmishes on who has final say continued, but the University of Paris gradually settled down as a hoary center of a christian patrimony more in the power orbit of the kings of France rather than under the papacy.

Oxford (founded later than 1167 but before 1190 AD) and Cambridge (c. 1225 AD) universities branched off from Paris, as it were, and

---

3   This *ius ubique docendi* (law of empowerment to teach wherever), however, was often torpedoed by local professors jealous to protect their own students' employment in a given university.

developed a college residential structure peculiar to England. The Universities of Prague (1347–48), Vienna (1365), Heidelberg (1385), Leipzig (1409), and others were founded by local governments, and thus were free to be more secular in spirit and bound to become more nation-oriented—although Latin was still the language common for scholarship everywhere.

One could sum up the legacy in the medieval formation of the university, which has remained as a pattern, this way: (1) *Universitas* is *societas magistrorum discipulorumque* (a corporate society of master teachers and younger scholars) with a fairly stable curriculum of disciplinary study (the seven philosophical arts) where students are tested for a degree that licenses them to teach and/or to enter advanced study programs for the vocations of medicine, law, or theology.

(2) The university wrestled for its own sphere of educational authority, but had to jockey constantly with the Roman church, with whatever political government was reigning, and with local neighborhood society on what various responsibilities are due to be honored by whom and possibly shared.

(3) Despite the centuries-long privileging of rhetoric as crucial to the style of an educated person, and despite the Humanist revivals of attention to classical languages and literatures (c. 1050–1200 AD), the tremendous impact of the Arabic-transmitted Aristotelian corpus of logic and natural science analysis upon university circles, while it did not exactly curb speculative Platonizing theology, did cause logic to squeeze out rhetoric for primacy, and firsthand examination of natural phenomena began to replace the production of scholia on ancient texts.

Variations on the medieval university setup

The Prussian Wilhelm von Humboldt (1767–1838) was instrumental in founding the University of Berlin (1809). The emphasis Humboldt gave to rigorous, unending *wissenschaftliche Forschung* (philosophically scientific research) brought a distinctive new focus to German university life. A university demands a genuine community of advanced thinkers wholly driven by the passion to cultivate themselves (*Bildung*) to reach the truth, which will be ever critically improving the individual's ratio-moral humanity. A university is not the place to prepare for a professional job: the vocation of university professors and graduate students alike (in seminars, not lectures) is to keep doing in-depth research, to be philosophically active searching for connecting links in perhaps obscure, recalcitrant realities, exploring the as-yet-unknown heights and depths of specialized knowledge.

This Romantic Idealist twist to university studies favored an elite group of individuals—students were expected already to be researchers—who were right to be wholly absorbed in their academic investigations, without practical worries, far from the madding crowd. Humboldt wanted the king to make the university financially independent so it could focus on its real task: research.[4] And it is precisely this self-contained, almost Faustian obsession with research, one might say, that left many German university scholars shamefully ignorant or negligent of their public responsibilities in society during the Nazi era of Hitler's dictatorial rule.[5]

Johns Hopkins University tried to transplant the German research model to America in 1876, and began its institution with only graduate students. . . . But before I conclude this brief backgrounding on the historical formation of universities with remarks about the American hybrid slant that affects the whole world today, I should just mention the influential work of John Henry Newman (1801–1890), who converted to Roman Catholicism in 1845 and became rector of an explicitly Roman Catholic university in Dublin (1852), which was begun because the Catholic students' predicament at Oxford and Cambridge had been that they must sign an affirmation to the Protestant Anglican Thirty-Nine Articles of Religion.

Newman believed that a university, a Catholic university, needed to be critically self-conscious of its basic assumptions (*principia*), and not inculcate faith beliefs but do research for and then teach knowledge to students. You have "knowledge," said Newman, when factual information is intellectually ordered in an organic network of meaning. He could almost have quoted Matthew Arnold: you "see things steadily and whole" when you know something. The mission of the university is to give students knowledge worth knowing for its own sake, not because it is useful or practical, said Newman, but because the knowledge gives you encyclopedic scope, moral resonance, a gentlemanly civility in society.

You can hear the Victorian British, class-conscious breeding bias built into Newman's Catholic program. Unlike von Humboldt's elitist Humanism, which counted on severe philosophically honed, inquisitorial analytic talent, Newman's unifying study at the university is literature, English literature, Shakespeare. So Cardinal Newman's idea of a university is more gentle than the German one, and Newman's ideal university, even though he opened a medical school at his Dublin University com-

---

4   Cf. Anton van Hanskamp, "Wilhelm von Humboldt" (1995), 36.

5   Cf. Eric Vogelin, "The German University" (1985), 25–26.

plex, is characterized by a chastened trust in rationality and the decorous outworking of study in the Humanities.

American higher education has usually displayed a mixture of institutional structures. (1) Early American church-run colleges like Harvard (1636) followed the literary liberal arts lead of the residential Oxford, Cambridge, and Dublin setup, and started colleges particularly to train ministers for their denominational pulpits, much as Kosin Seminary, as I understand it, and then Kosin College were begun. (2) The U.S. Congress's Morrill Land Grant Act of 1862, signed into law by Abraham Lincoln, gave states land for state universities, which were expected at minimal tuition costs to democratically serve inhabitants of the state with the traditional undergraduate liberal arts education and provide them training in applied research, particularly in experimental agriculture and industrial manufacturing needs of the country. This was closer to the kind of "useful" university Benjamin Franklin had wanted. (3) Certain American universities like Johns Hopkins (1876), Stanford (founded 1885), and Chicago (1890) were impressed by the German graduate doctoral research university, and pioneered such advanced studies in the USA.

All three kinds of American college-university institutions trumpeted equality of student opportunity, quality of professorial instruction, and actually became the privileged way in society for someone to become a "professional," a person certified to provide a service with specialized knowledge. Important is the fact that the graduated clergy for the church, lawyers for the government, physicians, dentists, and nurses for the populace, as well as other professional specialists in agriculture and commerce, all had a roughly common underlay of liberal arts exposure: Western civilization overview courses, English and American literature, with elementary knowledge of mathematics, natural and societal sciences, plus a hearty dose of extracurricular activities like choir and athletics. This was the American way of "institutionalized individualism" (*e pluribus unum*)[6] in a university system organized along the lines of "competitive merit" and "team spirit."

After what is called World War II (1939–1945) and the divisive war in your own country (1950–53), things changed in the American university. American war veterans who survived the horrors were given money by the U.S. government (GI Bill, 1944, 1952, 1966) to go to university for the education they had missed. In fact, in postwar America there was a surge of mass enrollment of students, because college and university

6   Cf. John W. Chapman, *The Western University on Trial* (1983), 5.

were no longer seen as places you entered to find out by studying who you were as a person (Socrates' *sé gnowthi*), but you went there to train for a job. Two-year community colleges and polytechnic institutes sprang up like dandelions, and even the big-name, pace-setting universities, which had been drafted during the war by the U.S. government to bend their scientific research more toward defense and space technology projects (grant money!); these universities, too, diversified, multiplied specializations, and looked for ways to provide vocation-friendly courses.

The Russian space success in launching "Sputnik" (1957) opened the spigot of U.S. government money to pour funds into American universities to beef up study in advanced mathematics, natural sciences, technology; and everybody was in a hurry! Teenage students as well as married war veterans did not want to be prepared for life "in general," but were glad to be recruited for programs in an engineering department or in business administration that led directly to an income after graduation. Many American universities became "multiversities," as Clark Kerr dubbed them, with myriad academic specializations that seemed to lack any overarching connection to the others—there was no center. Multiversities took on the character of high-grade educational cafeterias where majors and minors in different fields of information existed for a while, subject to the market forces of special interests, a kind of degree factory, often with excellent training, but scattered.

Student unrest, however, grew, not only because of warring in Viet Nam (U.S. escalated involvement 1964–69), but because something was missing. Not even an established university can live by bureaucratic administration and bread alone. Robert Hutchins inaugurated the "Great Books of the Western World" program at the University of Chicago in the 1960s, to try to recapture alive the historic tradition of Western civilization and make it palatable to a generation of students-as-consumers.[7] Harvard, which long ago had introduced the matter of "electives," now broached the requirement of a "core" curriculum, to try still to give a common civilizing knowledge to students passing through its hallowed gates.

It has always been hard to sell Americans on the value of history, and the riots of 1968 in Paris, the organized unrest at Berkeley campus in California (1964), the shooting of protesting students at Kent State (1970) and other rallies of revolt on American college and university

---

7   Allan Bloom (*The Closing of the American Mind*, 1987) and E.D. Hirsch, Jr. (*Cultural Literacy: What every American needs to know*, 1987) follow this old Humanist strategy too.

campuses, did not stop American multiversities from becoming the Big Business they are today. Often the educational crux of a professor of humane studies with an attentive apprentice student gets lost in the massive machinery of a teacher's needing to publish articles of expertise in refereed journals only the initiate can read, and the university's fixation with handling the grades of a student's "performance" efficiently rather than taking the time to judge the worth of the education given and received. And university administrators, rather than being held accountable for their visionary leadership of a community of scholars, often came to be evaluated by their success in raising funds. Large American universities today, I believe, are run more like business corporations, in consultation with government granting agencies, and have yet become cultural powerbrokers around the world on what higher education should be.

Implications of a History for Facing the Systematic Problem of Defining a University Institution

You have been patient to hear me narrate an historical sketch of certain steps that lie behind the universities we have on our hands today. My reason for taking the time to do that was to help us students and teachers who would follow the Christ in our advanced studies see that "a christian university" does not just drop out of heaven on a certain sunny afternoon. The university as an institution is alive and has a history, and a living university organization changes. Universities are communal human responses to God's call for educating a younger generation in the wonders of God's world. We humans are responsible for the institutional university response we make together. That is why at certain times for faculty, institution-building may be more important than advancing research in one's chosen discipline. If a university does not hang together, then the students hang separately in their multiversity specialist cubicles.

In our Reformation christian faith-tradition you do not go to the Bible to find a chapter and verse prescription that tells you whether to teach chemistry or add a department of painterly art to your school. The Reformed Presbyterian faith tradition takes seriously the belief that the creation also reveals our Creator's will,[8] and if our sinful eyes are corrected and directed by scriptural truth, we may fallibly discern in creation what way the Lord would have us walk. So, discerning carefully what has happened historically in university formation, de-formation, re-formation, should give us a clue as to what creatural realities humans have

---

8   Cf. G.C. Berkouwer, *Algemene Openbaring* [1951], translated *General Revelation* (Grand Rapids: Eerdmans, 1955).

had to wrestle with—from whatever faith position or perspective they acted—since the creaturely limits God has set for discovering and passing on knowledge in God's world give the parameters and cradle all human endeavors, whether they be pagan, christian, or secularized humans busy building its "university." Can we find out what kind of contours a normative university institution should have in our day?

When the oldest university in the world, Al-Azhar in Cairo, under Nasser's regime in Egypt, added an engineering program in the 1960s, the dilemma of current Muslim university education became painfully clear. Arab scholars note that Al-Azhar has two parallel, unharmonized systems of education next to one another: the secular liberal Western one, and the traditional Muslim theological one, under the same roof. But, they said, the Muslim nation is built on a common creed, and we need to have an integrated Islamic thought-world amid the morally destructive, materialistic culture all around us. Says Muslim scholar Syed Ali Ashraf:

> Unless we are able to formulate all basic concepts of knowledge from the point of Islamic metaphysics, we shall not be able to establish an Islamic university.[9]

The original Canadian universities were meant to pass on the traditional values of their elders to the aspiring leaders of the nation, but gradually Canadian universities followed, perhaps more slowly, the secularizing course of the American universities. Industrialists in Canada wanted more skilled occupational help. So Queen's University opened a mining school (1893), and the august University of Toronto began a forestry school on campus (1907), alongside the startup of independent trade schools (Industrial Education Act, 1911).

Much later, in the prosperity period after World War II and with the baby boom, the Canadian government began to give financial aid to the debt-ridden universities, since the populace supported this "investment" in helping Canada become a modern industrial nation, and most graduates found employment in their specialties. Around 1970, however, Canada experienced rising unemployment, spiraling inflation, *ad hoc* policy decisions by universities on what programs to develop, and cut-backs in

---

9   Bilgrami and Ashraf, viii. They continue: ". . . if we still follow the same syllabi that we are following now in imitation of the liberal West, we shall not succeed in making this education truly Islamic" (64).

A secularized Muslim educator takes a different tack: "There is no such thing as an Islamic viewpoint in the study of physics, chemistry, or any of the other sciences. . . . there is nothing wrong with the teaching of scientific subjects as such." So F.K. Khan Durrani, *A Plan of Muslim Educational Reform* (1989), 13, 15.

government funding: the costs of a Canadian university education came to be experienced as a burden rather than as an investment. "We want more scholar for the dollar," said the Ontario Minister of Colleges and Universities. Should Kosin University do that?

That is the time when the small graduate Institute for Christian Studies in Toronto began holding regular classes in philosophy, history of philosophy, philosophy of political science, philosophical theology, philosophical psychology, philosophical aesthetics, philosophy of christian education. . . .

When I read that even during the Choson dynasty (1392–1910) in your country, the Ewha Haktang College for women students (1886/1898) was supported by Queen Min, teaching christian principles along with natural science and manual skills quite strange to the confucian ideals, I became grateful to God for such an effort next to other christian colleges (Sungsil Union, 1906; Seoul Choson, 1915). And when I know how American christian missionaries stood by you as a people in mission schools during the Japanese occupations and wars for liberation, then I must confess the witness of Kosin University (with roots back to 1946) has much to teach us North Americans, since the persecution in which you have persevered cannot but have given your university studies and your decisions on priorities a sanctified caliber we academic believers in Canada and the USA do not know.

BIBLICALLY CHRISTIAN CONTOURS FOR A UNIVERSITY: SYSTEMATIC NOTES

Let me distill for you several matters I have learned from tracing somewhat the world history of universities. And in the back of my consciousness lies the directive of the LORD in Psalm 78 for fathers and mothers to recount *magnalia Dei*, the great deeds of the LORD, to their children, so that the coming generations will remember to tell it to their children, so that the great-grandchildren will

> set their foolish, unshakeable hope in God,
> not ever forget the deeds of the LORD,
> but instead, take good care of God's ordinances,
> so that they would not become like their ancestors,
> a stubborn, know-it-all generation
> whose heart never got settled,
> whose spirit never held steady, solidly faithful to God.
> (Psalm 78:7–8)

A community of scholars

A university is an institutional community of an older and younger generation of scholars/students whose calling together is to discover and cultivate God's world with informed, imaginative reflection, and then as responsible, responding human subjects *coram Deo* together articulate their acquired wisdom in awed thanks to God, sharing its blessings with one's neighbors, and by taking care of all God's marvelous creatures, including animals, plants, and stones.

A community of scholars is the crux to any university. The medieval community of scholars ate and drank, prayed and studied together, supported in their bookish life by family, friends, patron, or church benefice. A community of scholarship is not a church, and is not a family, but is a collegial union of capable, thoughtful readers and investigators whose faith identity does not assume unanimity or even consensus on every policy matter, but does attest to a fundamental communion of dedication to a common task.

I should like to propose that when a community of scholars as a body holds the Psalm 24 vision to be true—

> The earth with its profuse diversity,
> and the world with all its inhabitants
> belong to the LORD. (Psalm 24:1)

—and when as a body they breathe a holy spirit of inquisitive shalom tempered by "each [scholar's] humbly esteeming the others to be superior to oneself" (Philippians 2:1–11, v.3) as they all together "consider how to provoke! one another to passionately selfless love and good works" (Hebrews 10:19–25, v.24): then you have the heart of a christian university throbbing with life. Then heterogeneity of persons and interests, the wide diversity of fields and often hardly intelligible research problems, as well as possible unbridgeable cultural differences, are all still unified by everyone's commitment to communicate one's studies and insights to the other members. It's almost as if there is a tacit, transparent understanding percolating underneath among the various older and younger scholars that, because God's universe coheres, what we singular people do in probing its mysteries should also cohere in a uni-versity.

Secularized universities unfortunately tend to become multiversities, held together by traditional protocols or administrative glue. Inter-scholarly communication can be frustrated because there is really no transparency in the language used, no singleness of spirit or common lord, the way the early Christians experienced having common resources after Christ's resurrection, ascension, and the Pentecost arrival of the Holy Spirit (Acts 4:32–37). So competitive power-plays, pulling rank, and creeping fragmentation sap the morale of such academic institutions. Prestige and the role of managerial hierarchical authority can maintain a semblance of identity, but the positive, unfettered flourishing of communal researched study and teaching becomes pinched. The frame to what goes on inside the university seems to be more of an imposition than a wholesome bond of blessing you want to count on. Such emaciation of vital community can happen at scholarly institutions that carry Christ's name too, where, with the best of intentions, the operation is more like the time of the Older Testament judges, when each professor does what seems right in one's own eyes (Judges 17:6, 21:25).

A college or university that would be truly christian in its exercise of the scholarly vocation cannot be satisfied, I think, with having competent, thoughtful practitioners in the spectrum of the various disciplines who are devout, Bible-believing, learned *magistri*. An ordinary way-of-life that follows Jesus Christ by giving evidence of the fruits of the Holy Spirit (cf. Galatians 5:16–6:2) is of course basic and essential to every christian profession. It is also critical that a christian scholar, in whatever special field of investigation he or she works, comes to be conscious of and is able to articulate the vision of a world-and-life-view that commits one to discover and accept the lordship of Jesus Christ over every speck of creaturely existence. Such a comprehensive overview acts as the watershed that services each one's particular terrain of study. But there is one more crucial step, I believe, beyond living a joyful biblical style of life, and having a christian world-and life-view, that is necessary for a christian university to function in a way that fosters genuinely communal, redemptive scholarship. A christian philosophical systematics needs to be operative in the theoretical, conceptual world of the special scientists busy analyzing and teaching all the different disciplines.

Let me try to be very clear about this last matter because it has significant implications for university curriculum too.

A christian philosophical systematics

You do not need to have a philosophy or a developed world-and-life-view to be a bona fide child of God. You do not even need to be literate to be a person whose life is "securely hidden with Christ in God" (Colossians 3:1–4). But we are discussing what constitutes advanced university scholarly education that would be truly Christ-centered, Scripturally directed, Holy Spirited; and for this kind and stage of academic education you do need to be literate, you do need to be trained to think precisely, making connections, imagining hypothetical possibilities, drawing conclusions.

And I am proposing that if scholars who work with rigorous conceptual care in their chosen field of pedagogy—preventative medicine, literary theory, musicology, biology, mathematics, theology, or in whatever facet of God's world you examine phenomena—these specialized scholars also need to be serviced by a rigorous philosophical systematics in order to be prepared, at theoretical depth, to practice inter-relational, inter-disciplinary study that is integral to a university education. It is important for scholars to make the assumptions and implications of their conceptual work accessible to those with other world-and-life views by having their cross-disciplinary sharing of scientific knowledge also carefully chiseled to scrupulous theoretical intelligibility.

By a christian philosophical systematics I mean the practice of theory oriented toward probing the structured aspects of things, persons, acts, and events, ferreting out the interrelated meaning of the matters under scrutiny. A christian idea of philosophy, you could say, is that philosophy is more a set of fundamental questions than it is a number of answers; philosophy is a constellation of categories within which one proceeds to think and make conceptual judgments. A christian philosophical systematics itself will be a network of leading ideas that order how you analyze specific affairs and construe their encyclopedic connections, and this network of leading ideas or orientational categories will be marked by biblical wisdom.

For example, the biblical truth of the sovereign God's positing a raft of ordinances for creatural reality that are good, discrete, and interwoven ordinances that hold for all creatures after their kind (Genesis 1:1–2:3, Isaiah 40, Psalms 1, 19, 104, 119, 1 Corinthians 15:39–41) in spite of sin—humans don't ever become animals, they sinfully become inhuman!—has pivotal implications for structuring how academic disciplines limit the reach of their investigative findings and correlate their specialized knowledge with the contributions of other fields. Medical instruction operating out of a christian philosophical stance, confessing such an integral God-structured world, will recognize, I think, psychosomatic maladies, and will never treat whole persons who are physically ill as if they be an organic compound attached to or hosting a separate valuable soul. A christian philosophical anthropology assumes women and men are whole corporeal souls in the human race; and that basic presupposition will shape not only how medical doctors and nurses study medicine, but how one conceives and practices psychotherapy, school teaching, artistry, jurisprudence, the liturgy for congregational worship, and much more.

Another example: the scandalous biblical truth that Jesus Christ is God's veritable Archimedean point and Redeemer of world history,[10] whose Rule all humans are to be subject to (Micah 6:8, Isaiah 49–55, Habakkuk 2:14, 2 Corinthians 5:17–21, 10:3–5): that biblical truth spires the philosophical idea that all human endeavor—including agriculture, communication theory, music-making, scientific analysis of parasites, deciding economic policies, formulating the doctrines of a church tradition—will be following the Lord when humans do compassionate justice to the reality they study or administer. A christian philosophical view of society assumes that no one discipline may lord it over another, but that each kind of special study forges ahead in its field with the understanding that each washes the other's feet with the hands and towels and knowledge each specialized scholar has learned to employ. Economic theory couched in a christian philosophical systematics, as I understand it, will affirm in God's world that "profit margin" is a necessary condition for business. But if economic theory is aware of God's love for the poor, for fauna and the bio-diversity of plants, an economic theory couched in a christian philosophical systematics with an eye to justice will replace the "profit motive" with the category of "generous supply of resources for needs" as the guiding function for commerce which pleases the Lord.

Underlying biblical theology and redemptive historiography

It is the appointed task of a christian philosophical systematics to serve as this architectonic lynchpin for mediating a unity in the diversity of studies at a university. Biblical theological study, as I understand it, provides the rootage to a christian philosophy. Christian philosophical categories are conceived and born in sustained exploration of the Hebrew and Greek testaments of God's kerygmatic Word. There is practically a symbiotic relation between biblical theological searching of the scriptural revelation and a christian philosophical construction of redemptive categories that mesh with creational revelation. It takes a Reformational searching of the Scriptures, which reveals how the Lord God's *chesed* and *èmet* (covenanting mercy and reliable faithfulness), pinpointed in the grace of *torah* (the Lord's guidance), which when obeyed leads to *shalom* (abundant well-being) (Proverbs 3:1–4), all as the historical outworking of *basileia tou*

---

10 Cf. Herman Dooyeweerd, *De Wijsbegeerte der Wetsidee* (Amsterdam: H.J. Paris, 1935), 1:471–73, translated by William Young and David Freeman, *A New Critique of Theoretical Thought* (Philadelphia: Presbyterian and Reformed, 1953–1958), 1:506–508.

theou (the Reign of God) (Matthew 6:24–34, 9:35–38, Acts 1:3). That is the kind of biblical theology it takes to fructify a biblically christian philosophical systematics. There are other, sterile, theologistic ways to search the Scriptures too (cf. John 5:39–40, 2 Corinthians 3:12–16)! And it takes an on-going humble christian philosophy to keep renewing the biblical vitality of its underpinnings so that its basic categories and contours stay fresh, to keep on breathing a seeking, redemptive conceptual ministry rather than become a closed system with inelastic formulae that order standard answers for difficult problems. The epigones of many ossified philosophies have been a blight on university communities.

It may be important to note here the difference between wrestling with the canonic Scriptural text (=Biblical hermeneutics, biblical theology), which can be carried on in a university setting, and dogmatic theology, the systematic codification of biblical teachings aligned with a particular confessional tradition, such as the Roman Catholic, Presbyterian, Methodist, or Baptist slant on the Christian faith. Winsome doctrinal theology is as sound an endeavor as any other careful systematization of materials, such as one finds in legal codes, ethical standards, marketing or diplomatic protocols, and the like. Dogmatic theology deserves special prominence in a seminary, so that priests and pastors will have a thorough knowledge of the creeds and catechisms of their historical branch of the Church.

But dogmatic theology is not equipped, it seems to me, to play the role of philosophy, that is, to help critically examine and compare, for example, how Freudian concepts of *ego*, *id*, and *superego* are at odds with the Jungian postulate of a Collective Unconscious, and what their respective positions mean for understanding artists. That is a philosophical investigation, not a theological one. When dogmatic theology has tried to adjudicate theoretical, scientific matters outside its field of competence, there have been troubles, as when Galileo was censored and forced to recant what he said he saw in his telescopes and had figured out mathematically. (It could not be so—any fool can see that the sun rises and the sun sets around our mother earth; besides, the Bible says so in Joshua 10:12–14. . . .) In theoretical matters it is wiser to let a christian philosophical systematics translate the biblical orientation into a mediation of scientific disputes than to jump from a dogmatic theology into settling such matters.

Historical study that remembers what has unjustly been forgotten, and therefore redeems the meaning of significant past events that are getting lost, is a close partner of a christian philosophical systematics in promoting philosophical unity amid disciplinary diversity at an institution of advanced learning. Every field of study has a history, and a discerning historian sees how the norms posited for mathematics and music, psychology and economics, theology, literature, and philosophy, change over the years in staggered fashion. Yet there is often an overlapping similarity, unity, in the cultural dynamics of the different changing phenomena.

An Enlightenment spirit of ludic Rationalism can be found, for example, to be permeating rococo artistry, *des philosophes* of *l'Encyclopédie*, and the *gallant* politics of Louis XV and Louis XVI for a couple of generations preceding the French Revolution in Europe—the variegated cultures of different nations was of a piece. An American pragmatistic spirit of hang loose competitiveness has been driving postcolonial technological enterprise worldwide: judges, generals, and advertisers—at least in the Americas and Europe where I come from—all seem deeply committed to "whatever works." That pragmatistic spirit unifies so much of the incomparably different cultural phenomena extant. Yet so few (political) leaders seem to have any historical consciousness that the "normal" of today is abnormal in God's world, and frightfully destructive. Good history-writing will lay bare the divisive principalities and powers almost monolithically at work in diverse places of prestige and power throughout the world.

Historiography—history-keeping, history-telling, writing down the story of significant changes—makes philosophical meaning concrete, as it were, corporeal. And if it is redemptive historiography, it will have the eye to discover that there is nothing new under the sun as far as human cultural waywardness goes—there are patterns to human idolatry, good abilities, and wickedness. So a christian history-keeping discipline at the university will find a thread of continuity in the succession of noteworthy human events, as well as recognize the endings to periods of well-being and evil-doing over the years. To keep the history of a people or a culture, of a specific institution (like a university), or any thing, is to trace the surprising connections between quite disparate happenings, an itinerary, and to discern which changes contribute to the Rule of Jesus Christ on earth and which human responses are off track and lay God's good world waste. A just historiography details the relativity of human deeds under God's enduring faithfulness, and thereby encourages present-day professors and students who follow Christ to assume their allotted place and task with modesty: we never need to complete God's work! We only need to be faithful in bringing our cultural inheritance a step more normatively into the presence of the Lord (cf. Isaiah 60, Revelation 21:22–27).

The fact that a biblically anchored historiography unifies the incredibly fitful, disjunctive events scattered across the ages into a supple narrative of God's dealings with creatures, disturbs many so-called "postmodern" thinkers today who have decided to "wage a war on totality" and "master narratives" that offer false consolation to those who believe in them;[11] for example, in the evolutionary progress of the human race to an ever better life, liberty, and the pursuit of rational happiness. Because a biblically christian conception of historical wholeness allows for the surd reality of sin and does not whitewash atrocities of evil (Ecclesiastes 7:14, Job 19), yet still affirms the certainty of God's Rule a-coming, I call such a biblical overview a servant narrative. The biblically oriented servant narrative does not "mastermind" history into a utopian scheme, but situates a person today so that one knows surely what time it is: Today is the day the LORD has made! We are alive "in the last days" after Christ's ascension to God's right hand of power (Psalm 118:24–25, 2 Timothy 3:1–7, Hebrews 1:1–2, 2 Peter 3:1–15); we are alive in the time when we expect the glorious consummation of our human tending to God's world (Matthew 24–25, Luke 19:11–27). Bible disbelievers who have only "*petits récits*" (local narratives), for fear of falsifying reality in a grand scheme, usually suffer from inflating their own predicaments because they cannot relate their little journey to a public story that has intergenerational staying power. It is because followers of Christ know the biblically historical "Big Picture" in outline form, as it were, that we have the perspective to be critical of the status quo without turning revolutionary or anarchic.

A rainbow curriculum for wisdom

When a community of christian scholars has the grace to consider mapping the range and kinds of human knowledge there be within a christian philosophical perspective, and has the boon to acknowledge a relatively common record of God's blessing you, together with an imaginative, articulate thought-tradition spired by the historic Reformation in Europe of the sixteenth century, all undergirded by a consensual heart-commitment steeped in a biblical covenantal theology, then the university that institutionally frames your teaching and learning will validate a rainbow curriculum as cosmic as God's world. Any creaturely reality with its marvels and history deserves to be studied, because the LORD God does not

---

11 Cf. Jean-Francois Lyotard, "Answering the Question: What is postmodernism?" [1982], translated by Regis Durand, as appendix to The *Postmodern Condition: A report on knowledge* (Minneapolis: University of Minnesota, Press, 1988), 81–82.

make junk.

From the beginning humans were ordained to care for the earth and develop agriculture (Genesis 1:26–31, Isaiah 28:23–29); so the physical sciences, plant and animal husbandry studies are noble occupations. Early on in history there have been cities with problems of trade in manufactured goods, transport, and power relations within families and between neighbors (Genesis 4:16–26); so socio-economic and political sciences and psychological studies are important fields for sustained investigation, to try to order human deeds in good ways (cf. Matthew 22:15–22, Romans 13:1–7, Revelation 13). The fact that Adam greeted Eve with a poem (Genesis 1:23), that God had Moses incorporate wood carvings, goldsmith artistry, and vestments into the tabernacle worship even in the wilderness wanderings (Exodus 31:1–11), that later on God supported King David's emphasis upon training professional instrumental musicians and singers to lead God's people in praise and laments (1 Chronicles 15:16–24, 16:4–6), that there were free standing sculptures fashioned by Solomon's hired artisans for the LORD's temple (1 Kings 6:23–26), and that the psalms were booked so they could be read and studied: all these matters show that the imaginative arts and literature are dear to the LORD and deserve to be skillfully practiced by God's people (Psalm 33:1–3).

So, one might say, the whole rainbow of creaturely affairs, any colorful zone of God's universe, is grist for the mill of university education. Naturally no one can study everything, especially in our day of specializations. If 1 Corinthians 12 and Romans 12, however, provide the dynamic within your community of scholars, so that medicine does not think itself more important than church theology, and the seminary study does not hold its gift to be superior to the domain of christian school teaching, and the service of music-making is not considered less critical than nursing, then each specialty may glory in the contribution of the other members because you are all one diaconate body of rigorous scholarship. But there is still the problem of choosing which new fields of study should be selected for attention to fill out the rainbow roster. A single university like Kosin University seldom has the resources to do everything under the sun. How can a university with biblical stuffings be responsible to the Lord in our day, and make its choices as worldly-wise as a snake in the grass yet as innocent as a dove, in the pack of wolves where Christ sends us as educated people (Matthew 10:16)?

The pattern in the history of the university I just told suggests that one did well to study a core of philosophical and history-rich "liberal arts" as propaedeutic, to prepare students for the professional study of theology (to provide educated clergy for the Church) or law (to yield trained advocates for the Governing Powers) or medicine (to produce skilled practitioners for Public Health). It seems as if the professional services of nurse-physicians, prophetic priests, and political leaders came to the fore at the traditional university because these professions focused on certain pivotal points of human nature that surely need attention—body, "soul," and societal order.

It is significant, I think, that the Reformer John Calvin, who comes out of this medieval-Humanist university milieu as a reflective theologian, held up the training in law for ruling civic affairs as magistrate, to be the highest calling humans could assume, since unlike a pastor who shepherds a flock of believing, sometimes straying sheep, the lawful judge has larger scope and must administer God's justice to outright unbelievers as well as believers, says John Calvin.[12] So next to the hospital and seminary of a Calvinian christian university would probably be a law school, since in the end times the persecutions and violations of the pregnant woman (God's faithful ones) by the powerful Beasts and dragon (the Antichrist pseudo-World Rulers outfitted with the Lie) shall have to be fought in the courts and in the public square (Psalm 2, Revelation 12–13), and we will need christian lawyers and rulers to mitigate the evil.

There is also good sense, I think, in the long history of the university, as to why students have been required to study certain subjects like the *trivium* and *quadrivium* first, so they would be literate, able to read and interpret texts, and to think things through critically. What good is a Bible to a professional theologian or legal statutes to a professional lawyer if you do not know how to read with precision? And who wants a professional nurse or doctor who administers medicine and surgically removes diseased tissue who has not first learned to calculate proportions and angles exactly? Before one can enter the rigors of a specialized profession, one needs to master the basics of number and word and have the facility to identify differences and catch subtleties of meaning. Without an exercised founding in grammar, rhetoric, logic, and mathematical examination of phenomena, a prospective scholar is ill-equipped to advance one's professional specialty and to locate his or her specialty in the worldwide panoply of human tasks. Then there could be the temptation to do your technical thing and go it alone with your specialized competence.

Right here, on the matter of one's initial university studies, is a good

---

12 *Institutio christianae religionis*, IV, 20:4, 6.

spot for the biblically christian contours of a university to make a difference. When the flexible but basal canon of preparatory studies in the "liberal arts" will be couched in a christian philosophical perspective, flanked by a redemptive historiographic awareness of one's faith tradition stretching back to the LORD's dealing with God's elected people memorialized in Psalm 78, then students at a christian university begin by learning the fundamentals of scholarship in a way that forms their mentality to be at home in God's world. Apprenticed to an older generation that has thoughtfully matured in the Reformation faith tradition, the new generation is shown the general lay of the land, so a student does not become narrow minded, staring at just one small patch of ground in God's world. If one specializes too early, you can miss the breadth and depth of God's creational openings for wonderment and enrichment. Christian scholarship is not in a hurry, since study itself can be full-time service for the Lord, and to help a newcomer envision the richness of God's creational blessing and to own a habit of reflection that is wise to God's amazing, long-suffering compassionate justice in the world takes time.

This is why a university, I believe, should exist: to give able men and women the structured time to experience an intergenerational crucible for reflective shalom, so as to generate the wisdom of God abroad.

By "wisdom" I do not mean the ambitious, speculative knowledge promoted by Renaissance head turner Pico della Mirandola, who believed chameleon man could become an angelic intelligence.[13] Nor is "wisdom" finding out the alchemical secrets of the universe passionately desired by Goethe's Faust. Such godless, self-seeking Humanistic "wisdom" is demonic foolishness, according to the Scriptures (Psalm 14/53, James 3:13–18). What the biblical Proverbs call "knowledge" (*da'at*) is a firsthand, intimate experience of what God wants done, and what the Bible calls human "wisdom" (*hokmah*) is the Spirit-filled, disciplined ability to judge what God wants done, what it is right to do, what is just (*dikaios*).

Only God the Holy Spirit gives a human person wisdom (Proverbs 2, Job 28, 1 Corinthians 2). But we believing students and teachers may wrestle with God for the Lord's direction in discovering God's will hidden in the mines of precious stones, in the energy of the sun, in the labyrinth of a person's DNA, the quirks of pedagogy, and what God wants done to undo ignorance, to alleviate poverty, to rectify so much that has gone wrong in our complex, disturbed, secularized "civilization." Wis-

---

13 Cf. *Oratio de hominis dignitate* (1496), translated A. Robert Caponigri, *Oration on the Dignity of Man* (Chicago: Henry Regnery, 1956).

dom by formula is not possible, because the times are always changing, but Scripture encourages us to wait upon the Lord as we struggle communally, in all our getting of knowledge, to get wisdom (Proverbs 4:1–9).

Wisdom may seem to be a rather intangible rationale and reward for a university to exist, but Scripture celebrates wisdom as a redemptive conduit for God's effecting the Lord's will on earth (Proverbs 3:13–20). Karl Marx was wrong to disparage philosophers for only "interpreting" the world and to demand that thinkers "change" the sorry mess of society.[14] If a university is turned into a site where socio-economic and political issues are actually either imposed or resolved, that alteration violates the university's rightful space to be an institution of inquiry and consciousness-setting (cf. *nouthesía*, Ephesians 6:4).[15] But when Wisdom hovers over the give-and-take of teachers and students learning from one another at the university, as they parse through their disciplines and argue difficult matters: when wisdom attends their deliberations, the horizons of one's consciousness change. Under the tutelage of Wisdom, one is no longer caught in the mesh of a competitive society driven by the urge to capitalize on information that brings you success; instead, one's horizons for reflection have changed so that mentors and learners grow a vision of the Lord's imperative over their medical study, their formulation of doctrine, the debate about pedagogy and musical critique, horizons whose wise injunction is:

> let tried-and-true justice gush through the land like a rush of water,
> and let just-doing deeds overflow like an almighty river. (Amos 5:24)

Without wisdom at large in its operation, a university becomes a Babylonian citadel of vanity. With Wisdom blowing where it wills (cf. John 3:1–8) through the ongoing discussions of a university, there is a spirit of thankfulness in the study and promise of healing for the nations of the world in the classrooms (cf. Malachi 1:11).

The historical problem of priorities

Would a wise university today develop a specialty in the imaginative arts? What are sound principles for deciding priorities?

Jesus would look out over the world as he once did on the territory of Samaria, so despised by the Jews, and say, "Every field of human endeavor is ripe for being reaped"(John 4:31–35)!

Two-thirds world poverty is a scandal to shame every affluent coun-

---

14 *Theses über Feuerbach*, no. 11.
15 Cf. Edward W. Said, *Culture and Imperialism* (1993), xxvi.

try living by "the profit motive." We need a christian economics program to reflect on how loving money corrupts business (1 Timothy 6:6–10), and to think through what kind of banking system could operate by the guideline of "thrifty generosity" (2 Corinthians 9:6–15). The wanton violence against the weak in the monster megalopolises of the world, and the butchering of defenseless believers, gypsies, and outcasts in totalitarian lands cries out for the wise university to fund a program of jurisprudence to study the strains on international law, bullying tactics by the stronger, and how injustice leaves a curse upon the land when breaking treaties and deceitful cruelty is unacknowledged (Proverbs 3:27–35, 14:32–34). The terrible power of media technology to bear damaging false witness by sensational bites of reporting begs for a university concerned about truth to develop a program in the area of communications, rhetoric, and popular culture, in order to form a school of critical, investigative journalism that will avoid cheap muckraking but probe for connected commentary on current events that imaginatively supports what is wholesome, and expose to the light what is a hateful angel of light (Colossians 4:5–6, 2 Corinthians 11:12–15, 1 John 1:5–7). And artistry?

It is important, I think, to realize that in deciding priorities there is not only one right choice, and the rest of the possibilities are wrong.[16] Good judgment will not pit one avenue of service in partisan fashion against an other. It is good for medical study at a university to focus on the malady of cancer, a blight found particularly in an urban populace, but it is also good, it may be better, for a medical faculty to put its research energy into parasitology and diagnostics, in order to focus preventative medicine and healing upon problems experienced more by the helpless rural populations of our world—if you cannot do both. Which fields of study a university explores depends, it seems to me, upon deciding circumstantially where the most fruitful openings be to bring shalom at a spot where the miseries of God's people and our neighbors are worst, and where there is a source of gifted leaders able to carry through on bringing wisdom to that specific area of scholarship, so as to change by conscientization the demeanor of people and bring them hope.

There must be a holy spirited motivation behind deciding a priority, which generously sees the whole panorama of other needs too, and there must be the willingness by a few to commit to a generations-long haul in carrying out that specific program, because seeds need to be sown and

---

16 It seems to me Jacques Ellul falls into this mistake when he dialectically pits word against image in *Parole humiliée* [1981], translated by Joyce Main Hanks, *The Humiliation of the Word* (Grand Rapids: Eerdmans, 1985).

trees need to be grown before fruit can be harvested. If a secular government promotes bio-technology or engineering with a crash program of
awards and scholarships so that a university can assist a country to meet
the rabid international competition of industrial production, one needs
to ask whether the kingdom of God has those same priorities, before one
joins the crowd. Where and how can a christian university show a winsome alternative to the godless, dominant rush to serve Mammon?

No university should begin, and Kosin University does not need, an
arts program if it be conceived and practiced as a luxury, an ornamental
fringe on the garment of life,[17] something one dabbles in if you have
monied leisure. But artistry—music and song, theatre, poetry, graphic
art, the dance, architecture, typographic design—understood in a christian philosophical way has excellencies worth considering for serious
study:

(1) While the sciences generalize from phenomena investigated and
pursue the invariant law that holds the same everywhere, artistry latches
onto what is singular, unexpected, perhaps unique, in providing knowledge that may be characteristic of something we formerly overlooked.
(2) Artistry has the logic of defamiliarizing a person from ordinary experience. A poem forces you to read more slowly, so you are faced with
nuances of meaning you normally miss in words. Black-and-white photographic art throws up shadows that disclose a side of a person's character you never saw before in multicolor real life. Shakespeare's *King Lear*
makes you cry at the folly of a broken father's deluded love for a daughter.
(3) Art is God's gift that can protect us from reducing life to technical
knowhow, and primes children as well as adults, the uneducated as well
as the educated, to perform doxological acts that include the catharsis of
lament as well as a dance of praise.

The practice of artistry as a profession has not been an ancient fix-
ture at the university. American undergraduate colleges have given "the
fine arts" a place of sorts, but usually musicians, painterly artists, cerami-
cists, sculptors, and would-be novelists have gone off to the rigors of Art
Academies and Schools for Writing for their apprenticeships. But maybe
a christian university in Korea could find a way to integrate the professional practice and performance of artistry with the critical art historiographic and theoretical art study that would pioneer a comprehensive
art program that would research the place and task of artistry for people

---

17 Cf. Abraham Kuyper, "Calvinism and Art," in *The Stone Lectures on Calvinism* [1898]
    (Grand Rapids: Eerdmans, 1961), 151.

in society, and devise ways to have artists integrated next to nurses and teachers, police and preachers, as necessary figures in a normal society.

A flourishing literature in the *hangul* language that would bespeak a redemptive vision for our daily tragedies would be one important way for Korean culture to keep its voice amid the imperialistic pressures to be standardized in the American-English empire. Your ancient Korean tradition of crafted *hanji* mulberry bark paper and the exquisite, artisan paper objects that grace a home or office like butterflies of joy can be a way to encourage God's people in their troubles and to proffer a smile to engage unbelievers—why not harness such an art ministry to the outreach of a wise university? The peculiar glory of art's nature suits it to tell the truth tongue-in-cheek, like a jester, at special times of crisis and celebration in human life, when prosaic statements are inadequate. I wonder, could the Korean tradition of *han* lamentation be extricated from shamanistic and Buddhistic rituals, which effect a detached acceptance of one's fate, and be reclaimed, converted! into a biblically sensitive, voiced psalm lament that has the LORD God listen to your pitiful weeping and caress you gently, wiping away the tears from your cheek, as Psalms 6, 13, 39, 42–43, 51, 126, and 131 do?

That is, artistry—its reception and production—has had either a churchified or an uncertain history in the Western christian environs. My thought is that Kosin University as a christian academic institution of higher learning embedded in the rich heritage of the Reformation might have the unusual opportunity to find an alternative way of making art wise, giving artisanry a diaconal dignity that is so hard to manage in the differentiated chic art culture of New York, London, or Paris. If Korean artists have not historically suffered through the *l'art pour l'art* (art for art's sake) derailment of professional art's godly purpose to help the imaginatively handicapped neighbor perceive the wonders of God's world, maybe your university could translate indigenous folk artisanry into art-as-such (concerts, novels, *objets d'art*) that would be as chaste and neighbor-friendly as a Choson white porcelain vase. There is great, great need throughout the world today for dispirited people to have clean water, ample grain, clothing, shelter, and also the cheer afforded by a redemptive song, a sturdy image, by choice, wise poetic verse that banishes fear and instills hope (Hebrews 6:13–20, 1 John 4:16–18). Is there a small band of wise persons ready to lead a university program in this mission of the LORD to bring artistic shalom to the poor of the world (Matthew 5:1–16, Ephesians 5:15–20)?

I close this convocation address on "the university" with a special challenge for you who shape Kosin University's identity at present and, God willing, in the future.

The reason a university should exist is to glean God's wisdom from creation and its history, and to pass on the Lord's wisdom from one generation to another amid the cloud of faithful witnesses who surround us here and now (Hebrews 12:1–3). A university is called by the LORD God of the universe to do redemptive scholarship as a community, to lead God's people and our neighbors in good patterns of thinking, speaking, imagining, living. That means, I take it, not all God's children should become university students, but only those who are willing and able to dedicate themselves to the trials of disciplined study. There are many other ways to join the chorus magnifying the Lord's name among the nations and to offer up sacrifices that stay alive, which please God and are not conformed to the passing fashions of this world (Malachi 1:11, Romans 12:1–3, 1 John 1:15–17). A university education is not a preferred route of sanctification. But a university is necessary, I dare say, in our era of differentiated specialized studies, to provide an opening for concerted reflection that begets a communal wisdom our world desperately needs. To become a privileged member of such a university is an awesome responsibility.

May I encourage you in Korea not to simply take on the American Western model of university scholarship as the norm. Trust your roots in the living biblical Reformation christian tradition and the refining of faith your persecuted Korean ancestors went through, the missionaries who began this institution, to try to find alternative ways of practicing biblically christian scholarship that will be historically and internationally aware but may be folk-specific, and so brighten with color the rainbow diversity God loves in a communion of the scholarly saints.

The tiny Toronto philosophical Institute for Christian Studies is practically an anomaly in North America, an encyclopedic center of a university without the specialists; yet we have been blessed as an institution. Kosin University has a larger presence in the land, and I pray that our Lord keep you humble and imaginative as you explore God's world to disseminate the Lord's wisdom and shalom, so that God may surprise you with scholarly fruit one hundredfold (Mark 4:1–20).

All that the Lord expects of us professors, administrative presidents and vice-presidents, students and infrastructural staff, is that we be found, when Jesus Christ returns in glory, to be faithful and wise—worldly-wise! (*phronimoi*)—waiters and waitresses in God's academic household, says

Scripture, serving up nutritious scholarly food at the right time (Psalm 1, Matthew 24:36–51)! May the Lord God revealed in Jesus Christ equip you with grace and stamina for this joyful calling (Ephesians 4:7, 12–16, Jude 24–25).

I owe my colleague Bob Sweetman deep thanks for checking my wanderings in his field of medieval studies. It is a blessing to have virtuous friends. I thank my wife Inès Naudin ten Cate for special bibliographic help in preparation of this lecture.

Bibliography

Allan, George. *Rethinking College Education* (University Press of Kansas, 1997).

Altbach, Philip G. "The American Academic Model in Comparative Perspective" [1958] and "The University as Center Periphery" [1981], in *Higher Education in the Third World: Themes and variations* (New York: Advent Books, 1987), 213–31, 45–65.

Axelrod, Paul. *Scholars and Dollars: Politics, economics, and the universities of Ontario 1945–1980* (University of Toronto Press, 1982).

Badley, Ken. *Worldviews: The challenge of choice* (Concord: Irwin, 1996).

Barzun, Jacques. *The American University* (New York: Harper & Row, 1968).

Bilgrami, H. H. and S. A. Ashraf. *The Concept of an Islamic University* (Cambridge: Hodder & Stoughton, 1985).

Cabal, Alfonso Borrero. *The University as an Institution Today: Topics for reflections* (Ottawa: International Development Research Centre, 1993).

Chapman, John H. ed. *The Western University on Trial* (Berkeley: University of California Press, 1983).

Chung, Jun Ki. "Christian Contextualization in Korea," in *Korean Cultural Roots: Religion and social thoughts*, ed. Ho-Youn Kwon (Chicago: North Park College and Theological Seminary, 1995), 81–104.

Cobban, A. B. *The Medieval Universities: Their development and organization* (London: Methuen, 1975).

Durrani, F. K. Khan. *A Plan for Muslim Educational Reform* (Urdu Bazar: Lahore Islamic Book Service, 1989).

Giamatti, A. Bartlett. *A Free and Ordered Space: The real world of the university* (New York: Norton, 1988).

Giamatti, A. Bartlett. *The University and the Public Interest* (New York: Atheneum, 1981).

Haskins, Charles Homer. *The Rise of Universities* [1923] (Ithaca: Cornell University Press, 1957).

Illich, Ivan. *Deschooling Society* (New York: Harper & Row, 1971).

Jaspers, Karl. *The Idea of the University* [1946], translated H.A.T. Reiche and H.F. Vanderschmidt (Boston: Beacon Press, 1959).

Kerr, Clark. *The Uses of the University* (Cambridge: Harvard University Press,

1963).

Kuyper, Abraham. *Souvereiniteit in Eigen Kring* [1880] (Kampen: Kok, 1930); "Sphere Sovereignty," in *Abraham Kuyper: A centennial reader*, ed. James D. Bratt (Grand Rapids: Eerdmans, 1998), 463–490.

Lee, Sungho. "The Emergence of the Modern University in Korea," in *From Dependence to Autonomy: The development of Asian universities*, ed. Philip G. Altbach and Viswanathan Sevaratnama (Dordrecht: Kluwer, 1989), 227–56.

McIntire, C.T. ed. *The Legacy of Herman Dooyeweerd: Reflections on critical philosophy in the Christian tradition* (New York: University Press of America, 1985).

Morsy, Zaahloul and Philip G. Altbach, eds. *Higher Education in International Perspective: Toward the 21ˢᵗ Century* (New York: UNESCO, Advent Books, Inc., 1993).

Mourad, Roger P. *Postmodern Philosophical Critique and the Pursuit of Knowledge in Higher Education* (London: Bergin & Garvey, 1997).

Oliver, Robert T. *A History of the Korean People in Modern Times: 1800 to the present* (Toronto: Associated University Presses, 1993).

Pelikan, Jaroslav. *The Idea of the University: A reexamination* (Yale University Press, 1992).

Readings, Bill. *The University in Ruins* (Cambridge: Harvard University Press, 1996).

Said, Edward W. *Culture and Imperialism* (New York: Knopf, 1993).

Schipiani, Daniel S. *Conscientization and Creativity: Paulo Freire and Christian education* (New York: University Press of America, 1984).

Schwehn, Mark R. *Exiles from Eden: Religion and the academic vocation in America* (New York: Oxford University Press, 1993).

Seerveld, Calvin. "Footprints in the snow," *Philosophia Reformata* 56:1 (1991): 1–34 {infra 235–275}.

———. "Philosophy as schooled memory" [1982], in *In the Fields of the Lord*, ed. Craig Bartholomew (Carlisle/Toronto: Piquant/Tuppence, 2000), 84–89.

———. *Through the Waters: Christian schooling as a city of refuge* (Toronto: Ontario Christian School Teachers' Association, 1998) {infra 59–80}.

Sparshott, Francis. *The Future of Aesthetics* (Toronto: University of Toronto Press, 1998).

Sykes, Charles J. *ProfScam: Professors and the demise of higher education* (New York: St. Martin's Press, 1988).

Van Hanskamp, Anton. "Wilhelm von Humboldt: om de eenheid van de universiteit," in *Pluralisme, Cultuurfilosofische beschouwingen*, eds. Theo de Boer and Sander Griffioen (Amsterdam: Boon, 1995), 30–47.

Van Nieuwenhuis, Herman. Sermon on Mark 24:36–51. Toronto: Willowdale Christian Reformed Church, 23 January 2000.

Vogelin, Eric. "The German University and the Order of German Society: A reconsideration of the Nazi era," *Intercollegiate Review* 20 (Spring/Summer 1985): 7–27.

Weber, Samuel. *Institution and Interpretation*. Afterword by Wlad Godzich (Minneapolis: University of Minnesota Press, 1987).

THROUGH THE WATERS:
CHRISTIAN SCHOOLING AS A CITY OF REFUGE

The title to my remarks is probably a mixed metaphor. Because I was at first not certain what the convention theme "Through the waters" meant to convey, and since you are a gathering of educators and I figured you probably wanted some fresh, biblical reflection on schooling: for safety sake I added the subtitle, "Christian schooling as a city of refuge."

"Cities of refuge" come up in Older Testament history later than the Israelites' exodus from Egypt **through the** Red Sea **waters** (Exodus 14:1–15:21) to which Isaiah 43 is referring (43:11–13, 16–17). "Cities of refuge" were a provision by God's people settled in Canaan to nuance justice for unpremeditated crimes and accidental shedding of blood; the accused could run as fugitive to a city of refuge for safety from being lynched, and there await proper, timely justice.

I intend to highlight certain rough waters we teachers and administrators face today, and suggest how a christian schooling community can be firm ground for a rising generation (and their mentors) as we historically walk through great threatening turbulences, busy working, suffering, playing, and laughing in anticipation of Jesus Christ's glorious return.

A more succinct title now, which fits the convention banner too, might be: *Tough love in rough waters.*

Isaiah 43 occurs in the context of what we call chapters 40–48 of Isaiah. Isaiah 40 proclaims comfort! to God's beleaguered people in the cosmic panorama of our miraculous world, which belongs to this majestic almighty Creator LORD God who stretched out the heavens and calls the countless stars each by name, to whom nations like ancient Assyria and contemporary America look like drops in a bucket, before whom political leaders like Benjamin Netanyahu, Slobadan Milosevic, Mike

---

This lecture was presented to the Ontario Christian School Teachers Association (OCSTA) in Hamilton on 29 October 1998.

Harris, look like grasshoppers! it poetically says.

Both the prophet and God remonstrate with God's people in these chapters: has it ever occurred to you why—after your liberation from Egypt, after the insider Good News revealed to you at Mount Sinai certified you as a special people, and after you were brought into "the promised land"—why you ended up fighting among yourselves, having the "holy city" of Jerusalem destroyed, and are stuck again now in a Babylonian captivity? Do you realize your troubles often were punishment for your years of bitching about the daily diet of manna, always lusting for the juicy cucumbers of Egypt, playing footsie with the Canaanite sex goddesses, dazzled by the platinum credit-card Babylonian power trips? Thankless, godless idolatry and vanity is self- and neighbor-destructive, says the LORD.

BUT—God bends over crying, as it were—"It's enough now, you little worm, Jacob. I the LORD took you safely through the waters more than once before, and I'll do it again, so to speak, set you free from Babylonian culture to become a lighthouse for the peoples of the world (42:5–9)! I'm going to do something new: I am commissioning a pagan strong-arm military conqueror named Cyrus to restore you historically as a repentant peoplehood on the earth, where I the LORD God want my will to be done. I forgive you your ungratefulness and shall completely forget your sin and stupidities" (43:25, 44:21–22).

—Excuse me; are you talking to the Ontario Christian School Teachers' Association?

Well, Isaiah 43 in the context of chapters 40–48 is not talking to Jews dead in the grave. Isaiah 43 is talking rough waters and the tough love of God who cares for troubled people **and** trouble-makers, sinful ingrates: God's Older Testament word speaks live to whoever has ears to hear the comfort and reproof, God's regret at the mess of punishment and God's promise of blessing. The book of Isaiah you selected always comes with both in tandem—that's the unexpected way the LORD God does things! says the Bible, pleading with Canadian school teachers, administrators, parents, children, leaders, school janitors, whoever, to repent and become wise to the ways the covenant LORD God set up the universe and patiently works in history.

So Isaiah 43 in context means: (1) Creatures are God's wall-to-wall carpeting in the universe; better, creation is God's *glossolalia* we humans who have become adopted children of God are called to interpret for our neighbors so that **everybody** hears day and night, sun and moon, praising the LORD (Psalms 19, 148), and that we come to thank God! for the marvels of the way an eagle soars in the sky, the way a snake slithers on top of a rock, the way of a ship in the middle of the ocean, the way of a strong young man **in** a maiden able to bear a child (Proverbs 30:18–19). Our task, says Isaiah 40–48, is to discover creation as God's ordered world.

(2) Sin is a three-letter reality in history Humanists try to ignore, and disciples of Christ often tend to dwell on morbidly or act as if it's a problem more for unbelievers. Sin eats away at **our** innards and really caresses our intentions to hell. Sin obscures vision, perverts good direction, reduces respectable people to garrulous fools; and this is relevant for schooling. Christian schooling is never perfect, incorruptible schooling, but if you hear Isaiah you know that pride and indifference toward God's way of doing things can be forgiven, undone! redirected.

(3) The LORD God by grace has kept intact a tattered redeemed body of believing servants, says Isaiah, who are veterans of being up to their necks in water. The faith-line of Abel, Enoch, Noah, Abraham, Moses, the other motley characters mentioned in Hebrews 11, David, culminating in the LORD God's Servant the Messiah Jesus: this cloud of witnesses who, following up the apostle Paul, also "by faith . . . won strength out of weakness" (Hebrews 11:33–34), includes Augustine, Luther, Calvin, Wesley, Kuyper, and many, many more—this company is "the ransomed of the Lord," Isaiah later says (51:9–11), "the LORD God made a way for, to pass through some very deep waters." If the Ontario association of christian teachers is God's people, then this faith-line is your family tree. Isaiah is reciting **your** ancient history as the redeemed people of the LORD.

(4) You don't go through the waters, in Isaiah, just to get to the other side, and look back at the destruction of Egyptian and Babylonian no-gods and technological military culture (cf. Isaiah 46–47). That is the apocalyptic background God's people know is certain (Revelation 17–19); however, Isaiah 43 and the Psalms' assurance of refuge with God (Psalms 16, 30, 46, 61, 62, 90, 91, 121), of being at-home with the LORD God right in the midst of the turbulent waters of apostate culture: God's promise of deliverance expects you to keep on walking, following the LORD's presence by day and the Holy Spirit's pillar of fire by night, walking in Jesus Christ's footsteps with neighbors and enemies all around, filled with the Spirit of God, says Isaiah a few chapters later,

> to bring shalom to those who are buckled over, to those whose heart is in splinters,

to proclaim "You are free!" to the victims of war . . . so that all who are weeping shall be comforted.

The LORD has anointed you to provide for the sorrowing ones in God's city—to replace the dirty ashes on their heads with festive jewels,

to unwrap the mournfulness they have cloaked themselves in and rub on the perfuming oils of celebration!

to change their spirit of beaten-down discouragement for one of laughing hallelujah! (Isaiah 61:1–3)

Within this biblical frame of (1) discover creation, (2) struggle against sin, (3) claim your tradition of the ransomed remnant who went through persecuted waters, (4) in order to bring holy praise to God and the LORD's shalom to neighbors, let me posit for you a couple of chewable ideas about christian schooling.

A city of refuge, I said. Like a safety island for crossing a traffic-busy street, like a congenial waiting room before they operate on your life, like a secure asylum where you are free from attack, abuse, discrimination, persecution, a place where you are accepted as is, affirmed, and can take a deep breath and have the elbow-room time to reconsider things. A christian schooling community is meant to be a place where parents can thankfully send their children for schooling because the whole endeavor breathes a gentle spirit of hospitality for all kinds of students: diligent innocents, problem children, precocious youngsters, adolescent renegades—sinful persons are welcome to study!

So parents must not expect a christian school environs to be safe from sin, a kind of bunker against seeing, hearing, or scenting evil—that would be "out of this world," as Jesus says (cf. John 17:15–19). When my wife and I sent our children to Toronto District Christian High, trying to help school-proof them we made clear that not everything they encountered there would be "christian." But christian schooling as "city of refuge" means that there is a concerted effort to avoid temptation, to protect one and all from evil by communally engaging evil with awe for the LORD, and that even the most hardened fugitive to come to the school will experience this uncanny holy spirit that seems to hang invisible in the air like a melody hovering over the place being hummed under their breath by the teachers, secretaries, librarian, coaches, principal, older and even new students.

Christian schooling is not supposed to be a cozy and snug Hadleyburg, an institution where the wild character of holiness gets domesticated, and the hidden curriculum is to turn everyone into a pious, docile little conformist who follows instructions. Sure, there should be a red bathtub lined with pillows in the corner of every first grade classroom for the special times when a good reader can climb in with a slower reader to read books together; and there will be occasions after the last afternoon class when the high school teacher sits on her desk in an empty, darkening classroom and a shy, distraught teenager spills her guts, and finds a measure of healing. But a schooling city of refuge is out to invigorate all comers with God's handiwork, to face the disturbing waters of reality hemming us in, and to learn hand-to-hand combat with the reigning culture foreign to the LORD. Christian schooling is not omphaloskeptic but outward-looking, because the Rule of God in God's world with its buoyant eschatonic prospect orients the teaching and learning.

Perhaps it would be easier for christian schooling to practice being a city of refuge if the student body were not so homogeneous (because only certain parents can scrape together an extra $6000+ for tuition beyond our ordinary school taxes to enroll them). A few bright kids from a slum, several eager unbelievers who for whatever reason wanted what we teachers can give and will respect the christian ethos of the school—this is normal policy for Seventh Day Adventist christian schools—or refugees from bad secular schooling mixed in would give a pied color and grit to christian schooling. Not that normal suburban, nominally christian homes don't supply odd-balls, malcontents, and enough difficult challenges, but we need to recognize freshly how malnourished, confused, tranquillized, not to say impaired, many of our ordinary regular students be. This schooling city of refuge may be a last opportunity to stir some of them alive to be wise to what's really going on in God's broken world.

Paideia kai nouthesía kyríou. I am assuming—an assumption you may not share—that the bottom line for participating in the city of refuge called christian schooling is the ability and willingness to be schooled, to undergo the discipline and "multiple-intelligent" consciousness-setting that constitutes the nature of schooling. (I question whether schooling should be compulsory against one's will.)

A schooling community for me is not a family home, "the place where," as Robert Frost said, "when you have to go there, they have to take you in." A christian schooling community is also not a church organization, no more than the city of Jerusalem was identical to the temple in ancient Israel. The fact that Jerusalem was the city of God where the LORD was present so justice was done (Psalms 46, 47, 87) did not collapse the city administration into the temple precincts. Similarly, while christian schooling is a manifestation of the kingdom of God where the Rule of Christ's body is palpable, the schooling does not therefore become a church—a christian school is not a parochial (tax-exempt) church school. A schooling institution is not to be an arm of the nation-state where political authorities dictate what should be taught and for how many minutes, as was done in totalitarian Nazi Germany. Again, a schooling complex is not to be a business set up to sell products and make a profit—

I could go on: schooling is not mass therapy or an emergency crisis center, even though especially principals, where the buck usually stops, must often do counseling in the clutch and handle all manner of life disasters. But the point is: although a schooling community rightly gives first-aid, in some locations will prepare breakfast for children whose parents are poor, may perhaps teach little ones to pray in public because churches act as if infants have no mouths—although the schooling has a business side and bills to pay and rules to follow, all the varied activities are focused toward the defining quality of being **schooling**. A school is a school is a school.

This is not the place to spell out the complicated historical genesis of the differentiated schooling institution we have on our hands in Canada. And I can't begin to detail, with appropriate caveats, the intricate intra-mural and extra-mural relationships a schooling community has within itself and toward home, church, government, business, and neighbor-hoods. But we school educators need to have at least a careful, sound working conception of what in God's world the specific nature and lim-ited tasks of schooling is to be, if we are going to keep working toward building normative christian schooling.

To keep teaching the same old way we always have out of inertia, and hope for the best, in our changing, urbanizing culture, or to try to be as like the secular Ontario schools as possible (plus Bible courses, of course)—then we must be okay—is ostrich-headed, it seems to me, because to drift along without continuing prayerful, self-critical reflec-tion on our proper task or to suppose that what's normal in our culture is normative is simply wrong. What is normal in our culture is mostly abnormal from a biblical perspective. And once the schooling commu-nity starts to act like a home or a church or big-brother government, you really get trouble!

Not that you principals and teachers want to be everything under the sun for children; but if a home no longer holds family devotions, intelligent conversations at meals, nor have odd jobs or paper routes for children to be responsible for—if parents don't do **their home** work—

and if the church can't make catechism classes exciting and its church teen clubs are a drag, so church and home and other interest groups line up expecting the schooling community to pick up the slack, schooling can blow its circuits from overload! It's not fair. The hard truth is that for christian schooling to be obedient to the LORD as schooling, normative, there must be reformation in the rest of society too. That's not OCSTA's job, but it's part of the picture.

It is the nature of schooling, I think—and I probably just put words around what you already know and hold as true—for an older generation and younger generation to stand hand-in-hand facing God's creation, and the older generation shows the younger ones the wonders they together can find there, and tells about the twisted, scarred glories of human deeds in history under the LORD's providing hand. This communal show-and-tell activity engages the apprentice and gives horizons, direction, and a committed contour of vision to the operation that primes the wondering consciousness of the young to reflection as they are prepared to become skillful, imaginative, articulate, and thoughtful bearers themselves of cultural manna, which they are to gather in daily, according to their gifts, to share with their neighbors out of thanks to the Lord.

I am just rephrasing what you could read in A. Janse (1935), K. J. Popma (1947), S. C. W. Duvenage (1962), all the way up to Stronks and Blomberg's fine book, *A Vision with a Task* (1993). Schooling the way God wills it takes place when a communion of seasoned saints—convicted that all creation belongs to the LORD and that all cultural formation, the work of human hands, must be God-pleasing for the LORD to establish it—pledge themselves in concert with the next generation to enable those young to catch, own, re-live, and take up obediently under the LORD's merciful, judging faithfulness this very task of cultivating God's garden until the Lord returns; to see what good streets we have built for him to walk on, what nutritious food we have learned to grow and share, which rich novels, paintings, and song offerings we made for the Holy Spirit to enjoy, what interesting people from all races and multiple kinds of intelligence have been joined to Christ's body to withstand persecution: then you know how glorious it is to work in schooling.

You don't add certain devotional vitamins to make schooling "christian." Christian schooling is simply schooling the way the LORD structured it to be: this inter-generational activity of exploring the world together, and traditioning/modifying/adulterating/destroying/redeeming cultural heritages in force, while busily focused on stirring up and honing the gifted human activities children harbor of crafting things, imagining, speaking, and thinking.

That last wrinkle of mine, what I would call the **core four** activities to focus schooling structure—handicraft skill, imaginativity, language, and thought—to highlight priorities so as to locate and limit the teaching/learning task, is moot. For me it is a philosophical attempt to distinguish the interrelated callings of school, church, home, government, employment, and other institutions, all of which, I believe, are expected to follow, in their several limited ways, the injunction of Ephesians 6:4: "Nourish them [the less experienced ones] in the *paideia kai nouthesia kyriou*, in the discipline and 'mind-set,' 'consciousness-positioning'—you could almost translate the word 'conscientization' of the Lord God."

In our differentiated society, malformed by power-play hierarchies or institutions acting as autonomous islands on their own, God's people know there should be inter-institutional cooperative support if there be such specialization. Rather than that every institution does everything poorly, let each complement the others by fulfilling its primary ordained calling. If the nation-state's province is to install protection and justice, and the home is to nurture the young with healthy diet, emotional security, and love, and businesses are called to redeem commerce by generous, thrifty supply of resources for people's needs, and the church exists to pray and witness to the regenerative power of the resurrected Jesus Christ, the school, as I understand it, zeroes in on exercising the formative, imaginative, verbal, and thinking facets of the full human creatures who are acting for the time being as students; christian schooling exists to give a redemptive slant especially to these four activities, which issue into the worlds of professional thinking, artistry, media, and technology.

A community of crafty teachers, for me, is the crux of practicing such normative schooling. By "crafty" I mean both a craft-sure enabler of others learning and, picking up the admonition of Jesus as he sent his disciples out, anticipating rough conditions, "Be as crafty—prudential, savvy—as snakes and as harmless as doves" (Matthew 10:16). I know teachers as passionate professionals who are constantly, it seems, in labor pains (to gloss Socrates) to have students give birth, to bear fruit, to unwrap their gifts for others to be blessed.

I would not promote professional**ism**, that middle-class, career-conscious idol of self-satisfied achievement. I think there should always remain something homespun human about the mastery of a teacher, because a key ingredient to enabling students to learn is to have them overcome their indifference, to trick them into becoming self-confident enough to want to understand what it's all about. It takes skilled labor, a crafty, wily, patient, gentle, generous—fruits of the Spirit (cf. Ephesians 5:22–25)—playful, peaceable, wise artisan to challenge, encourage, even inveigle a dubious student to come look over your shoulder, as it were, while you think through the composition of a joke, speak about the glory of deep sleep, imagine with Ursula Le Guin (*Left Hand of Darkness*, 1969) that our sexuality is changeable and circumstantial, or demonstrate a judo throw . . . until they say: "Wow!—jokes are planned? Sleep is redeeming the time? Sexuality is complicated! The gentle art uses violence for its downfall? I get the gist—let me try it too!"

Because God's world and history is so rich but hangs together, and students are so utterly diverse but all deserve care, crafty teachers at a school do well to teach truly in comm**unity**, because communion of the teaching saints is a biblical prerequisite for giving our love the cash value to forge a working redemptive integral K–12 curriculum instead of a patchwork of start-and-stop courses. Genuine community in operation also distills into the joy of making up for one another's weaknesses.

Teaching at the elementary, middle-school, or high school level can be as delicate as brain surgery: conscientization of children to live, work, play, and study *coram Deo* (before the face of the LORD) is crucial, but must not slip into brain-washing; and *paideia*, rigor, for flummoxed stu-

With Stanley (Sietze Buning) Wiersma at
Dordt College commencement, Sioux Center, Iowa, 1985

dents usually should mean not more control but relaxed flexibility. We teachers need to be proactive as arms and legs, eyes and ears, for one another in the body (1 Corinthians 12), not only to bear one another's burdens (Galatians 5:25–6:2) and together seek to discern good from evil (cf. Job 28:28, Proverbs 8:13) in pedagogy, for example—so correcting students becomes elaborations rather than put-downs—but also to show students (who can smell a fake Christian at ten meters) and evidence to any secular onlookers that christian schooling is not a collection of idiosyncratic hotshots and mediocre individualists, but is one dedicated, vulnerable company united together by the holy spirit of fallible, searching diaconal wisdom.

Practice time. One more thing about the craft of teaching and school-learning: it takes a special kind of time, pedagogical time, I believe, for christian schooling to flourish. The schoolroom is the right place for mentor and child, guide and inexperienced ones, to have the tensed leisure to simulate, construct, invent, discuss, often in "Once upon a time. . ." story form, or to dissect with trial-and-error creatural marvels like animals, plants, and song. It is normative for *paideia*, for a student's being-seasoned-self, to take on a slowly maturing knowledge of something, to have as much time as it takes to bewonder what is unknown and to sort it out, to play hunches, and especially to make mistakes! Schooling time is practice time, and you violate the creational nature of school timing if you force it by the clock to get something finished.

I know this point upsets people in the unschooled or workaday world who are production-minded, but, in my judgment, christian schooling is not a finishing school. Elementary christian school teachers are seeding a forest! It is back-breaking, long-range work, a time-consuming endeavor where sometimes you have to wait ages it seems for the spark of insight to jump across the cleft generations, and a teacher may not even live to see what she or he began to sow, watered, and God let grow (cf. 1 Corinthians 3:1–9).

This odd kind of ample, deliberative, "academic" time to schooling is why teachers are sometimes thought to have a soft job and not to be in touch with **real life**—you only deal in books. Well, I can testify that good books are congealed concentrations of human gut life, *la gloire et la misère de l'homme*, which when met firsthand confront a reading person with **actual** temptations and the necessity to make choices in one's consciousness **now**; nodes of wisdom that are as **immediate** a reality as when you have to slam on the brakes in your moving car. But a student meets concrete life in schooling framed with the grace to be able to mull it over, to erase any too-quick reaction, to retract and re-do without penalty a response to what took you first by surprise. Such elastic, exciting propaedeutic time is an unusual blessing in our whole lifetime, and teachers deservedly cherish it, and able administrators jealously protect it as part and parcel of the schooling city of refuge.

The whelming flood of waters through which the LORD walks God's people in history are legion. For us schooling educators and administrators let me recognize briefly just two: Mammon and Cultural Amnesia. Particularly these two evil principalities today have the systemic power, I believe, to undermine and destroy the consecrated work of our schooling hands if we are not prayerfully alert and surely faithful in what God has called us to do. The very air Christians breathe in North America is polluted commercialistically, and memory loss, as I see it, has become epidemic also among believers in the Christ.

(1) **Mammon**, according to the Bible (cf. Matthew 6:19–24, Luke 12:13–21, 16:1–17) is the mesmerizing idol of Goods that stirs up an insatiable, obsessive drive for More Goods. A disciple of Mammon covets Success and More Successes because Always More is one's everlasting security—Never Enough! (cf. Proverbs 30:15–16). Mammon reduces human life to the single passion of cutting out whatever is not profitable, whatever is not time-efficient, outcome-effective, whatever does not work (for Money, toward a better Standard of Living) must go! When Mammon takes a Pragmatist guise in our day, the code words become "achievement," "full utilization," "maximize results," "growth." When Mammon gives shape to schooling, schooling becomes businessified. Schooling in Ontario, for example, is becoming businessified with a vengeance, partly because the secular political government images itself preeminently as a business. According to the government, its *Common Sense Revolution* "will demand that **government does business *like* a business** [their emphasis]. In other words, in an efficient and productive manner that focuses on results and puts the customer first" (*CSR*, 16). **Citizens** are to be treated above all like **consumers**; **political** concerns for justice give way to the **economics** of cutting taxes so that those who have money to pay will have more to invest to make more. The provincial government's Education Improvement Commission report, *The Road Ahead* (August 1997), is permeated, behind the fancy language, by the controlling idea that schooling is for skill training to enter the (business)

workplace, and teachers are the government's agency to provide it; the public expects the latest technology "to be used effectively by both teachers and students" (*RA*, 20, 24; cf. also *Ontario Curriculum Grades 1–8 Language*, 6). "Education reform is essential if Ontario's next generation is to find high paying, productive jobs in increasingly competitive world markets" (*CSR*, 8). Only the most successful survive! so "The formation of partnerships [of schools] with local agencies, businesses and industries will continue to expand in importance"; province-wide testing will measure and "ensure that achievement targets are met" (*RA*, 5).

Who could be against inefficiency and not for finding employment? But there is not a breath of God, let alone Jesus Christ, in these documents, and to treat schools as if they are in business for business is to make mincemeat of what God set up schooling to be: schooling is not to produce Darwinian survivors, but is to coax students to know God's covenantal Rule of the world, to recognize the powers of evil, and to disseminate shalom in the name of Christ. The "Revolution of Common Sense" is misnamed, in my judgment: it is actually the "Consolidation of Dollars and Cents." There are 600,000 copies distributed in Ontario at our expense of this Gospel of Mammon in a respectable three-piece suit.[1]

Don't get me wrong. 1-800-903-MIKE John Snobolen and Dave Johnson are surely honorable men, but their educational policies strike me as being in the grip of an evil principality that is stronger and more deadly than anybody made of flesh and blood—the protean no-god of Mammon is what we fight!

Our elementary christian schools may seem unaffected because they are subject, if I understand it correctly, only to provincial health and fire regulations; but our christian high schools are checked on curricular match. According to an extensive study published by the Institute for Catholic Education, which analyses the Ontario government plans to revamp schooling by legislation: ". . . the curricular changes . . . strike at the very soul of Catholic secondary education . . . they threaten the distinctive character and mandate of Catholic education itself" (*ETS*, 3),

---

1   It is worth noting that the 1994 Report of the Royal Commission on Learning, *For the Love of Learning*, has a less reductionistic, commercialized idea of the purpose for schooling than the Education Improvement Commission, *The Road Ahead*, does. Cf. for example, LOL 1:53–63, summarized in the LOL, short version: ". . . the primary purpose of schooling is not to train students for a particular job, or to turn out a product, or to make Ontario more competitive in a globalized economy, or to compensate for a broken family, or to install worthy values that others have neglected. On the contrary, there is one thing above all that teachers are singularly equipped for. First, and foremost, their purpose must be to ensure for all students—whatever their future jobs or careers—high levels of what we've chosen to call literacies . . ." (4–5).

unless one think the "Catholic" or the "Christian" to schooling is simply value-added vitamins to the basic skills curriculum rather than a pervasive vision that makes a profound difference to the curriculum as a whole. The provincial government's concentration of power at the top to dictate where "smarter spending" goes in dismantling the former "traditional" vision of schooling (for which they have invented! a crisis—which the media has seldom exposed, cf. *OCECS*, 5–6) bodes ill even for christian teachers and students who work in the secular system. We Christians who seem to be an **invisible** minority in society to the government need to become clearly **audible** lest our believing and unbelieving neighbors be drowned in the rough waters through which we hope to walk.

But even elementary christian schools are not immune to the pull of Mammon. When an elementary christian school board sinks the budget by ordering a goodly number of computers and consoles for the school (not even minding the later costs of servicing the machines) so that there are no funds left to make a room in the inn for the arts and music programs for the little children, you have to pause to weep at how good intentions—who wants to be left behind!?—can be fooled. A fine report for the Institute for Catholic Education rightly says: "a school board's budget is its functioning mission statement" (*CM*, 8), because where you put your money is where your priorities are. Technology always reduces knowledge to information. Dexterity with amassed information data can be valuable, but learning to make hand-made objects and being able to sing songs should have a very high priority, it seems to me, in a city of refuge where children gather. What's all the hurry in education?! If schooling would be an occasion for inter-generational sharing of wisdom, we need to remember wisdom needs to steep like a good cup of tea.

(2) **Cultural amnesia** is like communal Alzheimer's disease: because a communal memory has gone blank, society wonders where it is, and when orientation is lost, disintegration sets in. African Americans in North America have slavery, gospel songs, and the blues; Jews have the Holocaust and Israel real estate; Europeans have a Renaissance Humanism as remembered history to give them a semblance of their own identity; but what do secularized, middle-class Canadians in Ontario have for a solidifying, common historical narrative tradition bonding them with a unifying world-and-life view? Do the people of Ontario have a common deep memory today?

Much of the current *academia* pretends that every and any *grand récits* (an over-arching story with a past beginning and a coming future)

Did Love Hurt Heloise

7. Your sto - ry, Pet - er, though ve - ry old, still holds mean-ing a-
fresh: no man, no wo-man ev - er out-lasts spir - it war-ring with
flesh. Fal - len, down on your knees, ask God to tell you, please
(whis- per_ the weep ing trees), did love hurt Hel-o - ise?

8. Your sto - ry, Pet - er, though ve - ry old, still holds mean-ing a-
fresh: no man, no wom-an ev - er out-lasts spir - it war-ring with
flesh. Fal - len, down on your knees, ask God to tell you, please
(al- though no one a- grees), your love hurt Hel-o - ise.

Text: Calvin Seerveld, 1998, ©
Tune: Calvin Seerveld, 1998, ©

9696D 6666
DARK LADY

is necessarily exploitive and to be avoided, especially the Judeo-Christian, Western colonializing imperialist story, which has almost always carelessly invited "others" to be like "us." Meanwhile, on the streets of our life we are encouraged not to grow up—Toys"R"us—and TV bombards our consciousness with images of atrocity, celebrity scandals, "world events" in overload so we have no time or memory space to remember where **we** came from. Our culture is drilled to live in the prison house of the present.

The Power of Cultural Amnesia upon schooling is that it rubs out historical sense—students don't know whether Socrates came before or after Christ; so Shakespeare lived when the epochal "King James" translation of the Bible into English was made—what does it matter when things happened? Students are programmed by the media and advertising to become ahistorical—fascinated by novelty, impressed by trivia, encouraged to trade in living traditions for the show of rituals.

In a Pop song-writing and repertoire course I took at York University this past spring, after we studied "Starry, starry night" and learned pop songs sometimes address historical figures like "Vincent," I wrote a pop song entitled, "Did Love Hurt Heloise?" The prof liked it, so I got to play it in class; "but you better tell them first who Abelard was," he said. And it's true, those thirty-five undergraduate York students knew just about every contemporary band, performance, pop-song singer, the producers and song-writers of the last twenty-five years, but practically nothing before then.

Schooling needs to make historical connections in order to ground and situate knowledge. We need to lift high school students up and out of the narrow confines of their world and give them glimpses of richer cultural times than the sounds over CHUM radio. When you discover that the musical interval of the fourth is integral to both Rhythm-and-Blues and Gregorian chant, and that Luther and Calvin's cantor Louis Bourgeois used medieval modal figures to write melodies for their stanzaic psalms and hymns, you start to tie songs over the ages together and gather in a thicker knowledge of R & B that can lean toward wisdom. British education theorist Peter Abbs proposed that teachers ask students to write autobiographies as a step in locating, if not centering, their consciousness, saving it from cultural amnesia.

Many of God's adopted grownup children have a limpid, milk-like faith that is simple and sure: Jesus loves me a sinner, the Holy Spirit leads me a saint, God is love, PTL. Other Christians have what Hebrews calls a robust, meat-eating faith that wrestles with the full counsel of God (Hebrews 5:12–14). But such a faith as well as the milk-fed faith can suffer, it seems to me, from confessional Alzheimer's disease—believers become mostly ignorant of the persecuted faith tradition that has nurtured them and is congealed, for example, in the very christian school presence today in Ontario. When anybody takes a precious gift for granted, it begins to tarnish and fade.

In the face of the ubiquitous principality of Forgetting-the-past, which tends to thin out discipleship, dumb-down worship of the living God, and breed a manipulatable superficiality, christian schooling has the wonderful task of taking the time to remember our roots—whether you prefer Irenaeus, Augustine, Aquinas, Chaucer, Luther, Calvin, Pascal, Wesley, or whichever saints they be—and to bring alive for our students that **we** belong to the company of the born-again martyrs who walk through the rough waters Isaiah is talking about, witnessing to the Rule of Jesus Christ on the earth. We who follow the Christ are not flotsam adrift in a swirl of competing alliances and stymied, meaningless projects, but hold God's hand as we walk along, historically grounded, tending to our appointed schooling service. As Bob Goudzwaard says: "Teachers must consciously reflect a mirror image of Christ as the priest who heals broken memories" (46).

We end now with the prayer of **Psalm 115** and a **Song of "Tough Love in Rough Waters."** The waters of Mammon and Cultural Amnesia I find forbidding. I did not spend a lot of time on the Waters because the devil likes nothing better than to take your time, and we must never indulge the false comfort of pessimism and forlorn critique. But it is urgent, I think, to name these principalities, to self-critically recognize their brutal and corrosive power over us too, as well as upon the World Banked and Walt Disneyed culture at large. Then, given our Isaiah 43 passage as a directive, we teachers in the schooling city of refuge are called to become neither social activists nor mere spectators but to **act** as disciplined wise women and men who can help both prodigals and the elder sons and daughters learn not to cough up the correct, standardized test answers, but to ask the right God-fearing, neighbor-loving questions of any topic, like the ones Doug Blomberg genially formulated half a dozen years ago:

What is normative for this area of creation?
How has sin and God's judgment distorted this reality?
What needs to be done to bring healing and reconciliation? (*VWT*, 246)

The institutional schooling city of refuge is not meant to burden children with the ills of the world but to invigorate them, at their appropriate stage of responsibility, by preparing them to discern the demonic angels-of-light besetting us (cf. 2 Corinthians 11:12–15) and to expect God to unwrap their gifts in a blessed, new way so that "counting the costs" they also walk through the waters as bearers of faith, love and hope (cf. Isaiah 61:1–3). Schools will pass away when the Lord returns, but

When You Pass Through Rough Waters

1. When you pass through rough waters, when you
2. Though the out - come seem bleak, though the
3. God will do some - thing new-- God will
4. Thank the LORD for tough love, thank the

pass through rough waters, they shall not o - ver-whelm you, for
out - come seem bleak, re - main true to the vi - sion of
do some - thing new - if you tire on the jour - ney, re-
LORD for tough love: re - main joy-ful and pru - dent as

God stays near-by you, when you pass through rough waters.
Christ's ru - ling mis- sion, though the out - come seem bleak.
mem - ber past mer - cy: God will do some - thing new.
teach - er and stu - dent, thank the LORD for tough love.

Text: Isaiah 43:2, 13, 19; vers. Calvin Seerveld, 1998, ©
Tune: Heinz Werner Zimmerman, 1971
Music © 1972, Concordia Publishing House. Used by permission.

66766
LITTLE FLOCK

whatever redemptive teaching and learning goes on there now lasts forev-er, says the Bible (Ecclesiastes 3:14–15). That's why I think wise teachers, from kindergarten to OAC classes, are worth more than much fine gold, and good principals, like a righteous judge Scripture even dares compare to being "gods" (Psalm 82; cf. John 10:31–39), are veritably priceless.

Since one generation goes as another generation comes to walk through the waters, what we are daily busy with in christian schooling is much bigger than any generation's gifts or failings: we are witnesses to the glorious, tough loving providence of the LORD God Isaiah reveals. And the Scriptures promise that the LORD will renew the strength of those sinful saints who get weary, and shall certainly establish the work of faithful teaching hands with joy! (Isaiah 40:28–31, Psalm 90:13–17, 1 Corinthians 15:58).

PSALM 115 [for communal responsive reading aloud]

leader: Not for us, LORD, not for us,
but do something glorious for Your name!
Make something solid and shining to show Your
covenanting Grace and utterly dependable faithfulness!
Why should the peoples all around say,
    And where now is their God?"

people: **Our God is in heaven!**
Everything that pleases God, God completes!

leader: Their "gods" are solid gold and silver,
[but] made by a human hand.
Their fake gods have a mouth but cannot speak;
they have eyes but cannot see!
Ears they have but can not hear;
a nose is there, but they cannot smell—
Their hands cannot touch things.
Their feet cannot go for a walk.
No sound passes through their throat . . .

people: **Like them become those who made them!**
Like them become all those who feel secure with them.

leader: Israel! get to feel secure with the LORD God:

people: **a relief and a protection is the LORD for such people.**

leader: [Priestly] house of Aaron! bind yourselves only to the LORD God:

people: **a relief and a protection is the LORD for such people.**

leader: You [newcomers] who fear Yahweh! trust—trust the LORD God:

people: **a relief and a protection is God for such people.**

leader: The LORD God has kept us in mind: God shall bless—

people: **Bless the house of Israel!**
Bless the [priestly] house of Aaron!
Bless those who fear the LORD God!

leader: —the unimportant ones together with the very important ones. . . .
May the LORD God prosper you, you and your children.
May you all be blessed by the LORD God, who made heaven and
earth.
Heaven [you know] belongs specially to the LORD:
The earth is what God gave for the sons and daughters of man to
tend].
Dead men and women do not praise the LORD,
not one of those who have gone down to where it is deathly
still.
But we people here, let us bless the LORD!
from now on and for ever more:

people: **thank God—hallelujah!**

(translation C. Seerveld, 1969)

Sources for the lecture

Abbs, Peter. *The Polemics of Imagination* (London: Skoob Books, 1996).

Badley, Ken. *Worldviews: The challenge of choice* (Concord: Irwin, 1996).

Bledstein, Burton J. *The Culture of Professionalism: The middle class and the development of higher education in America* (New York: Norton, 1976).

Blomberg, Doug. "Teachers as Articulate Artisans," in *Nurturing Reflective Christians to Teach*, ed. D.C. Elliott (Lanham: University Press of America, 1995), 99–118.

———. "Wisdom at Play: In the world but not of it," in *The Crumbling Walls of Certainty: Towards a christian critique of postmodernity and education*, eds. Ian Lambert and Suzanne Mitchell (Sydney: Centre for the Study of Australian Christianity, 1997), 120–33.

Bruner, Jerome S. *The Relevance of Education* (New York: Norton, 1971).

Christians and Higher Education in Eastern Europe. Proceedings of the 1993 Debrecen Regional Conference of the International Association for the Promotion of Christian Higher Education. (Sioux Center: Dordt College Press, 1996).

The Common Sense Revolution, 5th printing (Toronto: Provincial Government of Ontario, 1994). [=*CSR*]

Curriculum Matters: A Resource for Catholic Educators (Toronto: Institute for Catholic Education, 1996). [=*CM*]

Duvenage, S.C.W. *Kerk, Volk en Jeugd: Die verhouding van kerk tot volk* (Zaandijk: J. Heijnis, 1962). Diss.

For the Love of Learning. Report of the Royal Commission on Learning (Toronto: Publications Ontario, 1994). 4 vols. 1: *Mandate, Context, Issues*; 2: *Learning: Our vision for schools*; 3: *The Educators*; 4: *Making it Happen* (especially chapter 16, "Equity considerations . . . religious minorities"). [=*LOL*]

For the Love of Learning. Report of the Royal Commission on Learning, a short version (Toronto: Publications Ontario, 1994).

Fowler, Stuart. "The distinctive character of the school" (1986), unpublished mimeograph, typescript 29pp.

Gatto, John Taylor. *Dumbing Us Down: The hidden curriculum of compulsory schooling* (Gabriola Island, BC: New Society Publishers, 1992).

Gardner, Howard. *Multiple Intelligences: The theory in practice* (New York: Basic Books, 1993).

Goudzwaard, Bob. "Towards a Future of Care," in *The Crumbling Walls of Certainty: Towards a Christian critique of postmodernity & education*, eds. Ian Lambert and Suzanne Mitchell (Sydney: Centre for the Study of Australian Christianity, 1997), 40–49.

Griffioen, Sander. *The Problem of Progress* (Sioux Center: Dordt College Press, 1987).

Hill, Philip G. *Ontario Catholic Education and the Corporate Sector* (Toronto: Institute for Catholic Education, 1997). [=*OCECS*]

Janse, A. *Het Eigen Karakter der Christelijke School* (Kampen: Kok, 1935).

McCarthy, Rockne and Donald Oppewal, Walfred Peterson, Gordon Spykman. *Society, State, and Schools: A case for structural and confessional pluralism* (Grand Rapids: Eerdmans, 1981).

Neatby, Hilda. *So Little for the Mind* (Toronto: Clarke, Irwin & Co., 1953).

Nietzsche, Friedrich. "Über die Zukunft unserer Bildungsanstalten," in *Werke*, Kritische Gesamtausgabe, eds. Giorgio Colli and Mazzino Mintinari. (Berlin: De Gruyter, 1973), III/2:133–257; translated by J.M. Kennedy as "On the Future of our Educational Institutions," in *The Complete Works of Friedrich Nietzsche*, ed. Oscar Levy (New York: Russell & Russell, 1964), 3:3–142.

Ontario Curriculum Grades 1–8 Language (Ontario Ministry of Education and Training, 1997).

Ontario Curriculum Grades 1–8 Mathematics (Ontario Ministry of Education and Training, 1997).

Palmer, Parker J. *To Know as We are Known: Education as a spiritual journey* [1983] (San Francisco: Harper, 1993).

Popma, Klaas J. "Opvoeding, Onderwijs, Schoolverband," *Philosophia Reformata* 12:1–3 (1947): 36–41, 86–93, 130–44.

The Road Ahead, A report on learning time, class size, and staffing, by the Education Improvement Commission (of the Ontario provincial government), August 1997. [=*RA*]

Schipani, Daniel S. *Conscientization and Creativity: Paulo Freire and christian education* (Lanham: University Press of America, 1984).

Schwehn, Mark R. *Exiles from Eden: Religion and the academic vocation in America* (New York: Oxford University Press, 1993).

Skillen, James W. "Yes, Wisconsin," *Capital Commentary*, 22 June 1998.

Smith, Frank. *The Book of Learning and Forgetting* (New York: Teachers College, Columbia University, 1998).

Spivak, Gayatri Chakrovorby. Interviews and discussions in *The Post-Colonial Critic*, ed. Sarah Harasym (London: Routledge, 1990), 1–51.

Stronks, Gloria and Doug Blomberg, eds. *A Vision with a Task: Christian schooling for responsive discipleship* (Grand Rapids: Baker, 1993). [=*VWT*]

TDCH *Programme of Studies 1997–1999* (Woodbridge: Toronto District Christian High School, n.d.).

Trafford, Larry. *Educating the Soul: Writing curriculum for Catholic secondary schools* (Toronto: Institute for Catholic Education, 1998). [=*ETS*]

Van der Laan, H. and A. H. de Graaff, H. W. van Brummelen, et al. *The Ideal of Christian Schools* (Potchefstroom: Potchefstroomse Universiteit vir Christelijke Hoër Onderwys, Institute for Reformational Studies, study pamphlet nr. 358, 1997).

Van Riessen, H., W. Sleumer, and A. la Fleur. *De Moderne Cultuur en de Christelijke School: Uitdaging en antwoord.* Proceedings of Het Groot Comité tot Organisatie van Christelijke Schoolcongressen (Kampen: Kok, 1962).

The Voice of Liberal Learning: Michael Oakeshott on education (1948–74), ed. Timothy Fuller (New Haven: Yale University Press, 1989).

Zuidervaart, Lambert, "Deep Water from the Kuyperian Well: The future of higher education," *Perspectives* 13:3 (March 1998): 6–11, reprinted in *Contact*, newsletter of the International Association for the Promotion of Christian Higher Education, Fall 1998. 4pp.

As well as:

Cayley, David, ed. series, *The Education Debates* on CBC "Ideas," heard 8–11, 14–18 September 1998; continuing in January 1999 (www. cbc.ca/ ideas/).

"Counting the Cost: Learning to be a faithful servant of Jesus in the local and global community," Schoolwide Conference at Toronto District Christian High School, Woodbridge, Ontario, 7–9 October 1998.

Resources and conversations with Harry Antonides, Doug Blomberg, Corrie Bootsma, Richard vander Kloet, Gerald Vandezande.

THE SONG OF MOSES AND THE LAMB:
THE JOKE OF A.R.S.S. EDUCATION

You must set yourselves to hear what John of the Apocalypse heard as he looked into heaven that day and saw the victorious saints standing on a sea of glass wreathed in harmless flames of fire, playing God's harps and singing The Song of Moses and the Lamb (Revelation 15:2–4). I shall read you the entire song of Moses that he spoke near his death to those who would lead God's people when he was gone, how he recalls the history of Israel, admonishes his hearers, and reports conversations of God firsthand. This is no swan song, but the holy Scriptures preserved and heard through the ages by believers in catacombs and battlefields, cathedrals and studies, even to the instruction of us gathered in 1965 Anno Domini in the Unionville barn. This is the Word of God:

Gather to me all the elders of your tribes, (said Moses) your judges and office bearers so that I may speak in their ears certain words so that heaven and the earth shall witness it, because I know, after my death you shall all become as corrupt as they come and distance yourselves from the Way I have laid out for you, and terrible disasters shall hurt you in those latter days, for you will be doing mean things as God sees it, your hands will perform matters that simply get on God's nerves—

Then Moses spoke into the ears of all Israel gathered (to him) the words of this song—he spoke until it was finished:

Listen! Heavens, for I am going to speak!
Hear! Earth, the words of my mouth!
What I teach shall fall soft like the rain;
My speech shall rest long like minute drops of dew,

The keynote address delivered at the Unionville study conference of the Association for Reformed Scientific Studies on Aug. 25, 1965; published under separate title (32 pages) in 1966 by the ARSS.

like April showers on spring green grass,
like a thundershower soaking the meadows,
    For I proclaim: the glory of Yahweh!
    That's right—Toast! to our God!
        The Rock!
        What God does is without a mistake;
        Every one of God's projects is right!
        God of utterly true, trustworthy faithfulness,
            without a speck of fault!
        Straight and right is the Lord God!
—God's sons have spoiled the covenant with God,
a really tricky, crooked group of men:
    is that the way you thank God? you foolish, stupid
    people! is God not your Father? who possessed you
    by creation! God made you, right? and covers you
    (now with a hand)?—

Remember the good old days?
Can you recall the years of bygone generations?
    Ask your father, he knows; the grandfathers here,
    they can tell you

        When the exalted (Lord) of nations parceled out possessions
        to the varied children of men,
        God set limits to the peoples (of the world), thinking of the
        children of Israel,
        Because Israel was Yahweh's special interest, God's people;
        Jacob was God's particular possession.
            God found God's people (long ago)
                in a land gone to waste,
                in a never-never land of howling desert.
            God surrounded God's people carefully, gave them
                attention, protected them as if they were God's own
                skin.
        Like a huge eagle that rustles out its nest and hovers over
            the young birds,
        So the Lord stretched out God's wing, caught God's
            (fledgling) people, and bore them aloft on God's
            wide open pinions.

        (In the good old days) only Yahweh led God's people:
            they had no strange god at all with them (then).

God brought them over hill and valley of the earth.
God fed them from wild fruit of the fields.
God breastfed them honey out of rock! oils out of bed
    rock! cream from cows! full milk from goats! prime
    wool on lambs!
    Bashan bred, thick chested rams,
    Full, fat kernels of corn!
    And spilled juice of grapes, (remember?)
    You drank it like brimming, heady wine.

Then good Jacob ate, got the fat sick look, became sulky and skittish

    —you became fat! (do you hear?) F-A-T, fat! stuffed with good
      things!—
And good Jacob let God who made him go:
He spit on the Rock that kept saving him!

    They egged the Lord's jealousy on by taking in strange gods.
    They flauntingly provoked the Lord by performing unnatural
      cultic rites.
    They sacrificed to evil spirits—no-god(s).
    They worshipped gods they didn't even know.
    New gods lately come to the neighborhood before whom your
      forefathers would never even have been startled. (They now
      stood in awe.)

    —You stopped thinking about the Rock that bore you!
    You forgot God! who twisted in labor pain
    to give you birth—
The LORD God saw the nose-thumbing of God's Sons and daughters
(grown haughty), and God had enough of it.
God said:

    I will hide my face from them (awhile);
    What happens to them I shall see later:
      what a rotten generation!
      Kids who do not know what "faithfulness" means. . . .
    They have gotten under my jealous skin with their no-gods!
    They have roused, prickled me into irritation with their
      divine imposters.
So I shall drive them to sorry jealousy with an un-people!
I shall disturb them with a no-god nation,
    For a fire smolders in my face.

A fire of anger burns (in me) all the way down to hell; it is
  singeing the ground, all the plants, setting on fire the
  foothills of the mountain—
I will pile up miseries on them!
I will shoot every one of my arrows (so that) they be exhausted
  with hunger, diseased by epidemics and poisoning plagues.
I will set the hook teeth of beasts loose upon them and the
  noxious excretions of wiggling, dusty, crawling things.
  Knives will abort children on the street, and
  Horrible things will happen in the bedrooms—virgins,
    draftees, babies, or grandfathers—(no difference . . .)
I would have said, "I shall exterminate them!
  I will wipe any memory of them out of history";
But I am afraid those who hate them would jibe, that the
  enemies (of my people) would misinterpret (my action) and
  say,
  "Not Yahweh did all these things,
  But o u r hand overthrew his people. . . ."

Yes, [continues Moses,] (Jacob) was a people lost to discernment;
  they had not a speck of sense!
If they had been wise, they would have understood these things,
  would have seen what was coming later:

How come one (enemy) could rout a thousand of them?
How come a couple (enemies) could make refugees out of
  thousands (of God's people)
    unless their Rock had left them?
    unless Yahweh had let them go out of God's hand!

    For our Rock is not like their rock(s)—even our enemies
      admit that—
    Because (their foundation,) the root of their vine is the
      grapevine stock of Sodom (rotting) on the terraces of
      Gomorrah;
    Their grapes are pure wormwood, (frigid) little bitter
      clusters;
    Their wine has the slime of killer fish to it, the fatal bite
      of slippery asps.
"Do not suppose I have forgotten the (dirty, tempting
  corruption of my people's enemies," says the LORD God;)
"I have it locked tight in my thoughts till the day of judgment

and their punishment come, until the moment their feet
begin to stumble;
And their day of desperation is coming soon; what they have got
coming is hurrying near."

The LORD God shall give God's people justice and shower mercy down
upon their servant heads when God sees that they cannot stand
up any longer and free men look like slaves.

And the LORD God shall say:

So? where are their gods? the "rock(s)" to which they ran for
support? the "gods" who got the most and best of their
offerings? who enjoyed their toasts of wine?
Let them stand up and give help; let them be for them a
protection.

Do you not see that I, I am (God), and there is no God but
me?
I am the one who brings death and who gives life.
I am the one who hurts (men) and I shall make them whole—
Without (the touch of) my hand there is no succeeding!

With my hand to heaven, I swear,

"As I live forever:
When the blade of my sword is whetted sharp and my hand
tightens for just execution,
I shall wreak vengeance on those who oppressed my (people)
and shall demand retribution from those who did not
love me.
I will dip my arrows in blood, and my sword shall cut through
the bloody flesh of the impaled, caught ruling figures of
the Enemy."

Unbelieving peoples!
(You too,) laugh hard and joyfully with the LORD God's folk,
for God avenges the blood of God's servants,
brings troublemakers their comeuppance, and
washes away the guilt God's people have on earth.

So Moses came and spoke all the words of this song into the ears of
the people, with Joshua son of Nun (standing) next to him; and when
Moses had finished speaking all these words to all Israel (gathered
there), God said to them:

**Set deep in your hearts all the words that I have festively
    proclaimed this day to you:
Instill them in your children in such a way that they receive them
    to do them—all the words of this Command (of God),
For the Word (here spoken) is not just sound (in the air) around
    you:**

it is your life!

**By this Word (of God) you all can stay alive till you shall possess the
land promised you on the other side of river Jordan.**

(Deuteronomy 31:28–32:47)

A remarkable passage: Moses is toasting God on his deathbed and God is taking an oath to assure God's faithless people of God's care. We do not generally appreciate the jealousness of God toward believers, maybe because we tend today to blur the line between God's people and those who do not confess God as Lord. And that point—God's people before the jealous Lord of heaven and earth—the Song of Moses, spiked by the cross of the Lamb in the age of the mark of the Beast, is the critical-focus for any biblical thought about Christian education, primary or advanced. Without it you spout more or less humanizing moralistic air. The indiscriminate sweetness and light of our hale-fellow-well-met secular society is too humane for the revealed love of the LORD God. That is why the Rock Yahweh is too rough and ready for the particular Ivy Leagued humanist. Yet St. Paul says (1 Corinthians 10:1–13): you people Anno Domini should not be ignorant of what I read, the passionate doings of the Rock Yahweh with God's people, because that Rock of offense was Christ, and what happened happened to "set our whole consciousness" (νοθεσίαν—1 Corinthians 10:11; cf. also Ephesians 6:4). Especially those who think all is well in Jerusalem or Corinth Chicago or Antioch Toronto must take heed lest they fall, says the Scriptures.

Before I follow up on the Song of Moses' "setting our whole consciousness" and how that contextualizes the joke of A.R.S.S. education, one little telltale point should be noticed and made clear if possible, namely, that I read the Scriptures and expect to keep it in the back—not too far back—of our minds as we talk education.

Some acquaintances of mine who have followed at a distance what has gone on at Unionville the last few years[1] ask, "What's all this preach-

---

1   The first educational activity of the Association was to set up a summer conference for university students to help them think about Christian perspective in their studies. These were held just outside of Toronto in the town of Unionville, the first one on

ing? Why all this testifying, this Messianic fervor and sermonic heat about being 'Reformational'? Nobody disagrees here in Reformed circles; we are all Reformed. Your conferences and publications should stop agitating so enthusiastically for Reformation and get down to the difficult business of finding Christian answers to the many difficult problems of the age: overpopulation, automation, federal aid, how to get Reformed folks into governmental office." *Minder geschreeuw en meer wol,*[2] they might say if they knew Dutch.

A reply to this feint gets at the heart of the A.R.S.S. I think.

(1) Testimony, "prophecy" if you will, weaves in and out of the scientific studies on pragmatism, art, politics, ethics, sociology, biology, and the rest most naturally because we understand scholarship to be directed by Scripture, and like a lover lapses into kissing his beloved as she passes by his work, so our scientific studies fall so easily back into showing where our first love is, that's all. The flow between Scripture and scholarship is not a forced one but a relation of easy intimacy. We really mean it when we say that the Bible gives direction for learning, not in a biblicistic way of finding chapter and verse answers to academic problems, but quite literally taking biblical revelation of Christ as the thesaurus of God's wisdom (Colossians 2:3), expecting it to give us guidance for godly living and right thinking (2 Timothy 3:16). A Unionville Conference without the cast of Scripture openly professed is unthinkable. Every time I come here, I remember Rev. Guillaume's reading of the first chapters of 1 Corinthians (1:18–2:5) in 1961:

> . . . not many worldly-wise men, not many powerful, not many good lookers, but the fools of the world God has chosen (for use) to shame the philosophers; God has chosen the world's weaklings to confound the strong . . . so that nobody can boast in God's face. Thanks to God you are in Christ Jesus who has been made our Wisdom by God. (1 Corinthians 1:26–30)

Only when study has been divorced from Christ-commitment will its testimonial character seem strange.

(2) Are all those re-formed who are "Reformed"? The Reformational "R" in the A.R.S.S., that's right, does not stand for strict adherence to the collected opinions of the man John Calvin and his Calvinists. Reformation here means being captured by the centrality of the human creature's existing before the LORD God, the radical fact that everyone is

---

1–3 September 1959.

2   "Less talk, more walk, people!"

either wedded to Christ or is living, eating, and sleeping with a false god. Reformation to the Association for Reformed Scientific Studies means rediscovery of the priesthood of every believer, those without ministerial status too, rediscovery of the Christian community's being called to exercise kingship on earth, without a churchy imperialism. This is the biblical Reformational spirit that drove Luther and Calvin at their best: Luther and Calvin did not drive the Reformation. And the offense of this Reformational "R" to some is that it is ecumenically broader than institutional church denominations with historically Reformed confessions and that it will not assume that membership in a Reformed church implies genuine re-formation of one's thought and deed. Hence the continual excitement for Reformation! that all take heed where they stand and know that their daily life and scientific study is dead, or alive in Christ! That some people in this room who look alive, think sharp, and execute plans may be really dead, not taking God at God's Word, is frightening, biblically agitating. It is true that God uses us, dead or alive; it is all alike to God in working out God's will, but it is not all the same for us. Those who are dead get deader: those who are alive are kept alive, made alive, by active refreshment in the Lord of Life, till their faith and hope end in the greatest of the three: love, pure and excelling.

It should be clear, then, to an informed observer that the openly biblical, reforming character of the *Christian Perspectives Series* and A.R.S.S. action is not abnormal but what you would logically expect from an association formed to found a Reformational center of higher education. I will not go into the confusing the A.R.S.S. with a "church." Kuyper made it plain long ago that when Isaac da Costa forcefully expounded the Word early in the morning at his home, perhaps in his pajamas, to all who congregated there, it was not an official church service despite the prophetic edification that took place (*Onze Eredienst*, 2). Just because God's Word was read tonight to be listened to, the Father's blessing was invoked, we sang "spiritual songs" together, and a deeply needed collection may even be taken, our meeting is still not a formal worship service; this, our informal worship, which Christian study and work always is, is not in competition either with the solemn assembly of saints gathered under those ordained to open and shut the doors of the Kingdom of God. We are a complement of the body of Christ come to praise God tonight by examining, discussing, and supporting Christian education.

History: The cure to Christian education
The focal concern of Christian education, I should like to propose, is

understanding and developing history. Excepting the few old style humanists left and the *magistri* of the Roman church of course, modern secular education has come to value this central matter less and less as— fascinated by our human power to revolutionize culture—it has aimed the training of youth more and more toward exploration and problem-solving rather than retrospection. The evil dehumanizing of the society that such rootless education affords is part of the thesis, but right now our main concern is to grasp the workings of Christian education, to see why history is its crux.

When the Song of Moses poetically recounts the dealing of Yahweh with God's people and the sons and daughters of men, that is history being festively chronicled. The providence of God for all those in time, especially for those who believe (1 Timothy 4:10), is the stuffings of history. What Almighty God does with creation, how God attends, prompts, blesses the progressive differentiation of all kinds of creatures, and how God since the fall of Adam has graciously gone about reconciling the world to God self through Jesus Christ (Colossians 1:20), this is what's up in the world. Historians of every stripe notice the complicated changes that take place when a primitively whole, closed civilization opens up to a more specialized culture, how human relations individualize, how society's action breaks up into more distinct sorts, how people become more self-conscious of their self-consciousness. And historians interested in land and plants and animals have always noticed new speciations and extinction, patterns of growth and destruction. But these observers who missed knowing what history is, who lack the biblical understanding of history, and did not find God's hand anywhere in the happenings, God's eagle wing, arrows, righteous judgment, or speech, they have to resort to unbelieving stratagems to make any sense out of it all. Historians of one stripe postulate the vicious circle of a brutal bio-physical process. Other striped historians honor "natural" law or admit somewhat exhortingly to an evolutionary progress and betterment. The presence of numinous power has been variously denied and ascribed to demons, to humanity, Reason, money-making drives— A fashion today is to say Nothing underlies what goes on. This nihilistic viewpoint tries to suspend historiography at phenomenological description of random events, recommending to society they just try to stay on top of the wave of what is occurring till they can ride out the surf to shore, if there be one.

Not these phantasms of history constitute the meat and drink of Christian education, but actual history: the wondrous spectacle of *magnalia Dei* and the blessed unfolding of creations to their full, God-created special ordering. Immediately from creation—God's bringing the animals to Adam, sending the flood, calling out Abraham, giving Law on Mt. Sinai to Moses, obscurely arranging the phenomenal Western civilization of Hellenes; the incarnation and resurrection of Jesus Christ, Pentecost, conversion of Paul, monastic perseverance and barbarian raids, the Reformation, printing, telephone, ice boxes, world wars: this is all history! and knowing cosmic catastrophe and national joy—

> *I* am the one who brings death and who gives life.
> *I* am the one who hurts (men) and *I* shall make them whole—

. . . down to the rather insignificant, private, twisted line of our lifetimes till we set foot in this building tonight for the first, second, or seventh time, knowing all this as the Way! the Lord God faithfully fulfills through the responses of God's creatures the promises made to the first man and woman to the end of time, knowing this is central to Christian education. Why? First, because it is the Truth, the Truth that sets one free from idols. History is the shining gossamer of God in which we live, move, and have our meaning. Misunderstood or disbelieved, it becomes a cobweb for death. Education that holds a false idea of history or slights this undeniable, concrete matrix of the redeeming creator God's ruling human and subhuman affairs leaves those so trained lost in a maze of abstractions.

I mean this: if education is the disciplined forming of one's consciousness enabling one to make distinctions oneself and to perform new actions within a certain perspective, current university education throughout America leaves students largely operating in a vacuum. Research physical scientists, engineers, mathematicians, political scientists, sociologists, and psychologists in graduate departments across the continent: who could care less about history, much less history as I have presented it? Chemists are deep in esoteric synthetics; physicists are deeper in space technology or instruments of war; sociological experts convert all their energies to find *modi vivendi* to ease race tensions and burgeoning urban troubles. Except for an occasional classicist like Whitehead, special scientists have no time nor reason for themselves or their students to pursue in-depth historical studies that are philosophically mature: the past is done, you cannot do anything about it; we live in the present and must find a formula to survive, even if it is makeshift one. I call this the unreal world of abstraction that clouds the current apostate mind. But somebody says, "That is a strange use of the word if you think the dress I have on is a synthetic abstraction, and the bomb that can level a modern city of steel is an abstraction, and a hammered out compromise plan to relocate minority groups among the Angelenos is an abstraction, because those abstractions are what makes the world go round." But I do not intend to spiritualize evil or disparage the fabrics, comforts, and heroic plans of scientific technology, as literati sometimes indulge. I only wish to posit that human life, thought, action not couched and rooted in a motivating fear of the Lord God is vanity; more narrowly, that human living/thinking/acting that lacks a sense of history, is ignorant or unmindful that our created timed existence is response to the Lord God's apocalyptic involvement in God's complex handiwork, no matter how brilliant, is (vanity, the biblical word for "hot air," a false god) in my book an "abstraction," particularly if you think it makes the world go round, even though it may in deed make the world go down.

Of course, special scientific study, at the frontier of human knowledge, is intrinsically theoretical, "abstracting" from concrete lived reality, to get at the law-side of things, at how, for example, micro-phenomena function. Astrophysicists naturally measure light-year distances between stars rather than wonder what name God gave each one they discover, and biochemists do not get paid for admiring the scarlet color with which anemone lilies are clothed but earn their keep for years by trying to reconstruct its photosynthetic process. This is as it necessarily is and should be. The evil slip comes when the scientific habit is adopted, casually or expressly, as final authority, as fundamental orientation, as a source of knowledge not relativized by history, a human contribution not subject to praising the covenanting God of creation. Education that effects this perspective in students without pontificating, simply by crowding out alternatives, forcing the impossible mastery of detail in medical school, perfecting case upon case study in law school, soft pressuring results useful to the government for its National Defense research grant: such historically void, intense university education that has crept up on us is so dangerous because it is essentially revolutionary. This Renaissance-inspired, scientistically powered education has been tremendously successful in making us F-A-T, but it has loosed our Western civilization from its moorings of fifteen centuries of Christianized Hellenism. By reducing its sights to what's now in front of us, purposely disregarding continuity with the past, pretending to be unconditioned, modern scientific scholarship has minutely mastered culturally explosive areas of information—but, again, it has shrunken our heads and hearts: cosmology has been reduced to natural science, methodology to the study of techniques, ontology mainly given up for epistemology, hermeneutics for language analysis, and the full joy of a man and woman's caressing love reduced to a bare-faced relation between "male" and "female," abstractions of a playboy philosophy. And with our technologically shrunken heads and hearts, with no ground under our feet, no realities of sin, God's Wisdom, or historical norm, the Pied Piper of secular post-Renaissance science has left us crazy with our hands to pay for the 400 years of tune.

You misunderstand, though, if you think I am recommending large doses of great civilization courses for university programs to put some old tried-and-trusted ground under our contemporary feet or that the task of a Christian higher education would be to page back through centuries of war and economics to find lessons in morality that could instruct atomic scientists today. Christian concern with history must go beyond morality, and I do not share the positivistic faith that fair-minded historical studies shall produce a common rational ground on which all nations, races, and creeds will be able to meet. Unless history, like art and literature, philosophy and theology, and all the special sciences are grappled with academically *ex Scriptura*, advanced studies will not make twentieth-century folks more humane; one might sooner expect it to make us more sophisticatedly inane. Nothing less than a radical reformation of scientific studies will set a direction that God shall bless; a reformation of scientific study that conceives it, practices it, wrestles with it, teaches and studies it, envelops it live in the context of history biblically understood, revealed by the Song of Moses.

If I may make an odd comment for a moment, I think that reformation of the bio-physical sciences has often been blocked in American Reformed circles by the fact that our Ph.D.'s in mathematics, physics, chemistry, and biology have been such good elders and deacons. Some people are tempted to fault ministers for everything wrong, since they are, after all, leaders, but you may not blame theological drowsing over approved commentaries for the unreformed, detached state of higher education in chemistry. Highly competent chemists and physical scientists who are also strong believers, who know the covenanting Rock of Moses as the source of life and blessing—it is basically their baby. On off-hours, some of these scientists labor tirelessly in the church, consistory, societies, school boards, and building committees, with fruits that one would judge acquit them well of salvation; but higgledy-piggledy back on the job it is chemistry in the laboratory, developing anti-submarine detection devices, experimenting for months on the thymus glands of 8000 chickens—that may eventually "save" the life of your great-grandchild someday—but all the while taking up a major portion of the one's conscious lifetime daily seems to be utterly unrelated to the faith. If it bothers her, the scientist can always pull out the Reformed Linus blanket "all things can be done to the glory of God"—*Can be!* Not *is*, just because one's "heart" is right with God; there's many a slip twixt heart and the lip, and scientific hand too. I think it is right as a curator of Trinity Christian College recently said in discussing these problems: "Until we get Christian scientists we need scientists who are Christians." I think it is right too that the bio-physical-mathematical sciences present particular problems to Christian novitiates: but it is wrong to give one's blessing by word of "Reformed" mouth or inaction, to autonomous science so long as it leaves off-hours room for the vigorous application of the Reformed faith, a life of shared time. All scientific action and knowledge is human work—it is not the doings of angelic intelligence—and shares human conditioning and human obligation. If we have any sense of the inhuman prospects of our revolutionary age and compassion for our contemporaries and remembrance of the LORD God's jealousy, we will institute post-haste the opportunity for scientists like professors J. J. Duyvené de Wit (biology) and Harry Vander Laan (astronomy)—who do not need to be convinced of its necessity or urgency—to tackle professionally in faith reformation of scientific studies, in a Christianly philosophically seasoned way, as token of our obedience and hope before the Lord. Reformation of scientific studies—that will look like a dislocation of science to the secularly formed mind: do you realize the Association stands practically at the beginnings! historically of such work? It is so preposterous one could easily laugh.

If Christian education is working one into fear of the Lord that disciplines one's whole consciousness, motivation, and output, and if Christian education fires one's being formed and forming further with a living awareness of the Word's significance for all life, then the unique strength, natural focus, and necessary crux to Christian education is knowing and developing history. This is the point I have been trying to get at. (1) Because it is the Truth that sets us free from idols, when believers grow up under the Song of Moses they know that God's concern is to avenge the blood of God's people, punish the troublemakers of the faithful, and wash away the guilt of God's body on earth. Believers moved by Moses' Song know that their Lord Yahweh's faithfulness outlasts their ungratefulness—they know what rainbows mean!—and that the Covenanting Rock of Israel is not a local arrangement but, as Paul reveals it in Romans 9–11, the saving reality of today: the children of the LORD God's promises are the believers in New Testament communion, which all the gathered forces of evil cannot separate from the love of Jesus Christ. And when the

Song of the Lamb rings in confirming the Song of Moses humming in their heads, proclaiming that in the final analysis history is the mortal, triumphant struggle of the woman with child (God's people) against the Dragon, against those marked by the Beast, who falsely confess the Lord or spurn God, then, knowing this, believers are freed from fear, from being bluffed and distracted from their God-service by the no-gods of Success, the unknown gods of Fantastic Power, the new gods-come-lately to the neighborhood like Scientific Reason. The believer knows they are real . . . idols, and also that the whole run of Cyrus, Nebuchadnezzar, Caesar, Pilate, Constantine, Charlemagne, Napoleon, Stalin, and whoever fills the White House shoes, is a grand parade used inscrutably by God to complete God's people's glory. This world of God is the promised land of us who believe; it is *our* land that is occupied—this is what the biblical perspective on history brings to Christian education. We do not have the Old Testament injunction to go out and raze God's enemies, but we do have the New Testament imperative to heap coals of fire on their heads, to offer also scientific food and drink that will quench the enemies' hunger and thirst (Romans 12:20). Christian education is not cultural imperialism but a faithful exercise in loving God and our neighbor in the world being prepared for us.

Just that needs mention yet: truly Christian education equips God's people for developing history (2) because it furnishes them a normative guideline for historical, cultural action. The larger biblical directive fashioning Christian education most people know, and fight or ignore: the clear-cut demand to seek the kingdom of God first (Matthew 6:33), that is, let *everything* of this world go so as to be kept from evil and able to serve the LORD God entirely whole, receiving back from God as pure gift everything multiplied by a hundred—with persecution . . . (Mark 10:28–30; cf. John 17:15). Christian education that loses this prime thrust upon its students has committed suicide. But here specifically I mean the insight discovered by Dooyeweerd (I mention that purposely even though it makes some people see red, because this Scripturally led idea of great significance is found nowhere else; it is original with Dooyeweerd I think): that within the cosmic redemptive plan of God to reconcile the world to God self through Jesus Christ, with the body and kingdom of Jesus Christ central and final to the process (*In the Twilight of Western Thought*, 112), the norm for this historical unfolding of creation, both in its workings unattended by human beings and in their responsible cultural molding, the historical norm is the differentiating of creatures and social groupings to more individually integrated forms in accordance with their created sphere sovereignty structuration. (When my wife hears me writing and shouting at the study walls "differentiating . . . to more individually integrated forms in accordance with their created sphere sovereignty structuration," she brings in the coffee with a smile and asks, "How's the jargon going this morning?" But you cannot red pencil this out!) "Sphere sovereignty" is not an abstract principle thought up by Kuyper and canonized by Vollenhoven and Dooyeweerd: it is a life-giving ordinance of God that they have brought to theoretical confession and made terribly, dynamically relevant. Believers who josh it aside are simply spiritually blind at that spot, and will lead blindly. If you have no historical norm to follow, you act in a hand-to-mouth fashion until it is your foot in your mouth, and then try something else to extricate the foot to keep going. Or, with a false strait-jacketed idea of Providence, one exclaims, "The Lord is in control! What happens is His Will!" and then adjust stoically to whatever happens, which is really letting the rest of the world go by, thinking that so long as we increase our contribution to missions, when it all comes out in the Judgment Day washing our faith shall save us, our family, and our close friends, forgetting that we are to be worshipping the jealous God of earth as well as of heaven. Or, with still more shallow aimlessness, professing Christians get on the cultural train today—the Twentieth Century Unlimited headed down the road to revolutionary Death—and take pious comfort in being at least the conservative caboose. Doing so is a drag on the church, which should indeed be conserving but not petrifying—rather reforming to the Word in the opposite direction of Life!

Christian education intent on leading men and women into scientifically unfolding creation's wonders, reforming the traditions of unbelieving centuries, and applying knowledge to society's complexities in a way that is worthy of those who work along with God in God's kingdom (1 Corinthians 3:9) have an invaluable help in knowing that the norm for historical development is differentiation to sphere-sovereign integrated individuality. I cannot exegete now what that means for interdisciplinary studies in Christian higher education, and must trust you realize that it is a guideline calling for much difficult explication and concrete implementation, not a rulebook type of thing. But its wisdom is as Bible-simple a wisdom as saying a grown up man and woman shall leave their father and mother and cleave together as one flesh, and if the newlyweds, at our stage of socially opened up complication, remain under the authority of a patriarchal father or matriarchal mother, there will be an unhealthy violation of the historical norm of differentiating toward one's created individuality-structuration. Not "common sense" but *Bible*-simple wisdom discloses this norm for historical development; and one is deceived who overrides it for apparent momentary advantage. Action that opposes this norm, shows Dooyeweerd, results in historical retrogression or totalitarian infringement of life. Both Barry Goldwaterism in my country and Nebuchadnezzar's Great Society plan[3] are guilty: the one would repress onward differentiation, and the other squelches sphere-sovereign individualization with political placebos.

Why do Reformed Christians do little more than meet in barns and church basements? Dr. Evan Runner asked two years ago. How come a couple of beetles rout the army of God from the attention of millions across the face of the world? The LORD God is the Rock, not so? rather than a rotting grapevine on the sunbaked terraces of Gomorrah. If we were wise we would understand these things and know what is coming. Has the Lord turned God's face away because we have forgotten who bore us, forgotten what "faithfulness" means because there has been no prophetic vision gripping the people and we have run wild (Proverbs 29:18), wildly after the American way of life, whoring respectably after the strange no-gods (Psalms 73:27) of affluence, Faustian knowledge, and power? Because the free sons and daughters of God can hardly stand up today at the job and are almost indistinguishable from slaves at the laboratory, and because the cold war at the universities in *our* occupied land is going to get hotter and the politics more frenetic, maybe tonight is a good time to listen intently to the Song of Moses and to pray that the Rock shower mercy down upon our servant heads so that the enemies cannot jibe.

That brings me to the other point I need to make, because you may be wondering, "That's all very nice about history and Christian education, but what does that have to do with me and the A.R.S.S. plans for a Christian university of America, and you said 'joke,' right?" Right.

Responsibility of the older generation:
university Christian education
God's Word is always aimed at people, and the Song of Moses is particularly aimed at the parents and grandparents here, the elder leaders of the tribes, the Christian men and women between forty and seventy who

---

3 About the only difference between "The Great Society" speech delivered at the University of Michigan on 22 May 1964 (http://www.h-net.org/~hst306/documents/great.html) and the text of Daniel 4:30 is Mr. Johnson's future tense. "We have the power to shape the civilization that we want."

may no longer have children in school and who themselves are too old for university training, especially to you comes the Word: Instill in your children and children's children in such a way that they receive it to do it all at the Command of God, for this is your Life! That is, says the Song of Moses, it is the responsibility of the older generation to get into action in the next generation the sense and performance of history, live recognition, and significant response to the generations-old doing, promises, and directives of the LORD God to God's people.

Transfer of simple information from person to person is very difficult. How much more difficult is handing over in working order a body of Truth, an articulated perspective, a Way of leadership, especially when the delivery taking place is complicated by its happening between generations—so much larger a matter than person to person. And it is right here at this critical juncture, the changeover between older and younger generation, that every college, seminary, and movement falters, and either grows stronger or imperceptibly weakens. Older ones who have set the pace and direction for years are reluctant to trust, to deliver the guiding hand to the younger; and the younger ones have new, inexperienced ideas of their own to add that they are impatient to try out. Given the idiosyncratic human pride of each man to create in his own image, historical continuity is a sometime thing.

Through the ages, one major attempt to solve the problem has been to commit as much as possible the thinking and the spirit of the parents to writing for their legacy to discover afresh. But then you get a new problem if what is to be transmitted is the living sense and performance of culture under God's covenanting Grace. The written *human* transmissions, traditions preserved, easily gather undue weight, precipitate as an authority rather than act as a conveyor (cf. 1 Corinthians 15:3 ff. and 1 Corinthians 11:23 ff., vs. Colossians 2:8). Then one becomes bogged down in a scholasticism the Roman church knows, to which Barth says rightly: Thank God we do not have Calvin the way some people have Thomas. But only so far is Barth right. Thank God we do have writings from servants of God that share us their grasp and presence in history so that we may accumulate and be enriched while reforming.[4]

The key to avoiding scholasticism yet effecting continuous developing transmission from one generation to the next of the Christian habit,

---

4   An unbelieving student from the Chicago community who did a long list of readings in a course of mine at Trinity said at the end: "I see now—Calvin was reforming Augustine; Kuyper reformed some of Calvin; Dooyeweerd reforms Kuyper, and now you are out to reform Dooyeweerd." Yes.

deo volente, is that the transfer, commitment, take place in a living communion where the old and young speak to one another, where the Song of Moses—God's faithful dealings—is sung, recounted, heard *together*, where the testimonial torch is handed over charismatically, where there is time to train, answer and question, pray, struggle, live together, so that new things as well as old can be drawn from the thesaurus of God's wonders recorded and remembered (Matthew 13:52). Cold documents put in someone's hand are not the best way to build a lasting community. The best teaching takes place in oral intimacy, just as preaching gets to peoples' hearts like no written tract can. It is no small detail that Joshua, son of Nun, stood next to Moses as he recited his final Song to the people of God. And it is a happy fact that, despite the professorial trappings, relatively young fellows speak, lecture, and officiate at A.R.S.S. meetings, because the Song of Moses points one to the long haul, past the individual, past this generation to those still not born. It is not that we must guarantee what only God can give—keeping God's people in the Way—but Moses was called on to acquit himself of his trans-generational office with God-fearing discretion, and we too.

This leads—if you catch the drift of the argument—to the necessity of a Christian university. If we take God at God's Word that it is the life of God's people, that it is the responsibility of the older generation to fill the younger generation with the riches of Yahweh's Wisdom and drive them lovingly to live it out daily with fear and trembling, then in our day and scientifically ripe age that means a Christian university. Tribal councils and craft guilds are no longer held by fathers, nor would they be adequate to the tasks of the twentieth century. Though the institutional church has its precious corner on instruction and ministry to the saints, education is not properly its task—we are not Romish or parochial: education belongs in the family structure, to the parents and grandparents who in the community, by delegated proxy, must oversee indeed hammering down the tent stakes more firmly as the ropes to the tent get lengthened, as God's people expand left and right and their children's children prepare to inherit the spoil of the nations—as the prophet Isaiah puts it (Isaiah 54:2–3). Fastening the tent of God's people more securely does not imply, I take it, hammering theological doctrines more firmly into the ground, but rather getting more of the stakes, non-theological ones too, rooted in the Power of the Word of God.

Again, that means a *Christian* university, as Dr. Henk van Riessen analyzed it: not just a batch of scholarly specialists under one roof, but a believing community of one mind to have the leisure and trust of a younger generation to formulate objectives and weave a Christian context into the highly specialized studies one needs to meet and lead historical developments today. A *Christian* university is the mulching ground for all spheres of Christian action. A Christian press, Christian labor, Christian art, or Christian political action will not long flourish or even get moving unless a Septuagint community of Advanced Reformed Scientific Studies gives leadership to the generations coming. And that is the responsibility of the older generation sitting here!

There are always piddlers who argue:

> We have no children, or no children in school;
> therefore, we have no educational responsibility.
> We do not have the joys of psalm 127 and 128;
> therefore, we should not have the grievances—

and they give only enough to education as it were, to keep from being mugged by youths on the street nights (assuming education makes one moral, which it doesn't).

But if you belong to the people of God, you have a hundred children even though you be as barren as Sarah before she laughed, because there is neither mother nor father, brother nor sister, child-laden or childless in Jesus Christ (cf. Galatians 3:28). Christian education is not the matter of teaching one child or more or not, but a matter of the older generation's setting the consciousness of the next generation in the Lord. It is precisely those who do not have any (more) children to give God that have money to give; and let each give the kind of gift one's got, says the Scriptures, as steward of the multi-sorted Grace of God (1 Peter 4:10). If God's people, ὁ λαὸς, laity, God's beloved, adopted children shall inherit with Christ the world—the race goes not to the intelligent but to the obedient—they should rejoice that they may suffer along with the Lamb now (Romans 8:17, 1 Peter 4:13) in dollars and cents—which seem sometimes to stick closer to a body than a child.

There is just one other thing I should like to show in its Song of Moses context, and let it hang there: Christian teaching at secular universities.

It is so that fervent Christians can be proficient teachers and do salting work at secular universities. It is probably often more exciting too than leading a band of stiff-necked Dutchmen through a wilderness of dry rock, levitical factions, and petty murmurings, where you are liable to get a Moses-complex or sit discouragedly under a juniper tree and think, "I, only I am left, with the knee unbowed to Baal." The waters of Damascus *are* more sparkling than the hometown Jordan, though no one may ever say Christian education is a comfortable, safe place. (That is so only for those with a dead faith.) It can be an agonizing, corrosive, courageous war against the devil and his hosts— Also, more satisfying for Christians who are teaching at a secular university is that they can see what they are doing: point to a life changed here, a moment of respect for the Christian faith gained there. In a communal body of Christian education you are not alone and cannot take credit so easily for specific things. And since you are in a movement to form generations to come, which you cannot *see*, unable to over-see what you are doing, you can only follow a direction of faith.

It seems to me that Christians teaching in faith at secular universities need never feel that they must defend following where God leads them. The melodic note I should like to leave hang, though, is the concern of not how a Christian teacher fares there but how shall the oncoming younger generation of God's people be formed in physics, biology, literature, and philosophy? Like their secular peers? And not with the blessing of knowing history at a scientifically developed level, not outfitted at a scientifically advanced level with the insight to practice historical action pleasing to God? That kind of consciousness-forming knowing and practicing (most often) comes out of a faithful, competent, united, older Septuagint community of reforming scientists cross-pollinating with the younger ones under God's smile.

And when there are talented scientists, deeply biblically Reformational, ready to band together sacrificially in university, can anyone sit there and say I have no money to form a place for them to set the scientific consciousness of our children and grandchildren in the Way of the Lord God?

Everything said up to now has really been said before. But I want to close by adding something more—maybe because I do not know the problems from the inside yet, and after I have sat through a couple of board meetings of the Association for Reformed Scientific Studies maybe I would not say it—but tonight I want to say it:

The Christian university of America is needed now; the A.R.S.S. is moving too slow. Seven years of Grace have seen wonders, but what now? Unless the forthcoming Institute is shown to be an act of faith rather than a cautious step toward a possible Reformed university in the future, the Institute will not stir the hearts of the nation. It is a bold act of faith that edifies, rallies, and receives the surprise of God's bountiful blessing.

In passing I should drop a footnote on all the critics, who, Shakespeare would say, "Methinks doth protest too much," for they are constructive. I do not mean those who are praying and paying members of the A.R.S.S.—the praying is even more important (because then you cannot help but pay double so much)—I do not mean members of the A.R.S.S. who are sometimes impatient or troubled and seek privately to question and improve. I mean the critics who need an audience, seem to have vested interests, and make a public noise.

Prof. Vollenhoven was being attacked at home and from the States for a long time. Finally I said to him, "Professor, why don't you answer them?" His reply, I think, was sage advice; "Het neemt doodgewoon te veel tijd; dan kom je nooit aan je eigen werk toe."[5]

The A.R.S.S. should listen hard to its critics, learn much, and move ahead in its own way doing the work of the Lord. God is at hand and shall answer those who try to dissuade.

The Christian University of America is needed now!
That's a joke spoken in a Canadian barn!

But the seven Unionville Conferences to date have been one joke after another.

The first *Christian Perspectives* (1960) volume was printed almost single-handedly by Mr. Glenn Andreas without the speakers being aware of what was actually being done because, if they had known, they would have stopped it. And it was done, and were they upset! But do you see to what it has led?

Prof. S. Zuidema came and spoke penetrating lectures on Existentialistic Communication, with just his head above English water, as he put it. A high school student who attended that year went home and his father asked him, "How was the conference?" And the boy said, "Verbarstend moeilijk, maar we hebben de voorzitter, helemaal gekleed, in het water gegooid."[6] Today he is studying classics and philosophy at the Free University of Amsterdam.

Then there was the meeting where Dr. Runner spoke using a manuscript for 25 minutes, followed by 35 minutes with just notes, concluding with nothing in front of him for 55 minutes, except the power of the Spirit moving us to "A New Consorting."

And there was the tense time with some kind of hassle about "membership," and two contrasting opinions seemed to be formed and conflicting, until Canadian Reformed pastor Rev. François Kouwenhoven

---

5 "It would simply take too much time; you'd never get on with your own work."
6 "Unbelievably difficult, but we threw the chairperson, clothes and all, into the lake."

rose to speak and said disarmingly, "I have been minister for twenty years; I can please everybody." And big Rev. Arent De Graaf from New Zealand led us in a rousing Dutch psalm.

And there is always the joke of the remythologized Egyptian plague downstairs, before you eat, shoo away the flies—

Do you see what I mean? That *élan* of faith we have at Trinity too, in our own small way going on seven years:

> our faculty cows give cream!
> our scrawny staff are Bashan bred, thick chested rams!

> Unionville students eat full fat kernels of corn
> They get honey and oils out of bed rock!

> And when a few smashed, ordinary grapes are tasted, remember,
> says Moses, you drank it like a heady, intoxicating wine!

Is it honey or sweat out of the rock? Wine or plain water? Are the whole impossible, jargon-blasted years of experiment a joke?

Certainly! It is the joke of faith! It is the joke of A.R.S.S. education. The sardonic sees only milk, hard chairs, and nut-cracking lectures. The eye and ear, mind and heart of faith knows otherwise, that the Word of Life has found weak scientific flesh here and that it is a joke worth laughing about!

The A.R.S.S. should laugh more, and I have proposed the new joke. Like Moses, at your next *borreltje*: Toast the Rock! To the Christian University of America now!

Now, before you become fat like the believing people on my side of the border, before the sense of Reformed heritage becomes a hall, an archive, before the languages for scholarship, the Dutch, the pioneering immigrating days are lost to you. *Now*, without coveting anything except the Kingdom of God in scientific study, stubborn in prayer, calling for prayer and monies openly from Europe and Australia and Africa and the United States, to begin the jokingly small Christian University of America without delay.

Set deep in your hearts all the words that I have festively proclaimed this day to you:

Instill them in your children in such a way that they receive them to do them: all the words of God's command,

For the Word (here spoken) is not just sound (in the air) around you: it is your life!

By this Word (of God) you all can stay alive till you shall possess the land promised you on the other side of river Jordan.

Background material

Congar, Yves. *The Meaning of Tradition*, translated by A.N. Woodrow (New York: Hawthorn Books, 1964), 155.

Dooyeweerd, Herman. "The Sense of History and the Historical World and Life View II," in *In the Twilight of Western Thought* (Philadelphia: Presbyterian and Reformed, 1959), 83–112.

———. "'Er is geschied' en het historisch aspect der werkelijkheid," in *Vernieuwing en Bezinning om het Reformatorisch Grondmotief* (Zutphen: Van den Brink, 1959), 58–63.

Scholarship in Biblical Perspective (Hamilton, Ontario: Association for Reformed Scientific Studies, 1965), 11 pp.

Seerveld, Calvin. "The Christian School in American Democracy" (1964), in *In the Fields of the Lord*, ed. Craig Bartholmew (Carlisle/Toronto: Piquant/Tuppence, 2000), 178–191.

Smit, M. C. *Cultuur en Heil* (Amsterdam: A.G.O.R.A. aan de Vrije Universiteit, 1959), 32.

Van Andel, Henry. *Vision and Obedience* (Hamilton, Ontario: Association for Reformed Scientific Studies, 1964), 11.

Van Riessen, Hendrik. "De christen academicus en de wetenschap," in *Mens en Werk* (Amsterdam: Buyten & Schipperheyn, 1962), 103–129.

———. *Knooppunten der Moderne Cultuur* (Delft: Waltman, 1964).

Vander Leeuw, Gerardus. *Menswording en Cultuurverschuiving: Een anthropologisch probleem* (Antwerpen: Standaard-boekhandel, 1948), 20.

Formal photo in the Institute for Christian Studies library, to go with recruitment
promotional statement, 1986 (photo by Carol-Ann Veenkamp)

"I would do graduate study in aesthetics at ICS because there I could read the books I have always
wanted to read that tie philosophy and the arts together. I would learn to read with Christian antennae, working with mentors who wanted to give me their best, reforming ideas so we could . . . discover and contribute in the area of art history or literary hermeneutics or a philosophy of playfulness
as part of a long range effort to serve God's people and my neighbour with insight."

THE DAMAGES OF A CHRISTIAN WORLDVIEW

Now large crowds of people were fellow-traveling with Jesus.
Turning to them, Jesus said:

"If anyone comes to follow me but is more attached to father and mother, spouse and children, brothers and sisters, yes, is more committed to one's own life than to me, that person cannot be one of my disciples. Whoever does not carry his or her own cross in coming to follow my [Way] cannot be my disciple.

"For who of you willing to build a tower does not first sit down to count up the cost, to check out whether you have (enough) to bring it to completion? Otherwise, when you have laid a foundation and are not able to bring the building to completion, all those watching will begin to ridicule you saying, 'This fellow began to build but was not able to bring it off!'

"Or, what ruler going to encounter another ruler in war will not first sit down and deliberate whether one is able with 10,000 to meet up with the other coming toward him with 20,000? And if not, while the other is still a good distance off, asks, by sending off a delegation, what will it take for peace?

"Somewhat like that then: all of you who do not say goodbye to all that you yourself own, cannot be my disciple.

"Sure, salt is good. But if the salt becomes saltless, in what way will you be able to make it salty (again)? It is not fit for the earth nor for the manure pile—they throw it out.

"Whoever has ears to hear, let that man or woman hear."

(Luke 14:25-35)

This essay was originally presented at the "After Worldview" conference at Cornerstone University in Grand Rapids, Michigan, in September 2004 and dedicated in loving memory of Pete Steen (1936–1984); it was subsequently published in *After Worldview*, eds. J Matthew Bonzo and Michael Stevens (Sioux Center: Dordt College Press, 2009), 55–80.

In preparing to come to this conference, as I reviewed some of the literature on "worldview" and "Christian worldview" published in the last twenty years—the essays in *Stained Glass* (edited by Paul Marshall, Sander Griffioen, and Richard Mouw, 1989), the solid book by David Naugle (Eerdmans, 2002) and publications he refers to in his Appendix A, plus various other readings—I thought, what an embarrassment of riches! You could get the impression that among evangelical Christians it is almost fashionable to have or consider having "a Christian worldview" as a tower of defensive strength to do battle with the "postmodern" enemy armies at the gates.

I wondered if, in the spirit of the theme of this conference as I understand it, "After Worldview," I could complicate matters a bit, join in the conversation, and suggest why the Christ's encouragement and warning to his fellow-travelers in Luke 14 might be an appropriate Word of the Lord to remember at this juncture. Have we who have been building a Christian worldview counted the costs of bringing a Christian world-and-life vision to completion as we introduce its contours to a public and rising college generation? The cost of genuine discipleship in following the Rule of Jesus Christ is quite stiff if it is not wholehearted, does not stay salty, or defaults on follow-through. What are the damages of a Christian worldview?

Defining "worldview" as a "world-and-life vision" distinct from a "way of life"

Let me begin *in media res* with the working definition I should like to be responsible for: a worldview is a conscious, quasi-synoptic world-and-life vision of everything all together, which is imaginative and literarily suggestive in quality rather than theoretically precise, which structures and can guide one's concrete experience in God's ordered cosmos.[1]

This terminology helps me clarify, I think, various matters found in the literature and lets me note: *not everybody has a world-and-life vision.* Every sane human being, whether aware of it or not, does have, in my judgment, a "way of life," a subconscious habit of activity that is not a studied reflective view but is a pattern that hangs together and gets beaten out in the press of daily life. A person is inducted into a way of life at birth along with one's mother tongue. Sometimes called "ethic," this *habitus* one unthinkingly inhabits is an historically worked-in formation corporately held, a tradition of wonts shaped by underlying faith com-

---

1 Paraphrasing a section of C. Seerveld, *Skeleton to Philosophy* (Chicago: Trinity Christian College mimeographed typescript, 1960).

mitment, passed on by common consent, certified by specific rites and rituals, which notably shows its assumed cohesive grip on one's life in crises.

In the provincial rural New York community where I grew up, sons routinely followed in the occupation of their father, married early, raised a family, became prosperous, and grew older, and their sons followed the same cycle. In pre so-called World War II–Italy, a similar way of life would be followed, except the eldest son would be offered to the priesthood.

Once upon a time there was a Western Humanist way of life called civility, where without question when the Titanic was sinking, children and women went first into the lifeboats.

If your way of life happened to be a walk with the Lord informed by the preached Scripture like Micah 6:6–8, Matthew 5–7, and Romans 13:8–10, when the Dutch teacher H. de Jongste (who translated the bulk of Herman Dooyeweerd's *A New Critique of Theoretical Thought,* 1953–1958) answered the knock on his door one night during German troop occupation in the 1940s and faced two downed American airmen, what do you instinctively do, knowing that if the Nazi informer who lives above you finds out, it could mean the death of you and your family? Of course, you take them in and hide them.

For me, a person's way of life is inescapably basic, the primary outworking of one's entrusting faith orientation in God's world, whatever the faith be. A way of life is the contour of what one tacitly takes for granted as meaningful. Sander Griffioen calls my subconscious way of life a *Weltbild:* "the common outlook of a people, society, or culture; it is apprehended and appropriated in an unconscious manner; it is relatively constant in time" (Griffioen 1989, 2). No wonder the persecutor Saul went looking for those "who belonged to *the Way*" (ὁδός), it says in Acts 9:2. The early Christians were not killed for their "views," but for their converted way of life described in Acts 2–8. And it is precisely because the apostate way of life inculcated subliminally in many postliterate American adults by the ubiquitous powerful pop-culture media and targeted advertising gets jolted into reflective consciousness by the culture critique of a Christian world-and-life vision that makes a conscious Christian world-and-life vision a valuable aid in redemptive education.

When one's subconscious way of life reaches sustained consciousness, when a life pattern becomes roughly understood as a pattern of sorts, gets expressed, articulated with connections and ramifications, then you have the network, in my book, of a *Weltanschauung,* a world-

and-life vision.

An indigenous tribal people can carry on living under its myths, but it takes a mythographer or a storyteller like Homer to weave a world of rudimentary powers (cf. Galatians 4:3, Colossians 2:8!) into a roster of superhuman gods and heroic demigod-like men to form a mythology that hangs together but still is not always systematically clear.

The Puritan world-and-life vision crystallized in John Bunyan's (1628–1688) robust tale of Pilgrim Christian's progress on the narrow road toward the Celestial City, with so many worldly sideshow attractions off limits, marshals together the tempting pitfalls and little accomplishments and blessings of a sober, persevering human life of faith with sure otherworldly horizons.

Gustav Mahler's (1860–1911) *Die Kindertotenlieder* (1901–1904, sung by Janet Baker or Shelley de Young) presents Friedrich Rückert's (1788–1866) Biedermeierish verse of Stoic grief transformed into a massive, poignant German Romanticist mesh of sound that encompasses human life and death with poignant Nietzschean *Weltschmerz:*

> Ein Lämplein verlosch in meinen Zelt!
> Heil! Heil sei dem Freudenlicht der Welt!

It would be wise, it seems to me, not to shrink the "world-and-life vision" designation down to a technical term "worldview," since it is *the pulse of life lived* that invigorates the imaginative narrative of a world-and-life vision. Fortunately, Abraham Kuyper (1837–1920) salvaged in his first Princeton Stone lecture (1898) from his intended *levens- en wereldbeschouwing* (life-and-world view) terminology, the emphasis on *life,* because he was concerned to counteract the accusation that Calvinism is only a narrow-minded dogmatics: "I desire to speak to you on Calvinism as an independent general tendency, which from a mother-principle of its own, has developed an independent form both for our *life* and for our *thought* among the nations of Western Europe and North America" (Kuyper's emphasis, 15). But Kuyper was ill-advised to call this principled world-encompassing consciousness "to furnish human society with a different method of existence, and to populate the world of the human heart with different ideals and conceptions" (17) a "life *system*" (11 n.1), because *system* overstates the conceptual form of a Calvinian world-and-life *vision.*

To approach an interrelating world-and-life vision, whether it be Calvinian, Marxian, Muslim, or American Horatio Alger–Walt Disneyan vision of world and life, from the side of its bringing to self-consciousness a way of life in the world—weighting structural features like order and change, what is good and what is evil, setting up choices of priorities, deciding what is worth dying for—highlights better the sterling integrity and service of a world-and-life vision than coming at it from the German Idealist perspective of a *Weltanschauung*'s being a pretheoretical, somehow supraindividual contemplative "view" of the world. Maybe we do not have to worry about getting a baptismal certificate for "worldview" (Naugle, 289–90; Rowe, 156) if we conceive a "world-and-life vision" in terms of its being grounded in the biblical hint on *hodos,* that a world-and-life vision is born out of a cohering way of life sprung from one's faith.

A world-and-life vision is a comprehensive world map and a draught for action (Griffioen 2002, 287) to which one may be *committed.* J. P. A. Mekkes shunned the standard phrase and deliberately used the term *levensovertuiging,* life conviction, life persuasion (Klapwijk 1989, 43). I myself prefer to speak of a "*committed* world-and-life *vision,*" to catch its far-reaching scope and its claim on one's heart—a feature Dilthey half-sensed in talking about *Streit der Weltanschauungen.* Now, I should like to introduce carefully a different uncanny dimension of creatural reality that intersects, I believe, the committed world-and-life visions (as well as ways of life) operative in many of us people.

If a committed world-and-life vision is an imaginative typical orientation that can be taken toward the *structural* features of our life world (what is there? how? why?), there is also the matter of *directional* choice on where are we headed? what Spirit drives you on in your world-and-life vision?

While world-and-life visions get at cosmic structure, direction is a matter of being spirit-led

There are biblical givens on how humans who, at heart, have been enlivened by the Holy Spirit and have become new(!) creatures (2 Corinthians 5:17, Ephesians 3:16–19) still struggle with the manifold power of *Sarx,* sin, in their bodily members (Romans 7:5–8:11, Ephesians 4:17–5:21). Holy Scripture makes clear that the resurrected Christ has indeed overcome the evil principalities and powers of this world (Ephesians 1:19–23, Colossians 1:15–23, 2:8–15), but all of us creatures alive must still contend with their demonic brutality (Ephesians 6:12). Evil spirits, often masquerading as angels of light (2 Corinthians 11:12–15), crave to reside in bodies, especially important bodies, officials, institutions, corporations, and only if necessary in a herd of swine (Mark 5:1–20). That's why Scripture says we must test the spirit of what is afoot and prophesied in society to know whether it be of God or the Lie (1 John 4:1–6).

I have been at important gatherings, I dare say, when you'd swear you could detect the acrid trace of a smell from some lower echelon devil lurking nearby in the room ready to befoul and derail the deliberations.

And I remember vividly a Friday afternoon meeting of Seventh Day Adventist leaders in Collonges-sous-Salève, France, I was invited to join (1989) where there had been hefty debates, but during the concluding communal prayers held as the sun quietly began to set and the Sabbath of rest began, you could sense a sweet communion settling like an angel down upon the group with a holy peace. Maybe that is why Karl Barth muses about angels as personal Power Point presentations/messengers of God's omnipotent will (*Die Kirchliche Dogmatik* III/3 par. 51).

When my wife and I attended a Black Panther rally in Chicago in the late 1960s, just to see what was going on, there was an altogether different spirit present than there had been in an assembly to hear Martin Luther King speak on nonviolent protest a year before. (There was no entrance fee to the Panther Rally, but you had to pay *to get out* of the meeting, a contribution to the Huey Newton Defense Fund.)

Before you think I am off track, let me quote you Walter Wink: "It is a virtue to disbelieve what does not exist. It is dangerous to disbelieve what exists outside our current limited categories" (Wink 1984, 4). Principalities and powers do exist, according to Scripture, and deeply affect our lives in the world.

"School spirit" is a much more fundamental matter than accrediting agencies may think, and it is the school principal or college president who usually functions as the lightning rod for the spirit of an institutional faculty and student body. One could also say that exorcism of written texts, images, and prophetic appeals called philosophy is at the crux of Christian education: teachers need to detect, expose, and cast out the evil spirit weaseling in the materials we deal with in classroom and lab. But then do not do exorcisms the way Pharisees do it, said Jesus, for show, with acclaim, triumphantly (Luke 11:14–23, 18:9–14, Matthew 23:1–12, Mark 9:38–41; cf. Acts 19:11–20). Scripture adjures us to reclaim those flesh-and-blood humans and their deeds, which are possessed by evil principalities and powers, and to do it by painstaking, prayerful probing that leads to the truth by doing justice to the writings and forging peace because one's own imaginative competence and humbled analysis—God help us—is led by "the sword of the Holy Spirit, which is the Word of God" (Ephesians 6:10–20).

If we keep this matter of *spirited direction* in humans (following

God's holy will though plagued by disobedience *versus* godless enslave-ment to evil principalities though kept human by God's grace) distinct from our human overall vision of the structural constancies and changes in God's world, it puts a more complicated spin on the nature and rela-tive salience of our committed world-and-life visions, which are also al-ways Spirit-driven.

Let me draw out just three implications for discussion purposes.

1. **World-and-life visions are not incommensurable and can provide knowledge to the wise**

There are different world-and-life visions to which people are com-mitted because different basic positions can be taken on various realities of world and life that impinge willy-nilly on our consciousness; namely, is everything a *uni*verse? what is the makeup of the world and the relative place of human life? where does the buck stop? and are there criteria for meaning?

One popular world-and-life vision throughout the ages has been the vision that change is constant and reality is an evolutionary (or devolu-tionary) process in which the fittest survive. That world-and-life vision shaped ancient Chalcedonian Thrasymachus's stance on political justice (might makes right), Renaissance Pico della Mirandola's (1463–1494) take on the chameleon nature of man (we can become devils or angels), and guided Milton Friedman's (1912–2006) unlimited free market mon-ey policy for the nation. *Good for the best!*

A quite different world-and-life vision imagines that sameness is heaven, absolute unchanging law and paradigmatic order is what counts as real; neglect what seems bad, troubles are illusionary. Such a station-ary world-and-life vision has permeated the contemplative quietism of Zen Buddhism from time immemorial: endure the *fata morgana samsura* and await to be transfixed by the state of *nirvana*. The so-called Interna-tional Style of architecture, a weakened derivative of Mies van der Rohe's genius (1886–1969), has carried a rationalized version of Mondrianic balanced stability and inhuman sameness throughout the whole world in its standardized rectangular high-rise domiciles and office buildings. *Remain unmoved!*

Another favorite world-and-life vision, considered to be as solid as the Rock of Ages, is the one that only counts the birds in the hand: your fitness health, your accumulated wealth, and a good conversation over a martini at the tenth hole is what it is all about. Hellenistic hedonists, even Borgia pope Alexander VI (1492–1503), and sybaritic yuppies today in both East and West all work out this simple world-and-life vision with gusto. *Carpe diem!*

Or a world-and-life vision of quite a different tack has people mesmerized by the occult, an invisible *mysterium tremendum,* what is alchemically hidden in the numinous Dark Night of Universal Unconscious Soul. This is the perennial world-and-life vision of Gnostics, Jewish Kabbalists, the Masonic lodge of Tolstoi's day (1828–1910), TM, and those who live by astrology and horoscopes. *Become initiate to the Secrets!*

But you know all of this. There are an indefinite number of world-and-life visions extant today, recurrent in history, available to format your consciousness because there are many ways to construe (misconstrue) the structural pressure points of the realties enveloping us. Each of these bona fide world-and-life visions are imaginatively consistent and hang together, depending on the tinted eyeglasses you accept to peruse life in God's world. "They are divergent, contrary, conflicting, but are not incommensurable" (Griffioen 1998, 125–26), because they are fabricated and held by nonstupid human persons dealing with the same reality, who grab hold of the elephant at a different place, and give priority to and valorize different structural features of world and life.

What I want to suggest is that opposing world-and-life visions are not mortal enemies for followers of Jesus Christ, but are just bad neighbors, *neighbors.* And a communion of Christians who consciously develop 20/20 biblical vision can *learn from* mistaken world-and-life visions even as we sinful saints examine such astigmatic visions and refocus what has been taken crookedly amiss, distorted, wrongly cleft, and reductionistically oversimplified.

Those who know that it is *not* "good for the best!" but have a vision of "blessed are the meek!" (Matthew 5:3–10) can still learn from Darwinian protagonists that "meek" does not mean "seek the martyrdom of being steamrollered." Christians who respond to God's injunction to become "mature" (τέλειοι, Matthew 5:48, Hebrews 5:14–6:3) rather than "stand pat unmoved," can still learn from the rock-ribbed who believe "the Western canon is the canon—that's it!" that "newer is not always truer" and "the latest is not necessarily the greatest." The biblical faithful who cringe at our *"carpe diem"* effrontery toward the millions of the world's poor can still learn in back-handed fashion from the self-indulgent that it is good to be content with one's straits (Philippians 4:11), but also to be joyful with "Amens!" for the gifts God puts in our laps (Psalm 136, the sevenfold refrain of Ecclesiastes). And Bible-believing Christians who are grateful that God's will is *not* hidden but is fully revealed in the person and Way of Jesus Christ (Deuteronomy 30:11–20, Colossians 3:1–4:6) can learn from a Jungian mythologizing perspective that there may be more about us humans than is dreamed of in many a rigid orthodox theology.

That is, by "antisympathetic vibration" (Seerveld 1995/1962, 20), to extend John Calvin's (1509–1564) metaphor of Scriptural eyeglasses (*Institutes of the Christian Religion* I, 5, 14), Christians with a biblically Christian, committed world-and-life vision are free to receive instruction from those who are confined to bad neighborhoods, because world-and-life visions are *relatively important*—they are not the pearl of great price (Matthew 13:45–46). And followers of the Lord Jesus with a steady vision of creatures *coram Deo* headed for the *eschaton* of Jesus Christ's return may also be able to *give* a corner of *vision* to those who may still be looking. It is not that a biblically Christian world-and-life vision claims to be more or the most "rational" world-and-life vision available, because *visions* are imaginative fabrics and not provable or disprovable by arguments (Griffioen 1989, 87). Christians may *give away* insights F.O.B. Be winsome with your wisdom, says Scripture (Colossians 4:5–6), and make those with poor eyesight and handicapped hearing jealous to envision the shalom you present amid a cloud of witnesses to God's providential mercy.

2. Different Christian world-and-life visions are still bound to submit to one Holy Spirit

The second implication that I want to draw from the fundamental distinction of *structural vision* and *directional mission*, which are always conjunctive, is a matter becoming more and more accepted in recent decades: *there are quite different committed Christian world-and-life visions around*; rather than "worldview" religious wars, maybe we need respectful cooperation in an apostate world culture where the Christian faith and way of life is no longer hegemonic but is fast becoming a minority position.

Whether one takes Richard Niebuhr's *Christ and Culture* (1951) taxonomy or David Naugle's more relaxed, rather churchly delineation of Protestant Evangelicalism, Roman Catholicism, and Eastern Orthodoxy (4–54), to which I should wish to add at least a couple more—the steadfast recurrent chiliastic wing of Christianity close to Anabaptist and Mennonite sensitivities and the definite community of "liberal" Christians focused on humanitarian needs, often named "the Social Gospel" movement and more recently "Liberation theology"—it is a fact that there are deeply cleft, long-standing Christian world-and-life visions that do not comport well and do aggravate one another.

Jesus' Solomonic judgment about why his followers were not ascetic in lifestyle as were Baptizer John's disciples is appropriate here: "Wisdom is justified by the deeds of *all* her children" (Luke 7:35; cf. Matthew 11:16–19). *Both* the wine-drinking Reformers *and* the Anabaptist "stepchildren" put the do-nothing caterwauling spectators to shame! So, rather than fight for dominance or submit the different Christian visions to arbitration to work out compromises, I suggest that we look to the alternate Christian world-and-life visions for wisdom to complement our own visionary lacunae or blind spots and take to heart that *all* of God's children fall under the stern injunction to be of one Holy Spirit (Romans 12:1–11, Ephesians 4:1–11).

I find it hard to take my own advice. It was great fun to bond with a Jesuit graduate student on the other side of the classroom at the University of Michigan in 1952 when he and I would challenge our brilliant Humanist professor Throop's exposition in a class on medieval societal history: that was a more enduring connection, I think, than when Communists and Calvinists worked together in the underground of Gestapo-occupied Netherlands.

My colleague George Vandervelde, who with a few dignitaries joined Pope John Paul II for after-supper prayers in his private Vatican chapel a few years ago, assured me the man is truly, phenomenally pious; but when I read the papal Easter Sunday 1999 letter to artists of the world with all its blatant Humanist blather about "artists . . . lead[ing] to that infinite Ocean of beauty where wonder becomes awe, exhilaration, unspeakable joy" (section 16)—good thing it is not written ex cathedra!—my supportive resolve weakens.

I remember that at the Jerusalem Synod, reported in Acts 15, it seemed good to the Holy Spirit and the brethren (v. 28) to remove circumcision from the essentials of the Christian faith; later, the apostle Paul was led by the Spirit to modify still further James's restriction on Christian non-Jews' eating food offered to false gods (1 Corinthians 8 and Acts 15:13–21). So, meanwhile, as different Christian world-and-life visions jostle with one another, I need to check first of all whether *my* spirit is holy and whether the witness of the Reformational Christian world-and-life vision to the truth is beyond reproach.

It might be wise to restore the shorthand formula often used to characterize this particular Christian world-and-life vision, in which I gratefully find myself at home, the full description Dooyeweerd gave *In the Twilight of Western Thought*: "the radical and central biblical theme of creation, fall into sin and redemption by Jesus Christ as the incarnate Word of God, *in the communion of the Holy Spirit*" (my emphasis, 42). A person could have an excellent Christian world-and-life vision, but if it be espoused with an ambitious, aggressive spirit, it is mere tintinabulating talk-show chatter or a clanging gong.

I do not expect a merger of committed Christian world-and-life visions, but I do believe the Lord asks us with our different Christian world-and-life visions to become one in the Spirit, with a unified witness to unbelievers and disbelievers testing out non-self-seeking *holy*.

3. Cultural dynamics of evil principalities need special attention

The third implication that I want to spell out for your response in thinking through the conjoined difference of *structured world-and-life vision* and *spirited direction/willed mission* is to be more definite and careful in delineating the ambit of world-and-life visions and in fathoming the locus and depth dimension of cultural turmoil.

The Holy Spirit is not a world-and-life vision but is God in person who mysteriously directs an obedient people toward shalom through tears. Principalities and powers are not a world-and-life vision but are uncanny perverse authorities "of the air," says Scripture enigmatically, evil "spirit(s) energizing persons right now into rebellion" (Ephesians 2:1–12). Unless we confuse the two, it makes sense to say: contrary world-and-life visions cause problems to their adherents because you need to translate what the other perceives, appraises, and hopes for into the shape of your own visionary perception, valuation, and expectation if you would understand what in God's world is being maintained by the other; but the opposition of spirits driving us human creatures and our deeds—which includes our world-and-life visionary constellations—entails outright war to life or death, no quarter sought or given. President George Bush, Billy Graham, the World Bank, the World Council of Churches, the city where I live, ordinary you and me ourselves are jackasses (*ceu iumentum*)—to use Martin Luther's (1483–1546) rough, colorful metaphor in debate with the erudite scholar Erasmus (c. 1466–1536)—on how human willingness relates to God the Spirit and the Satan who contend to ride us willing creatures ("*De servo arbitrio*," *Werke*, Weimar Ausgabe 635: 23–28~): we persons, communities, society with a mix of world-and-life visions are sites for mortal conflict between spirits that will drive us to fruitful cultivation of God's world or to desolation. *The root struggle and warfare in history is not between world-and-life visions but is one of spirited direction.* No wonder Scripture pleads with us double-minded (δίψυχος) followers of Jesus Christ at a loss as to which Way to go, to ask God for Holy Spirited wisdom on the direction to take (James 1:2–8, 3:13–18).

So-called "postmodernism," as I understand what this inadequate term refers to, is not a world-and-life vision but is a spirit. Spirits(!) δυνάμεις, to use biblical terminology. And principalities, powers, thrones and dominions captivate people craftily, sift like Chicago fog on cat feet into the crevices of one's *mentalité*. It is seldom a frontal attack.

Duchamp's harmless urinal "Fountain" in the New York Armory Show of 1913, Dada hijinks in Switzerland during so-called World War I, later Beat Generation poetry and the aging Picasso's parodies of masterpieces in the Fifties, 1960s "happenings," punk rock from England in the 1970s, MTV, John Cage frequenting Toronto, Jeff Koons at the Tate, are all weathervanes of a surging "cultural atmospherics" that dissolves the rusty chains of Rationalistic constraints and denies historical continuities, a kind of soft, destructive, no-hands-at-the-wheel nihilism. Parody kills with a kiss.

And there is another sophisticated spirit I think that one can detect that has gained cultural strength, especially in the academy, since Arnold Schoenberg's (1874–1951) twelve-tone music, Malevitch (1878–1935) paintings, and later Rothko's (1903–1970) icons, which makes practically a fetish of theory as interminable language games, where the trick is to remain seriously suspended in thought, achieving a deferring, noncommittal reflection on reflecting, driven as it were to be fixed in Lacan's (1901–1981) mirror phase of misrecognition. Virtuality beckons one on, flickers as if it be reality.

The principality I am naming "soft nihilism" and the principality I try unhandily to finger as a spirit of "Zetetic Agnosticism" are formidable powers loose in our generations—the ones that critics often lump together, I think, as "postmodernism." But these principalities are not the only game in town, although it may be the only one many academics are playing. A most pervasive power out to control and ruin human lives today, including mine, is the durable Beast of Pragmatism.

In 1967, as a traveling Fulbright Scholar in Germany, my wife and I went to a meeting at the U.S. embassy in Berlin, and I was able to ask a midlevel embassy official, "Why did you let them build the Wall?" His reply was: "We sent all the info to Washington; they put the data in their computer banks, and the answer came back: if you stop the wall here, they will build it further back; if you try to stop the wall there, they will build it still further back; so, unless you are willing to risk total war with Russia, let them build the wall around Berlin."

That same blinding spirit of trusting scientific, planned, experimental techniques to provide the right results, to base policy, norms, and action on, *for now,* rules today, it seems to me, the shifting fortunes in the West of what Eisenhower long ago called "the Military Industrial Complex," and it is not postmodern. Wal-Mart has a metanarrative of utility and is driven by the Pragmatist spirit of "Grow for maximum profits." And the wholesale armament industry, whose chief supplier worldwide is the United States, is not postmodern but cruelly Pragmatistic: "If your current military power does not bring your country security, you can afford more, bigger, and better weaponry—*it works!*"

The thrust of this third strand of my drawing out implications is that we do well not to overvalue our discovery of important world-and-life visions and not to abstract their formatting human consciousness from being embedded in persons, groups, and institutions that are dated and located battlegrounds of principalities, powers, and the Holy Spirit. It can be shown historiographically—though I cannot do that here now (see Seerveld 1980, 1989)—that the European Renaissance (c. 1420–1520) and the historical Reformation (c. 1520–1650), that later the Enlightenment (c. 1715–1770) and later Positivism (c. 1820–1920) are not just names for historians' shoptalk, but are actually "invisible authorities," the power play events in which people with committed world-and-life visions live out their seventy or eighty years, principalities that are pertinent for retelling history and for assuming cultural leadership in a given generation.

One should not inflate ruling cultural principalities à la Hegel into a single monolithic *Zeitgeist* phase of Absolute Spirit: different cultural δυνάμεις vie for human allegiance in the same chronological time frame. And there is no rationale, so far as I can discover, on why Pragmatism, for example, supplants, let's say, Positivism as a dominant cultural dynamics, unless there be a "logic" of idolatry—idols wear out—or maybe even evil spirits get tired and give way to another one of the Satan's legion . . . .

Would it make any difference in how you conceive world-and-life *visions* or alter where we should aim our marbles and gird for battle to *set* the younger generation's *consciousness* (cf. νουθεσία, Ephesians 6:4), if we kept distinct in this conjunct reality the force of *spirited direction*?

Literary biblical underpinnings
to the imaginative world-and-life vision of a community
Before I mention a few temptations and blessings of a committed Christian world-and-life vision, to add up the damages in my title, I need to

treat, however briefly, the biblical underpinnings of a Christian world-and-life vision. A Christian world-and-life vision, like a biblically Christian way of life, does not just drop out of heaven ready-made. Those who pick up a packaged Christian world-and-life vision on someone's say-so, learn the words, and are relieved to have more than a ragtag bag of bits and pieces—*bricolage*—to situate themselves, maybe even to complement a good homespun way of life, will only be fellow travelers with Christ's body until the hot sun comes out or the weeds overrun your packaged vision (cf. Matthew 13:1–23) if you do not spend time keeping your world-and-life vision pulsing fresh by hearing God speak in Scripture. Then your "vision" can become an "ideology," as Jim Olthuis reminds us (34), and you use it as a safety filter rather than as an ongoing explorative ultrasound detector of surprising realities.

Creation Regained: Biblical Basics for a Reformational Worldview (1985) by Al Wolters presents clearly the Christian world-and-life vision I heartily recommend investigating because it highlights God's revelation in *creation* and ties appropriating such disclosure to an underlying intimate *Bible knowledge*.

Let me throw into the conversation two considerations:

(1) The texture of a world-and-life vision is *literary, imaginative*. David Naugle's characterization reads "a semiotic system of *narrative signs*" (253, 291)—telltale vestiges, perhaps, of the Rationalistic Orr, Clark, and Henry penchant—but Naugle does emphasize the story character of a world-and-life vision (297–303). Sander Griffioen says it best for me: "a world-and-life vision is less dependent upon concepts than a philosophy, goes to work more suggestively and thus gives more leeway to the personal power of imagination, is less dependent upon a heavily technical terminology."[2]

I think that is right. That's why William David Romanowski[3] and Richard Middleton and Brian Walsh[4] can forcefully show how cinema and pop music culture are carriers par excellence of reigning world-and-life visions. World-and-life visions must not be propagated as simplified lay philosophy. Literature and artistry best embody the richly nuanced, deft, incisive, subtly connected insights of a world-and-life vision, which, when redemptive, can give luster, resilience, and incentive to one's daily walk.

---

2 "Omdat een wereldbeschouwing (of levensbeschouwing) minder op begrippen is aangelegd dan een filosofie, suggestiever te werk gaat en dus meer aan de persoonlijke verbeeldingskracht overlaat, is ze minder afhankelijk van een breed gedeelde taal" (Griffioen 2003, 242).

3 *Pop Culture Wars* (1996), *Eyes Wide Open* (2001).

4 *The Transforming Vision* (1984); *Truth Is Stranger Than It Used to Be* (1995).

(2) The biblical writings also have a *literary* texture. A very fine book by David Smith and John Shortt, *The Bible and the Task of Teaching* (2002), makes very convincing that the Bible—which is where the Holy Spirit particularly hangs out today—has the flexible, metaphorical distinguishing storied mark that allows God's Spirit to insinuate its godly wisdom into the silt of our consciousness. The Bible brings categorical guidance intuitively rather than logically, scattering sparks of disciplined understanding, which piques further wonderment and keeps on percolating imaginative responses, as parables do. The Bible's historical accounts do not just provide "control beliefs" to double-check *post factum* what one supposes to be so, but gives us reliable imaginative apriori promissory horizons in which to be communally busy in God's world—and to teach students (59–60, 70–77, 87, 117–19).

Much more must be said, but a crucial plank in my argument for the inadmissibility of not constantly swimming in Scripture to keep one's Christian world-and-life vision alive rather than deadly formulaic—and I know there are many nominal Christian fish on dry land—is the fundamental conviction that God's written Word has the power to break through the historiocultural veils over our sinful eyes, whether inherited or recently adopted, and set us straight, open to God's call (cf. 2 Corinthians 3:12–18), *outfitting us with the vision of Jesus Christ's Rule a-coming, so that our communal walk and our communal consciousness can be (fallibly) scripturally directed* rather than a church-going variant of the "normal" lifestyle, visions, and apostate powers so much in evidence.

I know this thesis is moot.[5] In his evaluation of Patristic culture, K. J. Popma asks honestly: both the Patristics and we ourselves want to ground our critique of culture biblically, but do we not speak with the accent of our crooked age as much as we may think the Patristics did of theirs? Even Christ's Church has, at times, in public made concordats with evil regimes! Yet Popma heartens my conviction by appealing to what he calls a basic "naive Bible-sense" (101–2, 105–8), what I would call a predogmatic, pretheo*logical* reading of Scripture, an historically and literarily aware listening on-your-knees reading of the Bible, swimming in it (Seerveld 2003, xii–xiii, 83–86), which allows God's Word to shatter the prejudiced visions we have picked up—what happened to St. Augustine when he finally reread Romans 13:13–14 (*Confessions*

---

5   Cf. my discussion of Jacob Klapwijk's idea of "transformational philosophy" and the
     approach of *spoliatio Aegyptorum* in "Antiquity Transumed and the Reformational
     Tradition," in *In the Phrygian Mode: Neo-Calvinism, antiquity and the lamentations of
     reformational philosophy*, ed. Robert Sweetman (Lanham: University Press of America,
     2007), 232–237 {see *AH*: 80–84}.

VIII, 12, 29), what turned Luther's world upside-down when he discovered *poenitentian agere* in Matthew 4:17 meant "repentance" instead of "penance" (Thesis 2), what can happen to us once we realize *torah* is the Redeeming Creator Lord's merciful covenantal embrace(!) rather than a big godly stick with which to knock us back into line. Holy Scripture as God's Word, *credo,* can convict us to believe *in* Jesus Christ as *kurios* (not just believe *that* so-and-so is true), *call us/outfit us* with survival gear (Ephesians 6:10–20) to be participants in God's reclamation project of world reconciliation (2 Corinthians 5:17–20), and *give* some the gift to *discern the spirits* of the age (1 Corinthians 12:4–11, v. 10).

Blessings and unnecessary damages in holding a reformational christian world-and-life vision

The not inconsiderable blessing of sharing in this evangelical Reformational Christian world-and-life vision continually being reformed and reconfirmed (not verified) by living with God's Spirit-breathed booked *chokmah* (2 Timothy 3:16–17)—those from other Christian faith traditions may speak for theirs—is that you are *conscious* of where you stand in God's world, where you are headed with your life, what kind of messed-up good environs constitutes your matrix and *modus operandi,* and what kind of Chaucerian company you probably will be keeping (1 Corinthians 1:26–29). That is, persons are blessed—some are more engaged than others—blessed by an integrated vision of what's going on in God's cosmic theatre, to use John Calvin's metaphor (*theatrum Dei, Institutes,* I, 6, 2), where many go through their seven stages of living; make their entrances and exits, to pick up Shakespeare's image (*As You Like It,* II, 7); and by God's Word and Spirit are given the wherewithal to persevere in "making the life of Jesus visible in our often decrepit bodies," as the apostle Paul puts it (2 Corinthians 4:1–11). A Reformational Christian world-and-life vision provides a person context with historic footing and prospects for fruitful service that consciously solidifies one's human identity and provides patience, joy, and strength to exercise hospitality to strangers. *It costs one's lifetime,* but the yoke fits the faithful well and the burden is light (Matthew 11:28–30).

The stability of *consciously* knowing roughly the scripturally inspired lay of God's world and the purpose of life within it can deeply offend people, other Christians, too, who may be living distracted lives or are not conscious of their way of life and are made to feel as though they are stupid or backsliders in the faith. A misstep here can cause a lot of damage in a community. Especially if one's Christian world-and-life vision becomes a cliché, is touted as the best thing since bottled spring water, or is believed to be a sign that the millennium is breaking—a mistake also made by Christ's original disciples (Luke 19:11–27), who did miracles but sometimes could *not* exorcize evil spirits (Matthew 17:14–21; Luke 10:17–20)! One's Christian world-and-life vision can be surreptitiously idolized, become a shibboleth, turn one's circle of compatriots into a Hadleyburg,[6] or serve as license to go hunt materialism, naturalism, spiritualism and then hang their taxidermied heads up like trophies in your den.

But such unseemly damages can be avoided if you realize that *your Christian world-and-life vision is a thetical orientation and not a judgmental condemnation, a program for doing good for the commonweal and not a plan of attack on enemies.* A Reformational Christian world-and-life vision, Sytze U. Zuidema taught us, provides "beginsels" (starting points), *not* [he made up the word] "endsipels" (final-line markings). Sander Griffioen and Bob Goudzwaard say it well: when you have a biblically Christian world-and-life vision guiding your way as an imaginative map, as you proceed, new vistas open up for redemptive deeds.[7] I take this to mean that a Christian world-and-life vision is not a cut-and-dried paradigm you can be cocksure about—one size fits all feet; it is also not just a tentative guess about what you should be duly hesitant. No, *the evangelical Reformational world-and-life vision I find to be an enriching, imaginative, path-finding project* worth working out and carrying on is as wary as a snake and as innocent, vulnerable as a dove (Matthew 10:16).

Counting up the real costs of a christian world-and-life vision

There are two very expensive costs built in to the project of developing a Christian world-and-life vision that I will mention in closing: (1) follow-through with sustained, communal, regenerative, reflective deed in society; and (2) practicing a prophetic bona fide Christian philosophical systematics in the academy while working with specialist scholars at the inner reformation of theoretical disciplines.

---

6   See Mark Twain's short story, "The Man Who Corrupted Hadleyburg" (1899).

7   "Het is het gaan van een weg die aan het individuele leven samenhang geeft. . . . vast blijft staan dat elk pad afzonderlijk een bepaalde 'logica' kent: op bepaalde stappen volgen andere. . . . toegegeven dat het huidige leven diffuser is dan voorheen. Maar zonder wegen kunnen we niet. In zoverre behouden ook levensbeschouwingen een oriënterende betekenis" (Griffioen 2003/1996, 193). "In een weg-georiënteerd beleid verruimt de weg zich namelijk onder het gaan: elke initieel genomen stap voegt de informatie toe die je nodig hebt om verdere stappen te kunnen nemen" (Goudzwaard 1999, 21).

(1) Sidney Rooy goes to the less famous 1 John 3:16–18 to say that "spirituality" is a cop-out unless you give your lives for brothers and sisters in need. Rather than stare adoringly toward icons of God, go "secular," man or woman! (in the medieval Roman Catholic sense of the term): go work *in the world* of ignorance, perversity, and hypocrisy. Unless you are empathetically suffering along with hurting fellow believers, to say from your tower high and dry, "Shalom, shalom" is merely a slogan (2002, 147–48, 152).

I am not talking about 1960s protest groups and countercultural demonstrations against the WTO, but I am speaking for long-range intergenerational movements like the Christian Labour Association of Canada, the Citizens/Center for Public Justice (Canada and United States, www.cpj.ca; www.cpjustice.org), the Work Research Foundation in Canada (now known as Cardus—www.cardus.ca), which, in our differentiated society, take the time to regroup institutionally to posit reformative/restorative actions informed by the vision of βασιλεία τοῦ θεοῦ, the Kingdom-Rule of God in which, Gerda Hoekveld-Meyer says, there are no rights—only the duty of just-doing (1998, 64). God's people do not need to be successful entrepreneurs and political leaders so much as faithful at instituting protective, generous, healing deeds in society, especially for the impoverished. Even lone individual persons in legislative office or corporations need communal support if they are trying to end the fiasco of privatized faith. If we followers of the Christ are busy fashioning a salty Christian world-and-life vision in whatever circles of society we find ourselves, it behooves us not to default on putting the brave words into reliable deeds (1 John 3:18, James 1:22–25, 2:14–26).

(2) A Christian world-and-life vision is not theoretically precise enough to capture the "limiting concepts" that analytically determine the terrain for special scientific study of biology, for example, psychology, jurisprudence or . . . theology. It takes hyperconscious, philosophically exacting concepts and technical terms, not metaphors, to approximate the structural insights needed to break into the cycle of experience so one can order what is perceived and scrupulously relate finely drawn distinctions. "Modal aspects of things," "anticipatory and retroflective moments," "kernels of meaning," "limited sphere of authority," and "subsidiarity" do not make good storytelling; but jargon matching meticulous analysis is the meat of theoretical dissection, and such severe, logical abstraction is necessary to investigate the joists where specialized fields of scientific investigation interlock and expose the foci where one's faith orientation makes a difference. Henk Aay has shown how Christian geography schol-

arship in the Netherlands missed the opportunity to deepen its field of study with sociography because the professionals lacked the theoretical acumen to formulate Christian categories that could prevent transforming geographic science into ethnography (1998, 120–22).

Please do not misunderstand me. Making a Christian world-and-life vision winsome in the academy is of capital importance. And scholars specializing in world-and-life vision studies should actively seek to engage especially teachers of literature, art, and music history in the endeavor, because the intersection of world-and-life visions and period principalities are veritably palpable in the poetry, novels, paintings, songs, and symphonies to be studied in college, and professors in "the humanities" can train students to find good knowledge of God's world in slanted perspectives. Literary studies and interpretation of artworks are as rigorous and fine-tuned as philosophy, but they are just two different universes of discourse, in the way that reading Goethe's *Faust* intelligibly (1808/1832) is different from parsing Kant's *Kritik der Urteilskraft* (1790).

A phenomenal book like Ken Badley's *Worldviews: The challenge of choice* (Toronto: Urwin, 1996) is worth its weight in gold: this text reaches the high school(!) crowd mentality with cartoons, arresting typography, exquisite color photos, incisive commentary, and pointed questions that face teen-age youth with the incontrovertible truth that Muslims, Hindus, Buddhists, Sikhs, Jews, and Christians *choose* different understandings of family, work, technology, sexuality, medicine, suicide—Hey! What is *your* world-and-life vision, pardner?

This Christian world-and-life vision textbook is harder to write, I dare say, and perhaps a more effective Christian witness than many a finely argued treatise on apologetics. I am reminded of Bill Rowe's trenchant remark: when philosophy at the university lost its prophetic character and became professionalized in the last 100 years, the prophets went elsewhere (1989, 161). Maybe the prophets went into "worldview" studies!

But unless persons who value a Christian world-and-life vision support, request, and contribute to the formation of a *rigorous Christian philosophical systematics* that works through the categories needed to orient specialized theory of art, commerce, government, belief, health, language—you name it—the Christian community professing to give redemptive leadership in higher education has left off, in my judgment, building the tower of witness in the world Christ spoke of. Theoretical ideas do grow legs. And it is the proper task of *philosophy* to assist specialized theorists in conceiving original orienting hypotheses and in mediating the knowledge of detailed results into wisdom for life.

It is unfortunate, I think, when Christian scholars seem satisfied to promote a *theology* of art, *theological* psychotherapy, or a *theological* approach to politics, rather than a *Christian philosophical* examination in these disciplines. I support both formal and informal efforts to bring different brands of the Christian faith into a sound working relationship. But the academy needs something more fundamental than good will among church people and a sense of common mission to grapple with the troublesome thought-problem of sorting out the nature of "Christian philosophy" and "theological theory." My hunch is that this conceptual struggle goes back to radically different positions on the eucharistic Church at worship, the *corpus Christi* at large, and the Kingdom-Rule of God. My Reformational Christian faith-thought tradition is skittish about topping up disciplinary study with theological doctrinal control to make it kosher, particularly if it surfaces as a kind of Protestant clericalism. . . .

So as not to end on a querulous note, I'll relate a couple of incidents, comment, and refer to a photographic artwork.

In early 2003, Margaret Bendroth and Henry Luttikhuizen curated an art exhibit of paintings and prints at Calvin College in Grand Rapids entitled *The House of God: Religious observation within American protestant homes*. Philosopher John Hare told me of being present in the gallery when persons who had driven hundreds of miles came to stand motionless in front of Werner Sallman's well-known *Head of Christ* (1940) and unabashedly began to weep in respectful silent devotion.

I recently visited Casino Rama, built and operated on native land in Ontario. In a huge cavernous amphitheatre filled with rows upon rows of packed-together slot machines, jingle jangling with exciting noises, colored lights flashing everywhere almost psychedelically, single individuals, some appearing dazed, often slumped in chairs, dropped loonies into slots and pushed buttons of rolling tumblers. Over in a quieter section around multiple ornate tables, tense, sharp-eyed persons placed bets down on a bouncing marble in a roulette wheel or on a few slickly dealt cards. I marveled at the magician-like quicker-than-the-eye skill of the croupier to sweep away the chips and with a fast dance rhythm set up the next trick nonstop for people to lay down new bets on the inviting bright green soft felt tabletop. I spent a hell of an hour as voyeur there, speechless, flabbergasted, crying inside at what appeared to me to be the public, humiliating exploitation of desperately lonely, unsatisfied neighbors of mine.

To complete the world and life picture on our hands, remember the distraught Muslim mother in Michael Moore's *Fahrenheit 9/11* film shouting/crying out to the heavens, "Allah akbar! Avenge this senseless destruction!" amid the smoldering rubble of her neighborhood homes and dismembered children. (I am afraid that the true God may be hearing her prayer.)

To become a disciple of Christ as student and educator is asking for trouble, a more severe judgment from God (James 3:1). It is a biblical norm for schooling, I believe, that the older ones serve the younger. A major task for Christian teachers is to offer and instill, God willing, in the rising generation, a biblically vital, redemptive world-and-life vision that has the horizons to encompass with compassionate meaning those served by pietist kitsch artistry, those addicted to gambling, and fervent, suffering theists who deny that Jesus Christ is the Son of God. Our calling from the Lord is to show and tell somehow to anybody who will look and listen—our students may be more poverty-stricken than they outwardly seem—that *to be inducted into the order of Melchizedek as priestly rulers following Jesus Christ* (Psalm 110; Hebrews 4:14–5:10, 7:15–28, 10:19–39; 1 Peter 2:9–10) *is the joyful crux of human life in God's world.* Our educative task is not to "empower" people, as I understand it, but to *give them the vision and the Spirited will to be diaconal.*

To avoid the damages of leaving tower-building half-finished and to capture the real cost of Christ's discipleship, I refer you, by way of example, to a series of five photographs [see *CP* #32–36] by the Czech-American Duane Michals (born 1932), which plays loosely off "The Return of the Prodigal Son" (1982).[8] They illustrate metaphorically for me "the encounter" Johan van der Hoeven, glossing Buber, poses as a way to put a covenantal seal (1990, 27–29) on communicating and giving in a Holy Spirited way a Christian world-and-life vision off your biblical back to an other person in our ravaged environs.

The naked son, like a mirror image of Masaccio's Adam expelled from paradise, enters from the right into a room where the father is leisurely scanning *The New York Times.* The startled older man looks at the youth bowed in shame. The father loosens his shirt to protect the other's nakedness, and then thoughtfully removes all of his clothes to give them to the younger one. Finally, the naked old man gingerly gives the returned son a hug offering reconciliation.

I think such a gestural sequence may be a good image of how a Christian world-and-life vision gets transferred between generations.

---

8   See, e.g., the Yale Art Gallery catalogue for the 1995 exhibition, organized by Ellen G. D'Oench, *Prodigal Son Narratives: 1480–1980.*

And the surprise in real life is that when you give somebody the visionary cloak of Christ's discipleship you yourself received once upon a time, when you help the other person put on the world-and-life vision God's Spirit has entrusted to you (Britt Wikström, *Caritas*, 2001 [see *RA* #101, 102, 137]), you *both* become clothed in the quiet glory of the Lord.

Select Bibliography

Aay, Henk. "Christian Worldview and Geography: Christian schools in the Netherlands 1900–1960." In *Geography and Worldview: A Christian reconnaissance*, eds. Henk Aay and Sander Griffioen (Lanham: University Press of America, 1998), 108–24.

Badley, Ken. *Worldviews: The challenge of choice* (Toronto: Irwin, 1996).

Curry-Roper, Janel M. "Christian Worldview and Geography: Positivism, covenantal relations, and the importance of place," in *Geography and Worldview*, 49–60.

de Graaff, Arnold H. *Psychology: Sensitive openness and appropriate reactions* (Potchefstroom: Potchefstroom University for Christian Higher Education, 1980), 23pp.

Dooyeweerd, Herman. *In the Twilight of Western Thought: Studies in the pretended autonomy of philosophical thought* (Philadelphia: Presbyterian and Reformed, 1960).

Giamatti, A. Bartlett. *A Free and Ordered Space: The real world of the university* (New York: Norton, 1988).

Goudzwaard, Bob. "Tussen de klippen door," in *Bewogen Realisme: Economie, cultuur, oecumene*, eds. Herman Noordegraaf and Sander Griffioen (Kampen: Kok, 1990, 5–27.

Griffioen, Sander. "Christian Higher Education in Europe: A Catholic view," *Christian Higher Education* 1:2–3 (2002): 281–301.

―――. "Is a Pluralist Ethos Possible?" *Philosophia Reformata* 59:1 (1994): 11–25.

―――. "Kleine typologie van pluraliteit," in *Pluralisme: Cultuur-filosofische beschouwingen*, eds. Theo de Boer and Sander Griffioen (Amsterdam: Boom, 1995), 204–26, 235–36.

―――. *Moed tot cultuur: Een actuele filosofie* (Amsterdam: Buijten en Schipperheijn *Motief*, 2003).

―――. "Perspectives, Worldviews, Structures," in *Geography and Worldview*, 125–43.

―――. *The Problem of Progress* (Sioux Center, IA: Dordt College Press, 1985).

―――. "The Relevance of Dooyeweerd's Theory of Social Institutions," in *Christian Philosophy at the Close of the Twentieth Century: Assessment and perspective*, eds. Sander Griffioen and Bert M. Balk (Kampen: Kok, 1995), 139–58.

―――. "The Worldview Approach to Social Theory: Hazards and benefits," in Marshall, et al., *Stained Glass*, 81–118.

————. "Tijd voor het levens-beschouwelijke debat," in *Aan Babels Stromen: Een bevrijdend perspectief op ethiek en techniek,* Feestbundel voor Egbert Schuurman (Amsterdam: Buijten en Schipperheijn, 2003), 118–29.

Griffioen, Sander, and Bert M. Balk, eds. *Christian Philosophy at the Close of the Twentieth Century: Assessment and perspective* (Kampen: Kok, 1995).

Guinness, Os. "Mission Modernity: Seven checkpoints on mission in the modern world," in *Faith and Modernity,* eds. Philip Sampson, Vinay Samuel, and Chris Sugden (Oxford: Regnum Books, 1994), 322–52.

Hoekveld, Gerard A. "Alien in a Foreign Land: Human geography from the perspective of Christian citizenship," in *Geography and Worldview,* 83–101.

Hoekveld-Meyer, Gerda. "God's Own Countries? Contours of a Christian worldview in geography," in *Geography and Worldview,* 61–82.

Jenkins, Daniel. *Christian Maturity and the Theology of Success* (London: SCM, 1976).

Kienzler, Klaus. "Ist vom 'Christlichen' nur noch 'nach-christlich' zu reden?" *Wertepluralismus und Wertewandel heute.* Eine interdisziplinäre Veranstaltung zur 10-Jahres Feier der Universität Augsburg (München: Verlag Ernst Vögel, 1982), 3–16.

Klapwijk, Jacob. "Antithesis and Common Grace," in *Bringing into Captivity Every Thought: Capita selecta in the history of Christian evaluations of non-Christian philosophy,* eds. Jacob Klapwijk, Sander Griffioen, and Gerben Groenewoud (Lanham: University Press of America, 1991), 169–90.

Kok, John H. "To Have and to Hold: Peculiar grounds for cultural engagement and civil disagreements," *Pro Rege* 31:1 (2003): 23–30.

————. "Vollenhoven and 'Scriptural Philosophy,'" *Philosophia Reformata* 53:2 (1988): 101–42.

Kuyper, Abraham. *Lectures on Calvinism* [1898] (Grand Rapids: Eerdmans, 1961).

Marren-Reitsma, Heather. "Reading and Comprehension Strategies for All Levels and Subjects." Session held for Northern Christian Schools Professional Development Day, Houston, British Columbia, Canada, 2 April 2004.

Marshall, Paul A., "Epilogue: On faith and social science," in Marshall, et al., *Stained Glass,* 184–87.

Marshall, Paul A., Sander Griffioen, and Richard Mouw, eds. *Stained Glass: Worldviews and social science* (Lanham: University Press of America, 1989).

Mekkes, J. P. A. "Methodology and Practice," *Philosophia Reformata* 38 (1973): 77–83. (Original Dutch version: "Methodologie en Praxis." *Philosophia Reformata* 43 (1978): 3–10.)

Morrison, Toni. *Playing in the Dark: Whiteness and the literary imagination* (Cambridge: Harvard University Press, 1992).

Myers, Kenneth A. *All God's Children and Blue Suede Shoes: Christians and popular culture* (Westchester: Crossway, 1989).

Naugle, David K. *Worldview: The history of a concept* (Grand Rapids: Eerdmans, 2002).

Olthuis, James H. "On Worldviews," in Marshall, et al., *Stained Glass*, 26–40.

Palmer, Parker J. *To Know as We Are Known: Education as a spiritual journey* (San Francisco: Harper, 1993).

Peck, John, and Charles Strohmer. *Uncommon Sense: God's wisdom for our complex and changing world* (Sevierville: The Wise Press, 2000).

Popma, K. J. "Patristic Evaluation of Culture," *Philosophia Reformata* 38 (1973): 97–113.

———. *De Universiteit: Idee en practijk* (Amsterdam: Buijten en Schipperheijn, 1969).

Rooy, Sidney H. "Education for Life: The search for wisdom in the supermarket of values," *Christian Higher Education* 1:2–3 (2002): 139–63.

Rowe, William. "Society After the Subject: Philosophy after the worldview," in Marshall, et al., *Stained Glass*, 156–83.

Runner, H. Evan. "The Relation of the Bible to Learning," in *Christian Perspectives 1960* (Pella, IA: Pella Publishing, 1960), 85–158.

Seerveld, Calvin. "Does the World Ask Europe to Sacrifice its Beautiful Art?" in *The Art of Living*, eds. Jan Peter Balkenende, Roel Kuiper, and Leen La Riviére (Rotterdam: CNV-Kunstenbond/Europäisches Zentrum für Arbeitnehmerfragen, 2001), 13–17. {See *CP*: 35–53.}

———. "Footprints in the Snow." *Philosophia Reformata* 56:1 (1991): 1–34 {infra pp. 235–276}.

———. "Idealistic Philosophy in Checkmate: Neoclassical and Romantic artistic policy," *Studies on Voltaire and the Eighteenth Century* 263 (1989): 467–72. {See *AH*: 131–136.}

———. "Philosophy as Schooled Memory" (1982). In *In the Fields of the Lord*, ed. Craig Bartholomew (Carlisle: Piquant, 2000), 84–89.

———. "Reformational Christian Philosophy and Christian College Education," *Pro Rege* 30:3 (2002): 1–16 {supra 1–26}.

———. *Skeleton to Philosophy 101* (Palos Heights, IL: Trinity Christian College, 1960), mimeograph, iv–45.

———. "Toward a Cartographic Methodology for Art Historiography," *Journal of Aesthetics and Art Criticism* 39:2 (1980): 143–54. {See *AH*: 61–78.}

———. *Why Should a University Exist?* (Pusan: Kosin University Press, 2000), 80 pp. {supra pp. 29–58}.

Sietsma, K. *De Ambtsgedachte* (Amsterdam: S. J. P. Bakker, n.d.).

Smith, David I., and John Shortt. *The Bible and the Task of Teaching* (Nottingham: The Stapleford Centre, 2002).

Smith, James K. A. "Determined Violence: Derrida's structural religion" *The Journal of Religion* 78 (1998): 197–212.

Spykman, Gordon J. *Reformational Theology: A new paradigm for doing dogmatics* (Grand Rapids: Eerdmans, 1992).

Strauss, Gideon. "A Nation of Idiots," *thINK* (Summer 2004), 1–2.

van der Hoeven, Johan. "Christian Philosophy at the End of the Twentieth Century," in *Christian Philosophy at the Close of the Twentieth Century*, 55–66.

————. "Development in the Light of Encounter," in *Norm and Context in the Social Sciences,* eds. Sander Griffioen and Jan Verhoogt (Lanham: University Press of America, 1990), 23–25.

Van Til, Henry R. *The Calvinistic Concept of Culture* (Grand Rapids: Baker, 1959).

Wink, Walter. *Naming the Powers: The language of power in the New Testament* (Philadelphia: Fortress, 1984).

————. *Unmasking the Powers: The invisible forces that determine human existence* (Philadelphia: Fortress, 1981).

Wolters, Albert M. "Dutch Neo-Calvinism: Worldview, philosophy and rationality," in *Rationality in the Calvinian Tradition,* eds. H. Hart, J. van der Hoeven, and N. Wolterstorff (Lanham: University Press of America, 1983), 113–31.

————. *Creation Regained: Biblical basics for a reformational worldview* [1985] (Carlisle: Paternoster, 1996).

————. "On the Idea of Worldview and its Relation to Philosophy," in Marshall, et al., *Stained Glass,* 14–25.

Zuidema, S. U. "Pragmatism," in *Christian Perspectives 1961* (Hamilton: Guardian Publishing, 1961), 133–57.

BABEL, PENTECOST, GLOSSOLALIA, AND PHILOXENIA:
NO LANGUAGE IS FOREIGN TO GOD

It was ten minutes past six o'clock P.M. on a Saturday evening, 5 September 1936, as I lay on my belly perusing the script of a book, when suddenly the letters of the printed text made sense. I jumped up, ran to my Mother who was washing dishes in the kitchen, and exulted, "I can read! I can read!" and she had to stop to listen to me haltingly read aloud a few sentences. Thereafter I discovered a library in a neighboring town where you could take out books about boys having adventures on the high seas. One time my Mother bought me a storybook with, it looked to me like, a movie star on the wrap-around cover; but after I read it, *Tom Sawyer*, I knew I had now read a good solid book.

In the New York Long Island country high school where we lived I parsed Latin for three years, and was introduced to French. Mr. Heeter made a fool of himself and us, we thought—*eu, eu, eu*—but I learned to read French in two years and matriculated into second year college French as a freshman. At Calvin College I picked up Greek, corrected Latin quizzes in W. T. Radius's class for food money, and took two years of German, accelerating to struggle through Schiller's *Wallenstein* in my final senior semester. In my English Lit Master's program at the University of Michigan I explored Medieval Latin, and had a Greek class of two persons plus professor where we spent the whole hour three times a week translating Aristotle's *Nichomachean Ethics* into English one semester and Thucydides' writings the next semester.

Next, as a U.S. Fulbright graduate philosophy student at the Free University of Amsterdam you were expected to know Greek and Latin and be able to translate Plato into Dutch at oral colloquia— a legacy of Erasmus, I think, on Dutch educational culture still operative in the

Originally the keynote address at the Ninth Annual NACFLA (North American Christian Foreign Language Association's) Conference held at Point Loma Nazarene College in California, this piece was first published in the *Journal of Christianity and Foreign Languages* 2 (2001): 5–30.

'50s—but I really learned to be bilingual Dutch writing love letters to the Dutch woman who became my wife, carefully consulting Kramer's Dutch-English/English-Dutch dictionary before I sealed an envelope. One summer I hitchhiked over the Alps to Italy to learn Italian. As I walked across the border into an Italian village early one morning someone said to me, "Bon giorno." So I repeated "Bon giorno" to everyone I met, and in response they taught me new words. What fun to learn a people's tongue in such wanderlust fashion!

I finally learned German at the university in Basel—not the best accented place to do it—hearing French Alsace-Lorraine professor Oscar Cullmann lecture in German with excellent enunciated clarity, and living communally with thirty-some theological students in a kind of fraternity house there—"Kartoffeln, bitte" (Please pass the potatoes). That's where I studied Older Testament Hebrew, and am grateful to this day that my dictionary is Hebrew-German. It gives me wonderful, imaginative slippage time to render the biblical Hebrew into colloquial, literate American-English, by way of thinking German. . . .

I took these three minutes to tell my thumbnail language-history because it explains why as Canadian I think I am more European than North American—I want to repeat my Calvin English prof Henry Zylstra's good advice to me in 1947, "Stay with a language long enough to get into its literature"—and because I want to thank God from whom all blessings flow for what happened in the plains of Shinar long, long ago, which we know by the name of "Babel." God's historical act of "Babel" has blessed my life with colorful excitement and sanctifying wonder.

Let me read you about that act of God in Genesis 11:1–9. This is the Word of the LORD:

> All over the earth there was just one way of speaking, the same kind of talk. And as people [descendants of Noah's three Sons and daughters, Genesis 10:32] migrated from the East they found a plain in the land of Shinar and settled down there.

> Everybody said to one another, "Hey! Come on! Let's bake us some bricks! Let's burn up some crisps!" So they had bricks for stone, and they used asphalt for mortar.

> Then they said [to one another], "Hey! Come on! Let's build for ourselves a city and a skyscraping citadel! Let's make a Name for ourselves! Otherwise we are scattered all over the face of the earth."

> The LORD God had to step down to see this city and [skyscraping]

citadel, which the sons of men were building. And the LORD God said, "Look at that! The people are all the same, and all of them have the one same manner of speaking. And this is [just] the beginning of their daily doings. Right now it's not impossible for them to do all that they intend—Hey! Come on! Let's step down and thoroughly mix up their way of speaking there, so that they cannot hear each other's speaking."

So the LORD God scattered them from there all over the face of the earth: they left off building the city. That's why its "name" is called "BABEL," because that is where the LORD mixed up [=had them bobble, Heb. *balal*] the way all the earth was speaking. The LORD scattered them from there all over the face of the earth. (Genesis 11:1–9)

The gracious Lord God likes creatural diversity

Contrary to most readings of the Genesis 11:1–9 pericope, I think Christoph Uehlinger is correct to propose that it was the uniformity of speech, a kind of monotonic cant utilized by the human race several generations after Noah to stick together that angered God. In the wake of militarist strongman Nimrod (Genesis 10:6–14), the people devolved a single, approved communication lingo, a kind of clipped, pidgin talk that cemented the solidarity they needed to vaunt their consolidated power and build this one fortified city that would signal the monolithic worldly rule (*Weltreich*) they coveted. But, as Psalm 2:4 would say, God just laughed and simply mixed up their in-house speech so they couldn't understand one another, and therefore moved off in their little hard-bitten, monolingual enclaves, inadvertently doing—disobediently—what the LORD had first asked them to do: fill in the earth, flourish, make the whole earth fruitful (Genesis 9:1–7).

So the thrust of the account in Genesis 11: 1–9 is, as Barbara Carvill and David Smith's wonderful new book says: "Babel" is God's judgment on uniformity and human empire building.[1] (The Genesis 11 incident is remarkably similar to the much later event where God puts Nebuchadnezzar down on all fours like an animal for boasting, "Is this not the great Babylon [Heb: *babel*] I myself have built to house Sovereign Rule by the strength of my own power and for my own majestic glory!?" [Daniel 4:30, Aram. v.27].)

Two matters should be noted to crystallize this biblical orientation for discussing language:

---

1 *The Gift of the Stranger* (2000), 7–8, 209–216.

(1) God's judgments on human sin in history always hold a loop-hole of grace. Instead of Adam and Eve's dying on the spot after eating from the Tree-of-the-knowledge-of-good-and-evil (Genesis 2:17, 3:2–3), God made them banished mortals with lives of pain and sweat, and out-fitted them with clothes (Genesis 3:16–24). Pain is good warning of me-dicinal need; sweat—as Chaucer writes (*Canterbury Tales*, "The Canon's Yeoman's Prologue")—can be a joyful celebration of bodily exertion; and clothes not only protect human intimacy but can enhance our human limbs and lineaments. Also, after God saw the monstrous cultural ab-normalities (*Nephilim*) born of conjoined godly and ungodly conception in the generation of Noah, and felt constrained to flood out the human race, the LORD still saved a remnant of animals and eight humans to start history over again, as it were, with leftovers under a rainbow in the sky (Genesis 6: 1–9: 17).

When humankind conspired to reduce speech to a monolithic tech-nospeak in order to bolster a totalitarian grasp for World Power, God pre-vented such warlike violence and vanity by dispersing men and women across the face of God's earth (Genesis 11:1–9) so they would not be able to centralize and capitalize their own utter destruction (cf. Proverbs 1:10–19). The diversity of speech in the mouths of humans then is like another rainbow from God, not in the sky but within the human voice: a rainbow promise made good with a down payment at Pentecost.

(2) God likes creatural diversity. The bio-diversity of plant life and the incredibly numberless shades of green to foliage in almost any land-scape, as well as the fantastic array of animal kinds, from dinosaurs to mosquitoes, rattlesnakes to Canadian geese, the Leviathan and butter-flies, testify that the LORD's imaginative taste for colorful variety (Job 8–39, Psalm 104) is beyond question, it seems to me. And no matter how the multiple nations and peoples developed, apocalyptic prophe-cies of Scripture, from Isaiah 60 to Revelation 21, detail the joy that the LORD anticipates in seeing the refined, variegated wealth of the various nations from near and faraway being finally assembled in service to the Lamb of God and the faithful body of Jesus Christ. It is sin that ho-mogenizes or stereotypes differences into a banal sameness, and it is we middleclass who are more comfortable with what is usual and familiar. But God—this is what Jesus was trying to teach the slow-witted men who were his disciples upset by the woman who broke a whole flask of expensive, anointing perfume over the Christ's body (Mark 14:1–11): God likes surprises!

The marvelous gift of human speech and written literature

The fact that God gave us humans (and also angels)[2] the special ability to relate to things by naming them and, as the Bible story tells it, waited in the beginning to see what Man would call the land animals (Genesis 2:18–20), hints at the marvelous inventive power hidden in human language. God said, "Let the earth bring forth creepy-crawly creatures!" and worms, ants, and chameleons came to be. The mother tongue of humans made to bear God's image enables a person not to "create" things, but to establish connections, to posit identities with vocal or gestural signs, to question matters and to clarify the relations of things with other persons. A human baby says, "Mama," and a mother bends her breast near to nourish the child with milk.

A child gradually comes to inhabit and voice a whole system of syntactically related phonemic words in verbal sentences with predicates, subjects, and objects. Animals like cawing crows, trumpeting elephants, as well as piping dolphins, communicate with one another by sounds too, and God hears their animal noises as praise and requests for attention, says the Bible (Job 38:39–39:30, Psalm 104:24–30). But only human speech has the glory, I think, to bespeak themes that show a self-conscious stance and bearing toward the matters narrated that is more than reactive, and is able to give, as Shakespeare says about poetry, "to airy nothingness a name" (*As You Like It*). Human speech is peculiar in having the depth for one to use it to tell lies, or to articulate the predicament of "It's me, it's me, O Lord, standin' in the need of prayer."

A characteristic of human speech, and even language, that seems important to me, as philosophical aesthetician, is its inescapably multilayered nature: *talk is always more than a lingual act that specifies something clearly (or unclearly)*. Vocabulary, grammar, intonation, pace and accent, the tilt to adjectives, the tense of verbs, all undergird (spoken) language with thick or thin texture. Is there a fresh breath of imaginative air in the precise word choice? The dimensions of decorum, certainty, informativeness, how listener-friendly or not, also adhere a person's speech.

Whether the actual language be Hungarian or Mandarin Chinese, Castilian Spanish or British English: the actual language spoken indelibly stamps the speaker with a history, usually with a geographic location, and embodies a whole fascinating world of idiom, customs, and a people. Speech inevitably reflects one's education, sometimes one's dated age, and frequently a person's prejudices. Although the mother tongue

---

2 Cf. For example, Isaiah 6, Job 1:6–12, Luke 1:26–38, 2:8–14. Also 1 Corinthians 13:1.

one receives or adopts takes on each person's idiosyncratic torque, possibly a dialect, *every one's base language acts as a cultural gyroscope in their life.* One's original native tongue is the place where one feels more than semantically secure: *one's mother tongue is one's particular, complex cultural homestead.*

When language is heightened aesthetically, that is, when the connotative layer embedded in every language is given free play, so to speak, so that the metaphorical underside of language comes to dominate the utterance rather than just remain latent, then the speaking becomes poetic. In an oral culture the flowering of public speech as an art becomes storytelling, and that act becomes crucial for the transmission of that language community's traditions and prospects, shaping the way the elders lead the people. When a language is written, in a literate society, the artistic intensification casts language in literary form. And literature—composing, scripting, reading literature—demonstrates how language that reaches the maturity of textuality has enormous suasive power for shaping and channeling a vision that accompanies that language community.

I am not referring to "sacred texts" like the Bible, Qu'ran, or the Te Ching collection, but to "ordinary" literature like Chaucer, Shakespeare, Milton, Wordsworth, George Eliot, and James Joyce, for giving English-speaking people a special literary inheritance. Luther, Goethe, Nietzsche, Kafka, and Brecht do something to and for a German-speaking public that sets them apart. If you have been raised on Racine, Pascal, Balzac, Baudelaire, Rimbaud, Proust, I wager you will have a different *mentality* than if you are a generation who was bred on Tolstoi, Dostoevsky, Checkhov, and Gorki along with your mother's milk.

I know, I'm talking literary canon, which is in dispute, under review, and polemical expansion today. But even if you settle for an ethnic *bricolage* of makeshift authoritative sources for the voices you want the rising generation to hear—if there be no settled, living literary tradition in force, one is apt to be prey to whatever is merely briefly fashionable—no teacher should fool oneself on the subliminal shaping power of what the rising generation reads or does not read of one's native language become literature. The writing down of aesthetically enriched language on papyrus parchment, paper, some material, gives the spoken language a complicated, double whammy of permanence and a kind of imprimatur that simple speech, however eloquent, lacks.[3] Textual significance is outfitted

---

3 Cf. Section IV on "History and history-keeping: tracking footprints" and "Writing and historiographic task" in my article, "Footprints in the Snow," *Philosophia Reformata* 56:1 (1991): 16–28 {infra pp. 254–268}.

with the warranty of additional affirmation to that of the author; a text demands slower, more considered interpretation to get at the congealed meaning than if you are just interactively taking in and responding to someone's live speaking.

This discrepancy is a grave problem when an oral culture like that of the Venda tribe in South Africa encounters literacy. Suddenly the older story-telling elders whose authority and wisdom reside in their memory and public ceremonial speaking are considered illiterate because they cannot read the forms and paper communications the government sends their tribal way. There is upheaval in the cultural leadership of a people. The most redemptive way I have seen to effect the traumatic transition from an oral culture to the literacy of our dominant civilization still in place is by a Christian Reformed World Relief Committee leader, Jan Disselkoen in Sierra Leone, who trained natives of the Kuranko tribe to write primers using the stories of their people for teaching adults and children to read, so that the text and the oral culture reinforced one another.

I think it is important not to set up a dialectical tension between the spoken and the (aesthetically enriched) written language, but to honor the different strengths inhering speech and literature, and discover how as language teachers we are to equip the next generation to handle both such precious gifts from God.

The history-impacted problem of teaching rhetoric

Along with the systematic point I have just tried to make, that language in all its richness is shortchanged unless you also deal with its literature, comes the historical problematics of how rhetoric has fared in the educational institutions—seminaries, university, colleges, language schools—where the relation of language instruction to other disciplines needs to be adjudicated. The drift of institutions, as Foucault overstates, has a quiet way of favoring and handicapping various fields of study. Are you (foreign) language teachers at peace with your place in the academic curricular sun?

While recently doing research for a different occasion on the nature

---

Plato wrestles with the relation of scripting language well in *Phaedrus* 274b6–278b6; and Jacques Derrida spars further with Plato's Phaedrus on the matter of reading/writing in "La Pharmacie de Platon" [1968], translated as "Plato's Pharmacy" by Barbara Johnson in *Dissemination* (University of Chicago Press, 1981), 63–171.

For a laconic, jesting macaronic treatment of getting conference speeches published in academic journals, see John Fisher's editorial in *Journal of Aesthetics and Art Criticism* 38:2 (1979): 119–120.

and formation of universities, from the oldest university in the world, Al-Azhar in Cairo, Egypt (begun c. 700? AD by Muslim clerics), to Kosin University in Busan, Korea (founded by American Presbyterian missionaries, 1946 AD),[4] I found out how certain longstanding feuds, rival orientations, and mistrustful changes in the nature of advanced schooling have impacted what we Christian professors face today, as Babel is being rebuilt, but not in the plains of Shinar. Let me make just a few moot historiographic assessments.

The pagan Hellenic and Hellenistic civilizations left the Church, which followed them, with a standoff between rhetoric and (dialectical) logic for how cultural leaders should be instructed in humanity. A sophist like Gorgias taught the technique (ἀρετή=virtue!) of winning arguments by persuasive speech, whether the cause was right or wrong, thereby defining for Socrates the nature of commercialized sophistry.[5] Plato, however, promulgated philosophy, one could say, which was understood as the never-ending devotion, search for wisdom (φιλο-σοφία) and certified true knowledge (ἐπιστήμη), a chore that left you eternally critical and logically en route to speculative, definitive answers that were never reached. Aristotle allowed the practical ethical person to make approximating logical, phronetic judgments.[6] But it was Isocrates (436–388 BC) whose antisophistic and antispeculative idea of the *orator* (disciplined speaker) as the moral thinker showed the most promise to coax speaking and thinking together rather than keep them in competition. "To speak as one ought is the surest index of a sound understanding."[7] This thesis by Isocrates was adopted by Cicero and Quintilian as the better way to promote civic responsibility than to train youth in philosophical logical arguments.

To make one literate, ready to study the divine text, Augustine esteemed the oratorical tradition of the *artes liberals*, as did the Venerable Bede and Alcuin, at Charlemagne's court, who believed that civil officials should cut their teeth on a canon of texts that inculcate virtue. John Scotus Erigena and Pierre Abelard who championed the Aristotelian position of Boethius, however, came down on the side of logic as the key discipline to school theologians in making the necessary distinctions when faced with *contrarium* in disputes—Thomas Aquinas's *Summa* is

---

4   "Why Should a University Exist?" {supra 29–58}.

5   Plato, *Gorgias*, 454e9–455a1, 463a6–463c7, 464e2–465a7; also *Phaedrus*, 262cl–262c4.

6   *Nichomachaean Ethics*, book VI, 1138b18–1145a11.

7   Isocrates, *Antidosis*, 256–257, 268–277, 304–305.

the epitome of this tack, which foregrounds logic. So different medieval universities took the rhetorical or the dialectical side of education for emphasis, even though ostensibly both the *trivium* and *quadrivium* were a common curriculum in the encyclopedia of university *studia*.

Matters between language and logic became more tense in the scholarly world in what followed: Christian Humanists like Petrarch, Lorenzo Valla, the Dutch Agricola and Erasmus, rediscovered Quintilian and Cicero's texts, and thrived on philological detective work (for example, Erasmus edited a better Greek text for the New Testament Bible), gleaning from classical literature the best that had been said and thought in the past in order to educate good citizens for today. Melanchthon, John Calvin, Beza, Comenius, and even Ignatius of Loyola, all felt at home in the rhetorical tradition, which assumed that truth is preserved in classical texts and that education is to make that persuasive knowledge live again to form stable, learned leaders in society. Colleges in the American Colonial Virginia, Connecticut, and Massachusetts took this rhetorical liberal arts tradition as guideline too.

But the Enlightenment spirit that followed up the secularizing trend called the "Renaissance" was fascinated with Nature and the mathematical experimental method found in the work of Copernicus and Galileo. The European Enlightenment methodical skepticism of Descartes and John Locke's rationalistic empiricism, claiming to have no apriori's, aligned learning with a logical, critical philosophy, again captured in Kant's phrase *sapere aude* (dare to know whatever), that rejects canonic texts, the weight of tradition, and chases specialized projects with scientific analysis. Post-Colonial America shaded with Benjamin Franklin, Thomas Jefferson, and Tom Paine, moved toward this Enlightenment ethos too, but colleges and universities are conservative institutions, and old-fashioned "liberal education," even "classical" languages, hung on fairly well at least until the War between the States (1861–65).

John Dewey's Darwinian pragmatism (refined at the University of Chicago, 1894–1904) balled together the Socratic process of endless search with an Enlightenment penchant for non-committal, practically engaged Reason, to wrench American education out of its Ivy League ways, with sanctified classics, into the bustle of being liberated from any absolute standards and normed values and freed for a truly experimental thinking approach to every situation encountered in life. Charles W. Eliot, while he was Harvard's president (1869–1909), introduced the laissez-faire elective system of courses, and the practice spread to other universities. When lack of unity in college programs was recognized after

World War I, the spot "survey course," like "Western Civ," came to be introduced, to provide cohesion.[8] But a pervasive democratic individualism worked like acid on American higher education to make vocational training paramount.

Perhaps your Christian college institution is not mainstream American, and you do not need Alan Bloom or Edward Hirsch, Jr. as apologists for a good old, of course updated, "liberal arts" educational program that still has vestiges of the millennium-old rhetorical tradition jockeying with the pressures of professional analytic science requirements for what may constitute a "core curriculum." But next to the general businessification of college and university education by the rampant Pragmatistic spirit is another cultural dynamic, conveniently misnamed "postmodern," that tries to honor what has for centuries been marginalized by the dominant Lie of Religious Fundamentalism, Scientific Rationalism, Eurocentric Colonialism, Patriarchal Chauvinism—its names are legion—and wants to manage human affairs with only *petits récits*, local stories, to avoid aggrandizement and totalitarian power plays. Such a diffident sophisticated spirit focused intently on deferral of binding judgments may allow odd, new, Christian (queer) voices to be sounded for a time in the marketplace, but on the whole I find this deeply intelligent quasi-skepsis to play a corrosive or parasitic role in public leadership. And this revolutionary current of turning-things-upside-down is not able to stop, maybe it even abets! the disintegration of authentic human differences.

We are called to teach languages and literatures of different cultures, none of which are foreign to God, in a world where differences are disappearing. Instantaneous communication on the net—for most of the world invariably in English—and jet plane travel around the globe for more and more tourists from all nations, allow the exotic to be familiarized or commodified as a collectible. The McWorld phenomenon is well known, and is not less imperialistic or neo-colonializing because its domination is a more invisible Commercialistic principality rather than an overt political one.

For example, as I stooped to enter the corrugated metal shack in a shanty town outside Potchefstroom in South Africa (1995) as a visitor, I

---

8   For a fascinating account of how "C.C." ("Contemporary Civilization"), required at Columbia University (and Stanford) in the 1920s, which attempted to provide curricular order and meet the perceived need to educate the many immigrant students into (national) American citizenship, later crossed with the University of Chicago "Great Books" program (led by Robert M. Hutchins and Mortimer Adler), see chapter 6, "Between the Wars: Aspiration to order," in W. B. Carnochan, *The Battleground of the Curriculum*.

could not believe my eyes: in the dimmed interior of the hut on a small TV powered by a car battery played a sit-com made in USA! This is no "global village." Ours is a global high-rise with the uniformity-congestion of a Babel where, as Yeats would say, there is no center holding things together, as the Beast slouches toward Bethlehem (cf. Revelation 12–13). And one does not need to share Ellul's jeremiad over cities or accept his unfair, dialectical diatribe against the "image," in his *Humiliation of the Word*, to agree that our pop culture does tend to be magnificently post-literate, indeed, is a visual culture.

What does that turn of events mean for redemptive teaching of languages and literature—verbal rhetoric—or, for that matter, being a Christian woman and man in God's world today, two millennia after Pentecost?

Let me read the brief account that is booked in Acts 2:1–13 as a conscious, God-breathed (2 Timothy 3:16–17) supplement to Genesis 11:1–9:

> Now when the day of Pentecost had fully arrived, [the core of Christ's disciples] were all together in the same place. Suddenly there was a sound from heaven like the force of a rushing wind, and the noise filled the whole house where the disciples were sitting, and it appeared to them as if there were tongues of fire distributed and resting on each of them. They were all filled with the Holy Spirit, and began to speak in different tongues, as the Spirit gave them utterance.

> Now there were Jews who resided permanently in Jerusalem, pious folk from every nation under heaven. At the [strange] sound a large crowd [of them] came together and were bewildered [mixed-up], be-cause every one of them heard the disciples speaking in his or her own peculiar dialect. The crowd was astonished and wondered, say-ing, "Wait a minute, are not these people who are speaking Galileans? How come each of us hears our own particular native dialect? Parthi-ans, Medes, Elamites, residents from Mesopotamia, Judea and Cap-padocia, Pontus, Asia, Phrygia, Pamphilia, Egypt, the parts of Libya belonging to Cyrene, Roman visitors, Jews and proselytes, Cretans, Arabians: we all hear these Galileans speaking in our own (mother) tongues, declaring the great deeds of God!"

> And they were all astonished and perplexed, saying to one another, "What will this mean?" But other persons mocking said, "They're drunk on sweet wine." (Acts 2:1–13)

Historical Pentecostal development: united diversity

Apparently God still enjoys the creatural diversity of speaking! Early in history, when the Babylon humans wanted to use a single language to make a Name for themselves, God stopped their vanity with the miracle of different ways of speaking, bewildering them with unintelligibility. Later in history, when the diverse speaking peoples of the world attended the inauguration of the Holy Spirit on earth, you might say, God surprised everybody, bewildered them again by having them hear clearly and understand people of a certain Galilean locality who were filled with the Holy Spirit, speaking in these different, strange languages and dialects about *magnalia Dei*, the Great Deeds of the LORD. Different ways of speaking at Babel in the plains of Shinar was the LORD's gentle, backhanded way of hindering great evil and giving humankind a fresh start. Different ways of speaking at Pentecost in Jerusalem was the LORD's redemptive way of happily blessing cultural differences in their diversity united by praise of the Lord's acts of salvation.

Maybe Pentecost was a kind of foretaste of what conversation will be like on the new earth: you effortlessly speak the other person's language intelligibly. That special gift of the Holy Spirit to those Galilean believers at Pentecost, according to the Bible (Acts 2:4), also happened when the apostle Peter, as an elect Jew, finally caught onto God's message that an Italian soldier and uncircumcised Gentiles can be at home in the community of Christ's followers too.[9] So the biblical point of the same person's being gifted to magnify the LORD in different local languages is that the LORD does not pick favorites in languages, and God's people also are not to consider "unclean" what is not foreign to God (Acts 10:34). God enjoys hearing "Hallelujahs!" sung indiscriminately in Arabic, Yiddish, Swahili, Frisian, Hangul, and Fulani speech, just as the LORD is not partial, say the Scriptures, to the rich, to male adults, or classicists, but contrariwise honors especially the poor, selects lowly handmaids for high honor, and inducts those who lack a refined rhetorical training into bringing strangers good news.[10]

It is wrong for anybody locked into a nationalistic mentality to assert, "If Spanish-speaking people want to live in Texas, let 'em learn English—it's our country!" Or, "If the Quebecois want to be part of Canada, why should they hang onto their French dialect?"—as if the English language be the law of the land, the law of the peoples of the

---

9 Acts 10:1–11:18, especially 10:44–48, 11:15–18.

10 Proverbs 22:22–23, Job 31:13–23, Isaiah 61:1–4 and Luke 4:18–19, Matthew 11:2–6, James 2:1–7; 1 Samuel 2:1–10 and Luke 1:46–55; 1 Corinthians 2:1–5.

world. The uncharitable temper of such monolingual fundamentalism, like other monolithic fundamentalisms, is its Babel-Babylonic presumption to exercise a coercive conformity that is at core totalitarian. And that conformist evil, which Pentecost dispels, is present also among the "outsiders" who idolize English today as the road to jobs, money, and happiness. For example, in the very America-focused South Korea (except for its food and the *kim chi* delicacy), the hot subjects in its high schools I am told are mathematics, electronics, and English. Teaching ESL is a high calling, especially when done for refugees, trying to alleviate their cultural homelessness; but if ESL would be done Christianly, one may need to exorcize the fraudulent expectations that give it allure to many students.

I should mention *en passant* that Spirit-tongue-talk, γλωσσολαλία, that ecstatic vocalization of humans whose sounds are unintelligible until somebody translates them into ordinary language, is one of the gifts of the Holy Spirit, according to the Bible (1 Corinthians 12–14); but *glossolalia* is a quite different phenomenon from what is reported to have happened at Pentecost and the time in Caesarea. *Glossolalia* is one of the χαρίσματα, like faithfully making God's Word known prophetically, or like teaching, says Paul to the Romans (Romans 12:3–8), or like the rare gift of cheerfully, generously giving away your money for the needs of neighbors (cf. also 2 Corinthians 9:6–15). But *glossolalia* is not directly intelligible.

Because the Corinthian congregation of believers misused *glossolalia*, that is, overvalued the personal edificatory use of this kind of mysterious, free-form prayer directly to God (1 Corinthians 14:2), maybe even made it a test of whether you had been baptized by the Holy Spirit or not (Acts 10:15–16, 1 Corinthians 14:16), the apostle Paul carefully laid down liturgical guidelines limiting its place in a worship service. Paul instructed that someone with the *charisma* for interpreting Spirit-tongue-talk should be nearby to explicate the content of what was revealed (1 Corinthians 14:6, 26–28), and admonished the believers always to consult those with the *charisma* to discriminate between spirits (1 Corinthians 12:10; cf. 1 John 4:1) to test whether the *glossolalia* manifested a building-up love of the brother and sister or was a show-off putdown.

The few times I have worshipped in England with a congregation that works *glossolalia* into its Sunday services, decorously orchestrated by the minister of music and musicians, it sounded as if a flock of birds had come to rest in a nearby grove of trees, chirping and twittering pleasantly for several minutes until the Spirit moved on elsewhere, and the keyboard, double bass, guitar, and saxophone led us, I suppose you could say loosely, into an "interpretation" of what had just happened—individuals softly vocalizing a devout babble of syllables out loud—led us into an "interpretation" by a song of praise up on the overhead. I found it oddly edifying, as if people were individually releasing their pent-up troubles and petitions to God in a place where they felt safe.

One time my father was leading a Bible study in a public senior citizens rest home in Colorado, and something he said triggered a 90 year old Dutch woman to say, "I hated it when I had to memorize the psalms every week in school, but now when I can't sleep nights I'm glad I can recite them:

> 't Hijgend hert, der jacht ontkomen
> Schreeuwt niet sterker naar 't genot
> Van de frische waterstroomen
> Dan mijn ziel verlangt naar God. . . .

As she went on for a bit, a large Afro-American woman sitting next to me threw up her hands, "Praise the Lord! Now I've heard speaking in tongues!"

I tell these anecdotes as comic relief to firm up two points about *glossolalia*:

With all our lingual-analytic philosophy and attention to pedagogical methodology we need to remember the reality of human speech, which has marvelous qualities holding much more than will be dreamt of, Horatio, in our academic philosophy or theology.

The human tongue, which language teachers lay claim to teach, is a truly dangerous, wild organ open to tempting, respectable demonic ambition as well as able to provide peace-making wisdom between people (cf. James 3). That is probably why the Bible says (James 3:1): "Don't many of you become teachers, brothers and sisters, because we will receive a more strict judgment than other people."

However, the drift of my remarks is much more upbeat, and is gradually, I hope, becoming clear: the historical Pentecostal pendant to Babel is the biblical charter for the North American Christian Foreign Language Association. Because human language is so rich and embodies in the idiom of a people the cultural diversity God likes, foreign language teachers are pivotal in the Lord's undertaking to provide first of all understanding and possibly even reconciliation among the different nations of the world by celebrating in mixed chorus together the *magnalia Dei*. The diaconal service of foreign language teachers becomes ever more urgent the more the world at large succumbs to the creeping domination of American-English as the *lingua franca* of a Commercialistic Empire, making other local voices virtually extinct.

I should like to develop John Calvin's judgment that the highest calling an educated Christian might perform is to be a magistrate because then you can administer the Lord's justice to both unbelievers and believers.[11] Such true judges and lawyers in the last days will still need mouthpieces for those who have been silenced, translators of the foreign tongues that have become taboo or "dead" languages. Being able to hear and understand, read and speak different languages so one can mediate between people is almost as critical for the well-being of world society as doing legal justice because you can do cultural justice to your foreign neighbor if you are able to speak more than your own lingo. An ability to speak other languages is primed for neighbor-love and is one of the most shalom-filled occupations because, unlike science, it is prone to honor diversity. (Second language teachers may be out of a job on the new earth, along with homicide detectives, surgeons, and evangelists; but you probably can quite easily retrain to be interpreters of *glossolalia*.)

In the meantime, foreign language teaching remains vital for helping all and sundry to obey the Lord's injunction to practice φιλοξενία, hospitality. (I shall be very brief on this matter since you can read Barbara Carvill and David Smith's exciting and insightful new book, *The Gift of the Stranger*.)

God's injunction to practice *philoxenia*
The Lord's original command for us to love not only the neighbor but particularly the stranger, "because you once were strangers in the land of Egypt," is very stern (Exodus 22:21–24, Leviticus 19:33–34, Deuteronomy 10:12–21, 24:17–22). The Newer Testament carry-over enjoining believers to "practice hospitality" maintains the same strong directive (Romans 12:9–13), and generalizes the motivation, at least in the first letter of Peter to the Christian Jews living as exiles in Pontus, Galatia, Cappadocia, Asia, and Bithynia (1 Peter 1: 1–2): because you are currently temporary residents sojourning in lands foreign to the peace of God, deal nobly with your unbelieving Gentile neighbors and practice hospitality ungrudgingly with one another(1 Peter 1:17, 2:11–12, 4:7–11). What a breath-taking injunction for a minority community beset with the trouble of being displaced "outsiders" in "a crooked and perverse generation" somewhere (cf. Acts 2:40, Philippians 2:14–18; also Psalm 120). And what a stirring challenge and galvanizing encouragement from

---

11 John Calvin, *Institutes of the Christian Religion* IV, 20:4,6.

the Lord to persist against all obstacles—ignorance, indifference, budget cuts—to learn and teach foreign languages.

You cannot practice hospitality unless you are at-home somewhere and recognize the person at hand as a stranger in your home territory; and you cannot receive hospitality unless you realize you are a privileged guest with a host in a strange land. What we call "foreign" language is central to strangerhood.

I hear the Scriptures say this world belongs to God who created it all (Psalm 24:1–2), and the LORD God revealed in Jesus Christ is our permanent at-home (Psalm 90:1–2). Since humankind sinned, however, the LORD has historically called out a people to be a company of saints, sinning saints, to be sure, but a company of Holy Spirited persons who are at home in God's world but at odds with—strangers in—the reigning sinful culture of society. (I've wondered sometimes, if I feel too much at ease in North American society, should I pretend to speak only Dutch or Hungarian, and see what happens, to simulate how God's people are supposed to experience the reigning culture?) The created world belongs to God; God's people are strangers in the reigning sinful culture; therefore—this is biblical logic for you!—knowing what it is like to be strangers in your own God-given home, as "a chosen kind of humanity, a royal priesthood, a holy peoplehood, a folk intended to be God's peculiar family . . . speak out the powerful glories of the One who called you out of darkness into God's wonderful light" (1 Peter 2:9–10, Matthew 5:14–16). Do that by sensitively loving to welcome strangers, to share a meal with a stranger, provide the shelter of bed and lodging, to visit, listen acutely, and talk slowly with the stranger in order to discover and celebrate the differences, which will enrich each other together *coram Deo*. You never know, says Scripture, the stranger may be an angel, a messenger from God (Hebrews 13:1–11), or even, says Matthew 25:31–46 (especially v.35), Christ in disguise!

Having a sure command of your own tongue and adequately speaking the stranger's language is crucial to hospitality that will not remain truncated. Speech, I suggested earlier, is not just a skill to pass on the barest of information. Speech is the language of living persons who have a history, possibly traumatic, and a home, whose body language, etiquettical language, gendered language, ethnic language, a good host needs to pick up as the mulching ground for the peculiar lingual idiom in which the stranger articulates his or her being-there. The spoken language of a stranger, like one's own, is full-orbed, coming from a certain viewpoint—maybe from the other side of the tracks—often tentative, in process, expectantly dialogic or self-absorbed and taciturn. Hospitality begins by making the stranger feel at home, coaxing the stranger to relax into being who one is. And every human is most at home in one's language when you can speak about what you believe in and hold dear. So whoever hosts a stranger well begins by listening rather than by talking oneself. Often listening intently to a stranger talk is a good way, as Robbie Burns would say, "to see ourselves as others see us!"

The writings of Claire Kramsch, and those of Carvill and Smith, give choice professional advice on how to engage students beginning foreign language study in listening to a stranger, and in being a stranger yourself in a foreign land, where you respectfully question the familiar and—learn most from your mistakes!—stay on hermeneutical alert and do not try to understand everything too quickly[12] lest instead of enriching your own world you dictatorially impoverish both. Their detailed advice—which I will not relate here—is good because they know that strangers like friends are mutually so. If strangers, as host or guest, try to absorb what is foreign, they domesticate the other person and ruin the playful glory of hospitality. If strangers remain distantly foreign to one another, afraid to venture beyond one's parochial confines into what seems utterly exotic, then too there may be formal, awkward encounter, but not the mutual trust and stretching openness of genuine hospitality, which enriches both, who remain strange to one another. Sinful power relations homogenize human differences: love allows differences to flourish.

That enigmatic point about *philoxenia* lets me close with an uncompleted comment on the art of translating literature, which I think has the opening to be practicing hospitality in a far-reaching way. And I shall give an oral example of translated poetry.

The doxological fermentation of imaginative translation

Once, trying to rouse an apathetic class from its consistent lethargy, Barbara Carvill handed out an assignment of several German poems with the instruction: "Don't translate everything. Just find one or two lines of German poetry tonight that you really like, and tomorrow tell us why."

I consider Professor Carvill a superb teacher of foreign languages, and this incident, not unlike that of the discouraged, imprisoned Paul who once wrote, "I'd really like to get out of here and be with Christ . . . but for your sakes . . ." (Philippians 1:15–26) I'll stay and prime the pump so you may grow in the joy of what God made possible for us, to talk face to face with a literate stranger: that incident carries the genial mark of trying to lift students out of their "shake-and-bake" attitude toward a foreign language

---

12 *The Gift of the Stranger*, 67–73.

so they might taste well-crafted bread from the best organic cereal grains leavened by love and surprise.

A foreign literary text has a fresh quality about it that can strip away your ethnocentric uniformity and egocentric fussiness if you give yourself up to its voice and charm. A good translator struggles to delve deep into the foreign literary text, learn precisely its grammatical DNA, become infected by its spirit and vision and bloody vitality, probing intuitedly the surplus meaning metaphorically compounding the diction, rhythm, and stresses. The norm for the translator's work is to present the original foreign text transformed, skillfully and imaginatively recapitulated, with its identity intact but now resident in the translator's mother tongue somewhat strangefied, so that the newly minted poetry is verbally translucent, showing through/echoing the original in its very contours.

Only purists think translations are necessarily the act of traitors. George Steiner may be correct that "Ninety percent . . . of all translation since Babel is inadequate and will continue to be so";[13] but God calls us to be "helpmates" to one another, not purists.[14] Yes, a translation of poetry is as delicate as triple bypass heart surgery, and is a matter of interpretation, just as history-keeping and history-telling is a (communal) subjective reading of events. But the translating endeavor, when it is right, is a matter of truly doxological import, and should keep us foreign language teachers thankful for our helpmateful task also when we have to pass through the doldrums. With a good translation the translator's language-world is graced with fresh bread/new wine, and the original strange poetry has not been ignored or lost but is given a new format of significance, its life restored, as it were, with a different place, also in its strangeness, to be at-home. Praise God! Love of learning a foreign language can be blessed with multiples of meaningful fruit.

Although I have not been able to work it out in the timeframe of this keynote lecture, I am interested in experimenting on translating foreign language poetry into English with accompanying commentary

---

13 George Steiner, *After Babel*, 396.

14 In the very chapter Paul addresses the problem of tongue-talk, 1 Corinthians 12:28 includes "helpmates" (*antilempseis*) among those whom God has placed in the body of Christ to serve the other members.

Mary's song in Luke 1:54, which uses the "helpmate" verb (*antelabeto*) in alluding to Isaiah 41:10c (*'azartika*), firms up the connection of this (verbal) ministration of mutually accepting each other, of mutually receiving and giving in return diverse goods—"helpmates"—with the provocative revelation in the Older Testament of persons being a (*'azer*) "helpmate" (as woman; Genesis 2:18–24, as God, Psalm 10:14, 30:10, 46:1, 54:4; as man, Job 31:21–22).

Translators, it strikes me, are specially blessed with the calling to be "helpmates."

by graphic art and music for teaching the *philoxenia* of hosting "foreign literature."[15] In our veritably post-literate, very dominating visual culture, I am wondering too whether foreign language song might not be a way to bring words, camouflaged by melody, into the verbal language classroom, singing the folk songs and possibly good pop songs of the foreign culture.

Would it not help the teaching of certain *Les Fleurs du Mal* (1857, 1861) of Baudelaire, for example, "Hymne à la Beauté" or "Les Petites Vieilles," to have them studied with selected "black" paintings of the later Goya, and hearing Henryk Gòrecki's somber *Symphony no. 3* in the background?

How about showing Luca della Robbia's ravishing, innocent children singing in his *Cantoria* from the cathedral in Florence with the translation of Gabriela Mistrale's "Canción de las Muchachas Muertas" or "Todas Ibamosa Ser Reinas" (from *Tala*, 1938) and be playing Johann Pachelbel's chaste *Canon* in the classroom?

Would not carefully chosen wood sculptures of Ernst Barlach reinforce a succinct translation of Geerten Gossaert's *Experimenten* (1954) while one also recalled the wiry "Passion" song of Heinrich Schütz? And so on. . . .

I end now with a translation of my favorite psalm, 39, since it is Lent, and Psalm 39 also happens to deal with the themes of my remarks: the human tongue as voice of our deepest longings and recrimination; the strangeness of a God-breathed poet daring to call God a moth! and the incredible request to have the LORD practice what God preaches—φιλοξενία.

I probably would accompany the translation of Psalm 39 with a slide of the large memorial sculpture by Glid Nandor at Dachau (1960), which I photographed through my tears, of emaciated human figures stuck in barbed wire, and then add a painting of the crucifixion by Haitian artist William H. Johnson, *Mount Calvary*, where thieves next to

---

15 Distinguishing a faithful translation from an insightful commentary instead of fusing/confusing these two distinct matters was a fertile point the keynote speaker at the 1998 convention of NACFLA, Ray C. van Leeuwen, made. Since I believe even the act of reading a textual passage is already hermeneutic activity, however, interpreting the text, the translation made or chosen to be read (especially a Scriptural passage in the circumstances of a confessing community gathered to worship the Lord) is already always more than a transliteration of an original text.

An excellent resource for the classroom to which Thea Van Til-Rusthoven introduced me for teaching French language and literature in a culturally rich way, accompanied by graphic arts, is the *Collection Henri Mitterand: Litérature, Textes et Documents*, 5 volumes, each dealing with a century, sixteenth through twentieth century (Paris: Édition Nathan, 1986–89).

Christ on the cross are men of color; a comment on Roman-American justice. The music would be Genevan Psalm melody 51, with Claude Goudimel's harmonization of open fifths, followed by the Black spiritual, "Nobody knows the trouble I've seen," and a few good guttural, raspy a cappella solo voice renditions of rural Blues laments heard in the 1920s from the Deep South of this country.

Psalm 39. This is the Word of God:

> Once upon a time I said to myself, "I have to watch my attitude or there will be sinning with my tongue; I have to muzzle my mouth as long as the wicked are nearby—or there will be sinning with my tongue."

> So I stopped my tongue from even moving. I kept still. But, instead of getting better, my vexation grew more agitated. I got hot inside; I started getting burnt up inside; I had to set my tongue loose and talk. So I said, "LORD God! LORD God . . . tell me . . . about the outcome, the end of the affair of me; and tell me how many days I still have left, so that I may realize what a perishable thing I am. Yes, You made the span of my days about as broad as a man's hand, and my life-time is like nothing to you—a little hot air, that's all a man can make himself out to be; he walks along like a shadow, getting steamed-up about nothing: he tries to get everything stacked-up, under control, and doesn't even know who will take it over after him . . .

> At the same time, Lord! now—what did I want? Oh yes, I want . . . my desire! my longing! what I hope for and expect! My request, which goes out to you, Lord, is:

> Save me from all my sins!

> Do not let me be made the laughing stock of the fools around me! —I'll keep quiet. I won't open my mouth. [I know] it is You who afflict me—

> [But—but, Lord—] take away the vexing burden under which You weigh me down, for I have been wasting away under the pressure of your hand. You discipline a man by punishing him for his sins and, like a clothes-closet moth, You eat away at his most coveted prize—yes, a little hot air, that's all a man is . . .

> [But—]
> Hear my prayer, LORD, listen to my cry for help!
> Do not be unmoved because I am crying.

Remember, I am a stranger here, a guest, just a sojourner
like all my fathers and mothers before me—
your guest, Lord.
Don't look at me that way!
Let me become a little more cheerful before I sink away and am no
    more. . . .

Bibliography

Asen, Bernhard A. "From Acceptance to Inclusion: The stranger (*ger*) in Old Testament tradition," in *Christianity and the Stranger: Historical essays*, ed. Francis W. Nichols (Atlanta: Scholars Press, 1995), 16–35.

Bammer, Angelika, "Xenophobia, Xenophilia, and No Place to Rest," in *Encountering the Other(s): Studies in literature, history, and culture*, ed. Gisela Brinker-Gabler (Albany: State University of New York, 1995), 45–62.

Bauman, Zygmunt. *Postmodern Ethics* (Oxford: Blackwell, 1993).

Berry, Wendell. *Standing by Words* (San Francisco: North Point Press, 1983).

Bolinger, Dwight. *Language, the Loaded Weapon: The use and abuse of language today* (London: Longman, 1980).

Breton, Philippe. *L'utopie de la Communication: Le mythe du village plantaire* (Paris: La Découverte, 1997).

Buechner, Frederick. *A Room Called Remember: Uncollected pieces* (San Francisco: Harper, 1984).

Carnochan, W. B. *The Battleground of the Curriculum: Liberal education and American experience* (Stanford: Stanford University Press, 1993).

Carvill, Barbara and David I. Smith. *The Gift of the Stranger: Faith, hospitality, and foreign language learning* (Grand Rapids: Eerdmans, 2000).

Davies, J. G. "Pentecost and glossolalia," *The Journal of Theological Studies N.S.* 3 (1952): 228–231.

Feldmeier, Reinhard. *Die Christen als Fremde: Die Metapher der Fremde in der antiken Welt, in Urchristentum und im 1. Petrusbrief* (Tübingen: Mohr/Siebeck, 1992).

Haughton, Rosemary L. "Hospitality: Home as the integration of privacy and community," in *The Longing for Home*, ed. Leroy S. Rouner (University of Notre Dame Press, 1996), 204–216.

Kimball, Bruce A. *Orators and Philosophers: A history of the idea of liberal education* (New York: Teachers College, Columbia University, 1986).

Kramsch, Claire. *Context and Culture in Language Teaching* (Oxford: Oxford University Press, 1993).

———. "Introduction: Making the Invisible Visible," in Claire Kramsch, ed. *Redefining the Boundaries of Language Study* (Boston: Heinle & Heinle, 1995), ix–xxxiii.

Kramsch, Claire and Linda von Hoene, "The Dialogic Emergence of Difference: Feminist explorations in foreign language learning and teaching," in

Feminism in the Academy, eds. C. Stanton Douma and Abigail Steward (Ann Arbor: University of Michigan Press, 1995), 330–357.

Noblitt, James S. "The Electronic Language Learning Environment," in *Redefining the Boundaries of Language Study*, ed. Claire Kramsch, (Boston: Heinle & Heinle, 1995), 263–292.

Rouner, Leroy S. "Introduction" in *The Longing for Home*, ed. Leroy S. Rouner (University of Notre Dame Press, 1996), 1–13.

Seerveld, Calvin. "Minorities and Xenophilia," in *Proceedings of the Seventh Symposium on the Role of the Arts in a Europe on the Way lo Integration* (Rotterdam: Christian Arts International, 1997), 7:38–43 {see *CP*: 1–16}.

―――. "We are not Pilgrims! We are called to build tent cities in God's world," *Christian Courier* 53:2545 (12 September 1997): 10–11 {see *BSt*: 373–379}.

―――. *Why Should a University Exist?* (with translation also into the Korean language). Pusan: Kosin University Press, 2000. 5–41 {supra pp. 29–58}.

Steiner, George. *After Babel: Aspects of language and translation* (London: Oxford University Press, 1975).

Tucker, Aviezer, "In Search of Home," *Journal of Applied Philosophy* 11:2 (1994): 181–187.

Uehlinger, Christoph. *Weltreich und "eine Rede": Eine neue Deutung der sogenannten Turmbauerzählung (Genesis 11:1–9)* (Göttingen: Vandenhoek & Ruprecht, 1990).

Van Leeuwen, Ray C. "Lex(icon), Lies and Bibliotype: Orality, literacy, and theory in Bible translation," typescript of keynote address to the North American Christian Foreign Language Association, 4 April 1998, at Eastern College, Pennsylvania. pp. 16.

Volf, Miroslav. "A Vision of Embrace: Theological perspective on culture, identity, and conflict," *The Ecumenical Review* 47 (1995): 195–205.

Wierlacher, Alois. "Mit fremden Augen oder: Fremdheit als Ferment" [1983], in *Hermeneutik der Fremde*, eds. Dietrich Krusche and Alois Wierlacher (München: Iudicium, 1990), 51–79.

Atop Buddhist temple Borobudur, Java, Indonesia, while lecturing at the University of Satja Wacana, Salatiga, Indonesia, 1987 (photo by Inès Naudin ten Cate-Seerveld)

JUBILEE ON THE JOB

To my surprise I found out that to celebrate a jubilee can be dangerous as well as exciting, if you take it seriously. For Queen Elizabeth II to reign for 50 years and go on tour in Canada, and for CBC Television to tout up 50 years of programming and hold an anniversary gala to congratulate itself on its accomplishments, doesn't quite have the biblical bite I understand the Christian Labour Association of Canada intends for its jubilee. According to the Bible the year of jubilee is not chronological—"49 and out!"—so much as God-almighty doxological!

Jubilee according to the Bible. Jubilee goes back to the special gift the Lord gave God's people in the wilderness: a day off from foraging for food, a "sabbath" from collecting daily God-provided manna (Exodus 16). Nobody else in the world had a regular day off from work except God's people: so you will know I have free time for you, says God, so you can taste a bit the jubilant fulfillment and peace I knew after creating the myriad kinds of amazing creatures in this world (Exodus 20:8–11; 31:12–17).

Sabbaths led the covenantal Lord God at Mount Sinai to initiate "sabbaticals" for later in the promised land: in the sixth year of your vineyards, olive orchards, and fields of grain I will provide you with an overabundant harvest, said God, so that every seventh year you may rest from your labors and let the poor among your people feast from whatever grows, and after the poor have eaten their fill, let my wild animals enjoy the leftovers (Exodus 23:10–11, Leviticus 25:1–7). Also, every sabbatical, directed God, let debts be canceled, with a smile! and any Hebrew man or woman who because of adversity and bankruptcy had to sell themselves into virtual slavery to you, set them free with enough capital to start a new livelihood (Deuteronomy 15:1–18). This is in the Bible!

Originally posted 1 March 2003, http://www.cardus.ca/comment/article/173/. An earlier version of this essay was presented as the keynote address at the Christian Labour Association of Canada (CLAC) 50th Anniversary Banquet, 26 October 2002, Hamilton, Ontario.

"Jubilee" is a supersabbatical, a sabbatical raised to the seventh power, you might say. God told Moses—Leviticus 25—to trumpet the supersabbatical jubilee after 50 years on Yom Kippur, that special one day in the year when the sins of the nation are to be forgiven! So jubilee means: after experiencing surplus blessings from the forgiving Lord God of the universe for more than a generation, we well-to-do humans who count ourselves to be obedient people of God: in a spirit of festive joy, as a witness to the unbelievers all around about the kind of incredible merciful Lord we serve (Deuteronomy 4:5–8), we rich people happily forgive our debtors completely, and we even restore the land and property we have acquired extra over 50 years to the original trustees of those goods whose descendants are now in need (Leviticus 25:8–12, 18–24).

Leviticus gives specific regulations to preclude people from making tricky business deals to take advantage of this regular 50-year restoration of capital by creditors (Leviticus 25:13–17, 25–55). But the point is that prosperity, real estate property, capital, and wealth are all not something anybody possesses in perpetuity, but are gifts and an inheritance entrusted by the Lord to us humans to work with for a while, for sharing with others. And jubilee is the-once-in-a-lifetime opportunity to actually show the grace of God in operation to those who are not expecting it.

A jubilee is not automatic. Jubilee is not a law somebody has to enforce. Nehemiah, says the Bible, talked and shamed bankers into canceling the impossible debt load of the returned exiles, and into abolishing interest on loans they needed for building up a new Jerusalem (Nehemiah 5:1–13). Isaiah called jubilee "the year of the Lord's favor" (goodwill), the time when imprisoned, addicted people shall be released from their captivities, and the broken-hearted shall be given a healing hope (Isaiah 61:1–4).

That jubilee is precisely what Jesus said, in his hometown sermon, that he was now fulfilling in history (Luke 4:16–21)! And jubilee is indeed what the early post-Pentecost body of Christ, the church of Acts 2 and 4 was practicing (Acts 2:43–47, 4:32–35): not the communist misreading of having spouses and children in common and everybody's holding the same, equal amount of stuff; but everybody among those early Christians had enough sustenance, including the widows, the single mothers, the homeless, and the foreigner Greeks—that's when they began a diaconate (Acts 6:1–7). And among those jubilee-celebrating Christians, says the Bible, with an odd expression, "there was a lot of grace, the joy of surplus grace!" (Acts 4:33)

I believe CLAC knows how to celebrate a biblical jubilee, not only after 49 years, but also on the job. Not in "the sweet hereafter," as revolutionary Marxists once promised. Not after you are given "the golden million-dollar handshake" certain CEOs take to their off-shore Caribbean islands. But jubilee ON the job!

What would that mean concretely? The National Board of CLAC will announce that next October all CLAC secretaries and office support staff will have six months leave with pay, leisurely to upgrade their talents? And the Board, the Council of representatives, trust God enough to believe that the necessary work for six months will still somehow get done?

Is jubilee really possible today?

Status quo of CLAC (third generation)
and the Canadian workplace (leaner and meaner)

Let me first sketch briefly where I think CLAC is historically, and sound a note about what time it is in the workplaces of Canada, before I mention a couple of problems and a few invigorating challenges we face as a Christian labor (trade union) association of Canada that is driven by the faith conviction to have the good news of jubilee grace permeate our very work guts and deeds at large.

A first generation of visionary leaders fresh off the postwar boat from Holland started this labor association on Canadian soil whose constitution (article 2) committed its members to base "its program and activities on the Christian principles of social justice and love as taught in the Bible." This first wave of charismatic leaders (1950–1972) sacrificed a lot of normality and braved wicked opposition from established secular unions, the provincial governments, and even churchmen. But God blessed CLAC originators with the 1963 McRuer Supreme Court of Ontario decision that set the Ontario Labor Relations Board straight on the nondiscriminatory legitimacy of a trade union simply wanting to be biblically just, and gave CLAC a foothold throughout Canada.

A second generation of CLAC leaders, who came up through the ranks, street savvy, has given a lifetime to building up a trade union of committed Christians that witnesses to integrity, compassionate fairness, and reliable work in the public arena of labor relations (1972–2000). The second generation has been busy to articulate and organizationally embody a confessional alternative to the tyrannical, closed-shop monopolistic way of doing commerce in North America. And God has blessed the institutional development of this biblical visionary labor movement, despite continual opposition, with good fruit.

And now a third generation (2000 AD) is poised to assume responsibilities for a going concern whose membership, numbering 27,000, is multi-faith but decide for a Christian union, and whose leadership comes from a variety of Christian faith traditions—including Mennonite, Pentecostal, Baptist—who have been stirred by the biblical Reformational dynamic to submit all creaturely activity to the reconciling Rule of Jesus Christ (Psalm 24:1–2, 2 Corinthians 5:17–19), and who rejoice in the fact that communion of the saints is not just a Sunday phenomenon.

This third generation of CLAC leaders faces the incredibly difficult task that comes with the complexities of organized size and age: how to differentiate specialist representatives with delegated authority but keep everyone integrated for communal decisions by the trusting élan of the original committed vision to wash each other's feet and to love the neighbors who wish to walk humbly with God (Mark 14:1–11, Micah 6:8, 1 Peter 4:7–11).

Once upon a time generations ago workers minded more the rhythms of day and night and seasons of the year: when the sun finally went down, laborers stopped for a meal and took time to sleep; winters were for repairing things and mending nets. But artificial light bulbs, factories manned by machines tended by women and children, unsafe mines, unsanitary hovels jammed with men who were treated like cogs in a never-stopping (unless sabotaged) moving line of trays spewing out products: such urban industrialization murdered the meaning of human work.

Antonides, Griffioen, Groenewold, and Vanderkloet in CLAC publications have documented how this mechanicalist curse on employment spurred on the formation of labor unions: see Edward Vanderkloet, "Why Work Anyway?" and Sander Griffioen, "The Future of Labor," in *Labour of Love: Essays on Work* (1980); Harry Antonides, *Renewal in the Workplace: A Critical Look at Collective Bargaining* (1982); Harry Groenewold, "The Church and Organized Labor in Canada: The Early Years," and Harry Antonides, "Canadian Trade Unionism on Trial," in *Us and Them: Building a Just Workplace Community* (1999).

People needed to protect themselves from exploitation by wealthy mercenaries whose god was Mammon, MORE MONEY, at the expense of one's neighbors. The benign $5-a-day evil of Henry Ford's famed assembly line which stripped workers of most initiative, simplified, economized, standardized, and monotonized your soul: I know an auto worker years ago who tried, unsuccessfully, to counteract the tedium by humming syncopated Genevan psalm tunes to himself as his hands moved tirelessly with the relentless line.

The assembly line and much clerical work had come under the spell of the American Frederick Taylor's (1856–1915) "scientific" stop-watch controlling, planning design—"Time is Money," had said Benjamin Franklin. Even Lenin was promoting this American time-clock efficiency in Pravda in 1918! And this ubiquitous plague of mechanical time and hot-house hurry to produce cars, armaments, or plastic bottles still brutalizes workers today, not only in Western sweatshops planted in Eastern low-cost-labor countries, but also in Canada, where collective bargaining often focuses down on higher pay for shorter work hours.

Still worse, I think, is the hardening-of-the-heart-arteries shift taking place in labor affairs precisely as the third generation of CLAC leaders comes onto the scene: computer-chip technology is fundamentally altering much human work and most industrial employment in a way that isolates workers with the illusion of increased autonomy and also has a neutronic fall-out that is intrinsically cruel to unskilled persons. There is a sea change from manual labor-intensive work to the so-called "service economy," where it takes skilled information-training on which buttons to push when on the flight panel of the airplane, in the cabin which slides the huge construction cranes over half-built high-rise buildings in our cities, or to change the angle of your liquid-filled bladder showing up on the TV monitor, to get a better picture of your enlarged prostate gland. A personal computer converts personal you into a technician, and technicians are valued strictly as means of production rather than as able-bodied humans who have a rich life when they are not nerved to be producing results on their contracted computerized work.

I am not Jacques Ellul or a Luddite castigating technics that lessens drudgery. But I am noting that self-serve gas stations, bank machines, and "Help Wanted only if you have computer skills" telltale a deep change toward gainful employment that is impacting labor unions and outmoding old-fashioned settlements with employers. Companies geared to cutthroat, competitive growth in the global marketplace who believe they must economize or die will automate what they can, hire part-timers as much as possible—more courier drivers are needed during morning and evening pickup/delivery rush hours, but not a whole eight-hour day; Starbucks pays more workers during busy hours and fewer during slow times—business flexibility. Or companies will engage manpower temporary agencies to avoid problems of worker benefits, tenure, and grievance procedures in firing "for just cause."

Meanwhile, people serve at McDonalds, Tim Horton's Drive-Thru, as No Frills stock boys and checkout cashiers, Mall security guards, or telemarketers at minimum wages maybe good for after-school, teenager first job experience, but hardly adequate for feeding a family. Our society today is leaner and meaner, I dare say, than when CLAC began in 1952 to bring God's grace to bear on the workplace in Canada. How can there be jubilee when there is so little natural rhythm and time to mature in our labors today, and so much internetworked frenzy of constantly changing helter-skelter rush to move it, do it, file it, or grin and bear it?

As I did research to make these jubilee remarks, I interviewed Harry Antonides, Gerald Vandezande, Gideon Strauss, and five stalwart representatives from the Grimsby CLAC office, read quite a number of reports, official minutes, submissions, and materials all the way up to the CLAC action plan adopted in September 2002. When I see the elderly faces of General Worker Local members who have supported this Christian labor association through thick and thin for more than a generation—some were active here well before I spoke "Christian Workers, Unite!" 38 years ago—and when I also see the fresh young blood eager to carry on the

Delivering the early speech "Christian Workers, Unite!" at the National Convention of the Christian Labour Association of Canada in Toronto, 1964

task, I can't help but be overcome by a sense of sweet thankfulness to have been historically touched by this improbable fellowship, warts and all, God has raised up on the face of the earth.

And I want to testify to the old-timers—Jim Joosse and Hank Kuntz, original and early National Board presidents, but to all those who have prayed for and sent in money to CLAC—the old-timers who know Psalm 128, which promises the coveted blessing of seeing not only your children but even your grandchildren living out of faith in the LORD (Psalm 128:6): so far as I can tell, CLAC third generation—the grandchildren of the founding fathers, so to speak—is preparing for the rigors of organizing the workplace in Canada so that the biblical witness to Jesus Christ's lordship over labor and commerce be obeyed. You veterans and founders may read Psalm 128 and exclaim: the LORD God is indeed faithful! (If I were younger I almost think I might apply for a CLAC job.)

Problems for CLAC:
(1) secularization, (2) dichotomization and fundamentalization
A problem that will creep up like fog on cat feet to test CLAC faithfulness in the coming generation is this: being tempted to let go of being a *skandalon*, a stumbling block following Christ, on the organized labor scene in Canada. Not that anyone would knowingly secularize and reduce the collective bargaining process to be simply lining up and balancing out company profits, adequate wages, calculating the rate of inflation—just a straightforward matter of crunching numbers. But if you have a $6,000,000 budget as a trade union, there will be subtle pressures to conduct business as usual, to expedite solutions for specific localities within the existing parameters so that our members, too, can be part of the contented, if a little disgruntled now and then, majority of people in the land. A human organization becomes complacent when it no longer takes time to view the big picture, to question the status quo, but settles for getting the best deal currently available.

That our normal culture is abnormal to God needs to percolate in our labor organizing consciousness. Western civilization has exchanged the Constantine birthright of the Sunday for a mess of potage called "a weekend," which has a very savory taste. And job satisfaction for me is much more important than whether the collective agreement is good for my Mexican neighbor, whom I have never seen! Does one ever wince when you walk into a dollar store, and faintly remember Psalm 8 that says we humans are made almost like gods! crowned with glory! outfitted to rule over the works of God's hands, awash in trinkets? If your job is structured along the line of getting commissions on sales of big-ticket items, say, at Future Shop, so jubilee on the job is practically precluded, should we not at least promote vacations of escape off the job? Who does not admire the entrepreneurial mentality of Robinson Crusoe, so long as you yourself do not end up as the "Friday" man who does the dirty work? And is our credit economy not a good normal practice? If you use a credit card you are rich! (Anyone with debts is rich, living off the resources of someone else.) But riches, according to the Bible, are a most precarious blessing unless you wisely give them away (Deuteronomy 8:17–20, 1 Timothy 6:17–19, James 4:13–5:6). . . .

Going deeper: all of us bodily inhabit a market economy. From a Christian viewpoint, a market can be the public place where providers of resources bring goods that merchants stewardly supply for needs of other people who thriftily recompense the goods and services; and the exchanges happen in a spirit of good measure, reliability, and caring liberality (Deuteronomy 25:13–16, 2 Corinthians 9:6–15). The laissez-faire market economy which dominates corporate world commerce and our daily lives today, however, breathes, as I experience it, an unbridled spirit of self-interest, often aimed at profit from luxuries customers can be induced to buy in the expectation of becoming happier. And the laissez-faire economic system in force worldwide cannot be trusted to do justice for the weak, because it is geared to the rights of the stronger, has a built-in ethic of "the fittest survive." This market system is free in Canada to build low-cost housing the poor could afford, as Habitat for Humanity does, but is apparently not willing and able to do it: the bottom line of profitability a business enterprise rightly needs is wrenched out of context and blown up to be the top, guiding line for commercial ventures, and is frequently driven by the principality of Growth, greed for MORE.

If our society is largely in the grip of MONEY, quietly fuelled by an established laissez-faire market economy system, concealing aggression and plumping for Success, and this setup is taken to be normal by management and labor and consumers, then the workplace will be disfigured into a bloody marketplace where "pure economics" dictates what comes and goes, and people—whether saleswomen, repair mechanics, or CEOs—come to function as cost factors, disposable merchandise, overworked "slaves" judged only on whether their work performance pays its way. Because a Pragmatistic Materialism is the very economic air we all breathe, it would be easy for CLAC to let itself be secularized and run with the madding crowd, give in to the tendency to put our own trade union members' interests first. However, if God remains first in our labor organizing consciousness, instead of being slipped off to the margins, and if CLAC prickles with awareness of the interconnected wholeness of human lives, then CLAC leadership will not "wobble" its declared rationale for existence of redirecting society to establish just-doing and shalom in the sphere of labor and industry, so help you God, and will never settle for the sop of getting a couple extra bucks into a paycheck.

Steffe Bak writes: "I am convinced that the Christian trade union movement can and must fill a crucial role in this whole process. It is ours to struggle with the spirit of the times, in the hope and certainty that it can be defeated. The Christian trade union movement must not in the first place keep itself busy with the question whether one more ounce of liverwurst is needed. Rather, it is about the turning-around of society."[1]

There is one other problem I want just to mention briefly, before I give content to the norm of expecting jubilee on the job. Beside the virus of secularization, a Christian organization that has outlived its first generations will likely face the insidious termites of dichotomization and fundamentalization. This is what I mean:

Once it becomes evident that forming a distinctively "Christian" labor union does not automatically solve all the misery, and the protean demonic principality of greedy Power, it seems, can worm itself also into Christians and "good people," and the millennium is not about to happen next month, then a later generation who inherited the glorious vision of revamping the crooked labor scene in Canada may dispiritedly lose their nerve of faith and decide, temporarily, to go for what you as an organization can manage: premium, professional nuts and bolts labor bargaining and grievance settlements on the shop floor, and strong "Christian talk" laced with Bible verses at conferences and solemn assemblies. Then you can also grow the union in numbers, because workers looking for a friendly, uncorrupted defender of their labor rights will be—and are!—attracted to CLAC even if they don't exactly believe the biblical inspiration of our praxis. This is a persistent historical difficulty when leadership of any organization changes. And if you go into the split maintenance mode of dichotomize (retrench to skills) plus fundamentalize (the old rhetoric), you tend to stagnate as an organization and lose your internal historical identity.

The current overlapping generations of CLAC leadership have wisely given funded priority to internal education, for example, to corral the 50+ Canada-wide CLAC representatives to mull over books together, like

---

1 Translated from "Vechten voor een werkelijke samenleving," in *Meer dan Ooit: Inspiratie, motivatie, presentatie, 100 Jaar Jong CNV*, 121.

Paul Marshall's *Heaven Is Not My Home* (1998) and Chuck Colson's *How Now Shall We Live?* (1999), so the representatives can mature and keep fresh the committed vision that has consistently animated the association as a Bible-oriented movement which knows that economics is embedded in more than economics, and concerns like spouses and children, neighborhoods and transportation, schools, government regulations and worship, patterns of leisure, all impinge on the workplace and deserve to be honored.

There is also Ed Bosveld's *Toolbox #1* training course for CLAC stewards, which introduces in no-nonsense prose whoever is elected to the post of steward in a collective agreement somewhere what sets CLAC stewards apart from other unions, the non-adversarial but non-apologetic stance with management in arbitrating conditions for the workplace that allow a laborer to exercise his or her vocation in one's occupation.

Precision on terminology here is good. "Our vocation is not in the first place to do a particular task, but to be Christian in all our relationships in God's creation."[2] "Strictly speaking, what we choose are occupations, where our vocations can be fulfilled."[3]

This fine *Toolbox*, which quotes cartoons instead of proof texts, fumigates the termite pests of sanctimonious accommodation, because the text matter of factly carries a congenial spirit not of "a company union," but of a Christian union that intends to live up to a bill of responsibilities as well as a bill of rights. This is worth celebrating!

But CLAC is not a church! That matter is critical to its genius, and is a point both the mighty secular Canadian Labour Congress and many Bible-confessing church communions do not understand because they have churchified the Christian faith. CLAC representatives are not lay evangelists. CLAC stewards are not chaplains. *Beds Are Not Enough* is not a tract, but is a recommendation for action to the Ontario government by a CLAC taskforce on "the hidden crisis in Ontario's long-term care facilities." Just because you translate biblical truths like "men and women do not live by bread alone" (Deuteronomy 8:1–10, Luke 4:1–4) into a Christian policy for health care workers that "beds are not enough" does not make you a worker priest: you are a priestly worker! It is a stunted, unbiblical conception to think that if you do just deeds which follow Christ's injunctions, then suddenly you are clergy or become "churchy." The historic Heidelberg Catechism (1563) answers question #32 "Why are you called a Christian?" without mentioning church: "I am called a

---

2   Paul Marshall, in *Labor of Love* (1980), 16.

3   Lee Hardy, *The Fabric of this World* (1990), 81.

Christian because by faith I am a member of Christ and so I share in his anointing. I am anointed to confess his name, to present myself to him as a living sacrifice of thanks, to strive with a good conscience against sin and the devil in this life, and afterward to reign with Christ over all creation for all eternity."

We need clergy—ministers, pastors, bishops—to pray from their pulpits that "the kingdom vision of Christ's Rule on earth" move more lay people to become General Worker Local members of CLAC, to swell the ranks of those who would support just-doing in the workplace in non-theological language and without the sanctity of a cowl, because it is precisely Christ-following obedience in daily life the Canadian populace, whatever its make-up, is aching to experience: jubilee on the job.

Prompting jubilee on the job

Jubilee according to the Bible, you remember, is not like winning the lottery: you have been a long-distance operator at Bell Canada for 13 years and suddenly you have $5,000,000; so you throw a blow-out of a party. Jubilee according to the Bible is also not something you achieve: you can't earn it, order it and the contentment comes. The special quality of a biblical sabbatical and jubilee is that it is a gift, a Godsend, and has the surprising character of a fulfillment you hardly knew you were anticipating but now that it has come you bask in this experience of relief, of being somehow restored, set free, forgiven, at peace with the living God present, and it's all right now.

If, as the biblical book of Ecclesiastes says, only God can give jubilee on the job (Ecclesiastes 3:12–13, 5:18–20, 8:15), how do we as CLAC prompt such a blessing?

Jeremiah 29:7 gives a clue. It is instructions God has Jeremiah write in a letter to God's people who were exiled in heathen Babylon but expecting their displaced woes to blow over fairly soon so they could get back home. God's startling message is: Work hard for the shalom of the city to which I have banned you people; pray fervently to the LORD God on behalf of Babylon's inhabitants, because shalom for you is inextricably tied in with the shalom of the city [where you find yourselves].

That Word of God means for us in our Babylon cities of Toronto, Hamilton, Montreal, Vancouver, or wherever, that with our own house in order as an organization—our biblical principles operational rather than as clichés—our orientation must be to propagate and practice our saintly wisdom for the good of Babylon! the inhabitants of the Babylon of Revelation 18 headed for destruction too. That is the way for God's people to experience jubilee on the job, crazy as it may sound (Matthew 7:12).

I'll mention just two tough matters: *(1) love your enemies.* God asks Christian workers to love your enemies (Matthew 5:43–48), whether it be an authoritarian Christian employer, an AFL-CIO union trying illegally to prohibit CLAC plumbers from working on sites in the Town of Vaughan (1980s), or the IMF.

Yes, the International Monetary Fund has become an enemy of working people throughout the world, I dare say. Although it was originally formed (Breton Woods, 1944) to tide over mortgaged nations by supplying World Bank capital (formed 1947, Washington, D.C.), the IMF has drastically overreached its limits, imposed megaprojects on countries, and demanded cheap exports of natural resources as collateral for debt, so that the indebted governments have no capital to spend on in-land schools and hospitals. A result is that now, arm-twisted by the IMF to contract their economies to the vagaries of unregulated market forces on interest rates set by financial speculators with their "hot money," many countries in the world, not even counting the attendant corruption of officials, are hopelessly mired in terrible destitution.

On a lesser scale perhaps, but still acting as an enemy, is any CLC union that thinks its monopoly over employment in a special craft in Canada and its monopoly on subcontracting work at a site in Canada is fine in a democracy, because monopoly works for majority-plus-one-vote them, even if it squeezes out the livelihood of others who don't play by the same hard-ball rules. And even confessing Christian employers who believe they know best what is good for the workers or teachers they hire—"Why do you need a raise or health insurance? This is the Lord's work we are doing!"—can be enemy-like, antithetical to the compassionate way God wants things done.

When Jesus Christ told the crowds "Love your enemies," it was so radical a commandment that maybe the Christ had a twinkle in his eye when he said it and meant it. To "love your enemies," biblically speaking, does not mean you lie down and let the enemies of God's way walk over your back. You love your enemies, as a trade union too, by giving good food and drink, showing hospitality to the enemy, overcoming the evil by doing good, says the Bible (Proverbs 25:21–22, Romans 12:9–21).

For example, when Bob Goudzwaard providentially had access to a World Bank executive and by extended conversations could patiently explain how "free trade" combined with "high tariffs" against agricultural products of poor countries was debilitating "aid," until the director

Bob Goudzwaard with Wynne and Gerald Vandezande, in
Seerveld home, Toronto, 2010

finally admitted that maybe World Bank policies were part of the problem rather than part of the solution, the angels in heaven could take a half hour sabbatical; and CLAC cleaners at Holland Christian Homes in Brampton, Ontario, if they were told about it, and knew that somebody was speaking up for the wretched of the earth on matters that affected their shrinking pension plan too, because even the Canadian government cannot independently set interest rates since workers and managers everywhere are caught up in a supra-multi-national world Juggernaut where good and evil battle furiously not only for your purse but for our very lives: if ordinary workers could catch a glimpse of what we little people are globally embroiled in, they could have a taste of jubilee as they continue to mop the floors.

Prime Minister Jean Chretien's brief speech to the United Nations General Assembly (New York, 16 September 2002) on the occasion of plenary debate on "New Partnership for Africa's Development" (NE-PAD) included this point: "Agricultural subsidies in rich nations remain a fundamental obstacle to African development. . . . These huge supports put a strain on treasuries, depress prices and effectively shut out producers from developing countries. Canada calls on developed nations to make the elimination of such subsidies a top priority."

To take the time to know and understand an antagonist is an act of love which God might use somehow, because such love takes seriously that behind the raucous rhetoric and often brutal tactical moves may lie a leader with a secular social conscience in thrall to an ideology that runs away with his humanity. CLAC's battle is not against flesh and blood, but against the principalities of this world which waste human flesh and blood! (Ephesians 6:10–12).

And when CLAC representatives must try to explain to paternalistic Christian employers who feel their God-given authority is wrongfully challenged when a co-determinative policy is put forward as the mature way for the redeemed to act, it may be, as Proverbs puts it, like "raking together live coals of fire on their heads" (Proverbs 25:22). But even in occasional failure, if as a Christian labor association you have loved the enemies by speaking the truth for employed workers to be done restorative justice in God's world (Ephesians 4:15–16), you may count on receiving a hint of the Lord's "Well done, faithful rep, for your unrewarded efforts; receive my quiet anointing of grace for continuing on the job of eliciting jubilee" (Matthew 25:14–30).

(2) *Witness to the government to do what is just.* In directing followers of Christ to pursue the shalom of the secular city, beside learning to love one's enemies, God asks a Christian labor association to call the governing state to administer the commonweal for working citizens, and especially for the poor, those women, children, and men who cannot manage to bring together food and shelter, clothing, and employment that affords true self respect in which they can exercise their God-created responsibilities.

Most people intuitively recognize that a church, synagogue, Muslim, and Sikh fellowship is by nature a different kind of institution than the nation state, and have different limited tasks. People also usually realize that a business enterprise with labor and management components is a different kind of institution than a government with legislative, judicial, and executive officials elected with power to enforce laws. The trouble comes in how to define the tasks of the different institutions and to decide how they are respectively interrelated.

One reason our society at large is seething with tensions and absence of peace is that the specific tasks of various institutions are ill determined, confused, wrongly subjugated one to the other, or are thought to be not interrelated. It is historically incorrect to mistake Abraham Kuyper's concept of "sphere sovereignty" for the Conservatist claim that church and state and business and school are "separated" and should have nothing to do with one another, as if the state should not audit the charity accounts of the church, and bishops have no place in calling upon the government to take part in housing the homeless.

Kuyper's correlative notion of "sphere universality" entails that each distinctive institution properly serves every other societal institution with its particular task, but limits its service from intruding upon the other institution's zone of authority and competence. So the state should set standards of literacy for schools, but schools decide curricularly how to generate literacy citizens need to have; businesses may request workers wear clothing fitting for a certain job, but cross the line if they demand you support a certain political party.

It is all much more complicated, but one point I want to make is that the God-given task of a governing state, as I understand it, is to do public corrective and enabling justice for everyone regardless of your faith fellowship and whether you have the money to pay for a lawyer. And when the federal, provincial, or municipal government makes a bad law, for example, a bad labor law, then faith fellowships need to pray out loud about it, and a labor union has to go to court to reform and get the law rewritten.

The Nova Scotia Court of Appeals recently upheld (May 2002) the Supreme Court of Nova Scotia which upheld the Nova Scotia La- bor Relations Board interpretation of the provincial statute concerning the construction industry in that province which declares that only the "fourteen international skilled trade or craft unions all with headquarters in Washington, D.C." have jurisdiction in the Nova Scotia "construc- tion industry"; so there is "no room for CLAC," since technically CLAC Local 154 is by definition of the act not a "trade union" in Nova Scotia construction because it is not one of the fourteen.[4]

Talk about totalitarian closed shop exclusion of fiber optic cable laborers of a bona fide Canadian trade union everywhere else in Canada! This signal injustice done by the Nova Scotia Labor Relations Board and the original provincial legislation needs to be overturned, just as Chief Justice J. C. McRuer overturned the Ontario Labour Relations Board decision denying CLAC accreditation within Ontario in 1963.

Can you imagine the jubilee excitement ahead in fighting this ardu- ous, very expensive battle for the justice of allowing in Canada, including Nova Scotia, a plurality of labor unions—no monopoly headquartered in Washington, D.C.—so that deeply different, faith-different conceptions and practices toward work may be exercised in the Canadian workplace! Citizens for Public Justice, Institute for Christian Studies, Christian Cou- rier, Christian Farmers Federation, Christian Business Federation, Chris-

---

4   Ruling N.S.J. No. 259, 2000 NSCA 73, Docket: CA 177004, by Nova Scotia Court of Appeal, Halifax, Nova Scotia, on Case: Construction and Allied Union (CLAC) Local 154 v. Nova Scotia.

tian colleges, churches, and other faith groupings concerned about just-doing should be rallied—each in their particular universes of discourse—to stand up for this fundamental freedom of association and responsible labor to work, to face not the fist of high-priced, coerced silence, but to be given the peace of sharing good work with skilled neighbors.

Jubilee will attend this difficult endeavor because the struggle is not for CLAC "to get its rights," but for CLAC to protect and do justice for the weak who simply are prepared to be worthy of their hire (Philippians 2:4, Colossians 3:23–24). This goes to the core of what makes CLAC tick: we do not run "hiring halls" which make workers beholden to the controlling union rather than to the employer, but CLAC will help unemployed meet prospective hiring employers; CLAC puts "binding arbitration" for unresolved disputes before a strike threat, since you don't go to war to make a genuine peace; and CLAC wants room for a more European approach to labor relations where labor leaders, management CEOs, and relevant government officials sit down together to plan an industry-wide sector for the next five years, which allows a Christian labor union and a socialist labor union to work side by side on the same job, rather than have to buy into the American power play of winner-take-all.

Standard rules in Canada (derived from AFL-CIO practices in the United States) allow only one union per trade to represent workers at a given enterprise, and often include control of subcontracting work. Jurisdictional disputes occur as to which craft union controls which phase of the work; for example, does the plumbers' union or the pipe-fitters' union lay the connections from the apartment building to the main outside line?

CLAC organizes all workers in a given workplace instead of only electricians or only welders or only carpenters. Such "wall-to-wall" organization of the work force in a given enterprise avoids jurisdictional arguments, and assures the employer of no work-stoppage because of dispute with one single trade.

In Europe normally the labor unions with different faith orientations show a more conciliatory (still competitive) attitude toward one another because they form a united labor front in arriving at a three-way joint agreement with representatives of management and the government for a large industrial sector. Strikes are less frequent in Europe because of this three-way, planned periodic arrangement.

The Canadian Auto Workers (CAW) in October 2000 challenged the CLC rule that workers are locked into one certain trade union permanently, and declared that workers should be able to leave one union and join another! The CAW is now presently angling for a sort of "wall-to-wall" organizing setup in Nova Scotia that would have their auto workers union include construction workers—precisely where CLAC has been excluded!

It is so that you cannot legislate "morality"; but you can make what is wrong legal. And that is certainly an occasion when Caesar needs to be given what belongs to Caesar (Matthew 22:15–22)! Christ did not mean: pay your taxes on time and keep your mouth shut. The Bible means: go after the unjust judges with the persistence of the wronged widow in the parable, and ask for vindication to work freely in this country; and the Lord shall hear that passionate request (Luke 18:1–8).

I know CLAC cannot singlehandedly effect just-doing over-all in Canada. But the Lord has done wonderful things in 50 short years with you men and women. I know too there is difference of opinion among us on the regulating role the state should take toward a country's economic life, especially now when international corporate financial transactions and fluctuating prices of oil and gasoline frequently override national competencies to control them. I personally think provincial governments abdicate their office of standing on guard for citizens when they fail to keep public utilities, public transit and transportation, a public postal system: fail to keep them public not-for-profit services (not-for-loss either), but "privatize" such matters and convert them into "for-profit" enterprises—which willy-nilly turns us citizens who need these essential services into customers, who then vote them out of office after the bills go up, and the assets are stripped from the commonweal. Meanwhile, the unemployed citizens sit in the cold without gas heat, they walk, and don't write letters. . . .

Serving the poor

I close with a note about the poor I mentioned.

CLAC is a labor union, not a political party. Every one of us as citizens still has to face the returning Lord at Judgment Day on whether we heard the cries of the poor for public justice. As CLAC we especially need to hear the cries of the poor in Babylon for bread, for employment. It is a marvelous opening to participate in jubilee on the job.

I don't mean only simple acts of redemptive generous kindness like a masseuse tithing time to massage indigent paraplegics so their cramped, knotted muscled bodies can relax momentarily and pulsate wholesomely; like a designer of cafeteria kitchens who takes extra time to plan the crucial sequential flow from refrigerators to ovens to serving bins to basins, to save steps and facilitate flawless rhythm for the servers; like an artist who makes a TV ad for Easter Seals with unsentimental imaginativity, asking support for those "who read with their fingers"; like an apprentice chaplain in a nursing home who softly plays an ancient German hymn tune on a native wood flute for an old woman who has maintained a cata-tonic silence for months, and her lips suddenly break into a thin smile as she begins to hum along: there can be jubilee, the mysterious presence of God's grace, showing up on all kinds of jobs when God's people give away peace to the neighbor.

I don't take the politicized line that Christ prioritizes the poor for special treatment, but I do hear the Bible say the poor represent Christ! (Matthew 25:31–46) And poverty in Babylon (or Laodicea) is not just about money, but is a matter of the least important, the little ones in society being incapacitated, stymied, ignored, or robbed from acting humanly. We need to find ways to employ the unemployed, the un-deremployed, or at least give them hope of being extricated from the historical pit where they are in Canadian cities and around the world. Labor unions, governments, churches, schools, media: all need to lend a hand—there is work to be done.

So I am proud CLAC is active in the World Confederation of La-bour, speaking up to the IMF about social justice in foreign places, and assisting independent trade unions struggling for a place to provide nor-mative work in Eastern Europe, South and Latin America, and elsewhere in the Babylons of today. I am excited that CLAC has brokered Northern Hire Agreements at the Ekati mine and throughout sites in the North-west Territories which includes a sizeable Metis, Inuit, and aboriginal membership, since until some kind of remedial justice and partnering work goes on between us kabluna and aboriginal Canadians there will be stigmata of curse upon the land.

I thank God that CLAC has had the sensitivity and strength for or-ganizing nurses and health care workers, those who are often considered less important, let's say, than surgeons; and I hope you go out of your way to unite those neglected workers who really need protection, like security guards, part-time assistants, shift workers. I deeply respect the effort CLAC stewards and representatives make on an on-going basis for the basics of safety, health, environment protection, computer literacy at CLAC Training Centres in Edmonton, Chatham, and elsewhere, and in the slow, step-by-step forming of new workers strange to the mind of Christ as together you formulate workplace agreements where what is "Christian" may seem nebulous to those who are "poor," especially if they make $30 an hour in heavy construction. But the "Christian" spirit is proved in the pudding of coming through for God's presence in these daily basics.

CLAC Representative Andrew Regnerus told me of trying to convince a worker to put the prospective raise in the agreement package into the laborer's pension plan rather than into his take-home paycheck.

"But the extra money means a case of beer a month I wouldn't have!"

"Money in your pension plan does not figure into the 1.4 percent of gross pay that goes to union dues. Believe me, it's better for you to put the raise into the pension plan so you will be able to have a can of beer when you no longer can work."

"You're telling me to do something which is less good for you Christian representatives?" Quizzical. "Okay."

To me that is Christian labor organizing in the rough—a genuine touch of educational jubilee on the job.

God alone knows what is in store for CLAC. Tonight is a veritable taste of jubilee, surplus grace.

If the Bible in your constitution remains a live, Spirit-filling directive for you third generation of labor leaders, and you work heartily for the shalom of the inhabitants of Babylon as obedient servants of the Lord, despite whatever persecution and tears come your way, nothing will be able to separate your generation and those who follow you from the love of God in Christ Jesus our Lord, who shall continue to bless you with a peace that surpasses figuring it out (John 14:27, Ephesians 3:14–19): jubilee on the job (Romans 8:14–17, 1 Corinthians 15:58).

CONCLUDING THESES ON TEACHING PHILOSOPHY IN THE NORTH AMERICAN UNDERGRADUATE COLLEGE

I am grateful to be here at Trinity, and thankful to those who had the vision to set up this intercollege symposium and make it possible. Just to have all of us present in one room talking to one another about our lifework and how to be more faithful is a great gift. Maarten Vrieze would be glad. It is a particular delight for me to hear what some of us might almost call the "younger generation" vigorously grapple anew with the key problems.

I was asked to focus, as best I could, on key issues that have surfaced in this symposium that deserve further attention if philosophy is to do justice to whatever its calling be in the Reformed undergraduate college. Are there actions that could be taken by us professors of philosophy that would be a fruitful faith response to what we have discussed?

I shall present a few clusters of theses with commentary that could perhaps orient our closing discussion.

Thesis 1. Insofar as philosophy has been refined to a specialized discipline that is run like a course in logic or semiotics, void of historically deep context, philosophy has forfeited its rightful task to be a curricular integrator.

To make the required philosophy course(s) a diverse selection of philosophic texts also serves students poorly as orientation since such a disjointed exposure in the initial course normally disperses or clutters rather than orders their beginning thinking.

In my lifetime I have seen the rise and fall of lingual analytic phi-

---

This piece was first published in *Philosophy in the Reformed Undergraduate Curriculum*, eds. John Roose and George Pierson (Palos Heights: Trinity Christian College, 1990), 79–89.

losophy.[1] But like the modern New York school of painting of the sixties, now being passed by in artwork, is still in the musea, just as no museum is going to deflate its prized holdings, analytical philosophy has the tenured power of position. As a philosophical aesthetician, and as a European trained person, I find so many articles in philosophy journals to be narrow-minded and boring, the trade talk of specialists; despite cute asides to affect real life contact, they seem to me to be utterly and solely in-house. Hence the chagrin of such specialists when somebody like Allen Bloom talks over their heads to the populace. This is the error of professionalistic specialism that professors of philosophy may have committed curricularly. And the wages of such error is rightly curricular death, a kind of marginalized limbo.

You cannot teach wisdom, I believe, but wisdom is contagious; you can catch it. Philosophy has no claim to be at the core of college study if it is not working at a discipline-integrative or key life-problem project of interrelational thinking, priming the *habitus* of theoretical wisdom, as my colleague Bill Rowe put it.

Thesis 2. Philosophy (in tandem with historiography) by nature is expected to deal in the interrelated meaning of things and events.

Philosophical activity deserves, despite this proper encyclopedic aperture, to be analytically honed and show systematic rigor in its reflective judgments, making careful distinctions and identifying precise relationships.

A philosophy will have definite contours, but in its character as a thoughtful categorial framing of thinking, philosophy is more a network of questions than a set of specific answers.[2]

In philosophy classes you ask "why?" questions. You do fundamental thinking about fundamental matters. Philosophy is perhaps the inheritor of *studium generale*, in a day of differentiated knowledge.

Christians should not remain "viewy." Philosophy is thought that stays thoughtful, remains thought provoking, but philosophy is not thereby "vague." Christian philosophers should use the current awakening to the significance of the "Christian worldview"—Ted Plantinga is

---

1 Cf. "Many, perhaps most, analytic philosophers have abandoned the ideals of 'ordinary language philosophy' (and rightly so, in my judgment) and resumed the traditional activity of theory-construction." Marilyn McCord Adams, 'Problems of Evil: More Advice to Christian Philosophers,' *Faith and Philosophy* 5:2 (1988): 128.

2 Cf. Susanne K. Langer, *Philosophy in a New Key* (New York: Mentor Paperback, 1942), 2. "In our questions lie our principles of analysis, and our answers may express whatever those principles are able to yield."

correct that "worldview" is a pre-philosophical orientation—to follow through now with a systematic Christian *philosophy*.

Thesis 3. Special disciplines of study like educational theory, literary criticism, art history, psychology, political science, physics, biology, and other fields of study at college are couched in a philosophy and assume a history.

Therefore, I think it is imperative at a Christian college, professing the Scripturally-led faith-integration of its teaching the rainbow of studies it offers, to have a Christian philosophy communally operative. Otherwise, the college courts becoming a hypocritical Babel of thought and talk.

As Bill Rowe's third sense of "foundational" has it: philosophy directs/grounds the basic hypotheses of the special disciplines, and further, in my judgment, philosophy is called to facilitate interdisciplinary thinking and knowledge. But philosophy must not try to replace the deposed Queen theology as Philosopher King, *à la* Plato's closed society.

Thesis 4. The philosophy (and historiography) assumed in the classroom teaching of any subject acts like a preemptive strike upon the student, because much as your mother tongue, which you learn even before you can speak, determines your world of conversation, so philosophy veritably functions as a schooled memory, and becomes the reservoir shaping the student's ideas and conceptual world.

Because a person's philosophical (and historiographic) thought-habit of consciousness embodies an underlying faith-commitment, to change one's philosophy is almost as difficult, deep-going, and traumatic as altering one's personality through years of psychotherapy.

Philosophy *is* being done in every classroom of the college—a capitalist philosophy of business, a Lockean philosophy of politics in those courses, a Matthew Arnold or Deconstructivist philosophy of English literature—albeit tacit or highly personalized.

Philosophy may be considered the *janitor/architect* (repairman and custodian; not the "mastermind") of the academy, and the Historian could be understood as *storyteller* spouse (local chronicler; not anecdotal gossip) to the janitor/architect.

Thesis 5. It is time we decided whether there is a Reformational philosophical thought tradition next to others, a philosophical habit of thought comparable to that of Thomist theism or a thought-habit of

evangelical piety and others, and then make earnest with the Calvinian-Kuyperian-Vollenhovian/Dooyeweerdian community of thinking, not scholastically, but imaginatively.

It is not parochial to know self-critically your historically rooted position and to be thoroughly at home somewhere philosophically. I think it is also not very helpful for a mature philosophy professor to waffle on what the contours of his or her philosophic habit be, for fear of abetting the ghetto mentality born of defensiveness.

Most of our thought habits are an amalgam of traditions in progress. We are all at varied, changing stages of our "schooled memory." And I am not recommending joining only EITHER the Society of Calvinist Philosophy OR the Society of Christian Philosophers. And I should prefer to think of a knitted community of philosophy rather than a monolithic "school," that is, a kinship of Reformation spirit and rough agreement on basics, thetical thrust, conceptual priorities, but not a set of precepts, yet blessedly free from needing to hash over the fundamentals still one more time. . . . I found moving Nathan O. Hatch's comment that so many "evangelical scholars are like historical orphans," so they tend to move toward an ideological traditionalism.[3] Reformed thinkers without a cohering philosophical systematics also tend to do the same.[4]

Thesis 6. From the standpoint of the Reformation thought-tradition, as I understand its contribution, a Christian philosophical systematics will be Scripturally directed philosophical thinking, but not captive to any particular denominational/ecclesiastical theology; in fact, a Reformation Christian philosophy, precisely because it is philosophical in nature, adopts a biblically thetical and critical stance that promotes a truly ecumenical confederacy of various (legitimately dogmatic) confessional theologies.

Much is lost, however, if Christian philosophy is taken to be theistic apologetics. Dooyeweerd offended many theologians on this point, designating dogmatic theology as a special discipline with philosophical presuppositions and without a corner on basic truth. Many read that

---

3   Nathan O. Hatch, "Evangelical Colleges and the Challenge of Christian Thanking," in *Making Higher Education Christian: The History and Mission of Evangelical Colleges in America*, eds. Joel A. Carpenter and Kenneth W. Shipps (Grand Rapids: Eerdmans, 1987), 165.

4   I have normally experienced in secular settings, and in Christian settings of wide diversity, that if you are not out proselytizing, there is a begrudged respect for the Calvinian tradition of thinking even though some find it hard to believe that at still exists today.

as if "general revelation" supplanted "special revelation." The fact that Thomists [con]fuse natural theology and philosophy adds to the continuing trouble.[5]

The current president of The Society for Christian Philosophers, Marilyn McCord Adams, wrongly proposes,[6] it seems to me, that we do well to conflate theology and Christian philosophy, while she rightly argues for the integration of faith and philosophical analysis she heard Alvin Plantings ask for in his inaugural address to that society.[7]

Alvin Plantinga exemplifies, if I understand him, what I think would be unhelpful:

> First [as a project for Christian philosophers], there is [needed in priority] philosophical reflection on specifically Christian topics—Trinity, Incarnation, Atonement, Sin . . . Election, and the like. . . . Third . . . developing from a theistic perspective a full-orbed, articulate, systematic set of answers to the main philosophical questions.[8]

To a Calvinian thinker, the first priority sounds like natural theology budding or in bloom; the third priority could be right, depending on what "set of answers" entails. It is clear to me that Al Plantinga wants to fight David's battle. My worry is about what appears to me to be Saul's armor.

We also need more than supervening "control beliefs" (propositioned creedal statements) regulating our thinking; that is not deep-going enough for me. I recognize a faith-commitment that knows creation is God's ordering duration toward the end, and knows there are relative interrelated structures (which are good) holding for entitles, and knows the historically needing-to-be-saved nature of being neighborhooded humans called to the order of Melchizedek, and so on. Such basic, inceptional knowledge underlies and gives from-within a Calvinian cast to my thinking.

Thesis 7. The first prerequisite philosophy course in the undergraduate program of a Reformed college should be a course in systematic Christian philosophy that, after a situating prolegomenal demonstration of currency, winsomely presents a Christian philosophical

---

5   John Wippel tries to update the old Brehier/Gilson controversy in "The Possibility of a Christian Philosophy: A Thomist Perspective," *Faith and Philosophy* 1:3 (1987): 272–90.

6   Marilyn McCord Adams, 139.

7   Alvin Plantinga, "Advice to Christian Philosophers," *Faith and Philosophy* 1:3 (1984): 253–71.

8   Alvin Plantinga, "Response to Keller," *Faith and Philosophy* 5:2 (1988): 163.

perspective (singular) in cosmology, anthropology, epistemology, and theory of history tuned to our circumstances.

Follow-up seminars that are field-specific and led jointly by philosopher, historian, and field-specialist professor, who share that common Christian mind, are a necessary mediation of the orienting instruction.

The way to integrate over-all Christian philosophical perspective and the necessary field-specialization in present-day college study is to practice it as faculty and students together. This means concretely: (1) on-going, in-depth communal faculty seminars; and (2) encouraging double majors among undergraduate students.

I remember a 1959 conversation that visiting Dean Ryskamp and President William Spoelhof of Calvin College had with Robert Vander Vennen and myself on the William Harry Jellema-designed curriculum of Trinity: "You should give an introductory course in 'straight thinking,' in logic" (as Aristotle proposed, prolegomenon to the sciences), it was suggested. We thought, however, we at Trinity would teach an introductory course in "Christian thinking"; and that gave birth to Philosophy 101 (3 hours), which first year students were required to take before the three-semester required sequence of ancient/medieval/modern philosophy (each 2 hours) and history (each 3 hours) courses taught in tandem.

In the 1960's Professor Marion Snapper at Calvin College always felt supportive toward, rather than disgruntled by, the Trinity Christian College two-year graduates who, at Calvin, put up their hands in his classes and asked, "What's Christian about that?" "At least they had structure to their thinking," said Professor Snapper.

There are many, many exciting philosophical topics to introduce: reorientation on the soul/body question apropos sexuality; a theory of knowledge dealing with imaginative knowing available in stories and films; historical exposure to unsettle ethnocentric Western parochialisms. The "singular" Christian perspective does not mean Niebuhr's classic options should not be discussed, but the introductory course needs to take a considered position, and then exercise dialogue in the teaching. As Lambert Zuidervaart said in comment on Ted Plantinga's "options"—one must participate and judge from an orienting, systematic position.

Our children went to Dordt College in the 1970s, because we knew they could get this kind of orientation there in a non-indoctrinating but formative, thetical way early in their college experience. One must neither brainwash nor pretend detachment, I think. James 3:1 is a most severe warning for teachers.

Thesis 8. The dated location of the educational circumstances (urban Chicago minorities, Iowan farmland, the Bostonian East, midwestern Grand Rapids, Canadian Toronto) gives the pedagogical clue into which language the philosophically careful terminology needs to be translated.

Once a philosophy professor knows street argot, the finesse of agricultural life, or the ins-and-outs of the pop-art scene, such a theoretician learns that one does not need to sacrifice precision in the pedagogical translation if you know both languages. Respect the life-world of your students, and know it thoroughly, rather than unwittingly pull the humorless, elitist putdown of professional experts before stupids.[9]

Good pedagogy will include, I think, the steps of surprise, precision, formulation, and experiment.[10] And it is especially the final stage of getting the student to "experiment" and enter into the thought empathetically and critically that takes doing.

Years ago at Trinity I put an ad in the University of Chicago student newspaper: "Wanted: atheist to discuss position with Christian students." I received four inquiries, and settled on an apostate priest who had thrown out the faith and was willing to come. He had to read the section on "Science impaired by sin," in Abraham Kuyper's *Principles of Sacred Knowledge* (a student assignment), make a critique of Kuyper's thought, and then present his rationale for being an atheist. Then my students were free to ask questions. I'll never forget afterwards, as I paid him, the atheist said respectfully, "My, you have a few very articulate students!"

In the years when I taught Thomas Aquinas, after I had had my say for several classes, I'd regularly invite a professor from St. Xavier College to come and lecture on Thomas and answer student questions. It was excellent teaching because the St. Xavier professor always said what I had said he would say, but my students saw he believed it.

I only got into trouble once, when the National Communist Party headquarters provided me with a Mr. Lightfoot (to follow up my critical teaching of Marx's philosophy), and a John Bircher got wind of it just before the college's annual drive for funds, misinterpreted my educational praxis, and telephoned all the church captains in the area that Seerveld was having communists teach at Trinity. The event was canceled. But

---

9   Cf. E. D. Hirsch, "How to Save the Schools," *New York Review of Books* 36:3 (2 March 1989), 29–35.

10 Cf. Calvin Seerveld, *Rainbows for the Fallen World: Aesthetic life and artistic task* (Toronto: Tuppence, 1980), 148–50.

the next year we spoke with an articulate communist by Bell Telephone conference hook-up. . . .

Thesis 9. Content, however conveyed, is crucial for solid interdisciplinary study, which Reformational Christian philosophy (and historiography) foster. To give/elicit contexted, in-depth knowledge of a few pivotal, representative philosophical texts (and a typical artwork of a period, novel, or literary essay) affords better Christian learning than a survey acquaintance from secondary sources.

Knowing the history of any discipline is central to being informed of the status quo, and cultural/philosophical history should be pursued both for its background in dated contribution and for its enduring systematic insights. The philosophy departments, I think, should consult and engage especially the fellow departmental resources of literature and the arts in this historiographic endeavor.

Decide communally on a number of basic texts that students with a B.A. (and their mentors) should have mastered. William Henry Jellema's Socratic style still gave you Plato. A. J. Ayer's deconstruction of the questioner gave you a brilliant method hard to duplicate, and certainly no notes. (Teachers proud of giving students nothing to hold on to are sophists, in my judgment.)

To get philosophy from a horse's mouth has authenticity that lasts; besides, the instructor does not have to fight the textbook's secondary perspective. This means that a teacher is to be busy philosophically. What about an Eastern/Oriental text in our history of philosophy teaching?

Thesis 10. Systematic philosophical thinking and its results need to be intrinsically God-thanking thinking if it would be blessed with educational fruit worthy of repentance before our Lord.

For God-thanking, Reformational Christian philosophical activity to become fruitful and wise, it may need to suffer through a lack of acceptance by colleagues and disaffection by career-minded undergraduate students, by sacrificing all ranked privilege and by serving them janitorially with integrative horizons and field-specific, life-pregnant understanding of the meaning of things and events.

Prepare submissions on the topic of this conference, meeting this criterion, for the manifold forums that already exist.

The proof of the Reformational Christian philosophy is in the special disciplinary puddings! When the colleagues and administrators at our college institutions can taste the foundational worth of our scholarship for other disciplines, then the necessity of a Christian philosophy becomes convincing.

Rather than recruit philosophy majors, we whose task is philosophy need to think of a philosophy major as "not designed for entrance into graduate school in philosophy," as Peter de Vos insightfully said. We need a philosophy major for people majoring in other fields like basket weaving or mechanics, a philosophy for soldiers, as Rosenstock-Huessey proposed, or a philosophy major for business majors (remember, the Good Samaritan was a business man), and a philosophy minor to reach out to inner-city black Christians. Then philosophy will have been humbled to service.

If we fail to be obedient in the current cultural crunch of fragmentary specialist career university-level studies, if we should fail to be obedient to the Lord in leading the next generation because of a party spirit or face-saving pride among us—the respectable sin academics are good at—then we deserve the millstones outfitted for our necks held in storage. Each of us together needs to be humbled by the calling of the Holy Spirit self-critically to subject our discipline to the project of edification rather than success, directed to thought-service rather than a lording-it-over kind of thinking, to the scandal of praise/love/care inside thinking rather than to be out to win the acclaim of a secular world. Our philosophy needs to be wholesome bread rather than that which hits stomachs like stones, or be like live ammunition handed out to shoot conservatives and liberals.

We all betray the background of mixed thought-traditions, which compounds our sin of being prone to temporize at being synthetic Christian philosophers. We must not condone that resident error, it seems to me, which stays with us a lifetime, by making it a principle we live by. "Reformed," as thorough-going Reformation, means at biblical bottom: being driven by the Holy Spirit of single-mindedly reforming our thinking (Philippians 1:9–11) until it conforms to the will of God, fully revealed in Jesus Christ, manifest in creation, and witnessed to our hearts by the Holy Scriptures (Romans 12:1–2). If we are busy biblically reforming our interrelational thinking we will have been obedient despite failures, in our philosophical calling, faithful to the ministry of reconciliation (2 Corinthians 5:17–19) and in doing justice to God's compassionate, judging redemption (Micah 6:5–8).

Bibliography

Marilyn McCord Adams. "Problems of Evil: More Advice to Christian

Philosophers," *Faith and Philosophy* 5:2 (1988), 121–43. Also in the same issue James A. Keller, "Reflections on a Methodology for Christian Philosophers," and Alvin Plantinga, "Response to Keller," 144–64.

Roy Clouser. "Religious Language: A new look at an old problem," in *Rationality in the Calvinian Tradition*, eds. H. Hart, J. van der Hoeven, N. Wolterstorff (Lanham: University Press of America, 1983), 9–23.

E. H. Gombrich. "The Tradition of General Knowledge," [1961], in *Ideals and Idols: Essays on values in history and in art* (Oxford: Phaidon, 1979), 9–23.

Nathan O. Hatch. "Evangelical Colleges and the Challenge of Christian Thinking," in *Making Higher Education Christian: The history and mission of evangelical colleges in America*, eds. Joel A. Carpenter and Kenneth W. Shipps (Grand Rapids: Eerdmans, 1987), 155–71.

E. D. Hirsch, Jr. "How to Save the Schools," *The New York Review of Books* 36:3 (2 March 1989), 29–35.

Eugen Rosenstock-Huessy, *Das Geheimnis der Universität: Wider den Verfall von Zeitsinn und Sprachkraft: Aufsätze und Reden, 1950–57*, ed. Georg Muller (Stuttgart: Kohlhammer, 1958), 17–34.

Max Weber. "Wissenschaft als Beruf" [1919] in *Gesammelte Augsatze zur Wissenschaftslebre* 3A, ed. Johannes Winckelmann (Tübingen: Mohr/ Siebeck, 1968), 582–613.

Christian Philosophy conference at Trinity Christian College,
Palos Heights, Illinois, 1990

Standing from left to right: Bill Rowe, George Pierson, John Roose, … ,
Ted Plantinga, Gary Weaver, Cal Seerveld, Mark Talbot, John Kok, Vaden House
Seated from left to right: Lambert Zuidervaart, Ed Echeverria, Lee Hardy,
John Van Dyk, Grady Spires, John Vander Stelt, Peter De Vos

A Final Lecture
at Trinity Christian College

There are a few stitches in the horse-hair shirt I wove while teaching at Trinity for 13 years (1959–1972) that I'd like to mention in about 23 minutes of remarks, maybe with time for a few questions from any former students. . . .

philosophical systematics: **Convicted eye-glasses for experiencing the real world** Psalm 148:7, Ecclesiastes 3:15

When Trinity opened for classes I was given an incredible opportunity to teach an introductory systematic philosophy course, to be required of incoming freshmen and freshwomen, that would be a Scripturally led philosophical analysis of the interrelated meaning of things in God's world of creatures.

Sometimes I mailed out ahead of registration an assignment students were to bring to the first philosophy class: a one-page précis of the Older Testament book of Ecclesiastes, and their thought on what it meant. That Bible book highlights, in my judgment, the joyful goods of **creation** in its sevenfold refrain, the violent unjust waste our human **sin** has wrought historically, and the need for **redemptive wisdom** already in our youth.

That assignment set up my mnemonic for examining how we temporal creatures exist in the theatre of the Covenantal LORD God who faithfully provides by setting the ordinantial limits for all creatures enacting God's purposes, as the psalms put it (e.g., Psalms19, 148), in a one-time history headed for the eschaton, which is cursed by sin yet mediated by Jesus Christ, our Archimedean Point of meaning, whose Holy Spirit can grip us human mortals at heart to persevere corporeally in the task of serving our neighbors by obeying God.

This talk was presented with PowerPoint diagrams and artwork images on 3 October 2009 at Trinity Christian College, Palos Heights, Illinois USA.

For those of you who know about the tin-can man, which broke conceptually with the traditional yet unbiblical soul-body dichotomy: in later life our eldest daughter convinced me in a student reading she gave at Dordt College (1982) that there should be a tin-can woman in the picture too. The latest development is that I have begun to use the metaphor of 1 Corinthians 4:7: the clay jar man and woman.

I am still firmly committed to this Reformational christian vision as a good set of glasses, John Calvin would say (*Institutes* I, 5:14), for **conceiving** our **life tasks** among the societal institutions we inhabit in our dated/located existence. And the Social Action Seminars we held at night in the mid/late '60s at Trinity, inviting in the surrounding community, were the lab sessions for the philosophy and history courses that, with Bible and English, were at the core of the Trinity curriculum. Those were evenings when Canadian christian labor leader Gerald Vandezande debated an AFL/CIO bigwig on open versus closed shop policy, Back to God Hour radio minister Joel Nederhood shared the platform with NAACP director Roy Wilkins, and student Mark Dykstra responded to evangelist Tom Skinner's packed-out presentation.

historiography: **A struggle not against flesh and blood, but against evil spiriting powers.**   Ephesians 6:12, Romans 8:28-30

The best brief way for me to sum-up the importance of studying the history of human reflection and culture, if you in your generation will to be outfitted with christian wisdom, might be, I thought, to cite a few representative quotations. Just because one may be outfitted with a biblically directed, systematic christian philosophical perspective does not mean you cannot learn from others not so gifted. And just as you can't jump out of your skin or avoid a slant to your committed vision, you can't avoid entering world history either. The ignorance of history, if it be a willful amnesia, is sinful, I dare say, born out of a revolutionary or pragmatistic vanity supposing WE can create our own cultural world *de novo*.

En passant I should say: the different languages are not meant to show off that I know almost as many languages as my wife, but to witness to the Pentecostal incentive to practice hospitality and careful scholarship: don't be proudly stuck in one language; if possible, show you love your neighbor by learning his or her speech—else we may compound misunderstandings, and one is at the mercy of (revisionist) translators, for example, of the Bible or Qur'an.

Plato and Aristotle were most exciting to teach: big encyclopedic thinkers, thoroughly pre-christian pagan theists whose perspectives have shaped Christian Western civilization, and traditional Muslim culture too. After my wife and I visited Egypt in 1967 with a German archaeological study group, I always started, before examining the Pre-Socratic Greek thinkers, with Egyptian wisdom literature, which pre-dates but ties into Older Testament biblical writings like Proverbs and Ecclesiastes.

Παις   ἔμοιγε δοκεῖ οὕτω.
Σωκράτης καλῶς· τὸ γάρ σοι δοκοῦν τοῦτο ἀποκρίνου.
(Meno, 83d1–2)

Mouthpiece Socrates for ventriloquist Plato (427–347 BC) often misused this good pedagogical advice by allowing his respondents only enough room to say "Yes" or "No" in Plato's dialogues. And it has taken me many years to realize that the "sophist" Isocrates' (436–338 BC) contribution on "rhetoric," depreciated by Realist philosopher Plato's prejudice for logically achieved ἐπιστήμη, needs to be critically retrieved and validated to correct so many philosophers' Rationalistic dependence on argument to get at "the Truth." Winsome **imaginative** thinking (which Plato often practiced!) may be more conducive to interactive communication and the peace of what is true than the opposition of analytically certified beliefs. (These are fighting words, some of you will know, needing various supplements.)

[. . . ἀλλα κρη; . . .] ἐνδέχεται ἀθανατίζειν . . .
(Nicomachaean Ethics X, 7, 1177b33)
[rather than act as a human mortal] an *anthropos* must, in so far as it is possible, pursue divine life (Werner Jaeger: make oneself divine), i.e., **become** noetic intelligent philosophical framework.

Unlike mathomanic Plato, biologist Aristotle (384–322 BC) trusted the senses, but since Aristotle also believed reasoning is divine (εἰ δὴ θεῖον ὁ νοῦς Ibid., 1177b30) his contemplation reinforced centuries of Humanist vanity.

1200s Catholicism meant to curtail such hubris of philosophy by conceiving philosophy, according to Thomas Aquinas (1225–1274 AD), as a subservient *ancilla* (hand-maiden) to the authority of theology, for Theology articulates the grace dispensed by the Church, which does not destroy but perfects/completes natural reasoning.[1]

However, Pico della Mirandola (1463–1491) rejected any ecclesial controls on humans and promoted a creed that resounds like a loveless

---

1   Cum enim gratia non tollat naturam, sed perficiat, oportet quod naturalis ratio subserviat fidei. . . . *Summa Theologiae*, Q 1,a.8 ad 2.

bronze gong throughout recorded history—East/West/North/South: we philosophically contemplative humans can, if we will, by *ambitio sacra* invading our souls become angelic beings and veritably merge with the very Godhead who made us.[2]

This driving, dynamic principality—To-Become-like-God (the Serpent's opening gambit, Genesis 3:5)—in a legion of empowering, captivating Faustian disguises has spooked world cultural history and dominates, I dare say, North American, Chinese, Japanese, Russian, Arab, and African dictatorship cultures **today**, in our Machiavellian politics, Darwinian economics, Double-speak media, Selfish Hedonistic entertainment— And if you don't know that this long-standing protean unholy spirit is the very cultural air we breathe, how can would-be followers of Jesus Christ not catch the prevailing toxic pandemic virus of "Godly-Me-First"?

A good dose of earthy gutsy Martin Luther (1483–1546) talk and song can inoculate a person against sheep-like following the bellwether crowd. **Maior est spiritus sanctus quam Aristoteles.**[3] The Holy Spirit is more important, is more significant than Aristotle, says Luther disarmingly, in analyzing the eucharistic sacrament, and in the process Luther enunciates a fundamental Reformation change in christian understanding of the Church: the Word of God preached changes humans at heart to become God's adopted children in Jesus Christ; salvation is **not** effected by sacraments performed by clerics!

> Nun freut euch, lieben Christen g'mein,
> und laßt uns fröhlich springen,
> daß wir getrost und all in ein
> mit Lust und Liebe singen:
> Was Gott an uns gewendet hat,
> und seine süße Wundertat,
> gar teu'r hat er's erworben. . . .

It cost God every bloody nickel to save us, so prance around joyfully!—that's Martin Luther's take on the christian faith alternative to ambitious Pico della Mirandola, Inc. The historic European Reformation

---

2 Invadat animum sacra quaedam ambitio ut mediocribus non contenti anhelemus ad summa, adque illa (quando possumus si volumus) consequenda totis viribus emitamur. . . . ut per eam ipsi homines ascendentes in caelum angeli fierent. . . . *De hominis dignitate*, 1487.

3 De captivitate Babylonica ecclesiae praeludium (1520), in *Luthers Werke in Auswahl*, ed. Otto Clemen (Bonn: Marcus und Weber, 1925), 1:442.

did not just change a few doctrines, but re-directed patterns of daily life and the grip of societal institutions! Monk Luther married nun Katerina von Bora and suddenly raised marriage to its biblical prominence instead of giving priority to the solitary life.

Reformer John Calvin's (1509–1564) deep-going thought, the one I treasure most, gives underlying grit and body to Luther's direct simplicity: . . . **omnis recta Dei cognitio ab obedientia nascitur.**[4] Knowing God is not esoteric γνῶσις, but is living in obedience to God's Word. And the most holy vocation—lawyer! John Calvin speaking—the most God-honoring task by a long shot, is to become a civil magistrate dispensing restorative justice to all and sundry, to believing **and** disbelieving neighbors.[5] Do you realize what that opens up? **All** of life is to be faith in operation! Preparing meals in the kitchen, filling bureaucratic routines in the office, teaching mathematics to children, can be as holy an activity as praying *matins* at 4:00 a.m. in the monastery. No wonder the Reformed Church Heidelberg Catechism (1563) stated answer #32 to "Why are you called a Christian?" does not mention "the church" (as ecclesial institution)!

The Dutch brand of Reformational thought is well-formulated by Abraham Kuyper: ". . . what we need is to be building up the whole of theoretical thought on a christian foundation. What we really need is a seedling of scientific theory thriving on christian roots. For us people to be content with the act of shuffling around in the garden of somebody else, scissors in hand [to cut the other's flowers], is to throw away the honor and worth of our christian faith."[6]

Kuyper believes Scripture can break through the hold on our consciousness bedeviled by "the traditions of men," and give us fallible servants a fresh start for a committed world-and-life vision of God's world and our dated/located human task, not to be successful in bringing on the philosophical or societal millennium, but in being faithful to prepare a welcome for the returning Lord of glory. It could be that our reforming sinful-obedient meals will look as severe as the diet of Daniel, Shadrach,

---

4 *Institutes of the Christian Religion*, I, 6:2

5 Quare nulli jam dubium esse debet quin civilis potestas, vocatio sit, non modo coram Deo sancta & legitima, sed sacerrima etiam, et in tota mortalium vita longe omnium honestissima. John Calvin, *Institutio Christianae religionis*, 1536, IV, 20:4.

6 "Wat we behoeven is een plant der wetenschap, tierend op Christelijken wortel. En ons te vergenoegen met de rol, om met het snoeimes in de hand, in anderer tuin om te drentelen, is de eere en de waardigheid van onze Christelijke religie wegwerpen." "De Wetenschap," 5, in *De Gemeene Gratie* (Kampen: Kok, 4th ed., n.d.), 3:527.

Meshach, and Abednego next to the high cholesterol gourmet feasts and sweets of Nebuchadnezzar's courtiers, but maybe we Christ followers will know better than others, as Bruce Cockburn's song has it, "wondering where the lions are" (1979).

My philosophy professors at the Vrije Universiteit in Amsterdam, D. H. Th. Vollenhoven and Sietze Zuidema, taught me, standing in this Kuyperian Reformational christian tradition, a most important truth that has guided me my whole life in Christ: **stel maar de thesis; dan zul je wel de antithese thuis krijgen**" ("Just posit the christian thesis; then you shall get antichristian theses thrown back in your face").[7] And I also learned from Karl Barth, with whom I studied during a post-graduate *Wanderjahr* (1955–56), when he explained why he himself was not a Barthian, the importance for a community of Christian scholars to work out of a faith-thought tradition with an identity, but not to be narrow-minded or fixated by the past:[8] Scripturally directed scholarship will keep its ear cocked to the enlivening, on-going re-directing, modifying power and focusing of God's Holy Spirited Word upon one's philosophical task.

philosophical aesthetics: **God's aesthetic injunction to be playful and allusive, imaginative adoptive children**

After moving on from teaching at Trinity to the graduate Institute for Christian Studies in Toronto (1972-1999), I was able to concentrate on exploring God's creational ordinance of ludicity/allusivity for our imaginative responsibilities. I spent time reflecting on our human "aesthetic life," which underlies "art making," and grappled with "the history and task of artistry and literature in society." Let me mention just a couple of theses in this field of investigation:

(1) Not everybody needs to be art-smart, but God does ask everybody to be aesthetically obedient, that is, to sound a note of redeem-

---

7   Calvin Seerveld, *A Christian Critique of Art and Literature* (Toronto: Tuppence Press, 1963/1995), 143.

8   "Es tat der Kirche nie gut, sich eigenwillig auf einem Mann—ob er nun Thomas (seien wir froh, dass wir keinen Thomas haben und brauchen!) oder Luther oder Calvin hieß—und in seiner Schule auf eine Gestalt ihrer Lehre festzulegen. Und es tat ihr überhaupt nie gut, prinzipiell rückwärts statt vorwärts zu blicken: als ob sie der konsequenten Eschatologie eben doch recht geben wollte, als ob sie eben doch nicht an den kommenden Herrn glaubte!" "Vorwort" to *Die Lehre von der Schöpfung, Die Kirchliche Dogmatik*, III:4 (Zollikon-Zürich: Evangelischer Verlag, 1951), ix. Walter Benjamin tackled the same problem: "In jeder Epoche muss versucht werden, die Überlieferung von neuem dem Konformismus abzugewinnen, der im Begriff steht, sie zu überwältigen" in "Über den Begriff der Geschichte," thesis 6 (1940).

ing imaginativity in your varied activities—perception (Philippians 1:9-11), speech (Colossians 4:6), parenting (Ephesians 6:4), friendship (Proverbs 17:17), or whatever.

(2) If you have the calling and determination, and develop the competence to become an artisan, an artist, an amateur or professional writer of literature, your happy stressful task is to provide nuanceful knowledge for the neighbor, especially those in society who are imaginatively handicapped, the unimaginatively obtuse or strait-laced.

(3) Authentic artwork is fallible metaphoric knowledge of nuanceful matters permeated by an awareness of the surd of sin and the joy of God's grace touching creatures.

(4) For artistry to be a wholesome presence in society there will best be a communion of sound artists, charitable art critics, down-to-earth art theorists, generous art patrons, and an informed or educable art public, intent together on giving away this normal gift to whoever will receive it. . . .

There are a host of wonderful, complicating problems: from my που στω Willem Claeszoon Heda's *nature morte* (1634 [see *NA* #4]) is a profoundly christian painting, thankfully relishing the glory of the creatural texture of pewter, glass, and linen tablecloth, wine and food, while simultaneously calling the viewer to remember with the drying out lemon peel's *memento mori* that we who eat and drink so gladly are mortal. Or a late Rembrandt (1606–1669) portrait [see *NA* #62; *AH* #13] captures the hurting gravity of elderly life, which like Job or the apostle (thorn-in-the-flesh) Paul's travail remains waiting not for Godot, but for the awesome blessing of God. That is, one does not need to produce liturgical art fit for Church worship, a fortiori not need to try to induce a transcendent numinous experience, to be fulfilling a godly artistic vocation.

With my particular picaresque bent I appreciate the comic relief—exaggerating what happens at a fiery "enthusiastic" Methodist church service—outsider William Hogarth (1697–1764) brought to the British scene at the time of genteel Academicians Reynolds and Gainsborough. Hogarth gave dignity to his servants! (1759) and to a girl selling shrimp! Hogarth was art historically important in getting through Parliament a graphic artwork copyright law (1735).

Käthe Kollwitz's *Woman with dead child* (1903) makes me quietly cry, since it tunes me deeply into the wretched misery of the lonely pain of the helpless nearby and worldwide. I am bound to mitigate such pain, and try to do so at least by showing you this artwork, Kollwitz's artistic offering to God [see *NA* #42]. Another artist from Inès and my local

William Hogarth, *Credulity, Superstition,*
Fanaticism – a Medley, engraving, 1762

congregation comments in oil on wood panel the bittersweet trials the
biblical letter booked by James says it is good for us to go through [see
Joanne Sytsma, 2001, *RA* #104]), since God keeps all our tears in God's
bottle—outfitted with the label of Matisse's "Dance of life"! And Trinity's Dayton Castleman uses a brilliant red-painted steel pipe perforating
cell doors onsite in a defunct Philadelphia prison, weaving in and out of

grey cinder blocks to leap over the prison wall surrounding the exercise yard (as Psalm 18:29 has it) and turn into a concert of organ pipes on the other side—a solid red thread of hope called "End of the tunnel" (2004) for the forgotten jailed in a labyrinth of confined, punished, suspended life. . . [see *NA* #83–85]. Rainbow-rich artwork, and events, can tell hard truths as well as sweet lies.

postlude   2 Samuel 23:2–7   Ecclesiastes 3:15   Psalm 31:14–15, 5

I'm glad for this ante-mortem rather than post-mortem opportunity to give a "final lecture" at Trinity. I'll end as I began, coming back to Scripture, which points to the source of everlasting life and insight: God revealed in Jesus Christ and made known in our hearts by the Holy Spirit.

The yearning pathos of King David's final words would be my penultimate words. Second Samuel 23:2–7 records how David failed doing what the LORD God required: rule justly (teach wisely) in awe of God so that his subjects (my students) would sparkle like fresh grass shining after a good rain as the sun rises on a cloudless morning. That speaks to me, interested in our generational responsibility to carry on and ramify the Lord's work,[9] because I resonate deeply with Augustine's moving plea: **"Da mihi castitatem et continentiam, sed noli modo"** (Give me chastity and continence, [O Lord,] but not yet!).[10] Given our failings, it is truly a miracle to be able to pass on the treasures we hold in us clay jars.

A good brisk translation of Ecclesiastes' opening "vanity of vanities" phrase (1:2) would be: "Hot stinking air! Utter stupidity! It's all a fart!" To which the refrain of the book answers (in 3:15): **"Yes, but God picks up the pieces"**[11] . . . of our lifelong activity, and will redeem the faithful false starts and the smell.

So my final testimony as philosophy teacher and aesthetician would be from Psalm 31: "My life time, my times, the timings for me, [LORD,]

---

9   My own grappling with this problem referred to in footnote 8 above, has been to try to reform Herman Dooyeweerd's threefold conception of "historical development" (differentiate, integrate, individualize) with the formulation: "regenerate, speciate, diaconate" one's inherited state of your cultural preoccupation or faith-thought tradition. Cf. my "Cities as a Place for Public Artwork: A glocal approach," in *Globalization and the Gospel: Probing the religious foundations of globalization*, eds. Michael W. Goheen and Erin Glanville (Vancouver: Regent Press and Geneva Society, 2009), 323 n.13. {See *RA*: 241–244.}

10   *Confessiones*, 8:17.

11   וְהָאֱלֹהִים יְבַקֵּשׁ אֶת־נִרְדָּף (Ecclesiastes 3:15).

are in your hand" (vv. 14–15).[12] And when the temporal earthly journey
for me ends (Psalm 31:5): "Into your hand, [Lord,] I entrust my very
life-breath," which the LORD gives and the LORD takes away; blessed be
the Name of the LORD (Job 1:21).

A clay jar model of human creaturely consciousness.

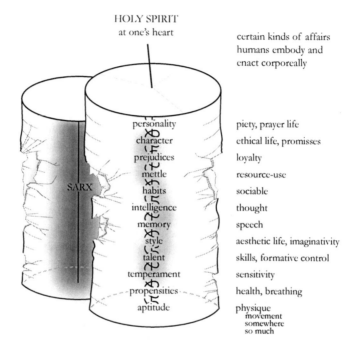

HOLY SPIRIT
at one's heart

certain kinds of affairs
humans embody and
enact corporeally

personality	piety, prayer life
character	ethical life, promisses
prejudices	loyalty
mettle	resource-use
habits	sociable
intelligence	thought
memory	speech
style	aesthetic life, imaginativity
talent	skills, formative control
temperament	sensitivity
propensities	health, breathing
aptitude	physique

SARX

movement
somewhere
so much

THINKING DEEPLY ABOUT OUR FAITH

So much depends on your standpoint when you start to tell what happened "once upon a time."

I thank God that a New Yorker like me was adopted by the God-fearing, Dutch-Canadian mavericks who began what has become the Institute for Christian Studies in Toronto. Just as parents in the United States formed Christian school societies to start Christian elementary schools, certain Canadian immigrants from Holland in the 1950s formed an Association for Reformed Scientific Studies to set up a Christian university.

1960s: Roughneck Beginnings

As a young philosophy prof from then-new Trinity Christian College in Chicago, I was made a trustee of the Association for Reformed Scientific Studies. I think I was appointed on the basis of my having spoken for the embattled Christian Labour Association of Canada: "Christian Workers, Unite!" (1964).

In 1965 I flew in late from Chicago to Toronto for my first board of trustees meeting and was brought by trustee Rev. Peter Jonker to Rehoboth Christian Reformed Church, pastored by trustee Rev. François Guillaume, who was a survivor of the Dachau concentration camp. As we entered the empty church building we could hear shouting going on behind closed doors. We entered the room, and there stood bookseller Peter Speelman and professor H. Evan Runner shouting red-faced at one another amid a table of eight seated men.

This introduction came to epitomize for me the passionate motivations inspiring what later became the Institute for Christian Studies in Toronto.

Grassroots Speelman knew that the student generation of post-World War II Dutch immigrants needed a Kuyperian university training so they would not be lost to the church in Canada; hence, student sum-

---

A slightly shorter version of this piece was published in *The Banner*, November 2008: 34–35.

mer conferences included speakers such as Hendrik Van Riessen, S.U. Zuidema, and Fritz von Meyenfeldt.

Wheaton graduate, Werner Jaeger/Vollenhoven-trained, professor Runner knew that what was needed was a high-caliber academic center doing advanced graduate studies that tackled current world problems, showing that an educated Christian, aware of history, could make a policy difference.

This double-focus meant that the Free University protégés of Runner who were first appointed to ICS—Bernard Zylstra, Hendrik Hart, and James Olthuis—had free rein to roam North America as stump speakers on many controversial topics, while also giving rigorous lectures in philosophy, political science, and ethics to disaffected college graduates crazy enough to come to this unaccredited place in Toronto.

Trinity Christian College gave a window of opportunity at that time for glimpses of the "Toronto" wedge into Reformed life in North America. In Trinity's Wednesday night Social Action Seminar series, for example, key player Gerald Vandezande debated an AFL-CIO bigwig on "open" versus "closed" shop policy. Trinity held *inter nos* conferences at which Calvin profs Nicholas Wolterstorff, Alvin Plantinga, and Institute profs engaged one another in mind-to-mind combat, with Ron Jager of Yale and Peter Schouls of the University of Toronto participating on topics of "christian philosophy"—if it exists, what is it? and if Dooyeweerd's thought is not it, what then? Meanwhile, ICS students formed a kind of brigade in Toronto to, in effect, scratch the open sores of the local Christian Reformed churches—out of concern for the Church, of course. The Sixties were heady days for the Toronto attempt to build up "a christian university."

1970s and 1980s: Settling down

By this time, the trustees had set up a body of academically trained folks, a *curatorium*, to oversee the workings of ICS professors, who now included Arnold de Graaff, C.T. McIntire, myself, George Vandervelde, Albert Wolters, Paul Marshall, and, later, Bob Sweetman. It was decided that the itinerant, circuit-riding professors should concentrate on teaching regular credit courses at 229 College Street in Toronto and on writing philosophical books, rather than roaming the continent connecting with the supporting community and raising the hackles of clergy.

When Calvin College administrators came to understand that the Toronto upstart was not going to solicit capital funds to build a university campus and would not crowd Calvin's undergraduate turf that much, opposition to the Institute as only an "institute" muted—although Calvin professor Lester De Koster, as editor of *The Banner* (1970–80), vented vigorous critique of everything Torontonian with editorials that seemed to many of us mean-spirited, hurtful.

When Robert Knudsen of Westminster Theological Seminary arranged for their faculty to meet with ICS faculty at a location halfway between Toronto and Philadelphia, and Westminster leadership discovered the Institute was not a seminary and therefore not a direct competitor, tensions eased there too. And when James Houston, president of Regent College in Vancouver, spoke at the Institute in 1974, and said, "I am glad you have stopped throwing stones at other people's windows; let our two institutions hold a conference together on the topic of Creation," the Institute got its second wind.

The presence of Dutch-immigrant Canadian pastors had begun to be appreciated at CRC Synods in the 60's—they had a certain vision of societal involvement that was refreshing and not parochial. With lawyer John Olthuis, the Rev. Louis Tamminga had formed a Christian Action Foundation and *Vanguard* magazine during his pastorate in Edmonton, Alberta (1960–65). That fledgling political consciousness raising endeavor eventually became the Citizens for Justice and Liberty organization in Toronto (c. 1961–63) and allied with its older sister, the Christian Labour Association of Canada, which won its accreditation as a **christian** bona fide labor union from the Supreme Court of Ontario in 1963, whose leaders were trustees of the AACS. There seemed to be a Reformed **Canadian** mentality congealing around the Institute, though it still sounded a little foreign and brash to CRC believers in the United States.

Lawyer John Olthuis and art designer Willem Hart were integral to the Toronto action. The few Americans busy in Toronto included Rev. Paul Schrotenboer, director, and Robert Carvill, editor of *Vanguard* magazine, and later Gordon Spykman as curator. Also, long before *worldview* became a household word in the American Reformed and evangelical communities, Iowan banker Glenn Andreas managed to get published the formative lectures given at the institute's early summer student conferences—a series of **Christian Perspective** books on "Life is religion": politics, philosophy, art, sociology, and education (1960–68). Thus God's Holy Spirit was mixed in with all the sinful, unwise, beleaguered actions of the Toronto "movement" becoming an academic center.

The fight for certification

In 1975 the first Junior Member (so named to emphasize the communal nature of teaching **graduate** students) to have completed **two** years of courses at the Institute, plus a thesis, was Japanese native Masuo Miyaza-ki. But he could not go back to Japan without a formal, certified degree, so the Institute awarded him a master's in philosophy.

When the Ontario government found out, it threatened to close down the Institute, calling it a "degree mill" because ICS lacked the legal authorization to grant degrees.

Thus began an uphill fight for legal recognition, led by John Olthuis, C.T. McIntire, Gerald Vandezande, and director Robert E. Vander Ven-nen—a fight that took ten long years. In Canada the provincial government has to pass a law to charter a *bona fide* higher educational institution. Even now, ICS is legally equipped (since 1985) to grant **regular** master's and Ph.D. degrees, thanks especially to Harry Fernhout's hard work, but it is carefully stipulated that the Institute will receive no government money. (The Ontario government and universities were really afraid of granting "Christian degrees"—ICS scholarly credentials and quality of study were not in question.)

1990s and beyond: Challenges for the next generation
When ICS president Bernard Zylstra (1982–85) was out raising money—something Institute presidents have to do relentlessly—he tried to explain why people should support a **graduate-level** Reformational studies institute, even though the donors could not understand what the profs wrote for their advanced students and secular colleagues. (Philosophy and art historiography can be as technically difficult as higher medical science.)

Institute presidents Zylstra, Clifford Pitt (1985–1989), Harry Fernhout (1989–2005), Morris Greidanus (2005–06), and John Suk (2006–08) also found that it can take years to live down a professor's controversial remark or misstep in the area of leadership. The history of an institution is an ongoing process, but traumatic loss of face on occasion and bad memories die slowly. Thankfully, followers of Christ continued to support and carry on building a school that bridges generations and outlives differing personalities.

Yet the vision of Speelman, Guillaume, Runner, and many others—including women like Marcia Hollingsworth and Barbara Carvill—who **sacrificed** time, health, money, and love to develop this Institute for Christian Studies is still underappreciated.

Worldviewy studies now are fashionable everywhere, but worldview studies need the sustaining rigor of **christian philosophically-developed**

systematic thinking in order for redemptive insights to pass muster in specialized fields of learning. Our apostate culture rightly demands more than critique and generalities from scholars who believe in the lordship of Jesus Christ. And why should the lynch pin of a Christian student's formal education be among a non-confessing group of scholars? Graduates of ICS are now respected professors at Redeemer University College, The King's University College, Cornerstone, Trinity Christian, Calvin, and Dordt College, and numerous other places; this is a fact worth being deeply grateful for to God.

My Dutch-born wife and American Europeanized me have been blessed by the years of engagement, turmoil, and bitter-sweet experiences at the Institute for Christian Studies in Toronto, nestled in christian societal organizations like the CLAC, CJL-CPJ, Curriculum Development Centre, Patmos, *Christian Courier*, Salem, and Work Research Foundation, which keep one's academic feet on the laboring ground. University-level professors, we have also learned (remember Peter Speelman), need to cultivate and hold the trust of God's "little people" (*kleine luyden*) in order to flourish, as Paul told Timothy, "Don't let people despise your inexperience, but show by your life the trustworthy faith you live by" (1 Timothy 4:11–12). We have truly experienced **communion** of the sinful saints **daily.**

If you care about christian **higher** education that shapes leaders who know that **Jesus Christ claims all of life**—from prayer to literary interpretation to disposing of garbage—**to be redeemed**, then ICS is worth investigating and supporting. The "last word" in anyone's higher education should be **an outright communal Christian attempt to think through God's world and its societal problems together with a Holy Spirit that affords surprises, tears and laughter, thanksgiving and wisdom**.

[Sidebar called "A Kuyperian Trademark"]

> There is not a square inch in the whole domain of our human existence over which Christ, who is Sovereign over all, does not cry: "Mine!" –Abraham Kuyper[1]

What has come to be known as "a Kuyperian perspective" is the position that Jesus Christ claims **all** human activity should be a thankful obedient response to the Lord for God's blessed order for life on earth. Homes, schools, businesses, governments, and churches are called by

---

1   A short clear account of "Kuyper's Inch" (breadth of a thumb) by Roger Henderson in *Pro Rege* 36:3 (2008): 12–14, gives a careful exegesis of Kuyper's famous saying.

God to carry out their particular special services in a redemptive way. Each different institution has an in-house responsibility, and also a duty to practice its proper task toward other institutions in society. For example, governments should practice public justice for all people with its tax monies, and not favor a Humanist school.

Abraham Kuyper was a Reformed preacher who became Prime Minister of The Netherlands (1901–1905). With Roman Catholic support, Kuyper helped pass into law a provision that schools receive the tax monies of their respective Reformed, Catholic, Jewish, Humanist citizens for their respective faith-based schools. Kuyper led God's people to set up a "Free University" in Amsterdam—free from direct ecclesiastic and political control, but committed to be directly responsible as an educational institution to the Lord for training students who would also be law-abiding citizens and devout believers. To certify teachers are Christians by having church membership is not adequate: genuine christian schooling must evidence a redemptive vision **in** the teaching.

DOOYEWEERD'S CONTRIBUTION
TO THE HISTORIOGRAPHY OF PHILOSOPHY

The main speaker at Wheaton College's annual philosophy conference in 1961, Prof. John Wild of Yale University, observed that during the day he had heard much from Christians doing philosophy but not much about a Christian philosophy. Émile Bréhier's judgment in 1931 that to date there had been no genuine Christian philosophy in history[1] was right, said Prof. Wild. But today one could speak of the beginnings of a radically Christian philosophy, for example, Herman Dooyeweerd's thought, which has finally broken with the Greek intellectualistic disparagement of pre-theoretical experience.

While such an observation could miss the biblically Christian bite to Dooyeweerd's work and range it simply alongside contemporary forms of *Lebensphilosophie,* so much is indeed so: rather than being satisfied with Christians busy criticizing other philosophies we need to be involved in developing a Christian critique of "classical philosophy." Christian thinkers can be grateful for the contribution that Dooyeweerd as well as Prof. D. H. Th. Vollenhoven have made in the last thirty years toward a Christian historiography of philosophy.

Controlling Thesis
For Dooyeweerd that means lay bare the *religious motive* grounding and shaping the core complex of *leading ideas* that searchingly guide and set up the kind of systematic coherence a man's *philosophical conceptual analysis* of things bears. As Susanne K. Langer puts it: "a philosophy is characterized more by the formulation of its problems than by its solution of them" because "in our questions lie our principles of analysis, and our an-

---

1 "Y a-t-il une philosophie chrétienne?" *Revue de Métaphysique et de Morale* 38 (1931): 161–62.

This essay was first published in *Philosophy and Christianity: Festschrift for Herman Dooyeweerd* (Amsterdam: North Holland, 1965), 193–202.

swers may express, whatever those principles are able to yield."[2] Now the inner spring of a philosophy's problematics, adds Dooyeweerd, is an underlying religious motive. The what-how-and-why of a philosophy's first questions, the fundamental cast to its basic ideas, is crucially determined by a usually hidden, always permeating and demanding religious motive. Therefore, head for the jugular vein in your critical investigations.

Christian about this attack is its recognition of the religious depth, nature, significance of all philosophical analysis—something denied or ignored by non-Christian and not-Reformational Christian perspectives.

Dooyeweerd's principle of philosophical historiography is working with the results of his critique of theoretical thought in which he showed, by analysis of theoretical (scientific) thought, its *gegenständlich* character and therefore its necessarily assuming something about the structure of ordinary experience, the nature of meaningful knowledge, and eventually about the possibility of knowing one's self, who we humans are. That this crux of three problems (how is reality set up and experienced? what makes action meaningful? where shall the answer to self-knowledge come from?) insistently attends all scientific philosophical activity is not surprising, Dooyeweerd could say, because reality is such that, however the world is thought to be made, and whatever is said to be the sense of humankind, and Whoever is posited as the final authority on γνῶθι σεαυτόν, the Christian knows that reality, the actual created state of affairs (ordained cosmos, ruling sinful man, Almighty God) forces its way willy-nilly into a person's reflection no matter on what object one sets one's sight simply because such is the ontic setting in which humans operate, thinking. The positive ideas any given philosophy entertains with respect to this trinity of inescapable problems, entertains even by default, constitute its cosmonomic idea for Dooyeweerd. And the makeup, thrust, the spiritual temper of a given philosophy's cosmonomic idea depends upon which religious motive drives it.[3]

Like John Calvin, Dooyeweerd states that religion defines man; that the *sensus divinitatis,* the inborn referential direction of all that a man or woman self does toward the true or a pretended absolute Origin, is what makes a human human. This statement, Dooyeweerd admits, cannot be theoretically demonstrated; the same holds for the fact that theoretical thought depends upon presuppositions (not of theoretical character) to

---

2   *Philosophy in a New Key* (New York: Mentor, 1953), 2.

3   Dooyeweerd, H. *In the Twilight of Western Thought* (Philadelphia: Presbyterian and Reformed, 1960), 52. (*T*)

meet the demand for self-reflection.[4] This conviction that all human life, including thought, is religion in operation, with a human on the road to eternal life or in the way of death as Deuteronomy 30 would put it, is simply a commitment prompted by Revelation, and, it seems to me, indeed a decisive assertion marked by Biblical insight.

By religious motive then (*religieuze drijfkracht*) Dooyeweerd means the actual transcendent δύναμις that takes hold of a person's heart, fills and dominates, consciously or unconsciously, one's every action. Religious motive is the moving power, the dynamic working of God's Spirit or an idolatrous Spirit at the very roots of a human, who so captured works it out with fear and trembling and curiosity. By "religious ground-motive" Dooyeweerd does not mean the *Grundmotiv* of Heinemann or the *großen Themen* of Heimsoeth, that is, the important motifs or central themes occurring in the history of philosophy. Brümmer is misled here into judging Dooyeweerd's religious motive as a "noetic theme," one which "loses sight of the ontic relation of man to the ground of his existence."[5] But that is exactly what Dooyeweerd catches sight of with the religious motive. What Cassirer was looking for—*die letzten Quellen und Antriebe . . . eine gemeinsame Grundtendenz*—at work in history so that one could escape being entirely historically conditioned, Dooyeweerd has pointed out.[6] Dooyeweerd has radically broken with all forms of rationalism and historicism, because the religious motive he recognizes as the starting point (*uitgangspunt*) of human thought is not simply a fictive transcendental synthetic unity of apperception postulated by human thought itself, not a vital psychological motivation absolutized, nor certain significant historical tendencies:[7] the religious motives are not a human construct so much as supra-individual commanding spiritual forces and compelling perspectives of Truth or unTruth given to or (mis)taken by human creatures, who are inescapably religious and therefore necessarily existentially attached to the Truth or unTruth.[8]

---

4 Dooyeweerd, H. *A New Critique of Theoretical Thought* (Philadelphia: Presbyterian and Reformed, 1953), I:56–57. (*NCTT*)

5 Vincent Brümmer, *Transcendental Criticism and Christian Philosophy: A presentation and evaluation of Herman Dooyeweerd's "Philosophy of the Cosmonomic Idea"* (Franeker: Wever, 1961), par. 34, especially 238, 240–242, 249.

6 J. Stellingwerff, "Problemen van het Historisme," *Perspectief: Feestbundel van de jongeren bij het vijfentwintig jarig bestaan van de Vereniging voor Calvinistische Wijsbegeerte* (Kampen: Kok, 1961), 220.

7 Dooyeweerd, H. *Reformatie en Scholastiek in de Wijsbegeerte* (Franeker: Wever, 1949), 43–44. (*RS*)

8 Dooyeweerd, H. *Vernieuwing en Bezinning om het Reformatorisch Grondmotief,* be-

Unless the difference between the nature of religious motives and the nature of cosmonomic ideas (as much as their intrinsic connection[9]) is clearly understood, Dooyeweerd will continually be misread back into the idealistic tradition from which he has been sprung (*NCTT,* I, 118–119) and even be accused of a beginner's *petitio principii.*[10] Such confusion will hinder understanding the complicated double-pronged critique Dooyeweerd actually makes of "classical philosophy."

Whereas nineteenth century idealists rested their introspective transcendental critical reflection at the level of ideas and tacitly, uncritically elevated certain of those transitional limiting notions to the status of final *allgemeingültige* realities, Dooyeweerd takes a critical step beyond idealism by positing that religious motives, which are not ideational but supra-human spiritual directives, are the Archimedean points from which one philosophizes (*NCTT,* I, 88). Dooyeweerd can take this step beyond idealism, because he takes it before he gets caught in the rationalistic dogmatic web of idealism, which at best has tried to confine (theoretical) thought a bit to make room for (practical) "religion."

Dooyeweerd starts by knowingly undemonstrably *assuming* that religious presuppositions *de quibus non disputare potest* condition the ideas underlying philosophic thought. Dooyeweerd does not claim to positively *prove* "objectively" that religious motives are intrinsically related to philosophic thought; he only claims, and I think rightly, to have argued and negatively proved by appeal to the structure of theoretical thought (naturally disclosed by his own admittedly Christian orientation), which is *common to all* theoretical thought irrespective of one's religious slant, that the answer to its possibility and workability cannot be found in theoretical thought itself.[11] To philosophies unwilling to face the problem Dooyeweerd's analysis treats, and to those that see the problem but dispose of the implied question about self as a pseudo-problem, nothing can be proved (*T,* 25–26)—until they speak out thoughts claiming scientific

---

werkt door J. A. Oosterhoff (Zutphen: Van den Brink, 1959), 8, 11. (*VB*)

9 Marlet notes it exactly: *Grundlinien der Kalvinistischen "Philosophie der Gesetzesidee" als Christlicher Transzendentalphilosophie* (München: Karl Zink, 1954), 46.

10 So D. Freeman judges him in *Journal of Religion* 38 (1958): 51.

11 ". . . the demonstrative force of our critique has been *negative* in character, so far as it, taken strictly, can only demonstrate, that the starting point of theoretical thought cannot be found in that thought itself, but must be supra-theoretical in character. That it is to be found only in the central religious sphere of consciousness, is no longer to be proved *theoretically,* because this insight belongs to *self-knowledge,* which as such transcends the theoretical attitude of thought" (*NCTT,* I, 56–57); i.e., is dependent upon religious presuppositions.

validity: then the dogmatic (extra-theoretical) character of their position becomes evident, and Dooyeweerd's point is made. To object, that nothing is demonstrated unless it be "objectively" demonstrated, is this not itself a *petitio principii*, assuming philosophical argument is valid only when it proceeds without any religious assumptions?

Gist of the Historiographic Critique

A Christian critique of Western philosophy for Dooyeweerd will expose the non-Christian religious motives there for what they are and show how these untrue standpoints pervert, emaciate, and hinder the important insights (*relatieve waarheidsmomenten*) such philosophies have posed for our civilization. Because a Christian critique has the mysterious Truth of Romans 11:36 ringing in its ear (that all is from-through-and-to Jesus Christ) and recognizes from its own true standpoint what non-Christian philosophies are distortedly trying to grasp with their ideas, a Christian critique can positively appreciate, will seriously appraise, thoroughly understand the struggling and brilliant contributions of non-Christian analysis and what they have meant for developing philosophic thought to where it is today.[12]

About the Christian πoῦ στοῦ, religious motive, Cornelius van Peursen has asked point-blank: is what Dooyeweerd designates by "creation, radical fall into sin and redemption in Jesus Christ's body filled with the Holy Spirit" considered to be *the* infallible absolute truth or is it not rather a humanly fallible summation of the Bible's witness to the Truth, a summation as imperfect as the human philosophy built upon it (*PR* 26 [1961]: 200)? I think Dooyeweerd must answer that this convicting dynamic of creation-sin-salvation-and-gratitude is the humanly accepted divinely revealed Truth, the very reforming Light and Power the inworking Holy Spirit brings to us humans moved by the Scriptures.[13] And one may not be scandalized, unless you existentialistically preclude the eternal Truth's being operative in time (deny actual Word-revelation) or subjectivistically reduce the reality of God's Direction to one or more possible commitments jostling among the saints receiving it: one may not be scandalized at the offense of someone's carefully proclaiming that what one's correctible, historically bound human philosophic knowledge is being-would-must be touchstoned to is the Truth, so help me God! because such a profession is simply the offense of a person thinking, out-

---

12 *RS*, 50–51 and *Philosophia Reformata* 25 (1960): 148–149. (*PR*)

13 Cf. H. E. Runner, *Christian Perspectives 1960* (Pella: Pella Publishing, 1960), 106–107, 110.

fitted with the sword of the Gospel. Unbelievers may ignore, dispute, reject, or ridicule such an approach, but evangelical Christians have no alternative, it seems to me, than to jostle along *with* Dooyeweerd, as Stoker and others do.

Working from the vantage point of revealed Truth, working with a cosmonomic idea spiritually derived from the Truth (not logically implied by it), that is, working with leading ideas primed by the radically integrating Biblical motive,[14] a Christian critique notices the fundamental antagonism, the disintegrating polar opposition in non-Christian religious motives and their companion cosmonomic ideas.

Plato's fabulous description in the *Timaeus* on the formation of the cosmos runs into a bind, for example, with χώρα. What is this permanently amorphous, originally shaking plastic, extended? nurse of a ὑποδοχή anyhow in which are fashioned by God what becomes copies of the ungenerated indestructible forms, αὐτὰ ταῦτα εἴδη καθ᾽ (50b–53b)? It is hard to understand, says Plato sagely, how utterly chaotic χώρα somehow can partake of τὸ νοητόν,[15] but Plato stoutly maintains (47e–48a) that the cosmos was generated by Νοῦς, persuasively overpowering the erratic Ἀνάγκη (χώρα "filled" with indefinite kinds of powers). Look, says Dooyeweerd, Plato's aporia with χώρα, how to fit this everlasting, formless generatrix into a mathematically rational universe, is not some logical inconsistency to his thought, a momentary blind spot. Plato saw sharply both the structured nature of things in God's world and their evident transiency, as well as the disturbing fact, that something was wrong. Because creation-sin-salvation in Jesus Christ's body was not the moving power behind his comprehension of what he actually saw, because as an inescapably religious man of the fourth century before Christ his heart was gripped by the daemonic faith in technical form versus a brute hurly-burly life-force (*RS,* 428, 430–431), whenever Plato's philosophical analysis led him back to the key matters of origin, meaning of it all, and how the world is set up, the intrinsic antinomy to his leading

---

14 So I interpret Dooyeweerd's (1960) polemic amplification of his (1948) scrupulous warning: "De transcendentale tijdsidee is niet aan dit uitgangspunt ontleend, maar slechts daardoor gericht. Een van haar [W. d. W.] grondstellingen is, dat uit haar centraal Bijbels uitgangspunt geen enkele van de drie transcendentale grondideeën, die in de wetsidee zijn samengevat, is *af te leiden. . .*" (*PR* 25:101). "Het bedoelde grondidee of wetsidee is niet identiek met de religieuze dunamis of drijfkracht van het grondmotief, maar slechts de *theoretische uitdrukking* van dit laatste, die als zoodanig afhankelijk blijft van dit grondmotief, dat zich zinvol in deze idee uitdrukt" (*PR* 13:57).

15 . . . ἀνόρατον εἶδός τι καὶ ἄμορφον, πανδεχές, μεταλαμβάνον δὲ ἀπορώτατά πῃ τοῦ νοητοῦ καὶ δυσαλωτότατον αὐτὸ λέγοντες οὐ φευσόμεθα (51ab).

philosophical ideas—due to the underlying dialectic of this informing religious motive—the builtin misconception of God's world, which runs through Plato's cosmology, anthropology, theory of knowledge, ethics, aesthetics, and what not, this hapless, keen distortion breaks out into the open. Νοῦς: χώρα or Plato's μέθεξις: χωρισμός or Aristotle's νόησις νοήσεως: πρώτη ὕλη or earlier thinkers' exaggerated fascination solely with φύσις: the revealing rationale to any Greek philosophy and to the whole evolution of Greek philosophy, says Dooyeweerd, is this single dialectical Greek religious motive of Form/Matter (*RS*, 30).

Or take Kant. Kant's philosophical genius and pathos are rooted in the religious motive of personal freedom versus causally determined nature. One could document how early Christians like Clement of Alexandria propaedeutically tucked Greek thought (and therefore the Greek religious motive) under the wing of an elevated Christian γνῶσις, and how this handmaiden affair scholastically firmed up into a distinct faith construct of a relatively autonomous realm of nature (includes philosophy) completed by a special supernatural realm of grace (theology here), with the understanding *gratia naturam non tollit, sed perficit* (cf. Thomas, *ST*, Iq. 1, a. 8). Dooyeweerd argues it is the Renaissance twist, which threw off Grace and ushered in with an élan Man as creator and savior of nature now defined mathematico-mechanically that formed Kant's horizons. Kant's first questions were posed by his faith in scientific understanding (for control of natural sense phenomena) jockeying controversially with his faith in practical reason (creatively applying moral ideals) to bring about human freedom, and his involved answers express only whatever this initial antinomic cosmonomic structure pendent from his embraced religious motive is able to yield. It yields contradiction. How can autonomous, timeless *reine Begriffe* ever be involved in a working relation with chaotic, later timed *Empfindungen*? Kant finally affirms their synthesis possible, dogmatically—on the very basis of his hidden religious dialectic, (*NCTT*, I, 89–90). And how come man's practical ideas are to have no real point of contact with his scientific analyses yet eventually, extrinsically should regulate them? Kant can only echo Thomas with a hollow secular sound: *Vernunft* cannot possibly disturb *Verstand,* but must contribute to its perfection.[16] Kant faced Hume's implacable threat to science honestly, and he understood piously the sober calling of man

---

16 "Es muss aber dennoch zwischen dem, was zur Natur der Vernunft und des Verstandes gehört. Einstimmung sein, und jene muss zur Vollkommenheit der letzteren beitragen und kann sie unmöglich verwirren" (*Prolegomena zu einer jeden künftigen Metaphysik,* par. 44).

to rule the universe, but he could not get the humpty-dumpties back together again because the modern motive of Freedom cleft from Nature in a single religious dialectic ruled his philosophical approach. It is not Kant's torturous non-answer to Hume that marked the truly significant and revolutionary act of his thought, suggests Dooyeweerd, but rather Kant's influential push for the primacy of practical (non-scientific) Reason, because this opened the door historically to the ichtisch Fichtisch sans-culottic romantic philosophies, which worshipped the aesthetically free creative *ego* alone and wildly believed it able to make the whole world as it wished unbothered by any (scientific) laws (*NCTT*, I, 90, 354–357, 362).

Precisely because persistent, fine thought has gone into such great philosophies as Plato and Kant's do they betray so clearly the irrevocable échec to systematic thought not dominated by the biblical motive, which openly focuses all creation in humanity through Jesus Christ out upon the living transcendent Sovereign God. Non-Christian religious motives offer some relative aspect of created reality as god with the inevitable result that whatever is not so deified is consolidated as an absolutely antagonistic antipode; and this broken-down, fenced-in radical disturbance at the base of human consciousness cannot be theoretically resolved but philosophically can only be muffled by muddled, inconsequent thinking (*T*, 36–37; *NCTT*, I, 63–64; *RS*, 54–55). That is the double prong to Dooyeweerd's Christian historiographic critique: non-Christian philosophies are as vitally in contact with created reality and genuine problems as are competent Christians (hence their cosmonomic idea), but non-Christian and apostate philosophies *cannot* give τὴν λογικὴν λατρείαν Paul asks of us humans, because the start and heart of their business is prostituted. Therefore, study them well! Dooyeweerd would say, as a warning catalogue of traps and antinomies thinkers (including Christians) by nature are prone to fall for *and* let their incisive distorted judgments of reality, their mis-taken knowledge, help us see, what *we* are analyzing ourselves in a reforming Christian perspective.

Contribution and Implications

Dooyeweerd's own philosophy and his criticism of "classical philosophy" teems with problems much because he simply writes with the carelessness of genius—is it so that book one of Aristotle's *Metaphysica* correctly typifies pre-Aristotelian Greek thought (*RS*, 20, n. 2)?—is it accurate to characterize Kant's *Kritik der Urteilskraft* also as a "dualistic" failure to solve the antinomy? One could picador Dooyeweerd for a long time. But it might be more fruitful to explore tightening up Dooyeweerd's historiographical method of analysis by grafting his insights into the careful approach of Vollenhoven.

Both Vollenhoven and Dooyeweerd are working out of the same philosophical perspective when they examine and evaluate the philosophical results of earlier and contemporary thinkers. While Dooyeweerd's main concern has been to expose the religious antithetical dialectic that informs a man's given philosophical standpoint, that is, how a pagan, synthetically Christian or secular *Archimedean point* disturbs one's philosophy with antinomies, Vollenhoven has focused his critical probing of the religious foundation to philosophical conceptions around the matter of *Arché,* that is, how God's Law-Word is viewed. This different locus of critique has made Dooyeweerd and Vollenhoven's historiographic methodologies seem more different than they really are, also because Dooyeweerd explains the cosmic fragmentation hidden in philosophic theory ruled by unbiblical meaning-motives loosely in terms of opposed modal aspects (hypostatized as form vs. matter, intellective grace above psychological nature, cultural freedom vs. material necessity) while Vollenhoven, more impressed with individuality-structure as an initiating point for analysis, explains mistaken reductions of Origin in terms of subject-ivism, object-ivism, and real-ism (absolutization of the cosmic structure binding individual subjects and objects). In addition, Vollenhoven's method documents consequently how a given philosophical conception breaks down the structure of world and the human (with monism or dualism) and approximates the relation of an individual to the universe—key philosophical problems, which when seen as critical points in a philosophical ontology aid the historiographer of philosophy in ordering and demonstrating the recurrence of somewhat similar philosophical conceptions throughout the history of thought.[17]

The fact, that Dooyeweerd and Vollenhoven's philosophical historiographical methods and results are complementary has not been sufficiently noticed, explored, and utilized. It would seem to me highly desirable that monographs of philosophical critique, as well as more sustained studies of periods that would bear witness to a Christian analytic bite, learn to move within the genial sweep of Dooyeweerd's religious-motive analysis and Vollenhoven's exhaustively precise treatment of the typically philosophical problematics that give away a thinker's religiously loaded

---

17 Cf. C. Seerveld, "Philosophical Historiography," *Journal of the American Scientific Affiliation* 13:3 (1960): 87–89. Note especially pages 11–16 in Vollenhoven's jubileum article in *PR* 26 (1961).

cosmonomic idea.[18]

Antagonists of such Christian historiographic philosophical critique must face Dooyeweerd's point that a christian historiographic critique of philosophy is not narrow-minded (*enghartig*) but evaluates a foreign philosophy from the inside out (*immanente benadering*) in terms of its own religious motive in order to veritably understand the other's attempted and attained service toward opening up (*ontsluiting*) creation in the ordained duration under Almighty God we call history (*VB*, 103; *RS*, 12, 52). In fact, Dooyeweerd claims rightly, for criticism of a given philosophical analysis and problematics not to realize that and to recognize which religious motive underlies the other is for criticism to slip its own grounding religious presuppositions into the works (*RS*, 42), and this makes a farce out of historiography, like making Plato, on the strength of a few late dialogues, an honorary member of the Vienna Circle, or like exegeting Thomas into the forefront of contemporary existentialism. Actually it is the *Ausschliesslichkeitsanspruch*, which Jaspers disdains, behind Christian critique that gives it the wherewithal to break out of the anti-historical! relativ*ism* of Historicism (where norms are sought in the present without any meaningful connection to past development) and to delineate the *relative* norm-bound sense of all philosophies (including Christian philosophy) within the slow movement of hard fought re-creation en route to the Last Day.[19]

Also, finally exposed is the idea of *philosophia perennis*. Famed Copleston "adheres to the Thomistic standpoint, that there is a *philosophia perennis* and that this *philosophia perennis* is Thomism in a wide sense."[20] K. J. Popma has interestingly shown that the Romanistic conception of *philosophia perennis* (a continuing core of naturally reasoned *Lehrgut*) was immediately at odds with the *philosophia perennis* conceived by the Renaissance figure Augustinus Stechus Eugubinus who coined the phrase with a book around 1540 (in which most of Christian theology was found in naturally reasoned philosophy): thus the tolerance of "*philosophia perennis*" has its limits[21] because it too has religious presuppositions! It will not surprise me if champions of "classical philosophy" subtly try

---

18 Henk Hart has recently signaled clearly a step that could lead in this direction. Cf. *Correspondentiebladen van de Vereniging voor Calvinistische Wijsbegeerte* 28 (Dec. 1964): 7–10.

19 M. C. Smit, "Historisme en Antihistorisme," *Wetenschappelijke Bijdragen door leerlingen van Dr. D. H. Th. Vollenhoven* (Franeker: Wever, 1951), 170–172.

20 F. Copleston, *A History of Philosophy* (London: Burns & Oates, 1961), I, 7.

21 "Philosophia Perennis," *PR* 55:2 (1955), 81.

to deny philosophic rights to Dooyeweerd's philosophy as non-perennial; but this would only be another example of the pseudo-broad-minded dogmatism afoot in every age. Dooyeweerd probes this same problem acutely in a little different context: "as long as there exists a fundamental difference in the philosophical views of meaning and experience, it does not help if, in line with contemporary logical positivism we seek to establish criteria for meaningful and meaningless philosophical propositions and require their verifiability" (*T*, 3–4). You have got to reach the jugular vein to break down dogmatism and establish dialogue, the kind of discussion that leads to an enriched understanding of one's position, not to universal agreement (*T*, 59).

Dooyeweerd's challenge along with that of Vollenhoven is not to cultivate *philosophia perennis,* but to build up a Christian community of thought that shall furnish the institutional setting for *philosophia reformanda.* An intrinsically re-formed Christian philosophy that goes back to and beyond the pre-theoretical (naive) experience Prof. Wild mentioned, to the very revealed Truth, that cannot be begun, says Dooyeweerd, so long as our philosophy willingly keeps on accommodating itself to this or that contemporary trend while bowing formally to the privileges of faith. Is this not limping between two opinions, between the natural light of reason synthetically connected to the realm of special grace? All a Christian does needs to be radically subjected to his Christian commitment, even his or her philosophy. No one shall ever have constructed a thoroughly Christian philosophy or made a final Christian critique of "classical philosophy": but what is required of us evangelical Reformational Christians is that we be busy at it together in the world when the Lord comes.

DOOYEWEERD'S IDEA OF "HISTORICAL DEVELOPMENT": CHRISTIAN RESPECT FOR CULTURAL DIVERSITY

> Since he identified apologetics by and large with defensiveness, Kuyper had little place for it, and he became a major source of whatever distrust of apologetics there is within the Reformed community.
>
> Within Kuyperian circles, Christian apologetics has been replaced, in great measure, by Christian philosophy.[1]

It is indeed the defensiveness of apologetics as a theological discipline that has always made me feel more at home with the positive task of contributing to a Christian philosophical systematics. I think I am grateful to those who would argue that the historical Christian faith is reasonable, but I would prefer to give an account of the hope I have in Christ's Rule a-coming (1 Peter 3:15) not by argument that shows that the disbeliever does not have a rational leg to stand on, but by making the secularist jealous of what Christ's body knows is true for right-doing culturally in God's ongoing world (cf. Romans 11:13–14).

Because Robert Knudsen has consistently supported the Christian philosophical endeavor stemming from the vision of Abraham Kuyper in the Netherlands, upon this occasion of honoring him as the retiring professor of apologetics at Westminster Theological Seminary, I should like critically to examine Herman Dooyeweerd's important, complex conception of "historical development" (*historishe ontwikkeling*) and "the opening process of temporal meaning" (*ontsluitingsproces*).[2] My intent is to exposit supportively Dooyeweerd's contribution begun in the 1930s,

---

1 Robert Knudson, "The Transcendental Perspective of Westminster's Apologetic," *WTJ* 48 (1986) 223–39; quotation from 225.

2 This matter is examined briefly in an early Knudson syllabus on *History* (1969, for classes at Westminster), in a section titled "The Norm of History," 29–31.

This chapter was first published in *The Westminster Theological Journal* 58 (1996): 41–61.

and also begin to update the concern to be historically obedient to Jesus Christ's Rule in cultural development and the allocation of institutional powers in society faced by Christian believers in the Western world today.

We who educate at Westminster Seminary in Philadelphia and the Institute for Christian Studies in Toronto need a honed, biblically directed analysis of historical change so that the many two-thirds-world students who come to us, suffering from a secularized Western educative neocolonialism, may find a conceptual place in the present generation to breathe fresh air.

Individual creatures are primed to mature

Creatural entities like mountains, trees, and animals have a panoply of object-functional possibilities given with their existence, which lie waiting for, ontically anticipating, the disclosure of such potential properties. Minerals wait to be mined for metal instruments; plants grow to be cut for food or herbs; animal skins can be converted into human clothes, as God did once for Adam and Eve (Genesis 3:21). And such opening-up and cultivated realization of stone flints, vegetation, and animal life is how the LORD primed God's creation (Genesis 1:26–31).

Human creatures too, as special self-hooded, neighborhooded persons in God's world, are each born to mature modally with their built-in responsibility to God's varied calls for obedience. In fact, humans are ontically prone to exercise their various subject-functional activities through the passing years so that one gradually builds up what one could identify as dispositions, like a temperament, a style, an intelligence, and a character. Among these relatively lasting identity traits and congealed, alterable, ongoing characteristics of individuality, one's more elemental, for example, physio-organic processes, tend to undergird and give tensile stamina to support the flourishing of one's more complex feelings, speech, and ability to be interpersonally social. If you always have a slight headache, it is hard to be empathetic, talkative, sociable. Such interconnected changing maturation is ordinary for human creatures.

God's ordinances, which together structure the varied filling-out and deepening of human life activity, elicit compliance, but with sin afoot in the world much can go awry. Even this transmodal process of realizing the different object-functionings of non-human subjects, and the cultural press upon humans to deploy and consolidate one's full modal creatural complexity prompt acquiescence, but do not insure such fulfillment happens. The LORD's mandate to "cultivate the earth" (Psalm 8:3–8; 115:16–18) is not a Platonic *eidos* or a threatening ancient Persian decree or a Jewish legal prescript. God's law for the process of unfolding creatural glories and for calling humans to a maturity of modal activity is a commanding blessing, which creatures may default on, neglect, or spurn.[3] Dooyeweerd aims to reject reading the creational propensity for cultivated disclosure as Aristotle did, as an entelechaic natural law, whereby little acorns necessarily wax into giant oak trees and the best noetic mortals attenuate themselves to a divine immortality (*N. Ethica* 10.7 1177b26–1178a2), or as Durkheim, Comte, and Herbert Spencer did, as a necessary bio-evolutionistic law (*NCTT* 2:260–61; *TWT*, 102).[4]

The biblical account of creation indicates it is normal to be born male or female and later on to leave mother and father to cleave to a wife or husband, and then bear children. But men and women who go childless, decide not to marry, remain or become a eunuch for the sake of God service, are thoroughly human, worthy of deep respect in spite of being short of certain fulfillment. Perhaps even because they are "unencumbered," single persons may be unusually gifted—those who *have everything*, hint Jesus and Paul, may lose the key childlike attachment to the Lord, which makes one truly rich (Matthew 19, 1 Corinthians 7). Yet it is creaturally normal for humans to learn to crawl and run, to see sights and speak the mother tongue, although too many children are physically or analytically lame, suffer sensational or aesthetic blindness, experience a mania, autistic impairment, or orphanhood, through no fault of their own. Such exceptional humans—although it is a hard saying—are awful openings for demonstrating the covenantal LORD's compassion through Christ's body (cf. John 9:1–4ff).

So, while the opening-up process, which envelops all created things, remains "broken in character," says Dooyeweerd, allowing meaning to

---

3   In a chapter on "Creation Ordinances," John Murray phrased the matter so: ". . . these creation ordinances furnish us with what is central in the biblical ethic. . . . Conditions and circumstances have been revolutionized by sin, but the basic structure of this earth, and of man's life in it, has not been destroyed" (*Principles of Conduct* [Grand Rapids: Eerdmans, 1957], 44).

4   Herman Dooyeweed's works will be referred to as follows:

CRPT = The Criteria of Progressive and Reactionary Tendencies in History (1958 address commemorating 150th anniversary of the Koninklijke Nederlandse Akademie van Wetenschappen; Amsterdam: Noord Holland Uitgever, 1959).

NCTT = De wijsbegeerte der wetsidee (3 vols; Amsterdam: H.J. Paris, 1935–36), in translation, *A New Critique of Theoretical Thought* (4 vols; Philadelphia: Presbyterian and Reformed, 1955–57).

TWT = In the Twilight of Western Thought: Studies in the pretended autonomy of philosophical thought (Philadelphia: Presbyterian and Reformed, 1960).

VB = Vernieuwing en bezinning om het reformatorisch grondmotief (ed. J.A. Oosterhoff; Zutphen: J.B. van den Brink, 1959).

be short-circuited, the full redemption of creation's promised unfolding normality still holds true for those secured in Jesus Christ (*NCTT* 2:334–37; cf. Isaiah 60–62, Revelation 21:1–22:5). I would add that along with the postlapsarian brokenness, and the apostate misguidance that can also bring misery to human flowering and environmental deployment, is the presence of an uncanny Evil still afoot in the world that does not rhyme with the knowledge humans have available. All the more vital then is our connected recognition that the creational promptings the LORD God has given us creatures for change and maturation continues providentially to undergird the hope of Christ's final redemptive Rule a-coming.

It is God's will for society to differentiate authorities while maintaining integration

Dooyeweerd seems to extend this conception of the opening-up, unfolding process of entities with individuality-structure to the more complex terrain of *society at large* when he names "differentiation, integration, individualization" as the three-in-one historical formative task put by God to humanity for developing the modally diverse, definite societal relationships, institutional bonds, and voluntary associations possible as typical cultural spheres of authority within humankind (*NCTT* 2:274–76; *TWT*, 102–12). Dooyeweerd also contends that differentiating to such zones of special competence as science, art, state controls, church affairs, business ventures, and schools aimed at training, is God's will for civilizing society when the workings of these diverse modally qualified areas of cultural activity are integrated in a particular physiognomy (*VB* 76–80, *NCTT* 2:287 n.1). Dooyeweerd readily admits that God's best laid plans for civilization can he thwarted, derailed, laid waste in time by human sin (*VB* 98–104, *NCTT* e.g., 3:271).

The biblical insight of Dooyeweerd's idea of God's creational "pull" on human society (cf. George Herbert's poem, "The Pulley") to differentiate itself into limited circles of human formative control is probably, in my judgment, one of his two or three most potent philosophical contributions, because it gives human leaders not a "universal" or oversimplified rule, but a deft regional *principium* for deciding contextually what may be historically obedient to the Lord, or misguided.[5] The statesman must decide whether a political policy does justice to the citizens, not

---

5   Sander Griffioen, "De betekenis van Dooyeweerds ontwikkelingsidee," *Philosophia Reformata* 51 (1986): 83–109, 107: "De diepste betekenis van Dooyeweerds ontwikkelingsidee ligt niet in haar vruchtbaarheid voor de vakwetenschappen, maar in het perspectief dat ze biedt op de concrete levenspraktijk."

whether the proposal is socially popular. The business woman must judge whether a given transaction provides resources generously for needs rather than promotes luxuries for sated tastes. An academician must learn to make precise distinctions that generate wisdom instead of entertaining students with fashionable slogans about esoteric trivia, if he or she would be historically significant *coram Deo* in the arena of learning.

This *principium* of integrative differentiation also gives historians the wherewithal to make fine measured principled judgments, without the supererogatory vibrato of certainty that a late-comer easily brings to a scene, or whether certain innovative acts or lack of action once upon a time were wise or regressive deeds. If the principle[6] of integrated differentiation and ensuing individualization indeed holds for what actually needs to happen historically in society, then the historian does not need to guess at personal intentions or mark significance by eventual success. Even historical failures, due to any sort of oppressive totalitarian empire in force at a time, can be very redemptive historical signposts of Christ's rule a-coming.

In Dooyeweerd's judgment, Clovis' founding the Frankish kingdom in the fifth century AD was historically fruitful for the political-cultural well-being of the German speaking peoples (*NCTT* 2:244). The Roman Catholic ecclesiastical institution, however formidable with its lethal power of excommunication, notes Dooyeweerd, bolstered well the fabric of feudal societal life after the dissolution of the Carolingian empire in the 800s AD, by city-generating building projects, balancing regional tyrants off against one another, authorizing monastic orders, which both preserved valuable manuscripts and did needful benevolent work among the populace (*NCTT* 2:288, my examples).

Working with Dooyeweerd's *principium* of historical development one would credit the ancient Greek sophists for professionalizing rhetorical education, despite their unscrupulous subjectivism. The more superficial sophist compelled, as it were, deeper-going philosophical objectivist Socrates' pupils to begin a philosophical "Academy," because institutional education does have a more pervasive societal presence and durance than a single gifted mentor.

One would also notice, for example, the epochal thrust *l'Accademia del disegno* had after being finally set up by Humanist painter Giorgio

---

6   "On Kuyper's view the Dutch word for principle, *beginsel,* has a richer meaning than its English equivalent. . . . For Kuyper a principle is something that impels and molds. Christian principles are major forces that direct and form the life of the Christian community" (Knudson, "Transcendental Perspective," 225).

Vasari at Firenze in 1563, which separated the grand Medici elected artists like Michelangelo from the ordinary run of the guild artisan. The differentiation of artist from artisans was historically significant for the incredible florescence of Italian Renaissance painterly art and sculpture, even though its elitist virus has cursed the field of "fine arts" with hauteur to this very day.

Dooyeweerd can designate the restoration of seigniorial rights in the Netherlands in 1814–15 as an atavism (*NCTT* 2:236) and condemn any Nazi *Blut und Boden* appeal to champion an Aryan Volk as historically reactionary (*NCTT* 2:274), as well as horrendously evil for many other reasons. And one does not need to be Marxian to challenge the monopolistic praxis of an international business corporation that expropriates independent commercial enterprise in the name of mass efficiency and stock market profit, because such action closes down economic openings and forces a political state-type of authority upon economic endeavors.

The wholesome thrust to the principle of societal historical development that Dooyeweerd has formulated as a creational principium is this: the LORD's concern is to spill over on people in time the liberating ennoblement of shared specific responsibilities. Violation of this primordial historical injunction to encourage differential tasks bearing an integrative prospect with definite openings for individual innovation is so destructive because the violation stifles being human and flourishing humanly in God's world.

A problem with Dooyeweerd's conception of "primitive" societies

However, this genial principle of God's "pulley" of speciating differentiation in world history is troubled by a few conceptual problems in Dooyeweerd's formulation that deserve thinking through.

That creation at large be initially given in order to be "opened-up," to have its potential riches disclosed by human cultivation, according to Dooyeweerd, and yet to blame an undifferentiated society and un-opened-up state of creaturely affairs as the result of sin and apostasy before God, seems antinomic. A fallen creation, observes Geertsema (1970: 141), is a prerequisite, in Dooyeweerd's view, for history. While that is a not unusual supralapsarian position, which locks God's redemptive plan and the fact of sin firmly into place, Dooyeweerd's tack has him identify tribal cultures dominated by mana and tabu as rigid, undifferentiated "primitive" societies caught in the moil of idolatry with a closed-down subsistence in God's world, because they have sold their transcendental birthright of worshiping the LORD for a mess of totem pottage (*NCTT*

2:259–62, 296–97). Then Dooyeweerd struggles to explain how there can, nevertheless, be opening-up and cultural deepening of meaning in such myth-ridden settings where all manner of gods, fetishes, magic, and demons degrade society and have replaced the sanity of worshiping the Creator of heaven and earth with blighted ignorance (*NCTT* 2:309–20).

Some of Dooyeweerd's 1935–36 observations on "primitive society," in his vigorous debate with Durkheim, James Frazer, Lévy-Bruhl, and Cassirer, seem inaccurate generalizations today, and not sensitive enough to the Europocentric slant in force when one identities our "higher cultural level" as if it could be the norm personified. It is questionable to me whether the presence of shaman, smithy, woman herbalist, praise singer, and chief in a tribal setting should be described as "the guardians of a rigid group-tradition, often deified by a pagan faith" (*NCTT* 2:259). There has always been more colorful variety and shared duties among the Fulani traders in sub-Saharan Africa, for example, than easily meets the Western eye.[7]

More serious for me is the matter of whether it is not speculative to posit a stage of undifferentiated society. Is "undifferentiated society" not still a hangover from the very macro-evolutionistic conjecture of an *apeiron* origin from which civilization rises in premillennial, biogenetic continuity—the very philosophical error Dooyeweerd forcefully rejects? Dooyeweerd himself spends considerable effort delineating "the *complicated* [!] structure [of various typical forms] of *undifferentiated organized communities* [my emphasis]" (*NCTT* 3:368, 346–67). So Dooyeweerd cannot mean by "undifferentiated" something amorphous or "simple"— neither Hobbes' original war nor Rousseau's pristine innocence. Dooyeweerd sees "primitive" societies as "mixed-up," that is, as not yet modally sorted out.

Since the Bible mentions that in the second generation of humankind the shepherd Cain built a city (Genesis 4:17), and in the second generation after God's flooding the world, the mighty hunter Nimrod built a city (Genesis 10:10–12), I doubt it to be sound to posit a prior "undif-

---

7   Griffioen says that Dooyeweerd follows Cassirer's mistaken idea that individuals of totemistic cultures *identified* themselves with the (mythical ancestral) animals ("De betekenis," 91). But Dooyeweerd is very careful in affirming the "disintegration of personality-awareness . . . in primitive peoples" (*NCTT* 2: 316), and pointedly qualifies and *corrects* Cassirer's "exaggeration" with Malinowski's denial of the effacement of individuals "by the group-mind" (*NCTT* 2:310–21). Cf. also, "At a primitive stage of culture . . . the guardians of the group-tradition remain responsible individual personalities. They cannot be denatured to a kind of indifferent passage-way of an unconscious group-will" (*NCTT* 2:245). However, Dooyeweerd does seem overly partial at times to Cassirer's leanings.

ferentiated society" from which much later urban civilizations evolve. Jane Jacobs' fascinating exposition of the thesis that cities are first and rural development comes later also supports the biblical narrative, and directly questions the reigning dogma of agricultural primacy, which she traces to Adam Smith's farrago that industry and commerce arise out of farming.[8] Jacobs argues that hunters become traders generate settlement centers of import and export, which gradually build a support system of animal breeding and hybrid seeds that became useful to farmers. Dooyeweerd himself emphasizes that fallen humans who live together under the inversion and restriction of their inalienable gift to be creatures of faith exemplify *devolution* of their human promise (*NCTT* 2:245, 309–10).

The conceptual mistakes I think we need to avoid are at least two: (1) a simple transposition from the structured opening-up of a human individual to the structured development of human society; and (2) an expectation that the ontologically possible schema of creatural complication functions as a necessary pattern of sequential duration. In my judgment a human is not a micro-society, and society is not a macro-individual, although both individual humans and society endure and have their meaning in God's good modal cosmic order. Entities rightly unfold their identity and fill out an individual human nature. But society, when it progresses normatively under "the demands of historical development" (*CPRT*:8) apportionates its nature, that is, portions out responsibilities, exfoliates specific ministries, not to round out a particular physiognomy but to diversify the whole, almost expand the intricacies, while remaining in concert.

I agree with Dooyeweerd that attempts to over-rule differentiation extant in society in order to reach a *simplified* integration is a totalitarian move that curses the inhabitants (*NCTT* 2:274). But we need, I think, to find ways to honor the relative strengths of less differentiated societies without abdicating a norm for their development.

A historically developed society can intensify evil

The vision that defines Dooyeweerd's whole philosophical reflection (*NCTT* 2:294–95, 363–65) is that the fundamental cosmic struggle between *civitas Dei* and *civitates mundi* will end with the sure ultimate historical victory of the LORD in Jesus Christ's Rule on the new earth. How that eschatonic struggle intersects with the historical process of "differentiation, integration, and individualization" is, however, somewhat ill-defined.

---

8 Jane Jacobs, *The Economy of Cities* (New York: Random House, 1969), 44–48.

Dooyeweerd can maintain that "Once *the progress of historical evolution* [in economic transactions] had reached a sufficiently *advanced stage* [viz., the modern credit system], this medieval norm [of prohibiting interest] *could not remain unaltered*" (*NCTT* 2:241, my emphasis). Likewise, for Dooyeweerd, Aristotle's posited norm in the *Poetics* for theater "is no longer valid in modern dramaturgy" (*NCTT* 2:240), but is superseded.

Paul Ricoeur would support the thesis that certain inventions like gun powder, writing and reading, moveable type for printing, the steam engine, and telephone, create "an irreversible situation for everyone" and establish "a *de facto* universality of mankind [sic]." Dooyeweerd might demur when Ricoeur goes on to assert that "The modern State, *qua* State, has a recognizable universal structure," thanks to "the rationalization of power represented by an administration"—Ricoeur credits supra-national science and technics for our becoming a one world civilization today.[9]

That is, Dooyeweerd and Ricoeur seem to say that certain technical development—improvement of tools accumulates cultural power that is never lost[10]—is inexorable; in the flow of cultural history, differentiation and (rational) specialization is on the side of the angels, as it were, and simply outdates less professional forms of human cultivation of reality. Yet both Ricoeur and Dooyeweerd recognize that certain "progress" is evil (*NCTT* 2:260–62). While Dooyeweerd believes Western culture is not a "closed" civilization (*NCTT* 2:268), and emphasizes that genuine "development as such" is the crucial idea for thinking through history (*NCTT* 2:281–84), he wants to keep distinct from the "process of an (increasing) cultural integration and differentiation . . . the leveling tendencies which in our days threaten the so-called underdeveloped cultures with secularized factors of Western civilization" (*NCTT* 2:260). Ricoeur also admits that the wonderful "massive" advancement of universalized culture we are witnessing since the 1950s "at the same time constitutes a sort of subtle destruction, not only of traditional cultures, which might not be an irreparable wrong, but also of . . . the creative nucleus of . . . great cultures"[11]—our worldwide civilization is becoming mediocre!

The upshot of this conceptual puzzle leads me to agree with Grif-

---

9   Paul Ricoeur, *History and Truth* (Evanston: Northwest University Press, 1965), 272, 273, 281. "The convergence [of capitalistic and authoritarian socialist economies] results from the fact that economies as well as politics is cultivated by the human sciences, which in their essence are supra-national, without a country. The original universality, with its scientific character, permeates all human technics with rationality" (ibid., 274).

10 Ibid., 275.

11 Ibid., 276.

fioen's sound judgment that while cultural and societal differentiation deploys amazing new features of creation's enriching possibilities, the process can also mean a deplorable loss of quality life and impoverishment of humanity.[12] As I followed a boy of the Kuranko tribe in Sierra Leone through a mesh of reeds towering over our heads, suddenly he stopped shock still. I who am schooled to hear the difference between major and minor chords in music and can discern the fine differences between Australian, British, American, and Dutch-spoken English was completely unable to sense which silences in that steamy tropical, insect-humming river environs meant safety or death by snake bite. Is a jungle-smart native who knows the medicinal value of hundreds of herbs and roots less "developed" in knowledge than an experimental scientist who can extract antitoxic serums from such plants? If you were to balance the "freedoms" of Gallic serfs in the relatively underdifferentiated feudal landlord setup c. 1100 AD against those of regimented British textile workers in Manchester during the mercantilist so-called "Industrial Revolution" in the mid-1800s, whose life would weigh humanly richer? When a person has gained entrance to the wide world of precise academic jargon, but lost the hang of slang and any poetic soul to one's speech, what does it profit your semantic humanity? And Griffioen is eloquent in pointing out the deserts of abandonment in the modern metropolises of the world—New York, London, Paris—because of "the sheer absence of normal rhythms" in every 24 hours, with the huge existential cost in drugged violence and despair.[13] Not all that "develops" a differentiated glitter is gold.

Dooyeweerd knows about such cultural checkmate, but his conceptual framework apparently fixes him ever close to the schema of *opening-up* faith-*closed* cultures to a *higher, deepened, developed* civilization (*NCTT* 2:245, 259, 265–67), as if a rigidly restricted faith is the major negative factor, and differentiation (viz., "the norms of historical evolution," *NCTT* 2:237) pries open such stubborn unbelief. But cultural differentiation does not, in my judgment, necessarily exorcise God-forsaking idolatry, and can just as well disseminate a curse and sediment human disobedience in cultural artifacts and societal formations, like cluster bombs, urban ghetto gangs, waste plastic, and Las Vegas, where aggression, efficient greed, and trivia deface the standard bearer Psalm 8 celebrates. To be sure Dooyeweerd notes that when an idolatrous cultural drive "bring[s] about great things in the development of civilization . . . it also [entails] historical guilt [and is] revenged by cultural tensions, conflicts and catastrophes" (*NCTT* 2:291).

---

12 Griffioen, "De betekenis," 94.

13 Sander Griffioen, *The Problem of Progress* (Sioux Center: Dordt College Press, 1987).

Yet I think we need a more delicate working hypothesis than that of open and closed cultures where the dialectic of Nature-bound tribalism opposed to the opening-up of social, jural, and moral law-spheres of fifth-century BC Greek culture with art and philosophy, for example (*NCTT* 2:321), tends to crowd out the truth that the wages of sin and the patience of God's blessing are not respecters of cultural "level" of civilization (*NCTT* 2:295, 322). Further, we need to recognize as inhabitants of Western civilization that differentiating human decisions taken in society by those who carry authority and power are intrinsically *directed* by one's allegiance to the *civitas Dei* or the principalities and powers of evil (Ephesians 6:12); and one has no credit with God if a people "develop" culturally only to disseminate motley waste products. Between the cultured deceit of selling weapons wholesale through an arms lobby cartel to poor nations or the systematic dislocation of a child's psyche by literate abusive parents and the notorious ancient Aztec cruelty, who would want to judge as to "savagery"? Post-Christian secularists, from the old unholy Roman to the current holier-than-others American empire, have the potential to be more perverse than an authentic pagan culture could be, because we have the onus of deciding, in our differentiated glory, to reject the gospel heard of Jesus Christ's mercy, and we possess greater power than in earlier days to rub the evil in.

Possible corrections to the tangent of Dooyeweerd's problematics

If it is so that less differentiated societies may have strengths worth preserving, thanks to God's grace, and if highly developed, so-called civilized society may be carrying out deeply destructive cultivating acts in God's world, in spite of the Lord's grace, what does that mean for our conception, assessment, and practice of historical normativity?

Before I try to posit schematically a cultural imperative that means to be biblically more supple than judgments prone to regard our (secularized Christian) Western culture as the embodied historical norm, let me note a few important revisions to features of Dooyeweerd's problematics.

(1) It would be good now after an initial critique thirty-five years ago to agree that for an orthodox cosmological theory in the line of Dooyeweerd and Vollenhoven, "historical" is not a modal aspect of things but is to be found in the transmodal change of "unfolding" and "differentiation, integration, and individualization" of all creatures, human cultural activity, and societal development.

"All creatures" includes, for example, glaciers, lightning-lit forest fires, tree line altitudes, and animal species going extinct. Significant changes that lay waste and/or enrich the status quo of anything constitutes its history, even if the subject of the significant change is not human.[14]

Historical change is never unspecifiedly global. Whether you trace it back to Hegel[15] or finger Troeltsch, Dilthey, Spengler, or Max Weber (*NCTT* 2:205–06; 3:82), the historicism Dooyeweerd constantly combats and rejects is the totalizing of an inexorable process that sweeps away any non-historical points of reference, and absolutizes the temporal related relativity of things into a radical relativistic flux (*NCTT* 2:200–201, 354–55; *TWT* 62–63). But to conceive "historical" to be just one aspect of creatural reality does not preclude its being totalized into any idol or ism.

There is indeed a "technoformative" mode of reality that underlies as foundational moment all acculturating artifaction. Dooyeweerd's equivocal talk about history "at bottom" (the struggle between *civitas dei* and *civitates mundi*) and history "as such" (formative control) is not satisfactory (*NCTT* 2:192f., 294–95) because the unclarity of "at bottom" and "as such" leaves confused the basic issue I raised earlier: how does the eschatonic struggle for Dooyeweerd intersect with the historical process? If one were now to collapse *historical* happenings to the *aspect* of "free (human) formative control," it would weaken even more Dooyeweerd's fight against historicism, since the cultural activity of humankind does not have the transcendental clout to hold at bay the total relativization of historical deeds. If history be conceived to be the modal activity of technoformative control, then it is no wonder that a highly differentiated society seems likely to be more normative historically than others. But only Jesus Christ as Archimedian point, as Dooyeweerd himself says (*NCTT* 1:173–77, 506–08), overcomes historicism, centers history, and points toward what will withstand the winnowing fire of final judgment (Hebrews 12).[16]

---

14 Cf. ibid., 47 and n. 40, where Dooyeweerd's restriction of history to (rational) human subjectivity (*NCTT* 2:229–30) is corrected, also by Van der Hoeven.

15 Knudson, *History*, 5.

16 Paternity for this would-be correction lies with Klapwijk, Geertsema, C.T. McIntire, Griffioen, Van der Hoeven, and myself. For the relevant articles see Johan van der Hoeven, review of *The Legacy of Herman Dooyeweerd* in *Philosophia Reformata* 52 (1987): 198; Griffioen, *Problem*, 47; C. T. McIntire, "Dooyeweerd's Philosophy of History," in *The Legacy of Herman Dooyeweerd*, ed. C. T. McIntire (New York: University Press of America, 1985), 89–106; H. G. Geertsema, "Transcendentale openheid," *Philosophia Reformata* 35 (1970): 135–37, 145–46; J. Klapwijk, "Een voorlopige standpuntbepaling t.a.v. de geschiedfilosofie van Prof. H. Dooyeweerd," *Correspondentie-bladen van de Vereeniging voor Calvinistische Wijsbegeerte* 29 (April

(2) It would be wise to carry through consequently Dooyeweerd's rejection of Rickert and Windelband's split of world reality into *Sollen und Sein* areas (*NCTT* 1:29–38, 531; 2:199–201, 207–8) by dropping the partitioning of God's covenantal ordinances providing gracious limits for entitary subjects into "normative and . . . non-normative law-spheres," divided by what is pre- and post-logical (*NCTT* 2: 189). The LORD's modal embraces for falling objects, combustion, digestion, and feeling call for human involvement too, to discover, posit, and therefore *norm* one's ways of being elementarily creatural in exercise, diet, and de-sires, as well as being busy norming social intercourse, trading goods, assessing lawful rights and wrongs.

"Norming" takes place, as I understand it coming from Vollen-hoven's orientation, whenever humans together enact from out of their spirited-hearted faith-committed stance and vision what they hold God's *hoqqim* to mean for whatever specific contexted activities are at stake in the concrete, connected travail of circumstances. Granted that migraine headaches, esophageal peristalsis, and psychic depression may normally occur subliminally more willy-nilly than packing clothes for a trip or promising to visit someone, still it is not *analytic* intelligence that is so crucial to setting and embodying normative responses as are one's apti-tude, temperament, memory, and the reserve of one's character and con-victions.

Because Dooyeweerd founds "all the later normative law-spheres in the logical or analytical sphere" (*NCTT* 2:238), he struggles, it seems to me, still overloading "the logical," to keep the Humpty of prelogical aspects together with the Dumpty of normative law-spheres by way of "anticipations."

In the pre-logical aspects of reality the modal laws are realized in the facts without human intervention, *at least insofar as* in this realization the normative anticipations of their modal structure are not concerned [*NCTT* 2:237–38, my emphasis].

It may be that natural laws of the pre-logical aspects of experience do not appeal to the human formative will for their realization, *insofar* as in the latter the normative anticipations of their modal structure are not concerned [*NCTT* 2:239, my emphasis].

But I think that within Dooyeweerd's own systematics the most el-

---

1965): 18–21; C. Seerveld, "Voor en uit de praktijk," *Corresponentiebladen* 24 (April 1960): 5–10; also "Dooyeweerd's Legacy for Aesthetics," in *The Legacy,* 76 n. 60 {see *NA:* 72}; "Footprints in the Snow," *Philosophia Reformata* 56 (1991): 16–17, 32–33 {infra 254–55, 274–75}.

ementary aspects of experience do indeed appeal to the human formative will for their realization.

So it makes good antirationalistic, biblical sense to deny analysis the privilege of being the gateway to normativity. *All* aspects of creaturely life become enacted normally when they are lived out normatively, that is, directed by one's pivotal, heart-deep recognition (even if ignorant à la Acts 17:22–31) of God's cosmic ordinances.

(3) To avoid Dooyeweerd's struggle to get leverage "above" temporal history with a "supratemporal heart,"[17] so that human deeds not be ontically dissolved in the fluidifying solvent of a never-ending continuous passage of past-present-future events, it may be wise to distinguish the human's hearted faith and faith-commitment from one's creedal modal activity of confession. Both of these matters—faith and believing—are called *geloof / geloven* in the Dutch language, and Dooyeweerd's translators have transliterated Dooyeweerd's technical term with the barbaric English coinage "pistical," tending to fuse the two states of affairs.

However, "faith" is a Spirit-given trust in (*fiducia*) and wholehearted commitment to (*assensus*) the true God or a deluded assurance in an idol. As K. J. Popma insists, the Scriptures talk about *pistis* as a substantial gift of God's grace, which results in an existential attachment of that human person to the LORD, the actual adoption of a woman, man, or child into Christ's body thanks to the working of the Holy Spirit.[18] Taking one's cue from Scripture (Ephesians 2:8–9, 3:14–19; Galatians 2:15–16, 3:24–27), then one may say that "faith" is not a modal phenomenon but a central matter for human nature. "Believing" or "confessing," however, "being certain about" (μαρτύριον) is indeed one way, the most complex modal way, one may say, of showing one's faith attachment, recapitulating it in fact.[19] The discipline of systematic theology has no corner on "faith" in its field of study, but attempts to give rigorous (*wissenschaftlich*) analytic cohesion to the *credimus* of faith-bound disciples and to draw out ramifications of human "confession" and examine the proper func-

---

17 Cf. Peter Steen, *The Idea of Religious Transcendence in the Philosophy of Herman Dooyeweerd, with Reference to its Significance for Reformed Theology* (Ph.D. dissertation, Westminster Theological Seminary, 1970).

18 "Het geloof is in zekere zin *niets:* het is het geopend hart, het toegewend hart, het ontvankelijk hart. . . . Daarom spreken we kwáád van het geloof, als we het een functie noemen" (K. J. Popma, *Levensbeschouwing: Opmerkingen naar aanleiding van de Heidelbergse Catechismus* [Amterdam: Buijten & Schipperheijn, 1958] 1:162).

19 Cf. my *Skeleton to Philosophy 101* (Trinity Christian College mimeograph, 1960) 7, 11–13, 16–18; also "Imaginativity," *Faith and Philosophy* 4:1 (1987): 56 {see *NA:* 43–44}.

tional tasks of institutions of confessional activity, the congregated *ecclesia* or church ("church" as distinct from God's "kingdom Rule"), if it be Christian rather than Jewish or Muslim theology.

This distinction between central faith and modal confession might help remove the occasional abrasive irritance Dooyeweerd developed toward the discipline of theology when theology assumed it must remain operating as *regina scientiarum* (*TWT*, 113–56).[20] A Christian philosophy is couched in *faith* and examines the interrelated meaning of things from out of that orientation, but Christian philosophy does not rightly compete with dogmatic (or apologetic) Christian theology, which examines human confession from out of the same *faith*.

Historical normativity and a scripturally directed cultural imperative
Given the ubiquitous ruling pragmatist dynamic and a commercializing Americanization of world culture today, the problem for un-American and non-European peoples is acute as to whether or not to accept the cultural assimilation that seems to come with the secularized differentiation and individualization the American way of life and death imposes. The faithful body of Christ in the West faces somewhat the same problem, perhaps, because their way of life has not quite kept pace with the secular maelstrom. Many evangelical believers still expect the official, organized church to answer their specific cultural problems (which the institutional church did do at an earlier stage of differentiated authority in the west); but many pastors, evangelists, and bishops do not have the competence and honed wisdom in our day to give counsel in the areas of burgeoning artistry, commerce, city planning, cyberspace, and politics, nor should the clergy be the only shepherds of God's people and neighbors. Many secular leaders, cannot take the institutional church seriously anymore because the church equates contraception with murder, sells God with

---

20 When Dooyeweerd openly wrestles with this problem of distinguishing a central act of faith from the confessional/believing aspect of certitude, he chooses unfortunately just the opposite English wording from the terms I propose. "But the modal-faith aspect may not be identified with the real act of believing which in its full reality comes out of the heart, and, though *qualified* by its faith-aspect, presents also other aspects in the temporal order of experience" (*TWT*, 137). Early on K. J. Popma was willing to accept a *geloofsaspect* of creatural reality, but then Popma conceived the task of theology to be scientific study of the faith-structure (*geloof-structuur*) of the believing understanding of God's Word (*De Plaats der Theologie* [Franeker: Wever, 1946], 70–71). Popma proceeded to make a rigorous distinction between churchly confessions (*kerkelijke belijdenis*) and theology, and warned against bringing theology so defined within the churchly gathering of the saints waiting to be fed by the preached Word of God (ibid., 29).

package tours and cosmetics in the media, and has a documented history of supporting colonialism and apartheid. So it is no wonder the current post-Christian ethos assumes all cultures are in principle equally worth-while.[21]

In this current climate of opinion a preliminary step Bible-believing followers of Christ might take, to be historically normative would be to admit that Western civilization has forfeited a claim to be the Christian prototype. Christians could consider whether less "Western-differentiated" societal complexes are less devoluted from creatural historical normativity than "civilization," and that other ethnic cultures may be able to teach us well-meaning North American imperialists certain features of human living, and show us cultural openings we have inadvertently or stupidly closed down, with all our haste and technocratic efficiency. At least we followers of the Christ need to reach back toward our less secularized Western times and seek out non-Western cultural formers today who have been born again by the Spirit of God, to refresh and variegate our typical cultivated offerings. For example, Jun'ichiro Tanizaki invites you to enter the Japanese world of outdoor toilets where one sits among the hollow bamboo stalks amid the fragrance of moss with rain pattering on the leaves, and where a person has the quiet time there in natural surroundings to meditate and write haikus.[22] The Ur-Swiss confederated canton conception of military training only for defense of one's *Heimat* has a pre-European spirit and tried to shuck the ethos of wars for conquest. *Can* we reconsider our ways and take the cultural diversity of humanity seriously?

As for the theoretical philosophical underpinnings to the problem of historical normativity, I understand Dooyeweerd to have described the transcendental conditions for historical activity when he delineates the developmental opening-up process of differentiation, integration, and individualization. When a creature, community, or society undergoes differentiation integrated with or fragmenting the rounding out of its specific full-bodied, God-appointed ministry, that significant change—chosen or not—constitutes its historical reality.

A problem comes to the fore when violence attends the affair. For example, before the Venda speaking people of South Africa received an orthographic script for their language in 1872, their oral culture was pre-literate and full-orbed: knowledge was passed on face-to-face by word of mouth, gesture, ceremonial rituals, and the elders conserved with author-

---

21 Griffioen, "De betekenis," 84.
22 *In Praise of Shadows* (1933) (New Haven: Leete's Island Books, 1977) 3–6.

ity the memory of the people. With the emergence of written language the Venda people became discriminated into the literate and the illiterate, and the traditional customs came under duress because of the power vested in texts to keep records, to authenticate oral cultural deeds for external authorities. And it was the literate who were best able to intermingle with the exogenous teachers and government who now colonialized by way of education in a foreign tongue with written literature. So the age-old Venda way of life is forced to change because of the irreversible (!?) differentiating step of literacy.[23] And it seems as if the primordial dynamic God set for creatures to develop expects the Venda people to become literate, or to become marginal in the world as it is, even though their haunting children songs are exquisite artistry.[24]

Is it historically normative for the Venda people to resist literacy as an encroachment on their way of life? Is the practically omnipresent availability of communication granted by the cell-telephone device an historically normative development for North American folk because it increases safety, although it may impede by speed and ubiquity the quality of spoken intercourse?

I should like to note two things in trying to formulate a cultural imperative that will be biblically wise: (1) I should like to emphasize that the cross-entity, cross-generational feature of historical deed must be remembered as one faces the creational injunction for historical action that Dooyeweerd has formulated. A historical connection is the unpredictable modification made across the break in willed continuity. Historical leaders are responsible for what they make of their circumstantial inheritance in passing on cultural goods.[25] Miscarriage in the transfer is frequent. The historical "process of unfolding" is not inevitable. Timing and modulation of the concentrated factors in the significant change is critical for its historical normativity.

While it is historically normative to be thirteen years old for a while,

---

23 Cf. Brian Stock, who traces in magisterial fashion the mixed blessing of literacy and textuality for the oral culture of the Church around the time of Carolingian Rule and following, c. 900–1200 AD, in *The Implications of Literacy: Written language and models of interpretation in the eleventh and twelfth centuries* (Princeton University Press, 1983), especially 3–87 and 522–31.

24 Conversations with Walter Muloiwa, and his paper, "The Place of the Written Word within the Venda Language" (Toronto: Institute for Christian Studies, Interdisciplinary Seminar, 1995); cf. also John Blacking, *Venda Children's Songs: A study in ethnomusicological analysis* (Chicago: University of Chicago Press, 1967).

25 Calvin Seerveld, "Footprints in the Snow," *Philosophia Reformata* 56 (1991): 1–34, esp. 16–17 {infra 254–255}; and "Vollenhoven's Legacy for Art Historiography," *Philosophia Reformata* 58 (1993): 49–79, esp. 64–65 {see *AH*: 47–59}.

and normal to be a parent, it is probably not historically normative to be a thirteen-year old parent.[26] One way for the literate Venda to avoid becoming an educated elite and to maintain solidarity with the now still illiterate Venda people is to write literature in the Venda language rather than opt for world markets in English.[27] And sometimes bringing a cultural project into conformity with the will of the LORD historically may demand that one abstain for the time being, or put the fire out.[28]

To resist developing the technoformative control in human artifaction is to commit cultural suicide because of the founding role technical control has in human cultivation of creatures. Willful neglect would constitute abdication of human responsibility to God and neighbor. However, to develop, in a historically normative way the meaning of differentiating technical skills means one must lead technique to deepen the quotient of joy, *koinonia*, just-doing, and peace-giving, for example—not just efficiency—within the panoply of society with its variegated tasks: that is the troubled proper calling of human leaders and followers in all fields of human endeavor.

(2) The guideline for historically normative decision and cultural action I should like to posit, which follows the contours of Dooyeweerd's "differentiate, integrate, individualize," is this: regenerate, speciate, diaconate. By this *principium* I mean (regenerate) that any given community intent upon following Christ historically always needs first and constantly to be Holy Spirit renewed so that they at heart have the identity of Christ's repentant body on earth; (speciate) that as a committed visionary unity with diverse, gifted callings, such specialties be encouraged to reach professional competence for challenging the enrichment of fellow members and neighbors; and (diaconate) that the whole cultivating process before God's face in schooling, missionary endeavor, artistry, or whatever, be not one of possessing things and counting returns, but a monstrous, tender *giveaway*, without guile, of insights and blessings.

It is not the province of any philosopher or theologian to dictate what should take place upon a given occasion. All God's children who mature as teachers, parents, missionaries, political, commercial, or media

---

26 I thank Jeff Dudiak, doctoral student at the Institute for Christian Studies, for the thought and example.

27 The Kenyan artist Nguigi wa Thiong'o now writes novels only in the Gikuyu language (cf. *Decolonizing the Mind: The politics of language in African literature* [London: Heinemann, 1986]). Jan Disselkoen, an imaginative literary officer for the Christian Reformed World Relief Committee, teaches literacy for the Kuranko tribe in Sierra Leone by inscribing their oral tales in primers.

28 Griffioen, *Problem*, 29–30.

specialists have the office to give leadership in their respective field for fellow believers and neighbors. It is normative, I think, for the different kinds of bodies with concerted authority extant in society, like business, family, political government, or media, to reach and honor certain diaconal limits of their respective sort, by having leaders within such communities or institutions exercise the power as shareholders with neighbors, not as dispensers of privilege. Whether the power of a given societal grouping is exercised protectively or violently within its confines or toward those who are not bona fide members within its particular bond does not depend on the stage of differentiation so much as on whether the leaders selflessly give away the good justly, move followers toward sharing such specific gifts rather than peremptorily demand acceptance, and can coax a relative unity, with (modally) appropriate sanctions, amid all the changes in one's different responsibilities.

I propose that it is biblical wisdom to resist whatever cultural policy standardizes practice to more sweeping uniformity or conformity (undoing! speciation), and it is biblical wisdom to support cultural professionalization that is kept humane by a diaconal character that honors plurality and diversity by facing the neighbor with an outstretched helping hand. Therefore, whenever leadership effects change that runs roughshod over blessings and gifts found in less differentiated settings, so that glories of the earlier state are lost, *aufgehoben* ("incorporated") rather than honored, or made obsolete without comparable replacement, such historical action is not normative. And whenever leadership overrules differentiated and differentiating specific cultural authorities in society by having a *specific power source,* like technological science, or money, effect a *simplified, pseudo-integrative move,* such historical action also violates the primordial societal creatural pull in eschatonic history that primes humans to share specific responsibilities in God's rainbow of a world.

I think the last several generations of post-Renaissance, post-Enlightenment, post-Positivist western society, fraught with the dominant pragmatistic *mentalité* current, have brought at large a de-differentiating curse on our on-going variegated culture. The idol of scientistic Reason has imperialistically dominated nonanalytic realms conceptualistically with monolithic oversimplifications; for example, in Freudian psychoanalysis and in propositionalist theologies. A similar oversimplifying cultural tyranny by Mammon has ruined much noneconomic life; for example, Reaganomics, which mistreated political rule as if it were a corporate business, and nationalistic contests of political opportunism, degenerating into racist wars. That is, analysis of our Western historical plight under the *principium* of "regenerate, speciate, diaconate" implies, in Dooyeweerd's terms, that Western society is really closing down rather than opening up other peoples, institutions, and human life, in a strange, cancerous way that destroys wholesome diversity.

As a Western Christian looks abroad, he or she does well to realize that the biblical Christian faith is *not* ethnic. Christ's historical centering and concluding world history is neither Western nor Eastern, not North or South.[29] So the biblical gospel has the wherewithal to change every ethnic city, undoing what is parochial and prospering whatever is rare among the human race, so that God's pleasure in the Lord's myriad creatures may brim over (cf. Revelation 21:22–27).

Such a realization does not entail that I must give up my American-born, European-trained, Canada-inhabiting child of God status to become nondescript flotsam in a universal intergalactic network. But I need to be so deeply pierced by the biblical voice, at home in the biblical idiom, that I can recognize and be recognized by others speaking in foreign cultural tongues that we are actually talking the same biblical language together, resounding thankfulness to the Lord, although our cultural (artistic) expressions be ethnically strange to one another. Without an underlying, active common idiom that vibrates Christ's redemption, efforts toward interethnic Christian culture will be stillborn.

However, we may trust that whatever is a truly biblical particularity in a given culture will be of universe-wide blessing. This truth is going to make eating as well as imagining incredibly exciting on the new earth. And once we realize that within the LORD's creational bounds there can be diverse normative responses,[30] like the wonderful motley medley of different languages one may speak, we who believe might even be able, as stiff Calvinists, to unbend enough to engage the sharply different rhythmic beat African music brings in praise to the LORD, and update the Genevan jigs corporeally so that there be blood coursing through the whole, full-bodied, dancing worshiper. While it is the blight of secularization to poison vibrant cultural richness, it is a mark of Bible-believing wisdom to show respect for cultural diversity, which Christian respect is integral to normative historical deed.

Although a divorced person cannot become a virgin and a hardened post-Christian thinker cannot become an ignorant pagan, an adulterer can again become chaste. It is correct that "Within history there cannot be an absolutely new beginning, as conceived by the purveyors of creative

---

29 Griffioen, "De betekenis," 106; *TWT,* 111–12.
30 Griffioen, "De betekenis," 104–5.

human reason. Everything new in history, every change that is normative historical change, must proceed from and take into consideration what is still living in the tradition."[31] But the fact that forgiveness exists in God's world means fresh starts in culture are possible. In order to reform the status quo in any secularized cultural field of human endeavor one needs, I think, to regroup societally at an earlier stage of differentiation in order to be able to reposit what has been historically misformed. If art schools are nests of ideological instruction that undercut the craft base to art, one needs to set up a guild complex where a skilled mentor makes drawing and basics an adventure. If philosophy took a wrong turn in the 1950s to become a kind of special science of language without encyclopedic reach, one needs to revive the practice of philosophy by having wise persons with vision engage non-specialists in thinking through troubled realities. If many American seminaries turned pop in the 1960s and downplayed the rigor of philosophical forming and the need to read Latin, German, French, and Dutch, in order to "go where the action is," it may be time to regain the theological grit sound scholarship with Hebrew and Greek can bring to the ordinary neighborhood preaching pastor.

A winsome, thetical handshake of witness to Jesus Christ

Dooyeweerd's method of Christian philosophical thinking can be aptly characterized as "empirical-transcendental."[32] Dooyeweerd probes ordinary human experience to detect the transcendental conditions for its existential, phenomenal meaning in God's world. Dooyeweerd's idea of "historical development," which I have examined here, resulted from this Christian transcendental approach too, where you ask biblically loaded questions and listen for the answers given by the cloud of believing and unbelieving witnesses as you examine what is happening around you.

A scripturally directed sense of what is historical (differentiate, integrate, individualize) in the world and how God's people together are to respond normatively thereto in society (regenerate, speciate, diaconate) is also relevant for conceiving the proper relational praxis of Christian apologetic, and Christian philosophy. From a Reformed Christian standpoint our stance toward unbelieving culture is antirevolutionary; so we are proponents for neither anathema toward nor interminable dialogue

---

31 Robert Knudsen, "Anathema or Dialogue?" *WTJ* 34 (1972): 137–51; quotation from 149.

32 Robert Knudsen, "Transcendental Method in Dooyeweerd," *Anakainosis* 1:3 (1979): 2–8, esp. 6; reprinted in *Roots and Branches: The quest for meaning and truth in modern thought*, ed. Donald Knudsen (Grand Rapids, MI: Paideia Press, 2009), 301–309, esp. 307.

with the disbeliever, neither the wormwood of spiritual accommodation nor the meandering Rortyan conversation. Our *Pro Rege* certainty that "the order God has placed in God's creation still asserts itself"[33] allows us the time to be thetical, without a nervous compulsion to make final judgments or carry out apocalyptic deeds, and to extend a hand even to one's enemy, because as God's folk we are saved to think historiographically and act historically with "a hope bravely contrived from things longed for, from things unseen."[34]

Once the Christian apologists and philosophers have detected where nodes of disbelievers are located in our generation—the dominated consumer as marginalized majority![35] the dislocated uncertain critical intellectuals wrapped in cryptic semiosis,[36] respectable apostate hypocrites inside the church (Hebrews 5:11–6:8)—then they can determine the cultural flash points where an offering of shalom may be deposited. The Lord's faithful are never asked to save the world in general, but are called upon to give away their particular joy and strengths where those gifts meet the world's pain.[37]

In my judgment current pockets of disbelief at the scandalous lordship of Jesus Christ on earth are ill-disposed for argument but desperately needy for something certain to hang onto, a vision that can shake one out of self-satisfaction, a touch or word that brings actual healing and a comforting hope. The gift a Christian philosophical systematics might offer the disbelieving student is an encyclopedic overview of interrelated creatural meaning that avoids false starts, misguided dilemmas, and patented easy solutions. The scripturally directed idea of "historically

---

33 Knudsen, "Anathema or Dialogue?" 145, 149–51.

34 Bob Sweetman, "Of Tall Tales and Small Stories: Postmodern 'fragmatics' and the Christian historian," *Fides et Historia* 28:2 (1996): 50–68, quotation from 66.

35 Cf. Michel de Certeau, *Arts de faire* (1974), in translation *The Practice of Everyday Life* (Los Angeles: University of California Press, 1984), xi–xvii, 29–42.

36 Secularist Edward W. Said pulls no punches: "Instead of discrimination and evaluation, we have intensified division of intellectual labor; objects of study both dehumanized and exorbitant have taken over the critics' attention, while intellectual debate increasingly resembles high-pitched monologue in narrow corridors. Most distressing of all is the growing resemblance between professed political neoconservatives and the religiously inclined critics, for both of whom the privatized condition of social life and cultural discourse are made possible by a belief in the benign quasi-divine marketplace" (*The World, the Text, and the Critic* [Cambridge: Harvard University Press, 1983], 292).

37 This insight comes from Marcille Frederick, librarian at the Institute for Christian Studies, Toronto, in her imaginative distillation of thoughts by Sarah Wenger Shenk and Kennon Callahan.

normative action" formulated here, for example, neither demands a final paradigmatic deed nor is satisfied with casuistic as-you-like-it attempts, but calls for a humbly principled and fallible enablement that provides merciful, specific service.

The gift a Christian apologist might present to the disbelieving crowd should probably not be a combative, rationalistic brief, if I gather correctly the thrust of Knudsen's article on "Progressive and Regressive Tendencies in Christian Apologetics." The respectful question asked almost twenty-five years ago about "whether Van Til's metaphysical notion of the archetypal intellect does not clash with the more central notion that man in the center of his being is constantly in the act of responding to God in God's self-revelation in Christ"[38] seemed, from the response, to touch a nerve about a great *logical* divide between saints and disbelieving humans.[39] Because what cleaves humankind in history, however, is adoption into Christ's body by the Lord's grace or not, not consequent conceptual analysis from true presuppositions, we do well, I believe, to make even our reasoned apologetics winsome[40] by focusing upon the vulnerable longings of those who are lost, also logically bewildered in avoiding an obedient response to God, and then giveaway to them saving thoughtful direction.

> Who shall do you harm if you all be eager to do good? But even if you suffer because of just-doing, you shall be blessed! Do not be afraid of fearing them; do not be intimidated. Hallow in your hearts the Christ as Lord, always ready with an apologetic for anyone who asks you all for an account of the hope in you, but do it with gentleness and a certain fearfulness. . . . (1 Pet 3:13–16)

---

38 Robert Knudsen, "Progressive and Regressive Tendencies in Christian Apologetics," in *Jerusalem and Athens: Critical discussions on the theology and apologetics of Cornelius Van Til*, ed. E.R. Geehan (Philadelphia: Presbyterian and Reformed, 1971), 275–98; quotation from 294–95; reprinted in *Roots and Branches*, 115–139; 135..

39 "Concept formation itself must presuppose the Christian world-order if it is to make any intelligible contact with the world at all" (Cornelius Van Til, in *Jerusalem and Athens*, 303). "The basic point of the matter, as I see it, is that whereas I attempt to show the non-Christian that *nothing*, no fact or law, can be seen as it is truly is except in the light of the revelation of God in Christ through Scripture, Dooyeweerd attempts to speak intelligently with unbelievers about laws and states of affairs which are intelligible up to a point *prior to the introduction of a Christian scheme of things* [my emphasis]. This difference between us is basic" (ibid., 305). For a more generous understanding of Dooyeweerd's approach, see the first paragraph in this section on "A Winsome, Thetical Handshake."

40 Robert Knudsen, "The Legacy of Cornelius Van Til," *New Horizons in the Orthodox Presbyterian Church* 16:5 (1995): 3–4.

Robert Knudsen, as I have known him, practiced both philosophy and apologetics in the way Peter commends. Thanks be to God for that witness.[41]

41 My colleagues Marcille Frederick and Bob Sweetman took valuable time to make me responsible for all the thoughts expressed in this article. I warmly thank them for providing me with a faith-thought community. I am also greatly indebted to contributions by colleague Paul Marshall, and especially the writings of Sander Griffioen from the Free University of Amsterdam.

FOOTPRINTS IN THE SNOW

Once upon a time a young angel who had a little spare time (very rare for an angel) noticed a devil doing something curious. The little devil had a broom and was whisking out the footsteps of a middle-aged person walking through the freshly fallen snow.

"Devils can be so stupid," thought the angel. "That poor devil doesn't realize the cold Canadian wind will blow the snow around to cover over the fellow's tracks. If the devils want somebody to lose their way, they could put their time to better use." But the angel reported it anyhow to Gabriel, just for fun.

Gabriel was not amused. "That little devil will go far in being a troublemaker," said the archangel. "Men and women resist believing that they follow beaten paths. But they really become insufferably proud when they look around and think they leave no tracks."

I

Taxonomy of major conceptions regarding tradition
There are certain major positions taken by persons who have reflected on the nature, meaning, and authority of tradition. I shall characterize just three and let these thumbnail profiles give us a sense of the topography we are entering as we prospect for a place to lay our own head.

Tradition as an up-to-date solid state of the past
Tradition for T. S. Eliot is the deposit of texts or monuments that "form an ideal order among themselves," and whose whole realm of the model canon is slowly augmented by any really new classics produced. "Tradition" is the historical consciousness of this great heritage of masterworks, an active reception of the presence of the past in our current consciousness. And nobody can be a poet after the twenty-fifth year of life if he or she is not traditional, says Eliot, that is, if the artist does not live and

---

This essay was first published in *Philosophia Reformata* 56:1 (1991): 1–34.

work in the awareness that one is continuing a tradition.[1] Tradition is a person's spiritual parentage and educational life-blood. Without an appropriated tradition a human is an orphan sick unto death with cultural anemia.

Jürgen Habermas would censure Eliot's unctuous valuation of the Great Books of the Western World and establishment Masterpieces. Yet Habermas's conception of tradition is similar to that of Eliot in that tradition for Habermas is the sedimented mass of norms that have accumulated over the years, but at present the canon suffocates those who would breathe freely. There is a whole network of supposedly value-free science (engineered by the Positivists) and interest-free language (trusted by Historicists in the humanities) that count as our tradition. Well, that "tradition" is a Romantic bureaucrat's dream on how to stifle the disenfranchised, says Habermas. Tradition is the ages-long hand-me-downs of privilege concealed in institutions, including schools and the media, that systematically violate human rights. Tradition, for Habermas, is a storehouse of statutes and patterns of behavior that is intrinsically ideological (= allegedly disinterested but hiding rationalized partisan interests).[2]

Whether it be esteemed or despised, both Eliot and Habermas conceive of tradition as a cumulative body of texts or laws that concentrate the past on the present and determine what we now do.

Tradition as an ongoing flow of traditioning current

In Gadamer's perspective every human is inescapably traditioned too, but tradition is not a backlog of achievements or a web of entanglements. Tradition is the process of handing-over-and-handing-on the common knowledge humans are inescapably undergoing.[3] "Tradition" is really the activity of traditioning, where you keep busy joining and echoing the chorus of voices that have been sounding from time immemorial, world without end.[4] Traditioning gives humanity sanity, says Gadamer. Con-

---

1   T. S. Eliot, "Tradition and the Individual Talent" [1919] in *Selected Essays* (London: Faber and Faber, 1951), 14–15.

2   See Jürgen Habermas, "Knowledge and Human Interests: A general perspective" [1965], as appendix to *Knowledge and Human Interests*, translated by J. L Shapiro (Boston: Beacon Press, 1971), 315–17, Also, Habermas, "Zu Gadamers *Wahrheit und Methode*" [1967], in *Hermeneutik und Ideologiekritik* (Frankfurt am Main: Suhrkamp, 1973), 52–55.

3   Hans-Georg Gadamer, *Wahrheit und Methode* [1960], 3 A. (Tübingen: Mohr [Paul Siebeck], 1972), 265–66, or *Truth and Method*, translated by Sheed and Ward staff (New York: Seabury Press, 1975), 250.

4   *Wahrheit und Methode*, 268 / *Truth and Method*, 252–3.

versing with Plato, for example, on being raptured by Beauty is traditioning par excellence, and will certainly convert any human prejudices (*Vorurteile*) into a "projudice" (*Vorverständnis*) that mediates understanding (*Verstehen*).[5] The human understanding that traditioning effects is not so much a subjective act resulting in a definite, finished *traditum* as it is your backing into the glorious process of mediating traditioning itself, dialogically fusing the past and your present.[6]

The point here is that for Gadamer tradition is a happening. "Tradition" is that inexplicable hermeneutic moment of truth when your voice and Plato's voice chime. And your activity exemplifies, resonates with, and carries on the nameless authority that cultivates what is humane under the sun. Traditioning is a dynamic usage only, a never-ending questioning,[7] and the best prospect we humans have on earth. "I believe in the chances of dialogue," says Gadamer.[8]

Tradition as the primordial rhythm of life one may ritually enter
For someone like Foucault, who believes that successive epistemic periods of culture are absolutely disjunctive, obliterating the possibility of any continuing progress, tradition is practically a misnomer.

Foucault diagnoses the (recent) modern man or woman of the Enlightenment to be like a finite watermark in the infinite text of Life, Language, and Labor-Desire; and Foucault believes the human has a probably endless, possibly hopeful, but monotonous journey because the human's mode of being is repetition (*la répétition*).[9] There seem to be certain continuing constellations of cosmic doubles and systems of regularities within whose inscrutable, fundamental recurrence specific positivities oscillate.[10] Limited individuals do not originate and then develop so much as enter into this originary welter of an empowering fertile Void

---

5   *Wahrheit und Methode*, 261, 452–65 / *Truth and Method*, 246, 432–47.

6   "Das Verstehen ist selber nicht so sehr als eine Handlung der Subjektivität zu denken, sondern als Einrücken in ein überlieferungsgeschehen in dem sich Vergangenheit und Gegenwart beständig vermitteln. Das ist es, was in der hermeneutischen Theorie zur Geltung kommen muss, die viel zu sehr von der Idee eines Verfahrens, einer Methode, beherrscht ist" (*Wahrheit und Methode*, 274–75 / *Truth and Method*, 258).

7   *Wahrheit und Methode*, 282 / *Truth and Method*, 265.

8   Comment made during a public conversation at the Institute for Christian Studies, Toronto, on 25 November 1975.

9   Michel Foucault, *Les Mots et les Choses: Une archéologie des sciences humaines* (Paris: Gallimard, 1966), 325–26, or *The Order of Things: An archaeology of the human sciences* (New York: Random House Vintage, 1973), 314–16.

10 *The Order of Things*, xiii–xiv.

(*le vide, la déchirure*).[11] This everlasting, all-consuming Solvent of any particular achievements is History, which nevertheless orders and enables unfixed communication between different creatures, societies, and significations.[12]

So Foucault's archaeo-geneological *modus cogitandi* discounts tradition as an accumulation of treasures (T. S. Eliot) or debts (Habermas), and also never positions the human as one who needs to initiate traditioning to be busy claiming and renewing one's humanity (Gadamer). The ongoing, endlessly repeated play of dominations[13] that preternaturally envelops every individual is as given as the primordial round of *ying* resonances to *tzu-jan* of Tao.[14] And the ritual—the rite of passage—of one's emergence into life, speech, and cultural activity reveals one's flowback into this residual, no-name Procrustean Ocean where the return of the Same is always imminent.[15] For Foucault the ritual of doing over such a charmed undoing of culture is the virtual occurrence of tradition—a cosmic web of ephemeral, hidden connections, that initiates read like a mandala.

II

An alternative, working definition of the nature of tradition

The three conceptions on "tradition" I have sketched call to mind the story of the three blind persons who were describing an elephant they were holding, one by the trunk, one by the foot, and one by the tail. Eliot with Habermas, then Gadamer, and also Foucault, are each describing genuine features of tradition, but each conception, in my judgment, is out of focus. There is assuredly (1) a given or perduring "content" to any tradition—the *what* passed on—since traditions have resulted from dated and located human formation. Tradition is also (2) in process, eventful, a happening, and not an entity—the "*passing on*" is essential within traditions, dead or alive. Further, traditions are (3) certain *kinds of human*

---

11 *Les Mots et les Choses*, 341–46 / *The Order of Things*, 330–35.

12 *Les Mots et les Choses*, 382–84 / *The Order of Things*, 371–73.

13 See Foucault, "Nietzsche, Genealogy, History" [1971] in *Michel Foucault: Language, counter-memory, practice* (New York: Cornell University Press, 1977), 150–52.

14 See Norman J. Girardot, "Behaving Cosmogonically in Early Taoism," in *Cosmogony and Ethical Order: New studies in comparative ethics*, eds. Frank Reynolds and Robin W. Loven (University of Chicago Press, 1985), 73–79, 86–88.

15 See *Les mots et les choses*, 396–98 / *The Order of Things*, 384–87. ". . . en découvrant la loi du temps comme limite externe des sciences humaines, l'Histoire montre que tout ce qui est pensé le sera encore par une pensée qui n'a pas encore vu le jour" (*Les mots et les choses*, 383 / *The Order of Things*, 372).

communal holding patterns, for the time being, rather than something unique or finished.

Because traditions have a nature, traditions are comparable, and do have a recurring feature—a coursing passage that remains in force. And tradition always conceals the founding figures and the ones being initiated, behind those active in bearing the passage—the *who* that are carriers—treading the water.[16]

But each of these matters—*traditum* (= a deposit of sorts), *tradendum* (= the needing to be handed on further, an activity of transmitting), and *traditio* (= the whole structured, configured course of needing to pass on some recognizable identity inherited, a fixed pattern)—should not be eclipsed by the other features if one wants an undistorted grasp of the nature of tradition.

Tradition is peculiarly human. Animals have no traditions. God is not subject to tradition. So far as I know, angels and devils lack traditions, since they do not admit of generations. Creaturely reality as a whole is set up, however, with God-ordered stability of duration, of temporality, imprinted with the mark of proceeding from the beginning to the end of history. Such an on-going fund of process[17] makes creation an eminently traditionable theatre of operation. All it takes for a tradition is a community of humans whose leaders, in their subjective responsiveness to God's creational provision for such transmission of acquired enactments, institute, or practice-patterned activity of some kind or other that is handed down from them to others (a younger generation), accept and continue somehow that particular, cultivated form of action.

A structured passing on of wonts
Tradition, let us say, is the structured transaction of passing on wonts from practiced to inexperienced human hands. Much traditioning normally occurs subliminally, although it is not necessarily unwholesome to be conscious of the formative happening. Because the new, willing, subjective reception and carrying on of the pattern being subliminally presented for adoption is crucial for a tradition, it is probably wise to say

---

16 I am indebted to Jeff Dudiak's treatment of Levinas on "the face of the other" as it relates to traditioning for this emphasis on keeping tradition peopled with persons. See his "Tracing the Track" (Institute for Christian Studies, Inter-disciplinary paper 1989, typescript), 16–20, 22, 38–39.

17 By "on-going fund of process" I refer to what I believe Johan van der Hoeven and Jan Dengerink call the "overgankelijkheid" (transitivity) of temporality. See Jan Dengerink, "Mens, kosmos, tijdelijkheid, eeuwigheid," *Philosophia Reformata* 54:1 (1989): 98.

with Edward Shils that transmission of *tradita* should occur at least twice (over three generations) before you can talk about a bona fide tradition.[18] A tradition by definition is a living praxis, a communal habitude, with a recognizable identity carried on similarly, wittingly or not, by a following of different human subjects. When patterns are flatly reenacted simply because they are precedents, in a "tradition-bound" or in an ideologically closed society, I would call such a process "traditionalism."[19] It goes without saying then that tradition is not new wine put into old skins, but is the old wine being drunk out of new glasses.

Let me add that like the resident treasury of imagery a grouping of persons may draw on—or like a common language people enjoy—tradition is "pre-analytic" in character,[20] and more extensive than a single person; a tradition is always shared by a limited number of adherents. These are basic factors in the power of tradition. Once a person participates in a tradition, you appropriate the past treasure of human wisdom (or folly) congealed in the wont that channels your activity. You give tacit approval to such forming, and benefit—or are handicapped by—that windfall of cultural formation you are inheriting and swimming within, provided you live within it as your own. Traditions like habits save an incredible amount of exploratory and indecisive time, because they apprentice the novice with a headstart—or a drawback!—in being formatively busy in culturing activity, depending upon whether the specific tradition be a good one or bad.

Varieties of traditions
A final comment is in order on varieties of tradition. It is the nature of tradition to be the most elemental "institution" or bonding in neighbor-

---

18 Edward Shils, *Tradition* (London: Faber and Faber, 1981), 15.

19 See Saburo Ichii, "Kein Fortschritt ohne Tradition," in *Vom Sinn der Tradition*, ed. Leonhard Reinisch (München: Beck, 1970), 117–8. See also Govert Buijs's reference to J. G. A. Pocock on "traditionalist societies," in Buijs, "Normativity and Historical Existence" (Institute for Christian Studies, Interdisciplinary paper, 1988, typescript), 1.

20 Adorno says: "Tradition steht im Widerspruch zur Rationalität, obwohl diese in jener sich bildete. Nicht Bewusstsein ist ihr Medium, sondern vorgegebene, unreflektierte Verbindlichkeit sozialer Formen, die Gegenwart des Vergangenen; das hat unwillkürlich auf Geistiges sich übertragen" ("Über Tradition" [1966], in *Ohne Leitbild, Parva Aesthetica* [Frankfurt am Main: Suhrkamp, 1979], 29). While I do not accept Adorno's "agonistic" (even "antagonistic") stance toward tradition or rest my analysis on the nature of tradition upon the "societal forms" that may attend or undergird a given tradition, and though I do not believe traditioned persons do so witlessly, I do hold that many a tradition, just as the acceptance of one's mother tongue, is usually subconsciously adopted, without foregrounded reflective analysis.

hooded human nature before God's face. Traditioning is an inescapable, pervasive reality that constitutively underlies all other kinds of human culturing and societal relationships. You cannot take up art without being engrafted as apprentice into some kind of artistic tradition; you cannot live into a neighborhood without learning social traditions (customs) already in force.

But it will be helpful to take good note of the fact that a confessional tradition (Confucian, Lutheran Christian, Zen Buddhist, or whatever) has a different sort of hold on a person than a political tradition (Whiggish Liberalism, Utopian Socialism, Fascism). A thought tradition (like empiricism, evolutionism, "dialectical materialism") impinges on human life differently than does an ethical tradition (celibacy, polygamy, promiscuity). Not any one of these various sorts of tradition has an apriori privilege of influence on human life, in my judgment. And the quality of a given tradition in a specific zone of human endeavor is a still different matter for concern. But an awareness of how mixed and complex an amalgam one's "tradition" always is—one embodies several kinds of traditions at once!—let alone how any one given tradition is also modified or compromised by one's personal strengths and faults, age, health, and experience, could caution us against oversimplified analysis.

There are other complexities too. Let me give an example or two. When the practice of dueling was a synecdoche for the tradition of war as at the time of David and Goliath (1 Samuel 17), or during the age when medieval knights met in chivalric jousts, dueling served a political purpose fairly well. But in the time when duels became charged ethical ceremonies presumed to settle breaches of honor in Bismarck's Germany, dueling had become a brand of aristocratic vigilante "justice" confused with a deadly sport.[21]

Or consider: the liturgical tradition for baptism (immersion or sprinkling) is distinct from the confessional tradition on what the sacrament testifies to (God's redemptive activity, or church certification of one's faith). If the difference and relation between (styleful) liturgical tradition and (dogmatic) confession tradition is ignored, then debating the issues tends to let one over-read or under-value what is at stake for the life of the church.

If we keep in mind that there are varied, irreducible sorts of traditions humans construct and simultaneously inhabit, that awareness could help us sort out some of the problems that seem to plague our coming

---

21 See V. G. Kiernan, *The Duel in European History: Honour and the reign of aristocracy* (London: Oxford University Press, 1990), 185–203.

to understand the nature of this rich, enigmatic, protean reality of tradition.[22] Meanwhile, granted the working definition I have sketched on the systematic nature of tradition—passing on wonts from a practiced to an inexperienced human generation who carries them further—I should like to explore the sense in claiming that humans are necessarily implicated in one most basic tradition not of their own making, the tradition of meeting and accepting or rejecting allegiance to Jesus Christ, a fundamental, historical faith-tradition that relativizes,[23] better, judges and orients all other kinds of humanly enacted traditions, as to the source of their meaning, and as a test of their vanity or sterility. (This will be section III.) But first let me describe what is at stake in discerning meaning and authority as inescapable features of tradition.

On meaning and authority of traditions

Let me say very simply that the central meaning of tradition is to be found in its being the fund that capitalizes human culturing activity.[24] A tradition of whatever sort provides the historical context for renewed continuation of such activity at hand. That's what tradition is for. If the thought tradition of Vollenhoven, Dooyeweerd, and the circle of *de Wijsbegeerte der Wetsidee* prompts your thinking, as it does mine, your analysis inherits a wealth of Kuyperian-Calvinian-Reformation insights and post-Neoidealist phenomenological baggage[25] that situates your analysis very precisely, and relates your probable concept-formation and decisions on judgment-priorities to a definite, long-standing way of thinking, however you presently, personally modify it. A person's thought tradition bodes a particular concentration of ideas; and the analytic schemata one comes to assume both limits and points your thinking further, but does not

22 See J. G. A. Pocock, "Time, Institutions and Action: An essay on traditions and their understanding," in *Politics, Language and Time: Essays on political thought and history* (New York: Atheneum, 1971), 234.

23 See Josef Pieper on "heilige Überlieferung" in *Überlieferung, Begriff und Anspruch* (München: Kösel, 1970), 71–72, 106–108, with reference to Yves Congar, *Die Tradition und die Traditionen* (Mainz, 1965). Also, Hans Urs von Balthasar on the "übermenschlichen Traditionen" of *imitatio Christi*, "Im Strom fließt die Quelle" (1966), in *Vom Sinn der Tradition*, ed. Leonhard Reinisch, 101.

24 This formulation does not commit me to a "Capitalist" ideology. In Marxist terms one could say that the central meaning of tradition lies in its being the means of production, the infrastructure, that underlies all human culturing activity.

25 See Robert Knudsen's careful yet loose designation of this tradition in "Transcendental Method in Dooyeweerd," *Anakainosis* 1:3 (1979): 2–8, esp. 6; reprinted in *Roots and Branches: The quest for meaning and truth in modern thought*, ed. Donald Knudsen (Grand Rapids, MI: Paideia Press, 2009), 301–309, esp. 307.

restrict a person from thinking abroad.[26]

Tradition means being primed

A traditioned person, as all of us alive today are in various ways, is not so much equipped with a thesaurus of knowledge for consultation in given cultural fields as that a person is set before certain options that temper your action.[27] Given the aesthetic tradition of William Morris's arts-and-crafts movement, for example, a moneyed person is liable to develop a gracious, genteel life style. Granted that other figures who are primed the same aesthetic way might veer into Biedermeierisch comfortableness,[28] or that three historical generations later Morris's heritage has been pragmatistically converted into Bauhaus style where clean lines and antiseptic space are next to godliness, the point is: anyone traditioned by the (Victorian) arts-and-crafts movement with Morris furniture and dance and a Mies von der Rohe chair will hardly go for the quirky lines of Rudolf Steiner's Goetheanum or anthroposophically freighted eurhythmics. Your tradition means your underpinnings and identifies your collaborators as you yourself proceed to posit norms (by leading or following) in that cultural area.

If a person comes out of the Anabaptist confessional tradition you are surrounded by a host of celebrated witnesses—John Hus, Menno Simons, John Bunyan, Roger Williams, C. H. Spurgeon, Dwight L. Moody—who adumbrate how you will confessionally face everything under the sun, whether it be Cartesian philosophy, political activity, schooling, or rock music and cinema. Maybe as a latter-day Anabaptist like Jacques Ellul you may flirt with Marxist Utopian themes as you censure the secular city and the established church, but again, the thrust of this example too is that *the meaning of tradition is its proleptic force.* A tradition outfits you for your cultural journey. Traditions mean nobody can be born yesterday. A tradition gives you your lease on certain cultural life. Unfortunately many people begin heavily mortgaged . . . thought-

---

26 H. van de Waal, *Traditie en Bezieling*, Inaugurale Rede (Rotterdam: Ad Donker, 1946), 12–13.

27 Shils, *Tradition*, 197.

28 I am hinting here that other sides of one's life and their traditioned filiation also affect how a person lives out a style tradition, for example. Such multiple coloration of one's aesthetic taste is not quite so sinister as Pierre Bourdieu implies. Bourdieu's skeleton key for unlocking the riddle of anyone's taste formation is the economic class position that figure has in society. But Bourdieu's overdrawn analyses are often trenchant, for example, on why middleclass people enjoy Impressionist painting but not Goya and Daumier. See *Distinction: A social critique of judgment of taste* [1979], translated by Richard Nice (Harvard University Press, 1984), 120.

wise, aesthetically, confessionally, in how they are initially traditioned.[29]

Are the traditions a person inherits fundamentally circumstantial? Can a person be circumspect in the tradition you come to own? Is it possible to act as if you were born yesterday? or assume you can begin fresh like Adam and Eve, and rid myself of these millstones hung about my neck?

Before we face such problems and then examine what tradition means for conceiving the outlines of an historiography with redemptive horizons (I treat these matters in section IV), we need to examine briefly the authority that tradition by nature assumes and properly exercises and find out if and when such claims to authority go wrong.

Traditions bear apriori canonic force

A tradition covertly exudes authority. Everybody who encounters a tradition always has a sense that it has been sanctioned—even those who question the given tradition's right to be there. Traditions always beat an individual to the punch, it seems, by having been mysteriously authorized once upon a time before you got there. Even founding a tradition cannot be done by oneself, by fiat. While it takes two to tango, it takes three to tradition: you need (1) the charismatic pattern-former whose face cinematically fades into (2) the initial receiver turned transmitter turning toward (3) a subsequent follower who accepts the meaning of the transaction and responsibly enacts it with others. This threefold institution of a tradition is why tradition naturally enjoins a given person's accord—the trans-individual pattern is actually in force, apriori as it were, legitimated by historical existence, even solemn with age, before one faces its embrace oneself. A tradition is like a silent, enabling injunction.

Schools are a good example of how this complicated triple action in-

---

29 I was left nonplussed at the age-old debt that seems to shape the October 1987 issue of *Faith and Philosophy*, intent upon presenting "Philosophy from a Christian Perspective." It seems virtually impossible for us thinkers to bring inner reform to philosophical analysis and develop a systematic Scriptural philosophy, if we remain within a thought tradition that virtually holds that "christian philosophy" is a theology dealing with philosophical problems. Cf. Etienne Gilson, *Christianisme et Philosophie* [1939] (Paris: Vrin, 1949); Herman Dooyeweerd, *In the Twilight of Western Thought, Studies in the pretended autonomy of philosophical thought* [1960] (Nutley: Craig Press, 1965); John Kok, "Vollenhoven and 'Scriptural Philosophy,'" *Philosophia Reformata* 53:2 (1988): 101–42; and my "Concluding Theses on Key Issues for Conceiving and Teaching Scripturally Directed Philosophy," in *Philosophy in the Reformed Undergraduate Curriculum*, eds. John Roose and George Pierson (Palos Heights: Trinity Christian College, 1990), 79–89 {supra pp. 173–182}.

trinsic to traditioning—where a hand-me-down becomes actually worn by a third party to whom it was given by someone other than the original wearer—now this "passing a wont down" exercises authority. Schools, like families, are par excellence institutional agents for passing on cultural inheritances and for issuing promissory world-and-life-view notes to potential heirs for signing.[30] Schools possess massive authority.

The student is at the mercy of a teacher because the teachers have (presumably) mastered the older knowledge and wont they mediate for the new generation to take in hand. The authority of the traditional way to "do numbers" in school, the authority of what the pupils learn constitutes their national literary treasury, the authority for how jobs and professions are ranked that a youth may prepare to take up, and myriad other kinds of tangential wonts embodied in the discipline of schooling: the authority of the preemptive choices made by the teaching community and being formally and informally transmitted in schooling is all the more powerful the more tacit the rulings be. Traditions passed on in the practicing arena of a school tend to be taken by the younger for the way things are or have to be. And it is right here that a pressure point in schooling elucidates a danger in traditioning.

The danger that the canonic character inhering traditions may be inflated into a sacrosanct infallibility by newcomers, or by transmitters, is mirrored in the fine but fatal shift in schooling from education to indoctrination. A teacher needs a learner to be a teacher, but if the learning novice is subtly pressured into becoming a disciple of the teacher, then the correct bond of pedagogical leadership has been twisted into a bondage of tyrannical control, benign though it may seem.

While there may be settings when the young are properly trained to mind strictly a given confessional or skill tradition (church school or dental school), ordinary public schools are the place to face students with the world and cultural history at large, to help them touch, analyze, imagine, and articulate everything under the sun, in the light of a chosen faith-tradition, to be sure. But schools are not the proper institution to

---

30 For myself the feature that qualifies schooling as schooling is the activity of "making distinctions." Learning to make distinctions, along with the particular foci of learning languages, exercising imaginativity, and achieving competence in various basic skills: all these disciplines occur—especially during the earlier academic grades—under an "ethical halo." See my "The Fundamental Importance of Imaginativity within Schooling," in *Rainbows for the Fallen World* (Toronto Tuppence Press, 1980/2005), 141–45; also K. J. Popma, "Opvoeding, Onderwijs, Schoolverband," *Philosophia Reformata* 12:1–3 (1947): 36–41, 86–93, 130–44. Schooling necessarily traditions students, especially in the faith-vision that guides the schooling, but schoolteachers do such traditioning in the solvent of reflection, speech, imaginativity, and skills.

catechize, proselytize, or tradition conformity to an established pattern of vision.[31] Similarly, a tradition in transmission needs respect and deserves to be maintained by the next generation absorbing its wont anew. If those accepting hand-me-downs are kept from making alterations to fit their body, then the traditioning is denatured into commandeering, which violates the very crux of the responsibility of human subjectivity to enact a normative calling.

Authority limited to its measure of obeying God's specific call

A given thought tradition, artistic tradition, or whatever kind, deserves the conforming authority it subtly asks for so long as its bonding pattern itself is in obedience to God's call for a tradition to promote the integrating speciated service of the human activity it sheathes. A tradition that protects the special glory of a given field of human cultivating and gives such culturing the room to be "professionally" (= committedly and skillfully) honed and developed while relating its acute blessing to the person and community or society's life as a whole is entitled to its authority of summoning proper compliance. The type of limited authority and acquiescence at stake depends upon the specific kind of human activity with which the tradition is dealing.

For example, the ethical tradition of lovers' engagement prior to marriage, no matter the untold variations throughout the centuries in East and in West, is basically a sound tradition because it beckons a couple to take betrothing time for testing and enhancing each other's tentative commitments in loyalty and intimacy, relativizing the crucial erotic from any besotted romanticism, with the outcome that the patina on their married sexual joy may have an enduring luster unknown to the unions arranged by quick elopement.

Or, take the scholarly tradition of footnotes in learned books and articles: if it be the posturing of conspicuous consumption or undigested thought, the documentation soon rings false. If the footnotes are humane and attest to researched care, sharing specialized knowledge while subtly making the point that enriched analysis involves a communion of thoughtful people and is not simply barefaced argument, then footnoting is a good traditional usage to be stipulated for academic work, even if it be out of fashion.

---

31 Josef Pieper (*Überlieferung*, 25–36) tends to keep "educating" distinct from "traditioning" too, but conceives the difference along standard Thomist lines where:

tradition is a matter of authority, accepted on faith

education is a matter of experience, accepted by reason

A last example: consider the ancient socio-economic wont of the business lunch. Unless I be mistaken, "the business lunch," under the guise of socializing sales, is a cost-efficiency ploy that commercializes fellowship. Whoever takes the check has gained the advantage of dispensing a company favor left outstanding, which the recipient in the deal good-humoredly weighs so as not to be outfoxed. I do not say this tradition is always a charade for Machiavellian manipulation of those who take the hedonist bait but as a time-honored practice it does not deepen human intercourse.[32] The common business lunch pattern blocks the gift of good food—let alone the second cocktail—from heightening eating into a celebrative meal by covertly turning mealtime into a "deductible expense" and simultaneously pretends it makes economic reality "personal" while actually cheapening people, uniting them for the occasion of intimacy by the glue of pleasure and money. The pulling power and authority of this suasive lobbying tradition is better to be shunned. No wonder Proverbs 23:1–9, centuries ago, warned those with ears to hear, "There are no free lunches."

The assumption that underlies the alternative, working definition on the nature of tradition I have been expositing in section II is that there be a creational law of God—as permanently there as God's Word—for human traditions and traditioning to be normed toward. Given that basic thesis, the existential problem then for anyone who wishes to make earnest with the human condition of being traditioned, is this: does the priming holding pattern for passing-on wonts (= the triple structured human response of tradition) that I have adopted—wittingly or not—engender good prospects for historically deepened fruitfulness in that cultural area? Does the human traditioning at hand in my life embody the nitty-gritty peace and wisdom to open up whatever activities are at stake for refined service in God's world?[33] If the answer is yes, those who lead or follow in that complexly traditioned way of life may pray with good conscience to be kept humbly faithful in the will of God. If the multiple traditions fall short of or run counter to this call of God for redemptive traditioning, then the carriers and custodians of the particular tradition, with the counsel of friendly observers from outside that tradition, need

---

32 Cf. John Gray, "Let's not do lunch," *Destinations: A Globe and Mail Magazine* 5:6 (1990): 40.

33 Cf. Dooyeweerd's "integrative differentiating formation," in *Vernieuwing en Bezinning om het Reformatorisch Grondmotief* (Zutphen: J. B. van den Brink. 1959), 63–76; "The sense of history and the historicistic world-and-life-view," *In the Twilight of Western Thought*, 83–112.

to consider policies of reformation, blood transfusion, or skin-graft surgery. But to suppose naively, as many North Americans do, or to pretend proudly—as is the custom of utopians and revolutionaries—that one can begin new, untraditioned, is foolishness.

III

Biblical direction for understanding tradition here and now
As I understand the Scriptures, it can be said that into whatever traditions one happens to be born, a person may believe God provides a way to go. This truth holds for the 1990s AD as well as for 1517, 451 and 60 AD. In fact, the dedicatory preface to the gospel according to Luke (1:1–4) and the testimony of the apostle Paul to the Corinthians (1 Corinthians 4:6–7, 15:1–1 1) and the letter of Jude (v.3) face any reader at any time with the truth: we have been given in writing an utterly reliable account of what happened respecting Jesus Christ and his revelation directing us to follow the saving Rule of the LORD God almighty in history (cf. Acts 1:1–3, Colossians 1:15–20).

That Word of God scripted in Greek once upon a time, along with the older covenanted sacred writings in Hebrew Christ held for authoritative (Luke 24: 25–27, 2 Timothy 3:10–17): the holy scriptures now present the Way God wants our entire human life and its traditionings to be focused. These specially God-breathed writings have a living power to face us time and again with the ascended Jesus Christ to whom they testify, as the Holy Spirit opens our human heart to hear their voiced direction (John 5:31–40, Hebrews 4:12– 13, 2 Thessalonians 3:1–5). The holy *scriptures* are instrumental in the deepest possible faith-traditioning of those who read and obediently hear them recite, narrate, and creedally voice the great deeds of God. Such believing faithful ones, just like Gamaliel's student Saul converted into the apostle Paul, are patterned into a basic godly *"Way"* of compassionate just-doing that is definite enough in life-contours and creedal tenets to be called "sectarian" by those who reject its orientation.[34] According to the Bible, this Way of life is the only underlying redemptive *faith-tradition* that humans shall find to fashion that "saves" and shows a face, provides openings, for "lasting" results. This biblically enjoined Way-of-life, if abandoned or compromised by humans, says Scripture, shall prime the destruction of their ensuing culture.[35]

With these last remarks the hermeneutic fat is in the historiographic

---

34 See Acts 24:10–26, v14 αἵρεσιν, v22.
35 2 Peter 2:18–22; cf. Deuteronomy 30:11–20, Micah 6:6–8, James 5:19–20.

fire. What precisely is this Biblically informed faith-tradition? Is it the kind of stuff that Paul commends and reproves the Corinthian believers, and instructs Timothy, in matters liturgic (1 Corinthians 11:2–16), sacramental (1 Corinthians 11:17–34), basic creed (1 Corinthians 15:1–11), church government (the whole first letter to Timothy), and the order surrounding marriage (1 Corinthians 7)? Can such human traditions "received from the Lord" (1 Corinthians 11:23) be privileged (N.B. 2 Thessalonians 2:13–15!) without becoming traditioned loopholes that help us crafty believers slip away from the complete, living obedience the Savior commands?[36] Can believers, after the historic Pentecost event, *add* to the tradition of what is posited in Scripture, update God's will with an authority equal to that of Peter, Paul, and John, or not (cf. Revelation 22:18–19)?

It is not my purpose here to try to "settle" this problem of a few millennia. But I wish to make two (necessarily simplified) observations before I relate the biblical givens to the matter of *writing* and historiographic task.

Four basic positions on christian faith-tradition

The first observation is this: The followers of Jesus Christ in history seem to have adopted certain basic positions on the matter of "authorized tradition" that are curiously similar to the taxonomy of major conceptions on ordinary tradition with which this essay began.

(1) There is the long-standing judgment of the Mother Church that Christian tradition is the exemplary reception of Scripture's faithful account of Christ's action and teaching, which is a legitimate way of regulating and edifying the conduct of the faithful.[37] The tradition codified by Church Counsels is an accrued Canon witnessing to its continuity with the inspired apostle Peter, and since Trent[38] the word of the Church is declared fully authoritative next to Scripture, and since Vatican I (1869–70) that authority is vested in the infallible *ex cathedra* pronouncements of the papacy.[39]

---

36 See Mark 7:1–23, parallel Matthew 15:1–20; also Philippians 3:2–11.

37 Jules Cambier, "Paul and Tradition," in *The Dynamism of Biblical Tradition* (New York: Paulist Press, 1967), 107–11.

38 8 April 1546; cr. Denzinger, #783–84.

39 Already Thomas Aquinas, appealing to 1 Corinthians 1:10, ascribes authority in matters of faith only ad Summum Pontificem; see *Summa Theologiae* II–II, q.1 a.10 resp. But the complexity of just how "sacred tradition" and "sacred Scripture" comport in the large Roman Catholic thought-world of today, since Vatican II, is incredibly nuanced and moot, far beyond what I am able to indicate here.

(2) A different strain of Christ's disciples have felt uncomfortable with such an accumulated deposit of tradition in the Vatican or in ecclesiastical archives. Taking their inspiration especially from the Johannine books, and filled with a passion for the *ecclesia spiritualis*, believers like (middle) Augustine, through Eckhart and *devotio moderna*, on to the modern Quaker movement, have distilled "tradition" into a habit of deep piety and personal experience that pits the living spirit against the dead letter, the future present against the past, and claim to be speaking *gospel truth* whenever someone is "in the Spirit." There is no binding Christian tradition except the Holy Spirit's stirring your spirit where the Spirit lists. When the Spirit speaks, even Scripture, as it were, recedes, and the original voice of God is reconstructed, because that reverberating Spirit testimony is the first and the last word on your union with Christ—what more could a Christian desire to have attend and shelter his or her life?[40]

(3) There has also usually been a chiliastic fringe active in the neighborhood of the church of Jesus Christ, for whom tradition reverts to elaborate rituals of mystery and secret doctrines preserved, known, and practiced by a select group of priestly figures. Elements of Christian sacramental tradition are usually so syncretized that one might better describe these strange deviations of churched community as cults. But for the "christian gnostics" and like-minded believers all the way down to the contemporary, bizarre Jonesville settlement, tradition becomes fundamentally certain archetypal rites that when performed are supposed to repristenate the primordial act of our release from bondage. It is significant that actual sects that disdain the mainstream community of faiths often seem to adopt this sort of atavistic sacramentalism as "sacred tradition," along with a concomitant fascination with exorcism.

I should also like to mention a fourth position that weights "Christian tradition" differently than these three, not as a classic canon coming up from the past, not as hindrance to the free play of the Spirit, not as sacrosanct ritual, but a fourth position that takes "Christian tradition" as counsel germinated by Scripture, current and always subject to commu-

---

40 Cf. R. Stupperich, "Spiritualismus," *Evangelisches Kirchenlexikon* (Göttingen: Vandenhoeck & Ruprecht, 1959), 3:1090–92. The (personal encounter) "Spiritualism" of Emil Brunner, according to D. H. Th. Vollenhoven's historiographic analysis, could be a (Neo-orthodox) variant of this confessional tradition, since Brunner privileges the apostles' "interior word of faith" response to Christ above any "mere words about" Christ (namely, Scripture), and Brunner conceives of the human subjective reception of the *testimonium spiritus sancti* as the *validation* (rather than a confirmation) of Scripture's God-Word nature. See Mike Goheen's Institute for Christian Studies 1989 Interdisciplinary paper, "Brunner, Ridderbos, and Apostolic Tradition," typescript, 5–9 and 16–19.

nal review. This fourth position (consonant with the alternative position on tradition explained above on pp. 236–38) is usually associated with the Reformation, which formulated its stand on the relevant factors with the precision of declared heretics. This position holds that the apostolic authority of those who saw Christ's deeds firsthand and inscripturated God's Word is historically unique. The authority of church bishops is of a different order than that of the apostles. The authority of elders and church overseers is secondary to that of the apostles; just as good, Spirit-filled preaching is not equal in authority to the original holy scriptures but is secondary, exegeted, guided, and to be touchstoned by the Scriptures. No ancient creed, no recent church doctrine, no new word by Pentecostal prophet brings a revelation that supersedes what is booked in kerygmatic *writings* of the God-breathed tradition-keepers of the Older Testament and of the Newer Testament apostles—this is the position of the Reformation.[41]

This fourth position of the Reformation, as I understand it and claim as mine, does not press the Bible into the rubric of "tradition." The Bible is a unique book, *writings* specially tendered into our hands by the Holy Spirit, where my God the LORD speaks directly and compellingly to those with ears to hear about God's great deeds in the world of living creatures and history. The canonic holy Scriptures are not unrelated to human traditioning, but are not enclosed within its Hebrew-Aramaic-Greek, dated-located human-language embodiment certified by the body of Christ once upon a time. As Jesus Christ is veritable God-man, and not merely a special Jewish human, so the Bible is a peculiarly God-breathed writing, and not merely a very privileged Tradition. Therefore, this Holy Writ has the gentle final authority of the Holy Spirit, to be trusted by its speaking for correcting "human tradition."[42]

So "Christian tradition" is not exempt from fallibility,[43] but insofar as the Reformational cloud of witnesses over the generations is Scripturally led—and as Reformational tradition not ideologically identified with the Scriptures—and therefore biblically *normed*,[44] its traditioning

---

41 Oscar Cullmann, *Tradition* (Zürich: Zwingli-Verlag, 1954), 27–31, 37–39.

42 Colossians 2:8, τὴν παράδοσιν τῶν ἀνθρώπων.

43 Such exemption is supported by those cited in n.23 above. The difficulty with the Roman Catholic stance on tradition for a Reformation person is very close to the equivocation Dooyeweerd finds in Thomas Aquinas on the referent for *sacra doctrina*. See *In the Twilight of Western Thought* (Nutley: Presbyterian and Reformed, 1960), 116–20, 131.

44 I put it exactly to avoid mistaking the normative calling of our traditioning response as if it were itself the divine law (or "final norm"). It is in this sense that I under-

wisdom should soften and comfort our hearts as it prepares our praxis for well-directed, insightful shalom in philosophical activity, art historical critique, setting financial priorities, writing a history of something, or whatever plow God puts into our hands.

Tack to take: historical knowledge of your chosen faith-tradition
My second observation on how the biblically traditioned Way of *life* relates to tradition here and now is this: the four delineated, different traditions on "Christian tradition" (247–49), and the comparable traditions on "tradition" (233–236), seem to be cleft from each other, each with a decisive, different ontological hold on a given community's life and perspective. This difference in "faith-traditions" seems to me to be of a deeper, more radical sort than the possible varieties of confessional tradition (Lutheran, Calvinian, Presbyterian, Anglican), or a (Nordic, Latin, Australian) style tradition, or other traditions of human activity whose contours are imbued with what I am calling a most basic "faith-tradition" (cf. above pp. 239–40) A congenial representative of any given, most basic faith-tradition, like David Tracy, for example, for the Roman Catholic Church tradition of faith, who is fully aware of Wayne Booth's tack on "the powers and limits of pluralism," may bend over backwards to "risk" becoming a genuinely "public" conversation partner; but he will still admit that one is immersed within a particular tradition.[45] Others like Paul Ricoeur gingerly try to avoid the offence of touching down too pointedly anywhere, determined like a simultaneous translator at the United Nations, to mediate others' entrenched positions into an intelligible dialogue;[46] but Ricoeur too knows where his philosophical thinking comes from and where it belongs historically.[47]

---

stood my colleague William Rowe's offhand comment during the opening session on Jaroslav Pelikan in the Institute for Christian Studies' Interdisciplinary seminar, 14 September 1987: "A healthy tradition is normative, but is not a norm."

45 David Tracy, *The Analogical Imagination: Christian theology and the culture of pluralism* (New York: Crossroad, 1981), xi, 99–102, 117–22. Cf. Wayne C. Booth, *Critical Understanding: The powers and limits of pluralism* (University of Chicago Press, 1979).

46 For example, Ricoeur says he aims to formulate a position that "without really contradicting Gadamer's hermeneutics, will rectify it in a manner decisive for the debate with the critique of ideology" (in "Hermeneutics and the Critique of Ideology," in *Hermeneutics and the Human Sciences*, trans. John B. Thompson [Cambridge University Press, 1981], 91). Ricoeur attempts something similar with Husserl and himself in "Phenomenology and Hermeneutics," Ibid., 101–28.

47 He dispassionately and brilliantly acknowledges his thought tradition in an article "On Interpretation," in *Philosophy in France Today*, ed. Alan Montefiore (Cambridge University Press, 1983), especially 187–94.

With Bill Rowe, Professor of Philosophy at Pennsylvania
State University, Scranton, Pennsylvania, 2004

The thrust of this second observation on the fact that humans seem to be fixed in certain faith-traditions, each of which tends to remain jealous of its own orientation, is this: it behooves everybody at the least to become self-critically aware *that* a person acts and breathes alive within the compass of a faith-depth-tradition, and it behooves everyone to become self-conscious of *which* faith-depth-tradition he or she has assumed. A person cannot experiment at a distance with one's faith-depth tradition or suspend that deepest traditioning for a trial period, because any tradition, like blood, has a coursing, on-going, in-force, once-only presence, fortiori the "all-consuming" faith-depth-tradition that you inhabit. Once a tradition is broken off, discarded, or bled, and a person undergoes a complete blood replacement of an other type, the earlier tradition can scarcely ever be restored.[48]

Although "religious wars" continue unabated in our day—Hindu

---

48 Max Huber, "Das Wesen der Tradition: ihre Voraussetzungen und Wirkungen in der Geschichte" [1929], *Heimat und Tradition* (Zürich: Atlantis, 1947), 203. Shils says, "A tradition once it has receded from regular usage cannot be deliberately restored" (*Tradition*, 329).

vs. Buddhist in India and Pakistan, Muslim vs. Christian in Lebanon, Jewish vs. Palestinian in the Mediterranean, Ulster Protestant vs. Roman Catholic in Ireland—its evil is more recognized by the body of Christ today than at the time of the Crusades and the formation of nation states in Europe during the 1500–1600s AD. As Christians of the several "Christian traditions" delineated above endeavor to join forces to do battle with the idols of our generation (including our own household idols), we should not, I think, buy into any "Enlightenment" project of taking "critical distance" from "our" traditions, but search out renewed Holy Spirit-led *biblical direction* for our traditions, which will drive us together. That search will include tracking the history of how we have been variously traditioned, and where we are today.

Thinking from within the Christian faith tradition of the Reformation, at the Institute for Christian Studies in Toronto, I know roughly where I am standing and walking historically in the Canadian wilds of the 1990s AD. My schooled memory[49] means to be wary of both traditionalism and the subversive tack of putting new wine into old skins (supra p. 240), and I prefer we put forward theses to be challenged rather than remain restlessly tossed in an ontological dialogic.

At this point I am prepared, for example, to propose a conception of historiographic praxis that might make a redemptive difference among the current options for recording history. That could be important: while traditions invisibly chaperone one's walk through the snow, historiography can serve as conscience to the traditions as the historian tracks the footprints of those walking or wandering through the snow.

IV

History and history-keeping: tracking footprints
"Historical" = *change that entails waste or enrichment of inheritance*

What constitutes the history (*Geschichte, res gestae*) of any creature is moot, but "significant change" might be a starting point for us on what it is of a mountain range or a ginkgo tree, a school of dolphins or some human person, the Kuranko tribe, the art of painting, "Germany," the discipline of philosophy or whatever, that is noteworthy for an historian. Any entity undergoes myriad changes during its temporal existence. Which changes are "significant changes" depends upon the specific locus or strand of modifications at stake, and how restricted or extensive the scope be. Historical changes are never unspecifiedly global, but are al-

---

49 See *Anakainosis* 5:1 (September 1982): 1–6. Reprinted in *In the Fields of the Lord*, ed. Craig Bartholomew (2000), 83–89.

ways harbored within a *topos* of the entitary reality whose history is being considered.

To take a relatively simple example: my medical history relevant for a prospective life insurance company would be the series of diseases, injuries, surgery, years of health and breakdowns of strength, impinging stress factors, and current dangerous living/working circumstances as they relate to my basically sound biophysical condition. My educational history pertinent for a Canadian Government grant application would include the schools and universities I have attended in different places, any especially suasive mentors, academic degrees I have achieved, key books I have read, the measure of disciplined learning my students show, prospective publications—all of which profile my scholarly journey so far. That is, the actual history of something is of a definite, limited sort (including the special instance of a biography) and the crux of what is historical ("significant change") is the conjunctive sequence of disjunctive alterations in the selected field that *fecundate and/or waste its treasure*.

This last criterion for what is "historical" is germinated, I think, by the Reformational Christian philosophical perspective, which is oriented to the biblical truth that the LORD God in generations-long, judging-mercy covenants shalom for the body of Christ that faithfully obeys God's multiple callings. Such a Scripturally directed setting takes the mania out of human culturing of the earth, because God's compassionate Word limits anyone's historical responsibility to his or her (communal) planting, tending, weeding, and bearing fruit, during that person's lifetime, in the cultivated ground one has inherited. Humans do not have to "make history" as if they be free-wheeling Adamic or Evesian figures. (Even a person's own history is by nature a response, not "free creation," conditioned by one's genetic and circumstantial, dated inheritance.)

Also, while change is normal to creaturely life, change is a creaturely gift needing to be normed. For me this means that historical change is handled responsibly in a given area if the change made enables the creature to be more fully conformed to God's will for administering that creaturely activity, whatever it be. Therefore, significant change can be destructive as well as enriching on the face of the earth. History and the historical nature of things is never simply whatever happens in the continental-drift, genetic flow of things, and is not the sum total of additions made to the state of affairs or received canon, and historical occurrence is also not an everlasting recurrence of a primordial truth. The history of something, especially the (cultivated) work of human hands: the history of anything is that sequence of deformative and corrective events or deeds or happenings that underlie where such matters now are and what the prospects be.

Different ways of keeping track of historical change

History-keeping, then, (*Historie, rerum gestarum memoria*) is knowing the path the footsteps have taken, and is being able to tell another person the twists and turns the track took through the snow. Many, many features of the footprints and their surroundings in the snow could be noticed, reported, and remembered—their number and size, the stride, apparent indecision, firmness, exact snow conditions at the time in that place, which roads were traversed, or was it cross-country and uphill, any blood in the snow, and so on—but the crux for history-keeping is (the normally subliminal decisions on) what are the memorable follow-ups among the footprints, and what is the overall route taken.[50]

History-keeping provides people with a memory of a walk that took place, and human memory by nature simplifies, correctly so, yet remembers particularly the crises that give contour to the whole. History-keepers cannot tell everything each time; so the Gestalt remembered may shimmer differently upon occasion. However there *is* a trail of footprints through the snow, and that track is what the trustworthy history-keeper recounts.

Practically everybody realizes that history-keeping leads to quite different trackings of the same path of footprints. There are important reasons for that troublesome phenomenon: (a) The history of many things leave faint footprints, because their passage is more like the flight of a bird than the steps of a beast of burden. And sin, which plays havoc in the history of human institutions, is usually all but invisible—tracking gossip that led to a suicide would be a nightmare for more than a strict philosophical Empiricist.[51] Also, an Existentialist history-keeper might credit a wink for the crime, while a Positivist colleague sees the wink as only a blink. (b) The altogether different, dated, and located subjectivity of the history-keepers leads to sharply diverse accounts of a course taken. An aerial point of view, an overview, of the rise and fall of Patmos Gallery,[52]

---

50 See W. Jackson Bate, *The Burden of the Past and the English Poet* (London: Chatto and Windus, 1971), 116. Also, Geoffrey H. Hartmann, "History Writing as Answerable Style" [1972], in *New Directions in Literary History* (London: Kegan and Paul, 1974), 105.

51 Eugen Rosenstock-Huessy, *The Christian Future or The Modern Mind Outrun* (New York: Charles Scribner's Sons, 1946), 30–31.

52 Patmos Gallery was a communal christian gallery for paintings, sculpture, and graphic art, originally organized around the Dutch Master artist Henk (Senggih) Krijger, in Worth, Illinois, and then Toronto, 1969–1979. See *Hommage à senggih: A retrospec-*

or of the establishment of the Institute for Christian Studies in Toronto, would be quite unlike the account of one who used bloodhounds to sniff out the trail through tunnels and kept going where snowstorms had obliterated tracks. Still different again: the diary of someone tramping the ground would authenticate colorful details ("I wuz dere"), but probably would not be unself-interested in shaping the tale.

These "points-of-interest" affecting history-keeping ("omniscient," third-person, first-person) and the difficulty of ascertaining where the footprints actually were can frequently be reconciled and checked out, with hindsight a more radical divergence in history-keeping stems from the traditioned visions of the history-keepers. For example, (1) the Nigerian town of Ijesha today charters any "new" important societal practices or taboos by *itan* (oral narratives) that reconstitute the past to act as ground for the present practice; and every new *Owa* (lineage chief) is ritually instructed into *itan*, certifying the present by making the past repeat itself.[53] Such "stereotypic reproduction"[54] affirms the mutual conditioning of past and present and unhinges history-keeping from remembering an irreversible *hapax* (once only) passage. Once a culture is literate, this tradition of history-keeping takes on an atavistic, repressive stringency. The most ancient pharaohs of Egypt, as I recall,[55] practiced such history-keeping by demolishing all previous pharaoh's records; and each began history with his own royal, divine regime. The Stalinist Soviet Union kept history by these revisional tactics.[56] Pop culture in North America does the same, and every decade retreads its tapes and canonizes a "new" old pantheon.

(2) Those who have a solid-state, conservationist outlook (supra pp. 235–236), like mature Toynbee, affect no bias in keeping track of footprints on the shores of time. Their history-keeping aims to identify patterns in the footsteps and to present global, comparative, encyclopedic summa-

---

tive of Henk Krijger in North America (Toronto: Patmos Gallery, 1989).

53 J. D. Y. Peel, "Making History: The past in the Ijesha present," *Man* 19 (1984): 111–115.

54 This Nigerian example is close to what Foucault both stigmatizes and practices as "archaeology of knowing"; supra pp. 237–38.

55 From conversation with Eberhard Otto (in Heidelberg, 1966). See also his *Ägypten: Der Weg des Pharaonenreiches* [1953] (Stuttgart: Kohlhammer, 1966), 64–65, 158. A later Egyptian way of history-keeping, during the Hellenistic period, had them legitimate foreign domination by incorporating these strange rulers into their genealogies (*Ägypten*, 247–53).

56 See Milan Kundera, *The Book of Laughter and Forgetting* [1979], translated from Czech by Michael Henry Heim (Middlesex: Penguin, 1980), 3.

tions of typical moves you might find in any number of particular journeys. Toynbee's orienting concern is to document the stages any civilization goes through (e.g., creative minority responds to environmental challenge; technocultural troubles ensue upon institutional stagnation . . .); his thrust is not to present a vivid narration of some definite, local significant change in the configuration of a people or nation's life. And you do not need to detect connecting links in a particular course of footprints so much as to note positive contributions we might emulate (cf. Burckhardt, Panofsky, Northrop Frye).[57]

(3) There are also history-keepers who consider themselves true to the footprints in the snow only if they enter into the footsteps, tread the same path as it were, not try to repeat what took place but to immerse themselves in and revive the operation. Such history-keeping tends to swallow up all previous exploits, and under the guise of dialogue, to absorb or dislocate the past into one's own present framing. After all, it seems to me, if you as history-keeper have to walk on top of the footprints in the snow to do your tracking, have you not extinguished the *différance* between the Original path and the dependent one? (Cf. Herder, Hegel, Adorno, Gadamer, Derrida.)

Historian subjectivity, event as object, and norm for tracking footprints
Given what seem to be well-intentioned but hopelessly divergent agendas for history-keeping accounts of footprints in the snow, a fashionable opinion today is to conclude that "History is not what happened but what people think happened."[58] History-keeping is like a Rorschach test where the narrator renders a plausible account of a pattern he or she finds in the footprints in the snow, and leaves it to public perception whether the story is acceptable or not; the test of history-keeping is not correspondence of a subjective version to an objective reality "out there," but simply whether the account is intelligible or not.[59] You may privilege a certain metaphor for a while (like a "control belief") to make your

---

57 Cf. Walter A. McDougall, "Mais ce n'est pas l'histoire!: Some thoughts on Toynbee, McNeil, and the rest of us," *The Journal of Modern History* 58:1 (March 1986): 21–22, 28–30, 39. Also, Arthur C. Danto, "Art, Evolution, and the Consciousness of History," in *The Philosophical Disenfranchisement of Art* (New York: Columbia University Press, 1966), 201–203.

58 Peter Munz, *The Shapes of Time: A new look at the philosophy of history* (Middletown: Wesleyan University Press, 1977), 208. Munz says this is "quoting from memory a remark I heard in a lecture" by Geoffrey Barraclough, 338, n.3.

59 Hayden V. White, "Historical Pluralism," *Critical Inquiry* 12:3 (Spring 1986): 492–93. Munz, *The Shapes of Time*, 220–21.

construction persuasive, just so long as you realize that privileged (even root or primal) metaphors are disposable as soon as they run amuck or no longer work in our changing world where determinate meanings in any exclusive and lasting sense are simply unavailable.[60]

In my judgment it is an error to treat footprints in the snow as unknowable *Dinge an sich*, and then reduce the deeds of other faces, including their races, to my/our intersubjective construction. It is clear to me that "objects" and "external events" are not the norm for history-keeping, and that the apriori committed vision of the history-keepers is irremediably subjective. But object realities do so far hold for an "interpretive community" in that the objects subject the history-keepers to tell what counted about them, the objects, and objects do demand that the subjects pay their subjective debt to the past, and bring to light the follow-ups that only hindsight can afford.

It may be as difficult for a history-keeper to track down certain footprints as it is for a court of justice to determine whether a given German man living in Canada for a generation has committed Nazi war crimes forty years earlier, but there are ovens and bones, dentures and disappeared persons, and documents (which could be falsified) that demand to be accounted for—matters independent of and other than the judging subjects.[61] Though the norm for history-keeping is not the "objects," and though the norm is always posited and embraced and judged applicable by human subjective history-keepers, the subjects are not the source and authorization of the norm.

To my understanding, a way to formulate the Scripturally-led norm for history-keeping is this: remember and witness to how the significant changes objectly taking place[62] initiated or consolidated more inclusive

---

60 Hayden V, White, "The Burden of History," *History and Theory* 5 (1966): 131. Svetlana Alpers presents this strategy in "Style is What You Make It: The visual arts once again," in *The Concept of Style*, ed. Berel Lang (University of Pennsylvania Press, 1979), 95–117. Stanley Fish, with his panache in the classic bout with Meyer Abrams, "entertains" the same position, with "Is there a text in this class?" in *Is There a Text in This Class: The authority of interpretive communities* (Cambridge: Harvard University Press, 1980), 305, 318–19.

It is my hunch that the current talk of "metaphor," to refer to ruling *topos*, is often an attempt to discount the personal life-decision and substantial responsibility admitted in owning up to the talking person's "categorial framework."

61 In Albert Cook's book *History/Writing: The theory and practice of history in antiquity and in modern times* (Cambridge University Press, 1988), he explains the slash in his title to mean: ". . . the Dinge an sich of 'events' *cannot be separated* from the act of writing, *or fused with* it either" (my italics) (7).

62 The phrase "objectly taking place" means "that which is the object of the history-

justice for the creaturely realities at work.[63] And I would be happy to direct history-keeping of theoretical aesthetics, for example, or the formation of the state of Israel, or the rise of video entertainment, along this line of wisdom, in contrast with those keeping history somehow before the bar of Reason, or in the court of petty factual claims, or in the undefined playing field of a Situationist aesthetics, politics, or economics. We should also not forget that along with this *historical* imperative—to be fecundive within a person's gifted callings and inheritance—is the most central, *directional* imperative for humans: to be holy before the face of the LORD.[64] History-keepers must not elide the directional imperative into the historical imperative, lest they be come historicists, who read significant change as necessarily normative rather than relative to the Way Scripture reveals human steps should take.[65]

Open-ended historical narrative vs. causality and plot scenarios

History-keeping goes best, I believe, when a given path of foot-prints has ended. Then whoever looks has the advantage of seeing the outcome of what took place, and can with more sureness describe the physiognomy of the whole given history, and even report on its afterlife. When a history-keeper has the blessing of hindsight, you can make contexted judgments on how the event met or failed the expectations of those trudging through the snow, and you can assess, with reflective distance, whether the sacrifices bore fruit.

It is a temptation, however, for hindsight to superimpose emplotment upon historical happenings, and so to over-read or misread the connected unity of footprints. Historical action, I believe, is by nature open-ended. How the subsequent, disjunctive step in historical action is conjoined to its predecessor, and how the follow-up circumstantially fulfills, undermines, or modifies its initial context, is not of a prefabricated character within an historical transaction, is not "causally" connected,

---

keeping subject's attention." The events that the history-keeper notes, like the art object that an art critic examines, make the subject dependent upon them, although it is surely possible for the inquiring subject as would-be history-keeper or art critic, in the name of co-dependence, to make the object over into its own subjective image. We might call such a mistake the Narcissistic fallacy.

63 M. C. Smit, "De Dynamiek van de Geschiedenis" (Amsterdam: Vrije Universiteit, Centrale Interfaculteit, Cursus 1974–75), 12–13.

64 See Romans 12:1–2 Hebrews 12:12–16, 1 Peter 1:13–16, 2:1–5.

65 M. C. Smit, "A Turnabout in Historical Science?" (1962) in *Toward a Christian Conception of History*, edited and translated by H. Donald Morton and Harry Van Dyke (Lanham: University Press of America, 2002), 315–17.

but also does not have a "plotted" link.

History-keeping unavoidably seems to exaggerate what happened historically, because history-keeping brings to consciousness and highlights in its description a conjunction that happened more unobtrusively. But even if the originating historical activity had been explicitly intended, the "significant change" was, I would maintain, *not* predictable, *not* enforceable, and does *not* have the imaginative connection of artistic composition.

Historical activity is *eventful* and not continuous; it happens *between different* subjective entities and *across* generations; so history is out of any creature's direct control. The historical norm can be violated, traditions defaced, interconnections ruined, and scandals enacted. And history-keeping is essentially a *telling* of such historical activity and its results, a semantic account of the contexted significant changes enacted, a narration that recounts the conjunction of fecundive and wasteful acts happening to an entity, community, or network of affairs with an identity. History-keeping is called to designate the critical sequences and to describe the broken line taken by the footsteps through the snow that the history-keeper has targeted for remembering.[66]

Again, it seems fair enough to me to have the history-keeper track a history at hand by recapitulating, with concision, the most poignant critical points on course (like tracking the parabola of a firefly's flight through the dark of a night). But it strikes me as a category mistake for Hayden White, and also for Ricoeur (if I understand him correctly), to view the narrative proper to history-keeping as one with a tropological formatting.[67] Both White and Ricoeur want to cut historiographic ac-

---

66 Several of these ideas were sprung from a long conversation with Marcille Fredericks, in discussion at the Institute for Christian Studies, Toronto, of her 1989 Interdisciplinary seminar paper, "Truth is Stranger than Fact: The difference between history and fiction." See also David Lowenthal, *The Past is a Foreign Country* (Cambridge University Press, 1985), 210–38.

67 Cf. Paul Ricoeur, *Time and Narrative* (1985), translated by Kathleen Blarney and David Pellauer (Chicago: University of Chicago Press, 1988), 3:184–85, 310 n.3. I am uncertain as to precisely what Ricoeur implies with his statement: "What is surprising is that this interlacing of fiction and history in no way undercuts the project of standing-for belonging to history, but instead helps to realize it" (3:186). Giambattista Vico's fanciful division of universal history into four periods, associated with the tropes of metaphor, synecdoche, metonymy, and irony (in *Scienze Nuova* [1744, third edition], par. 400–411), is the apparent source of this peculiar categorial framework adopted by Kenneth Burke and (altered) Northrop Frye. Hayden White claims these tropes are the "transformational system built into Foucault's conception of the succession of forms of the human sciences, even though Foucault appears not to know that it is there"! See Hayden V. White, "Foucault Decoded: Notes from underground,"

counts loose from all (positivistic) falsifiable, verification principles; but it seems as if Ricoeur at least claims that the performative, verdictive emplotment afforded by tropes is needed to shore up the historical narration with meaning.[68]

I thoroughly agree that the reliability of historical narrative cannot be one of logical falsifiability; but it would be wrong, I think, to look for the criterion for a history-keeping tale that "stands-for" and "refigures" a history, acquitting itself of "a debt we owe the dead" (so Ricoeur), in a penultimate form of the "poetic," "imaginative" limiting experience, because of its putative opening to "supra-narrative" eternity.[69] Historical narration is true, it seems to me, if it testifies clearly, with pertinent detail, to the orderly succession of significant changes needing to be remembered, and witnesses compassionately to the enriching and destructive contributions made. But histories, if we speak strictly, do not have happy endings or become tragedies (in an Aristotelian or Northrop Frye sense). Histories are busy opening doors for creaturely reality and effecting closure. And history-keeping is at the core oral, ostensive activity recounting such events.

Writing and historiographic task

When history is put in writing (*Archiv, annales*) something important takes place for the history of any footprints in the snow, and a fresh complex of problems with regard to history-keeping comes into view. Historio*graphic* activity, history-writing, is a two-step act: (1) you have detected, judged, and are prepared to tell an historical transaction as a rounded-off event worth remembering past your lifetime, and (2) you put it in letters, which turns the account into a record, the narrator into an author (*pace* Foucault), and the descriptive testimony meant to be heard into a scripted text meant to be read. Scripted history-keeping, in my judgment, is not only legitimate, but sharpens up and deepens the gift of history-keeping in forming the memory of a community.

A Methuselah witness for history-telling

To say that history-*keeping* is at the core semantic activity is to affirm that

---

in *History and Theory* 12 (1973): 45. This judgment may apply to Hayden White himself.

68 Hayden White, "Historical Pluralism" (1986), 488–89.

69 Cf. Paul Ricoeur, *Interpretation Theory: Discourse and the surplus of meaning* (Fort Worth: Texas Christian University Press, 1976), 59–63, 67–69. Also, Ricoeur, "On Interpretation," in *Philosophy in France Today*, 191–94; *Time and Narrative* (1988) 3:259–61, 271–73, 332 n.15.

history-keeping is eminently oral in nature and has intrinsically the witness character of pointing to historical events. History-keeping is structured to be the human act of an eye-witness describing eventful follow-ups to an other person. To "see," let alone recount, a sequence of deeds takes more than rigorous observation (as early Hume discovered), but a history-keeper making judgments has the cast of doing it vis-à-vis what has happened, tête-à-tête with a younger listener.

The model of history-keeping would be to have a Methuselah-aged witness sit down with us today[70] and relate firsthand about how the cathedrals were built in France during his youth, what the bubonic plague did to his neighborhood in Europe, what the couriers said about Columbus's return from the "new world," what Shakespeare's theatre did for London before the Bible was translated during King James' reign, and so on, provided our Methuselah witness was there somehow, kept current, and zeroed in on significant changes happening at the time in a variety of fields.

The spoken description of a history has a physical bodily presence contexting the history-keeping that is highly personal and comes replete with a kind of indisputable authority, especially to an impressionable listener. If the Methuselah testimony is accurate, vivid, and just, the next generation will be blessed with its memory intact. If the Methuselah witness has astigmatism or recounts mistaken hearsay, or betrays the past deeds of a suffering leadership and following by telling events in bad faith—was the Exodus from Egypt a liberation for that generation of Jacob's descendents? was the Reformation carried on by Luther and Calvin a secularization of Christendom? will the real (Carlyle, Marx, Groen van Prinsterer's) French Revolution please stand up?—if the tale told full of sound and fury is skewered and signifies falsely, then the memory of those who received that history is warped in a way incredibly difficult to overcome.

History-writing objectifies tale into text
Written history-keeping is not necessarily more or less reliable or fallible than spoken history-keeping, since both are dated and located, subjective

---

70 Paul Oskar Kristeller (1905–1999) actually did sit down with us at the Institute for Christian Studies in the late 1970's, and recounted the gradual demise of old-style, German Idealistic Humanism, for which he had given his scholarly life in Renaissance studies. The fact that he told this intellectual history as an eye-witness, yet generations later, gave the account an incredible feel of veracity, even though the painful failure of his own involved contribution showed through.

human activities.[71] Speaking is not necessarily more heartfelt or under-standable than written materials, since a speaker may be as cold and con-textless or as foreign to the listener, because of the speaker's idiosyncrasies and language, as the Nibelungenlied would be to someone who restricts his devoted ear to only country western music. It's true that a text can be treated with contempt by a reader as if it was not authored and bears no print of a human face; but denatured reading is no clue to the nature of writing and the spirited dynamic of a passionately written text.[72] Odi-ous comparisons between writing and speaking abound, but writing and speaking each has its own glory and responsibility.

The crucial juxtaposition for our understanding the treasure of history-keeping, as well as of traditionality, I think, is to recognize that engraving the history-keeping in "letters," putting the tale of significant changes to book, *documents* something historical. History-writing *objecti-fies* history-keeping by converting history-telling into a *script* for subse-quent history-tellers who would be shepherding history-keeping that of-ten continues mute, or begins to atrophy. But *inscribed* history is not the result of an unfactored, prime activity, as if inscripturation were a simple fixation by cuts in or marks on a medium.[73] A written history takes a scribe or engraver as well as a narrator (even if they be in the same per-son). To miss this duplex reality is to oversimplify history-writing, and to

---

71 Eric A. Havelock examines the difficulty for scholars, who are literate, to grapple with a general theory of "primary orality." See especially chapters 6–8 of *The Muse Learns to Write: Reflections on orality and literacy from antiquity to the present* (New Haven: Yale University Press, 1986).

72 Scripture credits its *writing* as well as the spoken word of Christ with life-bringing truth requiring obedience (e.g., John 2:22, Romans 15:4, 1 Corinthians 10:11, Rev-elation 1:3).

The old Marcion heresy of pitting Spirit against Letter, appealing to 2 Corinthians 3:6, mistakes the antithesis Paul wants to drive home in the epistles. Because Christ is the fulfillment of the Mosaic law rather than its abolishment (Matthew 5:17–20), our life is to be a letter from Christ inscribed (ἐπιστολή . . . ἐγγεγραμμέη) by the very spirit of the living God (2 Corinthians 3). The correct opposition Paul draws is that between an obedience marked by *literal* circumcision or by *circumcision of the heart*, a Spirit-humbled, holy writings-directed life (see Romans 2:25–29, 10:5–13, 2 Timothy 3:14–17). Gottlob Schrenk's exegesis is not wholly sound, I think, but the exposition is fine and complete on γράφω, in *Theologisches Wörterbuch zum Neuen Testament*, ed. G. Kittel (Stuttgart: Kohlhammer, 1933), I:743–73, especially 764–69.

73 Cf. Paul Ricoeur, *Interpretation Theory* (1976) 26–29. Also, I. J. Gelb's fascinating book, *A Study of Writing* (University of Chicago Press, 1963), discusses the pivotal role "phonetization of the script" had in making writing "largely a written substitute for its spoken counterpart" (11).

easily misread the written history as a one-step, empiricist transcription of data, packaged or not by the note-taker in some anecdotal fashion.

Writing is a craft with its own kind of artifactual results. The basic, nuclear character of a crafted work is to be an instrument, that is, its aim is to be a means, a means for accomplishing something else specific, like a vase for carrying water, or a stamped coin for facilitating the trade of bulky items. When history-telling becomes crafted history-writing, it is like having the spoken directions relayed to you by someone be put into a drawn map. A map documents the route to go (or trail taken by footprints in the snow) in a way that is not available to even an explicit telling of directions (with the added assurance, "You can't miss it"), to pointing, or even to a sign post. The drawn map or inscription of a history calls for an able *reading* subjectivity, in contrast to the attentive *hearing* subjectivity demanded by an oral account, in order for the written record and for the spoken address as objects to be serviced, so that the newcomer can follow the route. History-writing produces a *score*, a blueprint of sorts, on the path taken by footprints in the snow.

Derridean indeterminability and cultural amnesia

It is precisely the "deferral" of meaning in writing (as in a musical score), construed dialectically as a necessary ambiguous loss *and* possibility for inventive recovery, that exercises Derrida, according to my limited reading of his texts. Derrida seems to try to vaporize texts back into speech, but is foiled by the fact that texts for him are by definition *barbaros* to a reader, and speech for Derrida, to be authentic, must remain permanently glossolalia (tongue talk), in need of interpreters world without end. While I would grant that a written text of history-keeping (an inscribed signification, a tale placed, as it were, in a lettered time capsule) puts up front its mnemonic device character, quite differently from the history-keeping of a Methuselah witness (a straightforward utterance or semantic act), unlike Derrida I would cherish the map as a boon, for later travelers and pioneers in the snow, since they will be able to double-check, to review, to "trace"(!) on their own, ahead of time, the track of the footprints in the snow.

My quarrel with Derrida, as I understand him—best by recorded interview—is that (1) Derrida over-reads the inescapable connotative play within every text (and speech act too!) to be his ontological excuse to resist ever being caught dead himself with a position (an Archimedean ποῦ στῶ). That Derrida professes the phase of "interminable (interpretive) analysis" to be a structural necessity,[74] leads me to think either he is hiding something or he has bought into the uncritical, sophistic strategy of assuming you are without a (fundamental) position while you are looking for one. This is the old "neutrality postulate" of rationalism, it seems to me, reincarnated in very sophisticated, skeptical, royal undress.

(2) If Derrida turns the documenting channel of texts for historical knowledge into poetic mirrors that reflect what the interpreter sees, then Derrida's approach basically short-circuits not only hermeneutics but history-keeping and tradition as well. If a text is not a windowpane through which one sees however faintly another face, or footprints struggling through the snow:[75] better, if history-keeping texts are not (tinted) eye-glasses directed at realities, for the newcomer to try on for size and through which to notice and remember what was visible and eventful out there; if history-keeping texts only reflect one's own procreative dissemination, then Derrida's project, it seems to me, is to immerse all those under its spell in the streams of Lethe, especially because no one can step twice into the same river.

Granted the deconstructivists' serious desire to overturn the monolith of Positivist certainties that have canonized cultural violence for a

---

74 Derrida faults Ricoeur's movement to recognize an eschatological presence as falling into the closure of *certain* meaning, and thus of succumbing to an Hegelian Aufhebung. Cf. "Positions," *Diacritics* 2 (Winter 1972): 36–37.

75 I am open to David Carroll's consideration that American "deconstructionists" (and those in art historical circles?) may have oversimplified Derrida's thought into a "newer form of new criticism" (in *Paraesthetics: Foucault/Lyotard/Derrida* [London: Methuen, 1987], 81–89). Yet even Carroll notes that "a critical reading of Derrida should have as one of its goals to make a practical criticism derived from Derrida's work very difficult, if not impossible to realize" (207 n.3). Possibly Derrida's disciples, like those of Dooyeweerd or Dewey or Hegel, misrepresent his genius, but Derridean authority is constantly invoked on the world academic circuit today for its assembly-line scholarship of professional articles that continue to marginalize both philosophical and literary criticism. So there is more warrant than chagrin to André Lefevere's sardonic remark: "To produce more and more interpretations of texts that have been interpreted for centuries may appear to be a trifle redundant, except that it is a matter of bread and butter for most interpreters. . . . (quoting Vincent Leitch, *Deconstructive Criticism*, 1983:) 'There can never be "correct" or "objective" readings, only more or less energetic, interesting, careful or pleasurable misreadings.' Often the same person who writes this kind of thing then goes home and grades the 'misreadings' of others, so that they, too, can take their place within the academy, or be denied it, as the case may be" (Lefevere, "'Beyond Interpretation' or The Business of (Re)Writing," *Comparative Literature Studies* 24:1 (1987): 18.

William Rowe, however, asks for a patient, "more internal critical reading of Derrida's nomadic no-position. See his "Critical study of [Sander Griffioen's] *The Problem of Progress*," *Philosophia Reformata* 55:1 (1990): 80–83.

century and a half, at this point in my own development my hunch is that the contagious "anxiety of influence" deconstructionism has generated in art and literary historiography is often the bad conscience of secularized European scholarship lodged in North American breasts, and that the deconstructivist method idolizes the luxury of procrastination, and shall *weaken* the general (scholarly or popular) reading ability to read texts, and shall therefore further the disorienting history-keeping amnesia that is such a source of loneliness and sorrow in our day. Idols are indeed no-gods, but idolatry is a powerful reality.[76]

The gift of transcription

History-writing for me then is like a transcription and edited layout of history-telling.[77] The history-keeping that reached the focus of history-telling becomes set in the medium of inscribed letters as history-writing for a reading rather than a hearing public. There is nothing intrinsically illegitimate, mystifying, or suspect in this step of inscription. The historio*graphic* task is the same as that of history-*telling*—tracking footprints in the snow—with the difference that history-writing presents a map of the footprinted trail instead of a spoken recounting of the journey.[78]

Differences in history-writing or texts can be many, depending upon the dated-located variants and gifts of the history-writers. History-writing (like history-telling) can be wrong-headed, mediocre, or whimsical if the history-writer has a skewed perspective on what is historical, on history-keeping, on writing, is generally incompetent or given to special-pleading. But history-writing is not by nature cursed to misapprehend, misinterpret, or misdeal any more than scoring music or transcription

---

76 "Want een afgod moge niets zijn, afgoderij is een geweldige en te duchten macht! / For even if an idol is nothing, idolatry is a huge and dreadful power." D. H. Th. Vollenhoven, "Conservatism and Progressiveness in Philosophy" (1958) in *The Problem-Historical Method and the History of Philosophy*, ed. Kornelis A. Bril (Amstelveen: Haes, 2005), 15.

77 In technical musical terminology "transcription" means the arrangement, say, by J. S. Bach for organ of a Vivaldi concerto composed for violin.

78 Henk Geertsema posits that knowing grasped as *hearing* recognizes the relationality of other things and the proper changeability of enduring norms, while (Plato's) approach to knowing as coming by *seeing* tends to deprive knowledge of variability (*Horen en Zien: Bouwstenen voor een kentheorie* [Amsterdam: VU Uitgeverij, 1985], 20–22). Maybe still another "building block" is needed for a Scripturally directed theory of knowledge, since the reading of inscriptions (books) demands, it seems to me, a "metaphor" other than either "hearing" or "seeing." *Reading*, as an avenue for learning and knowing, is more complicated than our senses, and not reducible to them.

naturally miscarries. In fact, the special service of having an account of moving tones in a (sonata) score or the sequential events of a crime fixed in written documents is that anybody's memory of the happening is raised to a third power of recall. A text of whatever sort is at bottom a mnemonic device—not bare-faced, but colored by the inscriber's person—without which music may go lost after having been heard, and a trail of footprints may fade away under the cover of blowing snow.[79] Difficulties of correct reading remain, as do the difficulties of not mishearing a tale told.

The best *history*-writing will produce texts primed to give a new generation of readers a good sense of how to retell the way the tracks went, with a proper respect for making certain that the recapitulating needs to evidence the original tentativity as well as being able to assess the trail with additional hindsight. *Historical* change happens, as it were, behind the backs of the trekkers; so you have to be *after* the footprinted facts to be able to narrate or chart their course. And it is the gift of text and transcriptions to bring to book the synapses found by history-keepers. The visibility of such a booked record, because of its distancing objectivity (*not despite* the map making), throws the necessary and delicate pericope of history-keeping into relief,[80] and helps a prospective foot-sore wanderer discern paths taken.

So history-writers promote historical consciousness: a present-day mind imbued with knowledge of what should not be forgotten and with an awareness of what time and place it is now, and what needs doing for good right now, including later. Historical consciousness is never predictive, but historical consciousness, which has the panoply of traditions in force in the forefront of a person's reflection, is immensely wiser than a mentality suffering from cultural amnesia, with illusions of starting out tomorrow without having had any tracks behind you.[81]

---

79 Though music recorded on disk or paintings reproduced in high-grade color photography can be apparently "present" as the French revolution cannot be again represented, technical recordings and eye-witness documents *both* are once-removed replicas of the original event.

80 "Only the preservation and dissemination of historical knowledge through writing, and especially through print, sets the past firmly apart from the present." Lowenthal, *The Past is a Foreign Country*, 232.

81 "To be cut off from the past of one's society is as disorderng to the individual and to the society as being cut off in the present. . . . 'Civil amnesia' is as dangerous to society as the argument that the government should preempt the resources of society for the benefit of a particular 'class' or 'race'" (Shils, *Tradition*, 327).

V

Toward normative traditioning: the key of translation

History-writers can serve as a conscience for us traditioned people (as I said earlier, p. 252). Even when the historiography is framed in a categorial perspective we may not share, tracking the traces of a certain thread of footprints through the snow where horizon and destination may be less than clear, still engenders in an attentive reader some self-conscious reflection on whether you are a fellow-traveler or be busy walking a different path in the world (cultural) landscape. I should like to conclude this examination of tradition and history-keeping by pointing to the act of translating literature as a clue to normative traditioning.

Traditions are human responses to God's creational call for an earlier generation to covenant with a succeeding generation in the elders' giving the younger their prized treasures.[82] Handing on traditions, however—faith-tradition, thought-tradition, skill-tradition, respect-tradition, or whatever—is not like passing on a baton to the next runner in a relay race. True, the younger generation needs to take hold of and adopt (or is free to reject) what is being traditioned if the wont is to be carried on; but a tradition is more like the current memory of a community that is backgrounding and enveloping its very deeds, than like an inert stick or stone as heirloom. Human traditions of any kind have an umbrageous subtlety about them, whose identity of salient features is firm, yet whose mass seems to wax and wane and drift like a shifting swarm of bees. It is not possible to be traditioning a wont as if it had scientific exactitude and could be measured out to fit, or tried on like a pair of new gloves. Traditions are hand-me-downs, used goods, worn, and either come to cramp your attitudinal feet or to satisfy like your own pair of old shoes.

So traditions come embodied and have definite contours, but are living communal holding patterns not contained in any one carrier, representative, or custodian at any given time. This is a reason why traditions can be dismissed by hard-nosed fact-empiricists, declared "labyrinthine" by world-weary academics, and cashed in as current fashion by pragmatists. Its preconscious, sagittal quality as existential apriori is also why a tradition is often so intractable to being "faithfully" handed on *alive*: a tradition is a person's cultural blood in circulation.

---

82 My colleague William Rowe made me aware of the important book by Marcel Mauss, *Essai sur le don in sociologie et anthropologie* (1950) translated by I. Cunnison, *The Gift* (London: Cohen and West, 1970).

Translation of "foreign" literature

The craft of translation, translating literary art, can alert us to features of normative traditioning, even though what sound translation is and how literary translation is even possible, is hotly debated by conflicting traditions(!) and theories of translation.[83] To be brief here, let me just posit a few leading theses on the translation of foreign literature (that I hope shall be explicated and argued in another setting):

(1) The best translator is semantically at home in both languages, and is able and willing to be a rapt, *compleat listener* to the literary source-text.

(2) The proper goal to guide translation of literature is to aim not for a duplicate or a reenactment of the original, and not try to invent a new equivalent, but to fashion a text that *lovingly recapitulates* the source and lets the foreign literary artwork speak anew in accents that with metaphoric imaginativity freshen the target-language.

(3) The asymptotic resemblance that results from translating faithfulness is not an antinomy, but is the peculiar glory and mutually enriching reality of sound translation. A primary text that was initially confined to its resident language is now in translation given a new hearing, is graciously received not as a refugee but as a guest, a landed immigrant, and turning native, thoroughly at home, *enhances the idiom of the new language.*

There is mystery, not to say something miraculous, in fine translations of literature, because the translation is *giving birth to more of the same*—which is, strictly speaking, impossible—extending, midwiving, bodying forth new life to the original text in a different world concourse. The relation of translated text to original text is not one of secondary to primary source, performance to score, commentary to text, because the filiation is not derivative, supplemental, restorative, or even additional. A good translation of foreign literature gives the original a new artistic voice in its own right. The bilingual person finds both renditions rich; the pieces are not in competition. You don't have to give up one to enjoy

---

83 See George Steiner, *After Babel: Aspects of language and translation* (Oxford University Press, 1975), for perhaps the best comparative analysis of state-of-the-art in translation theory. George Steiner himself seems to prefer a special sort of interlinear literalist option (but *not* "a word-for-word" transference) that has the translator remain selflessly submerged within the original tongue, producing a centaur idiom in which one's own tongue takes on a "deliberate strangeness," and the product becomes virtually an unknown tongue that can "transcend the constraints of imprecise objective reference" (307-33). Steiner approves of Hölderlin's approach, and credits Chesterton on Du Bellay and Leyris on Hopkins as superb approximations of the true translation (407–13).

the other (cf. illustration of Sappho and Rossetti poetry). And for those who were blind to the foreign piece, they may now read, hear, and see the strange treasure indeed diffused and translucent in an alabaster light they happen to know.

Sappho of Lesbos

οἶον τὸ γλυκύμαλον
    ἐρεύθεται ἄχρωι ἐπ᾽ ὔσδωι
ἄκρον ἐπ᾽ ἀκροτάτωι
    λελάθοντο δέ μαλοδρόπηες,
οὐ μὰν ἐκλελύοντ᾽ ἀλλ᾽ οὐκ ἐδύναντ᾽
    ἐπίκεσθαι

D. G. Rossetti

Like the sweet apple which reddens upon the
    topmost bough,
A-top on the topmost twig,—which the pluckers
    forgot, somehow,—
Forgot it not, nay, but got it not, for none could
    get it till now.

Ramification and reticulation, not reification and simplification
Traditioning persons will do well, I think, to follow the translator's craft, and realize he or she is busy taking a source-tradition and translating its wont into the targeted present-day praxis. A good traditioner—of the older or the younger generation—needs to be culturally at home in both the ancient holding pattern and in the current vernacular. Those who mediate a tradition, which sutures two different generations, are not to be led by the desire to repeat, redo, or make obsolete the inherited wont, but to give it voice and force in the changed circumstances: not new wine into old wineskins, but old wine in new wineskins for festive drinking (supra p. 240). The traditioning custodian fulfills the calling of faithfully passing on a faith-vision or thought-pattern or journeyman skill or womanly craft—any sort of tradition—if the traditioning renews the given tradition's lease on bringing holy blessing to human activity. Traditioning an inheritance is normative if the traditioning act gentles the (reliable) wont into the inexperienced generation's hands so they do justice to its original obedience (granted it was relatively obedient) and find new avenues for its service.

Normative traditioning will ramify wonts rather than reify their practice, branch out alive rather than petrify. Normative traditioning requires that the tradition-givers extrapolate and reticulate what has been the wont, and that tradition-receivers complicate and integrate rather than simplify the wont in the new host of a living community. Traditioning goes wrong if the inherited wont is passed on dead, dead-to-the-world without the breath of passionate love infusing its original contribution, or if the wont is propagated and accepted in simplified form.[84] Crucial to normative traditioning is that the elders hand on the wont in a richer, more God-obedient format than that in which they themselves had received it, and the younger generation humbly and forthrightly exercise its promise and keep reforming its relative normativity while they come to own its gift as their own responsibility.

If a person is handicapped by the traditions he or she has inherited—monolinguality, world-flight faith-tradition, snobbish mores, or anti-intellectual thought habits that resist reform—so that person cannot with others be redeeming its mishandled moment of truth, then that person may have to undergo the rigors of not traditioning that tradition but of changing his or her cultural blood stream. Entering a different specific tradition than a person has inherited is not a matter of traditioning goods anymore, but is the excruciating struggle of orphaning oneself until you become a newly adopted child in that side of your ongoing (cultural) life. The difficulty of such blood transfusion goes beyond the scope of this essay, but it is a matter of integrity, especially for traditioning leaders, to recognize the ontological difference between *traditioning* a given tradition (both giving and the receiving) and *changing specific traditions*. Otherwise reformation is confused with revolution, which assumes any congealed *traditum* is wrong or suspect, and then a person makes the error of supposing riddance of one tradition for another is necessarily an act of redemption. Traditioning is like translation: changing traditions is like speaking in a different native tongue.

In closing this programmatic essay on tradition and tracking foot-

---

84 The Neoclassical penchant for simplification compromised Anton Raphael Mengs' important contribution to art historiography. See my "Canonic Art: Pregnant dilemmas in the theory and practice of Anton Raphael Mengs," in *Man and Nature/ L'homme et la nature*, volume 3, ed. Robert J. Merrett (Edmonton: Academic Printing and Publishing, 1984), 113–30 {see *AH*: 223–240}.

During a 1989–90 Interdisciplinary seminar at the Institute for Christian Studies, Toronto, William Rowe exposited the late Peter Steen's self-conscious teaching method of smashing the student's simple repetition of a teacher, since only when what is simplifiedly taught reaches "complification" has the matter been properly taught/traditioned.

prints in the snow, let me underline Gabriel's response to the novice angel in the opening story.

Because of the cultural distress many in Western civilization feel, an anxiety that there may be a Lie at work in our standard history texts and prevalent synthetic-christian traditions gone secular, there is a growing tendency by serious thinkers to treat traditionality as either an idol, a phantasmagoric curse, or a genuine sickness unto death. Christian theorists need, I believe, to present a reflective antidote to our "post-modern" generation so troubled by its cultural inheritance; better, we need to find a thoughtful, respectful way to foster healing in the worldly educated consciousness by bringing offerings of philosophical truth and shalom to the praxis of traditioning and history-keeping.

Let me just note and locate certain philosophical issues whose examination would enhance the conceptual prospects of taking the ontic privilege of tradition as a gift of grace to humankind, and the capability of putting history in writing as a treasure rather than as constant betrayal.

(1) *Ontology*

My assumption has been that the human reality of traditionality depends upon the eschatonic cosmic order as a whole, which holds for us creatures thanks to the LORD God's covenantal faithful Word. But as Vollenhoven once made eloquently clear, the whole once-only, dated duration of creatural process that goes on to the return of Christ cannot be proved or demonstrated.[85] For christian thinkers to make the ontic grounding of tradition winsome to all and sundry, there need to be lively thetical exemplifications of the biblical faith-tradition carried on in our generation. We need fresh humane studies from the Scripturally directed

---

85 Cf. the conclusion to D. H. Th. Vollenhoven, *Het Calvinisme en de Reformatie van de Wijsbegeerte* (Amsterdam: H. J. Paris, 1933). "Men versta me goed: hier valt niets te bewijzen. Maar één van beide: òf er is wetenschap mogelijk, die, althans in princiep, het geheel van den kosmos overziet, maar dan is deze gebaseerd op iets dat trans-kosmische zekerheid heeft, òf deze zekerheid ontbreekt, maar dan is ook een wetenschap die 't geheel kan overzien uitgesloten. Anders gezegd: alle wetenschap die neutraal meent te zijn komt, met betrekking tot de mogelijkheid het onderzochte in verband met het geheel van den kosmos te zien, vroeg of laat in moeite" (309) / "Understand me correctly: it is not a matter of proving anything. It is one or the other. Either science that at least in principle oversees the whole of the cosmos is possible, but then it is based on something that has transcosmic certainty, or this certainty is missing. But then science that can oversee the whole is also out of the question. In other words, all science that claims to be neutral eventually gets into difficulty as regards the possibility of seeing what is investigated in connection with the whole of the cosmos."

thought-tradition of the Reformation on basic problems[86] like creational ordinances (their provenance and directing promise), the coincidence of human transcendentality and suffering (the surd reality of sin), vestiges of native religion world-wide and the uncanny drive toward secularity, the wonderful presence of "objects" and of other subjects not reducible to our rightfully ubiquitous individual subjectivity. That is, systematic philosophical analyses of such foundational affairs would provide back-up orientation to the nature, crucial meaning, and limited subterranean authority of tradition for human action on the face of the earth, and give the matter scope.

We do not need an apologetics for a "Realist" ontology, I believe, so much as specialized studies focused on pivotal concerns giving sound content and direction to distinct fields of theory. After all, the best ontology is a convicting, worked-out cosmology and a wise, articulate cultural theory.

(2) *Philosophy of history*

My assumption has been that historicity is not restricted to human creatures, although only humans have the responsible office before God and staying power to be history-keepers and to engrave historical accounts on stone or paper. Rather than wrestle further with the vexed problem of what precisely Dooyeweerd meant by history,[87] perhaps Reformational christian thinkers could take a historiographic aperture—this is why I focused on "tradition"—in pondering the mesh of interrelated but different affairs that could be called (a) the techno-formative mode of skilled control that underlies all full-bodied human cultivating of God's world, (b) the structural principle calling for differentiation with integrated maturation (or the pain of fragmentation and atavism) recognized by many to

---

86 Here I simply highlight and add a few specific issues germane to "tradition," in the context of the careful, inclusive agendas laid out so well by Johan van der Hoeven and others in the 1986 jubilee number of *Philosophia Reformata*, and then the themes selected by Jacob Klapwijk in "Reformational Philosophy on the Boundary between the Past and the Future?" *Philosophia Reformata* 52:2 (1987): 101–34.

87 It is important, however, to note Johan van der Hoeven's corrections of C. T. McIntire's reading of Dooyeweerd on history (in *Philosophia Reformata* 52:2 (1987): 194–202). Jan Dengerink's precision on the respective understanding of "historicism" by Vollenhoven and Dooyeweerd, as he calls Jacob Klapwijk to precision on exegeting Dooyeweerd's view of "ontsluiting," is also, I think, on target ("Een brug te ver," in *Philosophia Reformata* 53:1 [1988]: 17–22). Sander Griffioen's incisive article on "De Betekenis van Dooyeweerd's Ontwikkelingsidee" is particularly helpful in delineating the nuances of Dooyeweerd's reflections (*Philosophia Reformata* 51:1/2 [1986]: 83–109).

be the outcome of historical initiative in cultural and societal settings, and (c) the cosmic battle between Christ's Rule and that of fallen principalities in the past, present, and future heading for the end.[88]

To take historiography as point of theoretical entry for shaping a philosophy of history would prompt a request for philosophical analyses of problems like memory (a crux in theory of human knowledge),[89] mediation and media (in interpersonal and inter-generational communication),[90] the nature of leadership and its relation to cultural periods, and also, as I have mentioned, translation of literature as hermeneutic touchstone. Philosophical studies in such areas, indirectly related to the theory of history but so close to actual daily human life, might bring new openings and insight for understanding history and for shaping the theory and praxis of writing a history of philosophy, history of artistry, history of "East" and West," and the many local histories of things we so easily take for granted.

The testimony of records is critical for doing justice to what takes place among one's cultural predecessors and neighbors and descendants: the evil of false witness in the certain face of a final judgment on human injustice[91] makes reliable history writing a most formidable, urgent task. As well as getting our theoretical "recipe" straight, with biblical vision, on history, we need the proof of edible, nutritious historiographed puddings.

As Western civilization undergoes the crisis of reaping its secularized cultural whirlwind, Bible-believing thinkers may hold on to the scandalous fact that the son of God, Jesus Christ, was a real Jew, whose sinful disciples happened to move predominantly westward at the time. That is no longer so. Within decades it seems there will be more followers of Christ in Africa and the East than on Western continents. But we West-

---

88 These distinctions are a refinement of my ancient note "Voor en uit de praktijk," in *Correspondentiebladen van de Vereniging voor Calvinistische Wijsbegeerte* 24 (April 1960): 5–10. Van der Hoeven considers the term "techno-formative" as possible for what Dooyeweerd named the "historical aspect" of reality, in Van der Hoeven's extensive review of *The Legacy of Herman Dooyeweerd*, in *Philosophia Reformata* 52:2 (1987): 198.

89 See Edward S. Casey, *Remembering: A phenomenological study* (Bloomington: Indiana University Press, 1987). Also David Farrell Krell, *Of Memory, Reminiscence, and Writing: On the verge* (Bloomington Indiana University Press, 1990).

90 Cf. Paul Ricoeur's argument that the necessary distantiation of media objectification does *not* necessarily entail alienation, in "Objectivation et Aliénation dans l'expérience historique," *Temporalité et Aliénation*, ed. Enrico Castelli (Aubier: Montaigne, 1975), 27–38.

91 See *The Belgic Confession*, article 37, and Matthew 12:33–37, Revelation 20:11–15.

ern Christians have a thesaurus of traditions whose encumbered words of life, often taken to be stigmata by current secularists, need reforming transmission, or we caretakers and philosophical chefs will have defaulted on being faithful to Christ's historical sacrifice under Pontius Pilate.

Since humans walk in God's landscape, no matter how devastatingly we pollute its seedtime and harvest, and build our ideological cities on the earth scraping the sky, theorists today are still called to make tracks, tracks of theory too, despite often showing, as Jean Brun says, "que l'homme a l'exigence du pèlerine mais le visage de l'homme errant."[92] We do know, as a motley band of Chaucerian pilgrims en route to the new earth, that even our theoretical tracks are able to be covered and saved by the blood of Jesus Christ who is a-coming.

Gathering of American students of the Vrije Universiteit of Amsterdam at a long day conference hosted annually by the Anti-Revolutionaire Partij at the Dr. Abraham Kuyper Stichting, Den Haag, Netherlands, 1954

Standing left to right: Ted Minnema, … , Harry Boer, Harvey Smit, … , … , … , Frank van Halsema, John Vriend, Calvin Seerveld, Henk van Riessen, Andrew Bandstra, Henk Kort, Gordeon Spykman, Lewis Smedes
Seated left to right: Louis and Ruth Rus, … , … , Jan Schouten, Margaret Vriend, … , Pieter Sjoerds Gerbrandy, Paul Schrotenboer, …

The best way to transmit a faith tradition affecting one's way-of-life and one's world-and-life vision, I learned from Bill Rowe, is to have its contours shared face-to-face between generations. The Anti-Revolutionaire Partij in the Netherlands was intent on having American students in philosophy and theology at the Free University of Amsterdam catch the thrust of Abraham Kuyper's vision for communal christian reflection on the believers' redemptive task in the areas of social, economic, and political affairs of one's country. We American students always finished the meeting by going together for an Indonesian rijstafel feast.

---

92 Jean Brun, "Le voyage dans le temps: De la chronophotographie au Futurisme," *Temporalité et Aliénation*, 364.

THE PEDAGOGICAL STRENGTH OF
A CHRISTIAN METHODOLOGY IN
PHILOSOPHICAL HISTORIOGRAPHY

The kinds of problems intrinsic to historiography and to philosophical historiography in particular are compounded when the question must be settled on how to teach the history of philosophy. For then, if one's methodology for philosophical historiography is defective, simplistic, or indecisive on the crucial matters, its exercise in the classroom will botch the philosophical development of a whole new generation.

I am persuaded that the Christian stuffings to the philosophical historiography initiated by Dirk Vollenhoven[1] provide a prospective student and instructor with important pedagogical advantages. Unfortunately, Vollenhoven's own specialized work in analyzing pre-Socratic fragments[2] and the several doctoral dissertations concluded under his tutelage[3] are poor places to look for models on how to begin teaching the history of philosophy. [4] And to try to press the full weight of Vol-

---

1 Cf. Calvin Seerveld, "Biblical Wisdom underneath Vollenhoven's Categories for Philosophical Historiography," in *The Idea of a Christian Philosophy*, ed. Herman Dooyeweerd (Toronto: Wedge, 1973), 127–43 {see *AH*: 1–22}.

2 Dirk H. Th. Vollenhoven, *Geschiedenis der Wijsbegeerte*, deel 1. Inleidingen en Geschiedenis der Griekse Wijsbegeerte vóór Platoon en Aristoteles (Franeker: Wever, 1950) and articles such as "Ennoëtisme en 'ahoristos dyas' in het praeplatonische denken." *Philosophia Reformata* 19:2/3, 4 (1954):58–88 and 145–68.

3 H. Evan Runner, *The Development of Aristotle Illustrated from the Earliest Books of the Physics* (Kampen, 1951); J. A. L. Taljaard, *Franz Brentano as wysgeer* (Franeker, 1955); Calvin Seerveld, *Benedotto Croce's Earlier Aesthetic Theories and Literary Criticism* (Kampen, 1958); Henk Hart, *Communal Certainty and Authorized Truth: An examination of John Dewey's philosophy of verification* (Amsterdam, 1966).

4 Vollenhoven's short survey of philosophy, *Kort Overzicht van de Geschiedenis der Wijsbegeerte voor de Cursus Paedagogiek MOA* (Amsterdam: Uitgave Theja, 1956), indicates better the potential of his methodology for teaching undergraduates the history of philosophy. J. M. Spier's attempt in *Van Thales tot Sartre: Wijsgeren uit*

This essay was first published in *Koers* 40:4–6 (1975): 269–313.

lenhoven's refined categories down upon the beginning student would be a little bit like encumbering the young David with Saul's professional armor. Critics unsympathetic to the sureness and fine analysis of such a Christian historiographic approach in teaching philosophy have sometimes stigmatized the attempt as putting tools for brain surgery into the hands of high school graduates who are not yet able to identify which person in the room needs the operation.

But on this occasion of honoring my colleague Prof. Dr. J. A. L. Taljaard, I should like to enunciate what seems to me to be the redeeming principle for teaching christianly the history of philosophy, demonstrate its method with an extended illustration, and then point up the pedagogical strengths of using this christian methodology in philosophical historiography.

Encapsulation of Philosophical Historiographic Standards within Pedagogical Norms

The struggle of modern historiography to acquit itself as a science, understood as a technical means for collecting exact data freed from traditional prejudices, and at the same time to proffer an integrated overview of what is truly happening: that struggle of some 300 years is truly instructive for checking out the task of Christian historiography.[5] The Christian may certainly take his cue from the current status of Western historiography, but not from its problematics.

A widespread "Pyrrhonism" toward scholastic precepts, as Emile

---

oude en nieuwe tijd (Kampen: Kok, 1959) to point toward the work of Vollenhoven mixed with Sassen suffers from the thankless and impossible task of old fashioned handbooks—cite the special commonplaces about a thinker and dispense with him in a page or two of print. Spier's book lacks the color and body of Gordon H. Clark's history of philosophy *Thales to Dewey* (Boston: Houghton Mifflin, 1957), which, however, tends to dissolve the seriousness of the enterprise into diffident wit. The introductory class syllabi of John C. Vander Stelt, e.g., "Survey of Contemporary European Philosophy" (Sioux Center: Dordt College, 1972), and John van Dyk, "Survey of the History of Philosophy" (Sioux Center: Dordt College, 1969–70), struggle with the dilemma of Spier too, and try to highlight the christian insight and conceptual results of Vollenhoven's work for the history of philosophy. But needed most at this time, perhaps, is to find a way of engaging others in the basic elements of this christian historiographic methodology, learning to use it on a defined problem. See John C. Vander Stelt's good article on "Kuyper's Semi-Mystical Conception," in *The Idea of a Christian Philosophy* (Toronto, 1973), 178–90.

5   For orientation see Friedrich Gundolf, "Historiography" [1936] in *Philosophy and History: The Ernst Cassirer Festschrift*, eds. R. Klibansky and H. J. Paton (Harper, 1963), 277–82; and Herbert Butterfield, *Man on His Past* [1955] (Cambridge University Press, 1969).

Bréhier puts it, carried on in the flush of Galileo's success, began to forge with Descartes and Spinoza a kind of conceptual iconoclasm that the Scientialistic mind of the seventeenth century thought was "critical."[6] Concern for such "critical" rigor modulated in the eighteenth century, under the ruling spirit of "Edify Humanity!" to a passion for dictionaries and compendia of culture—while the overarching historiographic girder of providence got thoroughly secularized into Progress. Subsequent nineteenth century attempts by Hegel and Ranke to assimilate past historians' accomplishments and to raise compilations of accurate detail and visionary optimism (in the face of Positivistic preachments on facticity) to the status of a critically constructed account of what actually took place somewhere: that cumulative (Neo-Idealistic) format became the working legacy of Toynbee and lesser general historians.

For our purposes, I am assuming that the christian historiographic method developed by Vollenhoven for expositing the history of philosophy has biblically reformed the directional set of this history of historiography and basically resolves the structural dilemmas that plagued it.[7]

Rejected is the implicit, soritical argument that for historiography to be professionally respectable it must be "critically" scientific, which entails it must be verifiably empirical rather than speculative, which necessitates that one rest with either "technical histories" or, perhaps, that the general historian may "add" his evaluative dimension. Instead, I have argued that Vollenhoven's categories have scientific precision and an intrinsically Christian bite, which nevertheless encourages the original texts to confront the historian of philosophy in their own terms. [8] Although "evidence" is a crucial constitutive element in every historian's conclusion, "evidence" may never presume to be a factor in the human historiographer's perspectival apriori, on pain of religious weaseling.[9] Vollen-

---

6 Emile Bréhier, "The Formation of our History of Philosophy" (1938), in *Philosophy and History: The Ernst Cassirer Festschrift*, 159–72.

7 Background materials for this argued position can be found listed in *Perspectief: Feestbundel van de Jongeren bij het 25-jarig bestaan van de Vereeniging voor Calvinistische Wijsbegeerte* (Kampen: Kok, 1961), Vollenhoven bibliography edited by C. Groen, 99–112; and cf. K. A. Bril, "A Selected and Annotated Bibliography of D. H. Th. Vollenhoven," in *The Idea of a Christian Philosophy* (Toronto, 1973), 212–28. Of special note is the monograph by Albert M. Wolters, "An Essay on the Idea of *Problemgeschichte*" (Amsterdam: Vrije Universiteit Interfakulteit, 1970), 69 pages.

8 Seerveld, "Wisdom underneath Vollenhoven's Categories," 135 {see *AH*: 12}.

9 It is an important question outside the purview of this article whether the problematics with which christian historian Herbert Butterfield (see, e.g., his *Christianity and History*, 1949) works is entirely free from such ambivalence. In evaluating Lord Acton and Ranke's use of Providence in historiography, Butterfield says: "The truth is that

hoven has shown that historiography of philosophy can be "scientific," while rejecting the covertly dogmatic neutrality proposed by the secular scientism that set the stage for so much of modern historiography.

Vollenhoven's tack of examining the development of strictly philosophical matters, within typical philosophical responses to creational meaning, for his history of philosophy, also has the makings of bringing peace to what Gundolf calls the "border feuds" in the history of historiography, as to whether historiography be a special science or essentially philosophy, and to what Bréhier pinpoints as the struggle to relate the historical "fact that" and the philosophical "truth of" certain ideas in

---

technical history is a limited and mundane realm of description and explanation, in which local and concrete things are achieved by a disciplined use of tangible evidence. I should not regard a thing as 'historically' established unless the proof were valid for the Catholic as well as the Protestant, for the Liberal as well as the Marxist. . . . Each of these can add his judgments and make his evaluations; and they can at least begin by having some common ground for the great debate that still lies open to them. Those who bring their religion to the interpretation of the story are naturally giving a new dimension to events; but they will not be less anxious than anybody else to know what can be historically established" (*Man on His Past* [Cambridge University Press, 1969], 139–40). It seems to me that limiting "what can be historically established" to "a limited and mundane realm of description and explanation" while yet making room for variously committed "evaluations" and "interpretation," still halts problematically between and tries to synthetically join two conflicting positions—the Positivist-inspired ideal in Ranke's *wie es eigentlich gewesen* and a vision true to 1 Corinthians 2:6–16. Dooyeweerd's insightful judgment can help us appreciate the ambiguity of such a struggle: ". . . in such a partial christian groundmotive the synthesis-in-appearance may be so arranged that the adapted non-christian motive is almost completely controlled by the specifically christian one. In this case the universal significance of the antithesis can indeed be recognized also for the issues of temporal life. But it will nevertheless not be understood as it would if the Scriptural groundmotive had penetrated completely" (H. Dooyeweerd, *Vernieuwing en Bezinning om het Reformatorisch Grondmotief* [Zutphen: Van den Brink, 1959], 13; translated by J. Kraay and B. Zylstra as *Reconstruction and Reformation* [Toronto: Institute for Christian Studies, 1970], sec. 1–6). Singleminded reformation and biblically-directed formulation of a creational norm for "description and explanation" seems imperative to me if christian historiographers are ever going to break with a synthetic-christian ideal, which misleads both children of God and disbelievers. Cf. Robert McAfee Brown, "The Reformed Tradition and Higher Education," in *The Christian Scholar* 41:1 (March 1958): 21–40; and the dialogue contributions treating the same problem in literary criticism by N. Vos, C. G. Seerveld, V. Mollenkott, E. C. Vanderlip, and K. Richardson, in *Newsletter of the Conference on Christianity and Literature* 16:2 (Winter 1967): 5–13; 16:3 (Spring 1967): 2– 4; 16:4 (Summer 1967): 10–16. My colleague C. Thomas McIntire enters the lists for christian historiography with his inaugural address, *The Ongoing Task of Christian Historiography* (Toronto: Institute for Christian Studies, 1974).

the historiography of philosophy.[10] History—the discipline of determining, with systematic exactitude what was "historical" about certain events ensuing in the unfolding of creation and culture—in my judgment, is an inter-relational science, similar to philosophy. The *Gegenstand* of historical investigation—"significant change" or "interlinking formative alteration"—will always give an encyclopedic cachet to historical research; but historical study can be practiced by professional specialists, just like philosophy, without thereby turning "historical" into a prime (modal) aspect of reality fit for a restricted, special scientific abstraction. It is true that historiography, the chronicling of results achieved by historical analysis, translates—as all writing does that is style-fully opened up—the science product into literature, whether grand or pedestrian; but that does not undo the original scientific precision of historical analysis, blur its inter-relational focus, convert it from history (focused on developmental, interlinking meaning) into philosophy (focused on structural, inter-relational meaning), or suddenly endow it with the character of true revelation![11] Vollenhoven's historiographic method incorporates, as I

---

10 P. Gundolf, "Historiography," 280–81; E. Bréhier and the striking quote from Lessing, "The Formation of our History of Philosophy," 128–30.

11 The complexity of historiography, as a defined task, concerns at the least professional historians, philosophers, and aestheticians. Gundolf raises the importance of the style question to influential historians from Herodotus, Thucydides, and Tacitus to Herder and Ranke ("Historiography," 277–78). Benedetto Croce struggled his whole life to lay the problem to rest, first tending to conceive historiography in the form of art that treats what is "individual" ("La storia ridotta sotto il concetto generale dell'arte" [1893], in *Primi Saggi*, 3rd edition [Bari: Gius Laterza and Figli, 1951], 1–41; see Seerveld, *Croce's Earlier Aesthetic Theories*, 4–6). Later Croce ascribed a rather "universalizing" power to historiography, so it could act as catharsis towards the past and as a propaedeutic instrument for moral (future) action ("La Storia come Pensiero e come Azione" [1938] in *La Storia come Pensiero e come Azione*, 6th edition [Bari: Gius Laterza and Figli, 1954], 31–33; Storiografia e Politica," Ibid. 177–81, 191–94; and "Storio grafia e Morale," Ibid. 211–19 e.g., "Si potrebbe altresì esprimere questo concetto nella formula: che la conoscenza storica è dell'individuo agente e non del paziente . . . e azione importa attuazione di valori o di universali," Ibid. 218). His final position on the unity of philosophy and historiography (cf. "Considerazioni Finali," Ibid. 333–35), in conscious polemic with Hegel (". . . lo Hegel mirava a risolvere la storia nella filosofia col darle l'andamento di un sistema che si svolga e compia nel tempo, e noi miriamo, invece, a risolvere la filosofia nella storia, considerandola come un momento astratto dello stesso pensiero storico e i suoi sistemi come sistemazioni storicamente transeunti e storicamente giustificate, e come ogni atto storico, di valore eterno," "Prospettive Storiografiche." Ibid. 277: cf. also "Hegel e la storiografia" [1951] in *Indagini su Hegel e Schiarimenti Filosofici* [Bari: Gius Laterza and Figli, 1952], 87–91), animated by a strong Lebensphilosophic spirit that confesses a lofty Humanism ("La Storiografia senza Problema Storico," Ibid. 77–79,100; "La Certezza e La Verità Storica," Ibid. 116–17; and titular essay in *La Storia come Pensiero e come*

understand it, the sound position that historiography articulates the fallible knowledge of an inter-relational science, which will be denatured if it is dissolved either into an "empirical science" (à la Positivism) or into philosophy (à la Neo-Idealism).

But right now, assuming a measure of settledness on christian historiography of philosophy, with Vollenhoven's beginnings as the working method, our question is: how can such a scientifically exacting philosophical historiographic method be made to serve teaching the history of philosophy?

The key, I think, is the simple wisdom of encapsulating the scientifically exacting method within pedagogical norms. That does not mean one relaxes scientific precision and uses a meat cleaver instead of a scalpel; but the principle of encapsulation means here that scientific features give way to pedagogical considerations, which take a superintending priority.

For example: scientific analysis requires definite categories with fixed meanings, univocal language (not to say jargon), and a proficient expert who executes the complicated examination with refinement, exhaustiveness, and dispatch. But good teaching starts with questions that surprise and stimulate wondering in the student: good teaching is playful, earthy, illustrational, until the student's imagination is aroused and he is willing to search-along as an apprentice and begin to research carefully with the repetition that develops skill and analytic precision. Therefore, somehow the firm philosophic historiographic categories of Monism, Dualism, and their important varieties, must be clothed in existential flexibility for the classroom. Terms like Universalism, Individualism, and Macro-microcosmoi motif must have their colorless scientific mark take on the exciting color of clues leading to new insights. Scientific determinations like Subjectivism, Objectivism, and Realism must keep their specially

---

Azione, 1–52 passim. This collection was translated by S. Sprigge as *History as the Story of Liberty* [London: Allen & Unwin, 1941]. See Seerveld, *Croce's Earlier Aesthetic Theories*, 102–104), still did not resolve the problem. In fact, this influential position, which makes philosophy the methodology of historiographic thought ("La Certezza e la Verità Storica," Ibid, 140–41; cf. also "Unità logica e unità mitologica della filosofia con la storiografia" [1947] in *Filosofia e Storiografia* [Bari: Gius Laterza and Figli, 1949], 188–192), was adopted by Collingwood in *The Idea of History* (Oxford, 1946) and practiced years before in Windelband's *Lehrbuch der Geschichte der Philosophie* (1891) and translated into English by J. H. Tufts, 1892; see also Windelband's essay on "Was ist Philosophie?" (1882) in *Präludien*, 3 A. (Tubingen: Mohr, 1907). It structuralistically confuses history with human "logical" "creative activity," historiography with "absolute spiritual" science, and leaves literarily formulated knowledge on the tenterhooks of a concrete universal. But a thorough-going critique of this tempting conception of historiography is beyond the scope of the present article.

defined, analytic sharpness, but again, adopt a tentative—not hesitant!—approximating elasticity. Teaching the history of philosophy should have the temper of a thorough medical examination and prognosis of the patient's health. But without encapsulation of the historiographic analysis within the pedagogical norms of surprise and apprentice-like detecting, you will only get an autopsy.

Or, to develop the same point further: scientific analysis is in principle conceptually definitive, and its method satisfied with a patient step by factual step, identifying sort of knowledge. But knowledge that would come across live in the classroom must have the lurch of being by nature unfinished, and at the same time show some silhouetted *Gestalt* integrating the learning in process. Scientific knowledge has a forbidding authority, dissects things, and relates abstractly: pedagogically interesting knowledge invites, playfully engages others, provisionally juxtaposes things, and carries on quasi-dramatically.[12] Therefore, history of philosophy should not be taught in the way of medieval, disputational indoctrination (*Utrum . . . sit, ad primum, ad secundum, sed contra, respondeo . . . ad primum, ad secundum . . .*), nor in the manner of professional journal articles where you state your concluding thesis first, parcel out your arguments, and close *Q E D*. Nothing is more tedious in the classroom than logical conclusiveness, even if banked by anecdotal persiflage and sophistic wit. So philosophic historiographic analysis of a certain philosophy must bring about limited mastery of its philosophical crux, in its culturally blooded setting, with the kind of simplification that encourages further exploration. Without encapsulation of the analysis within the pedagogical norms of patterning-open-for-further-response, history of philosophy will strike a student as cut and dried rather than as a source to be mined for healing knowledge.

---

12 See my "A Skeleton to Pedagogy: Christian Analysis," an unpublished address delivered at Westminster Theological Seminary, Philadelphia, December 1965, that develops certain ideas found in my *Cultural Objectives for the Christian Teacher* [1964] (Seattle: Pacific Northwest Christian Teachers Association, 1966), 18–23. For pertinent materials see: Alfred N. Whitehead, *The Aims of Education* [1929] (Mentor, 1949); A. Janse *Het Eigen Karakter der Christelijke School* (Kampen: Kok, 1935); K. J. Popma. "Opvoeding. Onderwijs, Schoolverband," in *Philosophia Reformata* 12:1–3 (1947): 36–41, 86–93, 130–44, especially thesis VI: "Het schoolonderwijs is niet primair-practisch en draagt een interpretatief karakter, zoowel in analytischen als aesthetischen zin": Jan Waterink, *Basic Concepts in Christian Pedagogy* (Grand Rapids: Eerdmans, 1954); Guido Calogero, "Educazione e istruzione" and "L'educazione e la tecnica," in *La Scuola dell'Uomo* (Firenze: Sansoni, 1956), 124–37, 163–76; Max Guzilowski, "Discussion in Teaching Philosophy," *Teaching Thomism Today* (Washington, DC: The Catholic University of America Press, 1963), 183–93; David R. Hunter, *Christian Education as Engagement* (New York: Seabury, 1963).

Good teachers in the history of philosophy, of course, come in all kinds of wrappers, and it is true that a sound pedagogical method does not guarantee sound teaching any more than good liturgical principles protect worship from uninspired liturgetes. But it would be a headstart for normative, christian teaching of the history of philosophy, if we became thoroughly conscious and convinced of the fact that the rightful scientific edge of philosophical historiography must be maintained and bound by pedagogical norms—this is necessary, legitimate, and desirable for professionally respectable teaching of the history of philosophy. While this principle of encapsulation may be simple wisdom, deep imaginative inventiveness is called for to bring it off responsibly with unformed students.

The illustration that follows does not pretend to exemplify a full-fledged model of christian pedagogy, and it does not propose to capture the push-and-pull élan of live persons engaged in classroom learning, the way a Platonic dialogue tries to do it. This somewhat bookish vignette (because written) means to exhibit the integrity and promise of pedagogically encapsulated, christian philosophical historiography, suggesting how one might go about it in the classroom in a way that avoids the sterilizing stare of manuals meant to help prospective teachers.

ILLUSTRATION: A CERTAIN PHILOSOPHICAL NEIGHBORHOOD OF GENETICISTIC, CONTRADICTORY MONISM

About the time BC when the Lord God Yahweh was teaching the children of Israel that if they do their daily work responsively to His Word they will certainly have an exciting future,[13] over in Egyptland ethnic reflection held a consensus that there is nothing new under the sun. An everlasting fixed order—MA'AT—kept the overflowing Nile and the third and fourth generations of men in a recurrent cycle with changeless patterns. And it was wisdom, according to the official scribes at Pharaoh's court, to become silent men fitting into that Cosmic, tradition-bound, unchanging Order.[14] In Ye Olde Greece of the same period, there gradually developed among that illiterate and unalphabetic people, a sense that the final lot of humankind, Μοῖρα, meant a cursed, implacable Doom.

As Homer came to narrate the syncretistic cluster of myths com-

---

13 Cf. the undying refrain of Proverbs 22:17–24:22, found in 23: 17–18, 24:14, and 24:20–21.

14 Cf. "The Instruction of the Vizier Ptah-hotep" and "The Instruction of Amen-em-opet' in *Ancient Near Eastern Texts Relating to the Old Testament*, ed. James B. Pritchard, 3rd edition with supplement (Princeton University Press, 1969), 412–14, 421–25.

monly believed by the Achaeans in the eighth century, the only way to make life meaningful among men under *Moira* was the way of Cunning Power. Prowess and daring that brought earth-bound κῦδος to the family name, in competitive struggle with a touchy family of limited, superhuman deities (cf. initiation of the Olympic games), is what counted. To be sure, during several centuries of civilizational turmoil in the Mediterranean, the Phrygian orgiastic cult of Dionysus captivated many Greek adherents. Boeotian rhapsodist Hesiod also introduced the element of Δίκη—a kind of regular, natural impartial equilibrium—into the heterodox mythology. Even strands of Orphic asceticism began to offer people a priestly alternative. But the Greek mind was originally formed and set by the heroes of Homer's sonorous hexameters, like warrior Achilles maddened by Ἄτη and πολυμήχανος (never-at-a-loss) Odysseus.[15] The basic idolatry behind Archaic, pagan Greek culture was cunning foolhardiness. Its monumental tomb art and regal κοῦροι bespeak the intrepid, measured *hybris* every young Greek admired.[16]

A πόλις economy developed in the Peloponnesus during the seventh and sixth centuries BC. Sparta and Athens jockeyed for power in an uneasy, peaceful coexistence, while Greek colonies started dotting Asia Minor and Italy. Money was invented, trade intensified, wars and rumors of wars began to dominate the news. And it was at this time that certain singular thinkers of Ionia (ἰδιῶται) speculated on what's behind it all? what is reality like? how is Φύσις set up? what's the point of human life?

Heraclitus of Ephesus

Heraclitus of Ephesus (fl. 500 BC) was one of those curious Greek thinkers. His abiding thought was that this world is a warring tension that

---

15 "Many poets since then have conjured up the gods and heroes of pagan mythology; but now we think of them merely as the shadowy puppets of poetic fancy. We might easily regard Homer from the same narrow point of view; but if we did, we should never come to understand what myth and poetry really meant to the Greeks" (I, 35). "And the greatest of Greek poetry does more than show a cross-section of life taken at random. It tells the truth; but it chooses and presents its truth in accordance with a definite ideal" (I, 36). "The Homeric epics contain the germs of all Greek philosophy. In them we can clearly see the anthropocentric tendency of Greek thought, that tendency which contrasts so strongly with the theomorphic philosophy of the Oriental who sees God as the sole actor and man as merely the instrument or object of that divine activity" (I, 53). Werner Jaeger on "Homer the Educator" in *Paideia: The ideals of Greek culture* [1933], 2nd edition (New York: Oxford University Press, 1945), volume I.

16 Cf. R. Ross Holloway. "Archaic Sculptural Form," in *A View of Greek Art* (London: Harper and Row, 1973), 31–44.

is constantly begetting opposites. This warring process is not subject to *Moira* but is itself divine, an everlasting, begetting, and consuming Fire—Logos![17] The hoi polloi act idiotically, as if an individual could think all by himself; and some πόλεις democratically decide this is right and that is wrong; but actually, whatever is, is right! and each man must simply be attuned to the common Logos-God-*Physis*.[18] The "best men" (ἄριστος) know there is a hidden harmony simultaneously, in the same respect, in all the contradictory transformations of world and cultural discord—salt water kills and gives life, depending upon whether you immerse men or fish in it—and the truth is that basically all things are One (ἓν πάντα εἶναι). One Universal Law of Natural Warring Tension.[19]

> It should be understood that war is the common condition, that strife is justice, and that all things come to pass through the compulsion of strife.[20]

Only when each I is We (cf. novel by Zamyatin, *WE*, 1920), and We lives κατὰ φύσιν with the skill to abide and take advantage of its own universally contradictorily flipping back and forth, utterly permanent Change, is there the justice and hidden repose of final meaning, says Heraclitus of Ephesus, about 500 years before Christ walked the earth bringing shalom (cf. figure 1).

TENSIVE NATURE (figure 1)

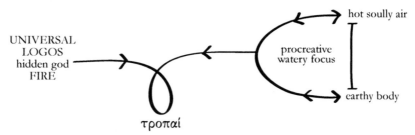

One should notice the threat this philosophical position of Universalistic Contradictory Monism would pose, let's say, for fifth century BC Athens, where a *polis* majority posited what's law. Heraclitus' perspective

---

17 Heraclitus in *Die Fragmente der Vorsokratiker*, ed. Diels-Kranz, 6 ed. (Berlin-Grunewald: Weidmannsche Verlagsbuchhandlung, 1951): γινοένων γὰρ πάντων κατὰ τὸν λόγον τὸνδε frag. 1; cf. frag 8, 30–31, 60, 67, 76–77, 103, 118.

18 Ibid. e.g., frag. 2, 29, 72, 114: τῶι μὲν θεῶι καλὰ πάντα κὰι ἀγαθὰ καὶ δίκαια, ἄνθρωποι δὲ ἃ μὲν ἄδικα ὑπειλήφασιν δὲ δίκαια frag. 112.

19 Ibid. e.g., frag. 33, 41, 49–50, 51 παλίντροπος ἁρμονίη, 61, 123.

20 Ibid. frag. 80, translated by Philip Wheelwright. *The PreSocratics* (New York: Odyssey, 1966), 71, as fragment 26.

relativizes any positive law and makes it possible for a strong man to claim he is in touch with a deeper Natural Universal Law that everyone should follow, superseding particular polis laws. Heraclitus' commitment to reality as being constant struggle is not altogether unreminiscent of Homer and Hesiod's attitude; but Heraclitus' affirmation of contradictory transmutation in the name of Logos, gives the whole flux a much more jurotechnical opportunistic character than one of bio-physical survival. Also, Heraclitus baldly approves something more than tricky talk and the doublecross to get fame:[21] analytic contradiction is thoroughly legitimate in his mind, because reality is fundamentally at odds, rightly so!

When, as a matter of historical fact, the Heraclitean "wisdom" entered the marketplace of fifth century BC Greece, and his cosmogonic Subjectivism got reoriented to the anthropocentric (not to say "anthropogonic") Subjectivism of *polis* society, the Heraclitean vision served as a cosmo-polis-an yeast in various sophists' feisty contribution to the demythologizing of Olympian gods, professionalization of *polis* education, their Individualistic support for demagogic tyranny, and the gradual undermining of classic Greek society.

And one should not overlook the crushing pessimism lurking in Heraclitus' fragments, despite their almost militaristic bravado and racist elitism that sounds their particular, Greeky spirit. There is no mediator for Heraclitus; no redemption for man is conceivable in Heraclitus' philosophical framework, except that he be tossed from his individual, provincial frying pan of warring contrasts into the universal Fire of constant contradictory harmony. When you realize that Heraclitus was figuring these things out in the dark of Asia Minor shortly after Daniel was given dreams from Yahweh in Babylon about the fall of civilizations foreign to God's Rule, and about the same time as Zechariah was receiving visions at night straight from the LORD, and Nehemiah was building up the little tumble down wall of Jerusalem, ending his diary entries at night so plaintively, "Please think well of me, O my God! for the little things I've been able to do for You," then you understand why the apostle Paul, after passing through Heraclitus' hometown 600 years later could refer to such patterns of thinking as ἄθεοι (Ephesians 2:11–22) and plead with Christians not to lose their minds that way but to get their whole consciousness truly new in Jesus Christ (Ephesians 4:1–24).

A good deal of philosophical water has gone over the historical dam

---

21 Cf. how the goddess Athena approves of Odysseus' lying straight to her face in *Odyssey*, 13:287–310.

in Western Europe by the time the Dominican Eckhart (c. 1260–1327), with his Master's degree in theology from the University of Paris, began to preach in Strasbourg and Köln around 1314 AD. "Church Fathers" like Clement and Origen from Egypt and Augustine from Africa had struggled in the first centuries after Christ's resurrection to keep the christian faith intact while they fitted its dogmas together with the great reflection of Greco-Roman humanity. The church headquartered at Rome had developed a world-wide establishment that officiated as the veritable custodian of Western civilization and for a millennium almost totally dominated human life. Worship services on Christmas and Easter in a twelfth or thirteenth century cathedral—overwhelming height inside, massive statuary in stone, gold-brocaded vestments in processions, with incense, stained glass colored light, mellifluously haunting plainsong crescendoing at the high point of the raised host and celebration of the mass, thronged by the whole countryside—epitomized incantationally the power and glory forever and ever of the church.[22] Only its priestly rites guaranteed you as a man or woman a heavenly eternity; so you were utterly beholden to it. And it was this "Mother" church that had given her blessing, officially and unofficially, to the habit of supplementing Platonic philosophy with the insights of supernatural revelation.

That certification, approval, program of the Roman church—call it what you will—to join the analysis of pagan minds with the truths made specially known by Scripture, led to its being the unquestioned method of educated leaders. The spirit of reinforcing the church's Latin theological deposits by combining to it the ancillary results of autonomous "natural reason" in order to arrive at a cumulative, definitive synthesis of truly authoritative knowledge on all matters—world, man, and God included: that driving spirit formed the Scholastic mind that controlled Western philosophy unchallenged from John of Damascus (c. 726 AD) till William of Ockham and the Black Death plague of 1348–50. Thomas Aquinas formulated a commonplace, an assumed framework, when he wrote *gratia non tollat naturam, sed perficiat.*[23] The fact that "the Philosopher" who got "graced" became Aristotle rather than Plato in the thirteenth century hardly batted a bishop's eye.

Eckhart of Strasbourg
German professor Eckhart called into question the administrative hold of

---

22 Cf. Émile Mâle, *L'art Religieux du XIIIe Siècle en France* (1913) (Paris: Librairie Armand Colin, 1948), 395–403.

23 *Summa Theologica*, I. q1. 8. ad 2.

the Roman church and its ritual upon the salvation of men.[24] He began breaking down the Scholastic mentality by using the unheard of formula—"*Die Meister sagen gemeinhin . . . Doch ich sage . . .*"—subtly recalling the way Christ corrected the tradition-bound Pharisees. He sidestepped the barriers of reasoned argument and the ecclesiastically wielded authority of Grace by claiming that his exposition of Scripture even went beyond Grace, passed all understanding, because it brought naked truth straight from the heart of God (*ein unbedahtiu wârheit, diu dâ komen ist ûz dem herzen gôtes âne mittel*).[25] And he did all this not as a rabble rousing son of the Church but as respected Vicar General of his order in Bohemia, from the pulpit with pungent, mystifying sermons in the vernacular.

God is divine, and once upon a time God created creatures. When the creating holy Trinity made man in their likeness, God sparked the soul to be His equal, everlasting, active counterpart. Only through man's active soul, an image of God, are creatures prepared for becoming and acting Godly.[26] That means, says Eckhart, in the beginning there was pure Divinity (*gotheit*) with nothing doing. Out of this utterly empty fullness of Divinity, God (*got*), of course, creates. Divine God is continually creating creatures that reproduce and re-create, after their fashion, like Him. It's clear that Father God, with the conceiving Spirit, gave birth to His only begotten Son out of His own reproducing, ever-generating Divinity. So you could say, in a way, God comes to be more and comes to be less. God becomes and even passes away! depending upon His begetting or the begoing of His handiwork. Especially when I who mirror God in the flint-like power of my soul (*vünkelîn, kraft*), able to unite all sorts of creatures into One by my activity: when I as God's image (*Bild Gottes*) return to God, in a sense, go beyond God back into the hidden,

---

24 "Wan swer got suochet in wîse, der nimet die wîse und lât got, der in der wîse verborgen ist" (Sermon *In hoc apparuit caritas Dei in nobis* in *Meister Eckharts Traktate*, ed. Josef Quint [Berlin: Kohlhammer, 1963], 1:91). ". . . gebete, an vastenne, an wachenne und aller hande ûzerlîcher üebunge und kestigunge. Ein ieglîchiu eigenschaft eines ieglîchen werkes, daz die vrîheit benimet, in disem gegenwertigen nû gote ze wartenne und dem aleine ze volgenne . . ." (Sermon *Intravit Iesus in quoddam castellum* in *Eckharts Traktate*, ed. Quint, 1:28–29). "Dise menschen heizent heilic von den ûzwendigen bilden; aber von innen sint sie esel, wan sie enverstânt niht den underscheit götlîcher wârheit" (Sermon *Beati pauperes spiritu*, 2:489–90).

25 *Beati pauperes spiritu*, 2:506.

26 ". . . Alle crêatûren verzîhent sich irs lebens ûf ir wesen. Alle crêatûren tragent sich in mîne vernunft, daz si in mir vernünftic sint. Ich alleine bereite aile crêatûren wider zuo gote" (Sermon *Nolite timere eos* in *Meister Eckhart*, ed. Franz Pfeiffer (Göttingen: Vandenhoeck und Ruprecht, 1914, reprint of 1857 edition), 180.

inner abyss of Divinity from whence I came, then an epiphany of eternity passes, and Godhood is all in all . . .[27]

Can you not simply be astounded at the staggering truth—even if you don't understand it—preached Eckhart, of man's being "born again" by the fructifying Spirit of God?! When a man is really "regenerated" in the wholly spiritual, uncreated power-point of his soul, which emanates from the Spirit itself, that man is begotten Son of God by the unique power of the eternal Father, as truly as Father God ceaselessly begets his eternal Son in Himself.[28] In fact, when you deny yourself and empty yourself of everything creatural, lose your will completely, for God's sake, so that your own knowledge becomes the purest ignorance, a dark un-consciousness, then God—who abhors a vacuum—shall wholly fill you. You will blend with God into Godhood when you forsake and are purged of the divisive life contrasting, for example, happiness and sorrow: when you become dead to the whole world in your soul, then you become singlemindedly alive in Being, in the eternal Being where you were before your creation.[29]

---

27 "Allez, das got würket, das würket er in dem einen im selben glîch" (Sermon *Ego elegi vos de mundo* in *Meister Eckharts Traktate*, ed. Quint, 2:63). "Her ûz drücket im got, der êwige vater, die vüllede und den abgrunt aller sîner gotheit. Das gebirt er hie in sînem eingebornen sune und daz wir der selbe sun sîn, und sîn gebern das ist sîn inneblîben, und sîn inneblîben ist sîn ûzgebern" (2:68). "Si enmac niht gelîden, das iht ob ir sî. Ich waene, si joch niht gelîden enmüge, daz got ob ir sî . . ." (Sermon *Consideravit semitas domus suae*, 2:143). ". . . got und gotheit hât underscheit als verre als himel und erde. Ich spriche mê: der inner und ûzer mensche die hânt alse verre un-derscheit als himel und erde. Got hât vil tûsent mîllen dar obe. Got wirt unt entwirt. . . . Got ist in der sêle mit sîner nâtûre, mit sûne wesenne unde mit sîner gotheit und er enist doch niht diu sêle. Daz widerspilen der sêle das ist in gote. God unde si ist doch daz si ist. Got der wirt dâ alle crêatûren. Gotes sprechen dâ gewirt got. Dô ich stuont in dem grunde, in dem boden, in dem river und in der quelle der gotheit, dâ frâgete mich nieman, war ich wolte odor was ich tête: dâ enwas nieman, der midi frâgete. Dô ich flôz, dô sprâchen al crêatûren got. . . . Got wirket, diu gotheit wirket niht, si enhât niht ze wirkenne, in ir ist kein werc. . . . Got unde gotheit hât underscheit an würken und an niht-würken. Swenne ich kume wider in got, bilde ich dâ niht, sô ist mîn durbrechen vil edeler danne mîn ûzfluz. Ich alleine bringe alle crêatûren ûz ir vernunft in mîn vernunft, daz sie in mir eine sint. Swenne ich kume in den grunt, in den bodem, in den river und in die quelle der gotheit, so frâget mich nieman, wan-nen ich kome odor wâ ich si gewesen. Dâ vermiste mîn nieman, daz entwirt" (*Nolite timere eos*, 180–81).

28 "Wan der êwige vater gebirt sînen êwigen sun des vaters und sich selber den selben sun in der einiger kraft des vaters" (*Intravit Iesus in quoddam castellum*, 1:32). "Diu selbe kraft, dar abe ich gesprochen hân, dâ got inne ist blüejende und grüenende mit aller sîner gotheit und der geist in gote, in dirre selber kraft ist der vater geberde sînen eingebornen sun als gewaerlîche als in im selber. . ." (1:40–41).

29 "Dâ diu crêatûre endet, dâ beginnet got ze sînne. Nû begert got niht mê von dir, wan

So the soul resembles God when it achieves a perfectly immovable disinterestedness (*unbewegelîchiu abgescheidenheit*): a mere conduit for Divinity.[30]

> The authorities say that God is a being, an intelligent being who knows everything. But I say that God is neither a being nor intelligent and he does not know either this or that. God is *free* of every thing and therefore he *is* everything.[31]

God in his Godhood, Divinity, is the inexhaustible source of meaning, the Origin (*Urbeginne*); our intuiting-soul (*Vernunft*) must shatter in if it would be taken up in untrammeled *Abgescheidenheit*. Therefore man must expunge God-knowledge and Godhood-distracting godliness ruthlessly out of his inner life and outer deeds and become perfectly nothing! so that the fishhook of Divine love may make you more free—even though you twist and turn—the more you are caught. Trust God, who is a God of the creating present (*God ist ein got der gegenwerticheit*), to turn even your sin into what's better for you.[32] If this all sounds like a

---

daz dû dîn selbes ûzgangest in crêatiurlicher wîse und lâzest got got in dir sîn" (*In hoc apparuit caritas Dei in nobis*, 1:92). ". . . diu sêle gesast sî in ein lûter wesen. Daz ander ist, daz ez in mi treit widersatzunge. . . . Dar an liget der sêle lûterkeit, daz si geliutert ist von einem lebene, daz geteilet ist, und tritet in ein leben, daz vereinet ist. Allez daz geteilet ist in nidern sachen, daz wirt vereinet, als diu sêle ûfklimmet in ein leben, dâ kein widersatzunge enist" (Sermon *In occisione gladli mortui sunt*, 1:135–36). "Dô ich stuont in mîner êrsten sache, dô enhâte ich keinen got, und dô was ich sache mîn sebles . . . Das ich wolte, das was ich, und daz ich was, daz wolte ich, und hie stuont ich ledic gotes und aller dinge. Aber dô ich ûzgienc von mînen vrîen willen und ich enpfienc mîn geschaffen wesen, dô hâte ich einen gôt; wan ê die crêatûren wâren, dô enwas got niht 'got,' mêr: er was, das er was. Aber dô die crêatûren gewurden und sie enpfiengen ir geschaffen wesen, dô enwas got niht 'got' in im selben, mêr: er was 'got' in den crêatûren' (*Beati pauperes spiritu*, 2:492–93). "Alhie, in dirre armuot sô ervolget der mensche daz êwic wesen, das er ist gewesen und daz er nû ist and daz er iemer bliben sol" (2:501). ". . . wan ich enpfâhe in diesem durchbrechen, das ich und got einz sîn" (2:505).

30 *Von abgescheidenheit* in *Eckharts Traktate*, ed. Quint, 5:412.

31 "Die meister sprechent, got der sî ein wesen und ein vernünftic wesen und bekenne alliu dinc. Sô sprechen wir: got enist niht wesen noch vernünftic noch enbekennet niht diz noch daz" (*Beati pauperes spiritu*, 2:497), translated by R. B. Blakney *Meister Eckhart* (Harper, 1957), 230.

32 "Vernunft diu bliket în unde durbrichte alle die winkel der gotheit unde nimet den sun in dem herzen des vater und in dem grunde und setzet in in iren grunt. Vernunft diu dringet în, ir genüeget niht an gûeti noch an wîsheit noch an wârheit noch an gote selber . . . Si geruowet niemer, si brichet in den grunt, dâ gûete und wârheit ûz brichet, unde nimet ez in principio, in dem beginne, dâ gûeti und wârheit ûz gânde ist, ê si ûz breche, in eime vil hoeheren grunde denne güeti und wîsheit sî" (Sermon *Modicum et iam non videbitis me* in *Meister Eckhart*, ed. Pfeiffer, 144–45). "Wan den

contradictory mystery, said Eckhart, don't worry your head about it. Remember that those who try to gain their life shall lose it and those who lose it disinterestedly shall find it for ever and ever, directly flowing in the heart of God (see figure 2).

GENERATING GODHOOD (figure 2)

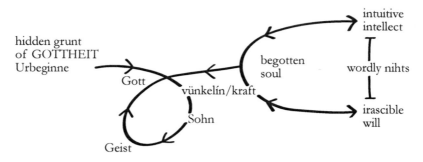

No wonder the Church of Rome anathematized Eckhart's writings two years after his death.[33] There is always a party-politics side to heresy, and the Franciscans were out to get Dominican Eckhart, who had defended himself point by point in 1326 (not in German, of course, but in church Latin); but the basic philosophical perspective informing Eckhart's sermons, if adopted, would unhinge more than the churchified society of thirteenth century Europe. Its Contradictory Monistic Geneticism conflicts sharply with any Structuralistic position, for example, Thomism or Utilitarianism. Eckhart's position cannot stand to think of (the christian) life, let's say, in terms of so many right and wrong deeds, so many credits and so many debits, about which one can take specified, hierarchical steps to get settled: life is a constant struggle of back and forth, an ongoing process *by nature*, so that every gain and loss is radically relativized—our life is simply, only, and finally a Becoming. So one should not expect a systematic theology in the neighborhood of Meister Eckhart. At most a theogonic odyssey of God with man in tandem, an attack, perhaps, on official christendom, and a deep-going, mystifying, unsettling . . . conservatism.

---

guoten koment alliu dinc ze guote, als sant Paulus sprichet, und als sant Augustînus sprichet: 'jâ, ouch die sûnden'" (*Die rede der underscheidunge* in *Eckharts Traktate*, ed. Quint, 5:231). "Aber dû solt gote wol getriuwen, daz er dir des niht verhenget haete, er enwölte denne dîn bestez das ûz ziehen" (5:233).

33 Cf. Denzinger, *Enchiridion Symbolorum*, 501–29, for the exact errors Pope John XXII cited on 27 March 1329, which the Roman church said *damnamus et reprobamus expresse*.

There is an unrelenting, muted stridency within Eckhart's pastorally warm sermons, because he assumes at bottom that change is the order of the day and one has to be caught up in the unpredictable yet rigorous process of flurrying activity that somehow demands renunciation if you want to be in touch with what's real. So there is agitation. But the call for continual return to a more simple, undifferentiated, unified Oneness acts steadyingly. However, that too is deceptive, because the call to return to Oneness is deeply anti-institutional. Eckhart's perspective has no compunction against dissolving church, state (or even 'God"!) into the stream of ever creative and recreative Divine Love and Power. Eckhart's Objectivism stops him short of being satisfied with "personal experiences" of purgation or rapturous God-union: the juro-technical quality of *Abgescheidenheit* (a balancing, professional, umpire-like disinterestedness)—which gives God his God status![34]— is a norm he posits that human subjects must meet. But that Objectivistic horizon is small comfort for the Church, since Rome has no monopoly on dispensing *Abgescheidenheit* as it did have on specifying the supernal (sacred) truths of a Realistic philosophy, which one needed in order to be saved.

It is noteworthy that Eckhart's basic philosophical conception and the whole set of his to be sure weary-of-Scholasticism temper is *not* conducive to all the quietistic mysticism that cropped up in Germany at the decline of the fourteenth century. Such introverted, ecstatic theoreticism takes its conceptual inspiration from a different neighborhood (like that of much sixteenth century Spanish mysticism), for Eckhart's commitment to surging, parturient activity does not brook the state of interiorized contemplation as ideal. Yet how woefully sad, it seems to me, when all is said and done, that christian believer Eckhart broke the back of the gospel, subverts the communion of saints, and puts stumbling blocks in front of any would-be believers, all by joining his love for God to and under a Geneticistic Contradictory Monistic misconception of reality. Because Eckhart sees the estrangement of man from God not as a call to men for a change in direction to obedience through Jesus Christ but as a necessary return in ontic structure of man directly to God, a biblically envisioned reality is ruled out. There can be no sense of creaturely man's being covenanted to the merciful, just, and faithful Yahweh fully revealed in Jesus Christ and attested to by the Holy Scriptures: God is fundamentally a hidden God who discloses his whereabouts like a man

---

34 "Wan das got ist got, das hât er von sîner unbewegelîchen abgescheidenheit ..." (*Von abgescheidenheit*, 5:412).

in the dark who happens to clear his throat.[35] Sin is not something historically subsequent to creation that can be rectified and healed: for Eckhart, evil is a furtive feature of creatureliness somehow, so that it becomes either/or between Godhood and creation for man. And man is not an adopted serving son of God, through faith, thanks to the Grace of the Lord: instead, thanks to his soul's *vünkelîn* (empowering spark), man is wrenched into the superhuman task of unending mediatorial work, making him a Christ actually, and therefore burdening him like a Sisyphus in an everlasting chain of Becoming perfect. Eckhart's genial sermons of encouragement have a permanent, disconcerting edge underneath, and his "Book of Divine Comfort" is spiked with wormwood.

An utterly different Spirit than the absorbed piety of Eckhart's sermons wells up out of a tract like *Il Principe* by Machiavelli (1469–1527) 200 years later. Times have changed from the day of Giotto where solid gold-leaf or a heavenly blue background graced the statuesque figures in a fresco with sanctified stillness. Now Paolo Uccello and Piero della Francesca have been introducing Florentines to a more turbulent world with three-dimensional, open space perspective, and Botticelli has canonized the pagan ethic of *kalok'agathon* for the Medici with winsome, wispy, gentling finery, not in the name of the Church. An authoritative Christendom promising security where moth and rust do not corrupt had lost its unquestioned control of men's hearts and minds. It's true, there seemed to be continuing attempts to keep a hybrid of grand humanism and Roman (catholic) culture intact: Cola di Rienzo tried to reinstate at Rome the good old *Roman* days while the pope was in and out of Avignon, but too many longed for *il papa's* return; even Boccaccio, master of the vernacular, spent the last years of his life, after he got to know bookish Petrarch, finishing up his *Latin* writings; and Castiglione's influential eulogy of the courtier covered over its idolatry of refined sensuality with a quasi-spiritual, Neo-Platonizing sheen. But the "christian" to such syntheses became more and more a transparent veneer for outright Humanism.

In fact, a Spirit foreign to any biblical christianity began to excite European society in the fifteenth century. A bald desire to enhance Human dignity by striving with Faustian ambition for secret knowledge

---

35 "Got möhte niemer nieman funden hân, als der wîse sprichet 'herre, dû bist ein verborgen got?' Wâ jet dirre got? Reht als sich ein mensche verbirget, sô rünstert er sich unde vermeldet sich selber dâ mite, also hât ouch got gotân. Got künde niemer nieman funden hân; nû hêt er sich vermeldet" (Sermon *Laudate coeli et exultet terra* in *Meister Eckhart*, ed. Pfeiffer, 301).

and occult power, with the use of cabala writings and magic if necessary, anything, to let man exploit this-here (*diesseitige*) Nature and achieve *humaniora*: this syncretistic spirit drove the deeply anti-synthetic-christian Renaissance mentality onward—this-here *saeculum* is what counts![36] If wandering Franciscan friars want to preach sermons on the mount for the birds, let them go their harmless way. If the powerful Roman church wants to play politics, then it will have to use the rules of the secular game. No matter which, Christianity as a distinctive way of cultural salvation is passé: we men must pull ourselves up by our own godless boot-straps and give birth to a culture worthy of Man's chameleon-like potential for divinity . . .

Machiavelli of Firenze

Machiavelli witnessed firsthand the governmental instability of his native polis, Renaissance Florence. The Medici bankers pulled political strings there like an Alcmeonidae dynasty, warding off papal assassinations, till Savonarola got them expelled and faced the city with theocratic hours of decision for four straight years, till he got himself burned at the stake in 1498. Then Machiavelli became Secretary of Defense for the ensuing republic and served thirteen years, until he was exiled by the returning Medici, who were recalled to stave off French domination. Out in the country Machiavelli wrote *Il Principe* (about the same time as Luther's theses, 1517) and shamelessly dedicated it to the junior Lorenzo Medici in power, fishing for a portfolio in the new Florentine administration —

By nature most people are evil, says Machiavelli; therefore, if you mean to rule people well, jockeying the masses off against the privileged elite, you must learn yourself how not to be good and use that knowhow when necessary.[37] A good prince will also realize and cope with the basic reality that armed men prevail over unarmed men: force determines what happens.[38] Yet things are more complicated than brute power and survival of the strongest, because reality is structurally a process wherein whimsical *fortuna* and the freely willing abilities (*virtù*) of man intersect in an uncertain, unpredictable coexistence. Time is essentially an indifferent

---

36 Cf. Pico della Mirandola: "*Invadat animum sacra quaedam ambitio ut mediocribus non contenti anhelemus ad summa, adque illa (quando possumus si volumus) consequenda totis viribus enitamur*" (*De Hominis Dignitate* [1488] ed. E. Garin, Firenze: Vallecchi, 1942, 110).

37 "Onde è necessario a uno principe, volendosi mantenere, imparare a potere essere non buono, e usarlo e non usare secondo la necessità" in *Il Principe* (no. 15).

38 ". . . tutt'i profeti armati vincono, e li disarmati ruinarono" (no. 8) uses Savonarola's fall as case in point.

well of constant circumstantial Opportunity, whose crest a good prince knows how to ride to more power and whose flipflop lapse he knows how to adapt to—in whatsoever stadium he be therewith to take advantage.[39] Therefore, an unsettled, factional tension of interests is permanent: war is unavoidable; sustained progress is impossible; peace is actually an illusion; and the prince maintains his precarious, fulcral civic post in the dynamic balancing of societal powers only by fortuna-ted cunning (*una astuzia fortunata*)[40] (cf. figure 3).

SOCIETAL REALITY (figure 3)

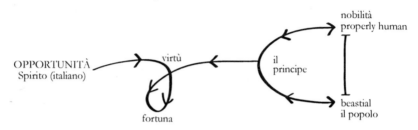

The watchword for Machiavelli's prince, since this is the way the world is actually set up, is: deceptive, impetuous force (*essere gran simulatore e dissimulatore*).[41] Rule by fear rather than by devotion; keep the populace off-balance, astonished, watching the unexpected results of your foxy, apparently generous, yet truly stealthy, leonine deeds. Be pious and humane, yet be able to switch immediately without compunction to ruthless, irreligious cruelties if necessary, ever mindful that a reputation for being magnanimous will cover a multitude of doublecrosses. The ability to take the least evil option, put the best face on it for the public, and carry it off with a flair, adapting to the most contrary winds of fortune: such *prudenzia* marks a good prince.[42] Cesare Borgia, son of pope Alexander VI, epitomized for Machiavelli a true prince of a man,

---

39 "Non di manco perché il nostro libero arbitrio non sia spento, iudico potere essere vero che la fortuna sia arbitra della metà delle azioni nostre, ma che ancora lei ne lasci governare l'altra metà, o presso, a noi" (no. 25); ". . . el tempo si caccia innanzi ogni cosa, e può condurre seco bene come male, e male come bene" (no. 3).

40 No. 9.

41 No. 18, no. 25.

42 No. 17, no. 19. "E però bisogna che egli abbia uno animo disposto a volgersi secondo ch'e venti della fortuna e le variazioni della cose li comandano e, come di sopra dissi, non partirsi dal bene potendo, ma sapere intrare nel male, necessitato" (no. 18). "E sopra tutto uno principe si debbe ingegnare dare di sé, in ogni sua azione fama di uomo grande e di uomo eccellente" (no. 21).

a ruler who redeemed his ferocious escapades by a megalopsychic ambition for the glory of Italy (*L'animo grando e la sua intenzione alta*).[43] What distinguished Cesare Borgia from the run-of-the-mill villany of the day was the fact, in Machiavelli's judgment, that he lived by the law of *virtù e prudenzia*.

A man must trust only his own power, but might is not *virtù* unless it show the quality of *gloria*. Cunning must disclose refinement; cruelty must be done with the clean-cut character of excellence (*bene usate*). Strength that even gains control is not enough in Machiavelli's world: the deed of strength must have the quality of virile forcefulness, the aura of great achievement—its craftiness must be heightened by a sleight-of-hand, daredevil, brilliant καλοκἄγαθος guile, or the princely action lacks the prerequisite for lasting ἀρετή.[44] And action of such quality is not out to achieve results just for the individual prince, but expects all principalities to be conjoined as One to liberate Italy from the barbarians.[45] Although one must remember that the last chapter of *Il Principe* goes with the fawning dedication, a commitment to *la virtù d'une spirito italiano . . . la virtù italica . . .* the superior Italian race . . . is genuine there, visionary, and historically trenchant, as well as nascently fascist.

Our largely Individualistic, Subjectivist-ridden day easily overlooks these last points and misreads Machiavelli to be simply justification for cynical, power-play politics out to aggrandize things for your own interests. But Machiavelli's political philosophy has the stature of (Socrates') Objectivism, and is not on a par with the old sophists' strong-arm Subjectivism. The fact that Machiavelli would recommend intrigue, bluff, and slow poison rather than hand-to-hand combat or a hatchet job is not just a Renaissance idiosyncrasy. Machiavelli's thought assumes human life has more to it than visceral and manipulative activity; if that further horizon of controllability constituted by style, intelligence, and courtier breeding—which holds for every controlling subject—if that objective horizon is disobeyed, then you do not have a Prince on your hands, but only a meaningless, brutal, or boorish villain. Machiavelli's final law for men to follow is not skill or success but *Opportunità*: an openness-to-be-formed, an optionability-to-be-controlled, an availability of means-to-be-exploited and mastered. *Opportunità* is really Machiavelli's god—you

---

43 No. 7.

44 "E quelle difese solamente sono buone, sono certe, sono durabili, che dependano da te proprio e dalla virtù tua" (no. 24). "Non si può ancora chiamare virtù ammazzare e suoi cittadini, tradire lì amici, essere sanza fede, sanza pietà, sanza religione: e quali modi possono fare acquistare imperio, ma non gloria" (no. 8).

45 No. 26.

are for or against *Opportunità*—and you live by that Word of technical formableness if you want to have τὸ εὖ ζῆν.[46]

It is partly this technical Objectivism that accounts for the durability and fascination of Machiavelli's position for so many post-Renaissance political opportunists, who usually cheapen the quasi-deified *Opportunità* circumstantially into a matter of pragmatic trickery. Machiavelli got at the creational reality that power is the basic ingredient of sound political action, that camouflage, timing, and undisclosed alliances rightly belong to diplomacy and policing the body politic, and that decisive, forceful response to culture-making choices is normative for men in God's world. But Machiavelli puffed that discovery up into a hideous idol. The fact that his idol of princely power came dressed with a hint of Macrocosmic *virtù* (*la virtù italica*) conned secularized modern statesmen into applying machiavellian principles so long as it was done for the SUN NEVER SETS on the British empire, LA GLOIRE de la France, or Deutschland ÜBER ALLES. Along with the dressing, however, came the inevitable militarism, cut-throat expansion policies, and forming of uncertain power blocs.

The fact that Machiavelli's Contradictory Geneticistic Monism has a decidedly secular Spirit gives its fix on reality a specially heartless character. Machiavelli's *prudenzia*, for example, is not like Scholastic Structuralistic Thomas' juro-analytic casuistry, applying universal precepts to individual cases in order to insure an infallibly good act in Nature that supports the legislature of Grace.[47] Machiavelli's prudence is a gutsy pounce on rough and tumble breaks in a stream of continuously changing, helter-skelter, irregular activity; and the prince is not only not subject to any law but in an amorphous, *exlex* fashion simply shadowboxes *fortuna* to gain advantage—there is no law but seizing Opportunity with grace. And note well, Grace is no longer understood as a gift of God, blessing from Yahweh, but is taken to be merely the quality of expert, human sureness. There is no Prince of Peace mediating Machiavelli's setup: only aggressive princes of proficient deception (=grace!).

Machiavelli's perspective, historically, has been a mixed curse. Ma-

---

46 Socrates commitment to ἀρετη (cf. Machiavelli's *virtue*!) led him to make this kind of Objectivistic point in a somewhat different neighborhood of thought. Cf. *Crito*, οὐ τὸ ζῆν περὶ πλείστου ποίητέον ἀλλὰ τὸ εὖ ζῆν 48b5–6.

47 ". . . ad prudentiam pertinet non solum consideratio rationis, sed etiam applicatio ad opus, quae est finis practicae rationis. . . . Operationes autem sunt in singularibus. Et ideo necesse est quod prudens et cognoscat universalia principia rationis, et cognoscat singularia, circa quae sunt operations" (*Summa Theologica*, II–II q47 3 res). ". . . prudentia proprie est circa ea quae sunt ad finem; et hoc ad eius officium proprie pertinet, ut ad finem debite ordinentur" (II–II q49 6 res).

chiavelli contributed to the emancipation of political life from ecclesiastic hegemony; his conception normally works integratively in society, unifying and centralizing quite conservatively powers at variance, and therefore has helped prevent anarchy in societal crises. But the thrust and very build of Machiavelli's conception is deeply diabolical: legal commitments are ways of fighting your neighbor, the state is not a continuing entity but simply a temporary instrument of Higher Force that does well to act both as a lion and an angel of light in the endless pursuit of . . . not happiness, not survival, but of continuing, unstable, equalizing, restless tension! That is, there is no room in Machiavelli's philosophy for forgiveness, for amnesty from the consequences of sin, for magistrates to exercise a most holy calling before God of setting crooked things straight.[48] Instead, Machiavelli affirms the bad news of turmoil and the groaning for redemption of frustrated men as itself good! thereby turning the truth into a lie and the lie into a hopeless yoke of ceaseless and permanently endless striving.

The forthright secularity that breathes through every inch of Machiavelli's philosophy has continued since his day to direct the mainstream of Western civilization. So the godless Spirit of trusting human ability for the Way, the Truth, and the Life of generations to come has mustered a majority consensus among cultural leaders now for almost half a millennium. The thought of Copernicus and Galileo, partly because they were concerned to rhyme it with Scholastic church dogma, helped settle the pristine, anti-synthetic-christian temper of Renaissance thinkers into a less revolutionary-appearing mould, where one paid unconditional allegiance to "Reason" in matters of this world, but could still honor God for the next. Such a compromise soothed the historical conscience of many, but it only insured the increasing hold on human hearts by the idol of secularity. God brooks no other god next to God self, and if men and women persist in their willfully God-less ways, God often silently leaves them to their own forlorn devices.

The restless history of Rationalism betrays just such a vaunting,

---

48 To hear a holy Spirited insight to which Machiavelli's is diametrically opposed, see Luther's "Ein feste Burg ist unser Gott, ein gute Wehr und Waffen. Er hilft uns frei aus aller Not, die uns jetzt hat betroffen . . ." Also John Calvin: "Quare nulli jam dubium esse debet quin civilis potestas, vocatio sit, non modo coram Deo sancta et legitima, sed sacerrima etiam, et in tota mortalium vita longe omnium honestissima" (*Institutio Christianae religionis*, 1536, IV 20:4). The Heidelberg Catechism (1563) also posits the Scriptural thesis in Lord's Day 10 on providence, to which Machiavelli's considered stance is a rigorous anti-thesis.

woebegone, secularizing development. "Reason" is the fiction concocted by men and women who, ignoring God and God's Word, outfit creaturely human understanding with final, universally binding, and absolutely certifying apriori's that guarantee truth and reliable meaning to everyone following it. "Rationality" thus assumes the status of God's Word.

When post-Renaissance men took up the belief that a mathematically honed rationality would introduce the indubitable truth in philosophy (e.g., Descartes), they were optimistic that Reason would also insure tolerance in ethics (Spinoza), lead to a politics safe from "religious wars" (Locke), and solve all kinds of problems from physics to theology (Leibniz). But the seventeenth-century Scientialistic reason seemed to reduce human affairs to what could be measured, and presumed as if whatever did not fit the rectilinear pattern, say, of the formal gardens in Versailles somehow was beyond the pale of civilization. The Aufklärung sensibility, however, confessed a more popular, socially intimate Reason as savior of society. The middle generations of the eighteenth century championed taste (Shaftesbury), sentiment (Rousseau), a skeptical, latitudinarian urbanity (Hume), and encyclopedia-type education (Diderot) that belied the ruinous, bankrupt superficiality at work behind their generation's rococo makeup. In the Enlightenment one could become enthusiastically secular, and therefore thinner as a man.

An Idealistic reason, which Kant professed, seemed to be a conservative hiatus in the worship of rational Baal: the certainty of science was contained to make room for faith . . . in ethical noumena (*ideas* of God, immortal soul, plenary world) that could serve as North stars for men in uncharted waters, if they chose to be critically human. But Fichte, Hegel, Schelling, and others left behind the Emersonian tones of oversoul and speculative, pious transcendentalism and built altars to a brave new world of unlimited "freedom," German university scholarship, and an utterly Romantic Humanism. Then the sobering, hard facts of machines, coal dust, and the industrial slave world of misery that Dickens and Zola saw replaced the fantastic reaches of Beethoven's Ninth Symphony, the "Ancient Mariner" of Coleridge, and Delacroix's heroic turbulence. In the nineteenth century of philosophy AD men by and large served positive, scientifically-determined bits of knowledge. It was a very tough-minded, professional universe of thought; but thinkers like Comte, Feuerbach, Herbert Spencer, J. S. Mill, and Freud prophesied that this time—if men will only shuck their mythical prejudices and we can make our scientifically reasoned method foolproof—we shall achieve a rational millennium of sweetness and light, liberty, and balanced personalities.

It was in the shadow of such a Positivistic Reason-god, offering quantified certainty and scientifically guaranteed security, that Western men and women really began to lose their cultural roots, daily life bearings, and disintegrate into aimless atoms of unrelated, specialized activities. It is also in this setting of hard-core secularity that a big figure like Ernst Cassirer (1874–1945) began to make his contribution.

Cassirer of Berlin, Oxford, and Yale

Physical facts are known by observation and experiment that ends in your getting their measurements and in determining their causal relations, says Cassirer.[49] But Positivistically spirited thinkers dogmatically miss two points: (1) factual truth is not a matter of mental duplication of simple sense data impressions, because senses themselves are a viable form of the human spirit and even resultant sense-fact knowledge always depends upon the act of (subjective) judgment;[50] and (2) historical facts and the living reality of language, for example, are simply not "natural" phenomena and cannot justly be treated like external, inert, unhuman affairs.[51]

Support for (1) comes from the very nature of science, says Cassirer. It was not until Renaissance philosophy, when Galileo and Kepler converted "space" as a substantial substratum and "being" as an objective entity into a mathematical function and form of human knowing activity, that there existed for thought the universality required to order empirical occurrences into a logically controllable continuum of apodictic verity, i.e., scientific fact knowledge.[52] And these necessary, mathematical concepts, which deal with sub-sensible reality, do not derive from experience,

---

49 *An Essay on Man: An Introduction to a Philosophy of Human Culture* (1944) (Doubleday Anchor, 1953), 221. At present it seems to me that the philosophical position Cassirer has around 1923 remains basically the same until his death.

50 *The Philosophy of Symbolic Forms*, trans. R. Manheim (1923) (New Haven: Yale University Press, 1970), 1:87; *Essay on Man*, 220; ". . . the naked core of mere sensation, which merely *is* (without representing anything), never exists in the actual consciousness; if it exists at all, it is the prime example of that illusion which William James called 'the psychologist's fallacy.' Once we have fundamentally freed ourselves from this illusion, once we have recognized that not sensations but intuitions, not elements but formed totalities, comprise the data of consciousness, we can only ask: what is the relationship between the form of these intuitions and the representative function they have to fulfill?" *Philosophy of Symbolic Forms* (1929), 3:141.

51 *Symbolic Forms*, 1:167–176; *Essay on Man*, 241, 246–54.

52 *The Individual and the Cosmos in Renaissance Philosophy*, trans. Marlo Domandi (1927) (Harper: 1964), 182–84.

but are, rightly so, mental apriori's of the human subject.[53]

Support for (2) hangs together with that historically important functionalizing of substance, says Cassirer, because even though science is the highest possible attainment of human culture, our veritable Archimedean point of constancy,[54] there is more to the universe than is dreamt of in mathematical categories. In fact, mathematical-physical science is to be defined in terms of the unifying general, human cultural activity, not vice versa, and the realm of meaning and human life is much more important and original than any brute world facts or "being."[55] What mankind needs above all, says Cassirer, is self-knowledge. That means we need even more than a critique of Reason: it means a critique of culture. "Our objective is a phenomenology of human culture,"[56] a rigorous exposition of the polydimensional ways we men perceive, constitute, yes, construct reality. That makes me an idealist, says Cassirer, I know.[57] So what?

Cassirer is also, knowingly, a committed "Subjectivist." That is, for him, "objective," "intrinsically necessary," is a proper designation for whatever is culturally configured. Is the English language or great art of the ages any less "universally valid" than scientific concepts? he asks. Whatever free formative activity man exercises, thereby revealing his self-contained, human endeavor, is unquestionably valid, holds utterly objectively![58] When man says, "Let there be!" then there "is," and that

---

53 Cassirer affirms the Kepler-Galilei position of Rationalism in its Kantian "critical" format. Cf. his article on "Rationalism" in *Encyclopedia Britannica* 18 (14th edition, 1929): 991–93.

54 "It is science that gives us the assurance of a constant world. To science we may apply the words spoken by Archimedes *dos moi pou stô kai kosmon kinêsô*. . . . In a changing universe scientific thought fixes the points of rest, the unmovable poles" (*Essay on Man*, 261).

55 *Symbolic Forms*, 177: ". . . das, was wir den Gegenstand nennen, nicht in der Art einer festen und starren *forma substantialis*, sondern als Funktionsform zu fassen ist. Und es zeigt sich zugleich, wie sich der wahre Reichtum des *Seins* erst aus dem Reichtum des *Sinns* entfaltet . . ." ("Das Symbolproblem und seine Stellung im System der Philosophie," *Zeitschrift für Ästhetik und Allgemeine Kunstwissenschaft* 21 [1927]:312).

56 *Essay on Man*, 75.

57 ". . . the fundamental view on which this book rests: the conviction that language, like all basic functions of the human spirit, can be elucidated by philosophy only within a general system of philosophical idealism" (*Symbolic Forms*, 1:72).

58 "Every authentic function of the human spirit has this decisive characteristic in common with cognition: it does not merely copy but rather embodies an original, formative power. . . . Each of these functions creates its own symbolic forms . . . each of them designates a particular approach, in which and through which it constitutes its own aspect of 'reality.' They are not different modes in which an independent reality manifests itself to the human spirit but roads by which the spirit proceeds towards its

is the only kind of "objectivization" that counts. Or did you suppose "things" were in the saddle and ruled mankind?! Man is lord over reality. Of course there are "subjective" (=naturally personal, expressive) and "objective" (=consciously explicated, significant) poles oscillating within human consciousness;[59] but any form of human consciousness—and that includes the mythical mode of active presence in the world—is "objective" and normative simply because it is an "authentic function of the human spirit."[60]

Kant was too timid. In pivotal chapters 76–78 of his epochal *Kritik der Urteilskraft*, says Cassirer, Kant held back from going all the way in dissolving *Dinge an sich* into regulative Ideas of practical *Vernunft*; he still allowed das *Übersinnliche* to be an objective possibility for grounding the *Erscheinungen* with which *Verstand* must reckon. And Kant waffled dialectically on whether Nature could be completely understood in terms of mechanics or had to be fundamentally purposive; he affirmed *Naturzweck* as a regulative Idea of reflective *Urteilskraft*, as a heuristic principle for investigating the particular laws of Nature, yet he recommended we explain products and happenings of Nature, *selbst die zweckmässigsten*, as mechanically as possible![61] We should finish Kant's Copernican revolution: "things" and "the physical world" are *theoretical constructs*, and what we call "reality" and experience is a dynamic *spiritual life* that bears the stamp of inner necessity and hence of objectivity.[62] And it is the ideal

---

objectivization, i.e., its self-revelation" (*Symbolic Forms*, 1:78).

59 *Essay on Man*, 177.

60 "Its (myth) objectivity—and from the critical standpoint this is true of all cultural objectivity—must be defined not thing-wise but functionally: this objectivity lies neither in a metaphysical nor in an empirical-psychological 'reality' which stands *behind* it, but in what myth itself is and achieves, in the manner and form of *objectivization* which it accomplishes. It is objective insofar as it is recognized as one of the determining factors by which consciousness frees itself from passive captivity in sensory impressions and creates a world of its own in accordance with a spiritual principle" (*Philosophy of Symbolic Forms* [1925], 2:14).

61 *Kant Leben und Lehre* (Berlin: Bruno Cassirer, 1918), 372–84; *Essay on Man*, 79–80.

62 *Symbolic Forms*, 1:111; "Objectification is always a constructive process. The physical world—the world of constant things and qualities—is no mere bundle of sense data, nor is the world of art a bundle of feelings and emotions. The first depends upon acts of theoretical objectification, objectification by concepts and scientific constructs; the second upon formative acts of a different type, acts of contemplation" (*Essay on Man*, 204). ". . . the reality we apprehend is in its original form not a reality of a determinate world of things, originating apart from us; rather it is the certainty of a living efficacy that we experience. Yet this access to reality is given us not by datum of sensation but only in the original phenomenon of expression and expressive understanding" (*Symbolic Forms*, 3:73).

possibility of this spirit-life, with its autonomous, rich symbolic form creativity, says Cassirer, not "mere actuality," that should engage us as men.[63]

So Cassirer's vigorous, Neo-Idealistic Subjectivism approaches the world through man's creative *Wirklichkeit*, defining world and man in terms of human cultural functionality. There is a

> system of human activities, which defines and determines the circle of "humanity." Language, myth, religion, art, science, history are the constituents, the various sectors of this circle.[64]

> Not only science, but language, myth, art, and religion as well, provide the building stones from which the world of "reality" is constructed for us, as well as that of the human spirit, in sum the World-of-the-I. Like scientific cognition, they are not simple structures which we can insert into a given world, we must understand them as functions by means of which a particular form is given to reality and in each of which specific distinctions are effected.[65]

And these various species of symbolic form, better, formative cultural energy, are in perpetual strife, says Cassirer, as conflicting forces in extreme opposition. Sophisticated scientific thought busy classifying the "relations" of things in a methodologically deterministic way contradicts and would suppress mythical feelings, characterized by an elemental, physiognomic sym-pathy with life in a deep kind of uncritical, primitive way; and art may appropriately claim to be "perhaps the most durable and intense pleasure of which human nature is capable," but striving for such sensuously concrete spirit life rules out formal, structural elements like language, which needs to be a vehicle for careful thought.[66] Yet these oppositions, and even an inherent polar tension, an "inner contradictoriness" that shows up in each specific symbolic form itself, does not sunder but only reinforces the dynamic unity and eruptive, living force of Human cultural, formative power.[67] *Human life* is a single (harmonious

---

63 "... image-worlds whose principle and origin are to be sought in an autonomous creation of the spirit. Through them alone we see what we call 'reality,' and in them alone we possess it: for the highest objective truth that is accessible to the spirit is ultimately the form of its own activity" (*Symbolic Forms*, 1:111). See also *Essay on Man*, 82–86.

64 *Essay on Man*, 93.

65 *Symbolic Forms*, 1:91.

66 *Essay on Man*, 95–96, 109, 163, 202, 273–75.

67 "The world of the spirit forms a very concrete unity, so much so that the most extreme oppositions in which it moves appear as somehow mediated oppositions" (*Symbolic Forms*, 3:78). "... here there is a demand that consciousness—contrary to its fundamental character, contrary to the Heraclitean flux in which alone it seems to subsist ..." (3:115). "The symbolic process is like a single stream of life and thought which

contradictory) process, Cassirer believes, of *becoming culture*.

In contrast to the holy exclusivity practiced by so many Dualist analyses of creation's fabric, the thrust of inclusiveness found in Cassirer's Geneticistic Monism makes a happy impression. He delineates an interwoven order to the jumble of symbolic form moments;[68] he makes a special point of affirming mythic consciousness as a permanent, legitimate configuration of the human spirit;[69] and he takes pains to show how, in varying stages of being "posited," "internal antitheses" of sensuous-spiritual/being-meaning /life-spirit (=*tropai!*) permeate commonly and determine together our structurally different "modes of seeing," viz., myth, language, art, and historiography (although science seems to have exorcized the dialectic from its rarefied realm of pure signification)[70] (see figure 4).

COSMOGONIC HUMANITY (figure 4)

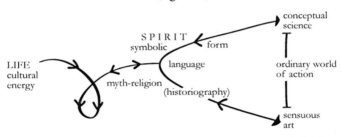

flows through consciousness, and which by this flowing movement produces the diversity and cohesion, the richness, the continuity, and constancy, of consciousness" (3:202). "The inner contradictoriness, the polarity which necessarily dwells within every such form, does not rend or demolish it; rather it constitutes the condition whereby its unity may again be established out of that contradiction and may thus again present itself to the outside world" ("Spirit' and 'Life' in Contemporary Philosophy" [1930], trans. R. W. Bretall and P.A. Schilpp, in *The Philosophy of Ernst Cassirer*, ed. P.A. Schilpp [Evanston: Library of Living Philosophers. 1949], 880).

68 "Language stands in a focus of cultural life, a point at which rays of quite diverse origin converge and from which lines of influence radiate to every sphere of culture" (*Symbolic Forms*, 1:175). ". . . language, as a general cultural form, stands on the borderline between myth and logos and also represents an intermediary between the theoretical and aesthetic approach to the world" (1:297–98).

69 *Symbolic Forms*, 2:4.

70 *Symbolic Forms*, 1:318–319; 2:245, 250; 3:54.93. See also *Essay on Man*: "If there is any characteristic and outstanding feature of the mythical world, any law by which it is governed—it is this law of metamorphosis" (108). "Language is, by its very nature and essence, metaphorical. Unable to describe things directly, it resorts to indirect modes of description, to ambiguous and equivocal terms" (142). "In aesthetic life we experience a radical transformation" (204). "It is this 'palingenesis.' this rebirth of the past, which marks and distinguishes the great historian" (225).

The trouble with this acute depiction comes when the mesh of symbolic forms itself is declared "a mobile order" and the differing levels of consciousness are interpreted ontogenetically as begetting one another dialectically.[71] The trouble comes when the origination of cultural activity is sought in "the *ultima ratio*, the power of the miraculous and mysterious," Life itself, and keeps receding till one agrees that man "remains a *homo absconditus*," and the circle of symbolic forms remains unbroken as a constantly recurring, continually changing "dynamic equilibrium" of circling, coexistent contraries in contradictory unity.[72] The trouble comes because the wages of a Contradictory Geneticistic Monism are an introvertish darkness as to source, an uncertain threat as to whether the concatenated framework enveloping everything will have the resilience to surprise us once more with its protean maneuverability; and always there is that logically irreproachable, inevitably necessary reversion to the hidden rootage—replenish the vitality of culture with elemental formative energy—an everlasting shadow that plagues development . . . nevertheless, affirmed![73]

Always above the sound of cultural strife and excitement Cassirer keeps his eye fixed on Humanity, not so much on so many men or "the individual consciousness" as on "the universal subject."[74] When individual Goethe coins new language as poet, his "single act of speech flows again back into the great river-bed of language itself, yet without being entirely lost," maybe even altering the current as a whole "in its direction and intensity, in its dynamics and rhythm."[75] So individuals and their acts serve the cosmic Cultural process as tiny centers of formative energy microcosmically duplicating and contributing, at different loci, to the One main activity. Men, for Cassirer, are monadic eddies or little springs

---

71 *Symbolic Forms*, 2:235; 3:115; *Essay on Man*, 215.

72 *Symbolic Forms*, 2:xv; *Essay on Man*, 29; "The various forms of human culture are not held together by an identity in their nature but by a conformity in their fundamental task. If there is an equipoise in human culture it can only be described as a dynamic, not as a static equilibrium; it is the result of a struggle between opposing forces" (Ibid. 279). *The Myth of the State* (posthumously, 1946) (New Haven: Yale University Press, 1983), 279.

73 For example: Cassirer genially explains why Nazism and racism, for example, cannot be refuted by argument—political myths have to be grappled with as myths, not as ludicrous arguments (*Myth of the State*, 279, 297). There seems to be an onus on reverting to "myths" as a man of twentieth century culture and science. Yet Cassirer insists upon their relative, anthropological values (*Essay on Man*, 103).

74 *Essay on Man*, 88.

75 "'Spirit' and 'Life' in Contemporary Philosophy," Schilpp, ed. *The Philosophy of Ernst Cassirer*, 879; see also 877.

pointillating the huge maelstrom of Humanity, that is, the great Culture-forming that shall make us free indeed?

> Human culture taken as a whole may be described as the process of man's progressive self-liberation. Language, art, religion, science, are various phases in this process. In all of them man discovers and proves a new power—the power to build up a world of his own, an "ideal" world.[76]

The fact that this great mission of Man is Utopia—in Cassirer's own words!—only stirs man alive "and endows him with a new ability, the ability constantly to reshape his human universe."[77]

Such faith in Humanity is an old-time religion, and Cassirer's volumes are an exceptionally grand confession of it. Anyone whose vision is shaped by the biblical Word of God, however, sees immediately that the Cultural King in Cassirer's procession has no clothes on. The stirring and intricate, probing and insightful Culturalism of Ernst Cassirer is a no-god made by a man's hand, and those who feel secure with such a brilliant man-made "god," says Psalm 115, will become like it (Psalm 115:4–8): busybusy, principled, little old-style idealists aware of tradition, open to innovation, toughened by Positivism, curbed from Romantic excess, but incurably sold on building, through ups and downs, advances and reverses, a richer and more noble Babylon in the hearts and lives of humankind. This particular idol worship allows no sabbath rest (not for disciples of Heraclitus, Meister Eckhart, or Machiavelli any more than for those who follow Cassirer). There is no opening for the Holy Spirit's healing, Christ's reconciling, the Lord God's establishing the beginning of *God's* gentle Rule upon the earth (see Isaiah 65:17–25): only an unceasing, combative (cultural) imperialism proper to this Geneticistic Contradictory Monistic universe of thought. There is no opening for the Holy Spirit, because Cassirer's favorite hymn, so to speak, would be, "Dwell in me, O blessed Cultural Activity . . ."

Evaluation of Cassirer's contribution makes a Christ-believer sad. Babel was no shucks as architecture either. Cassirer rightly latched wrongly onto the coram Deo response-ability peculiar to humans in creation's covenant to praise the Lord. Cassirer saw that man's glory did not have the transparent muteness of moon and stars, plants and animals; there is indeed a tête-à-tête, reflexive play inside the human's initiative and action in the world. Because Cassirer rejected grounding man's cultivating task in the body of Jesus Christ as ποῦ στῶ he tried to affirm the cultural task itself unconditionally. He had the insight not to champion culture to the

---

76 *Essay on Man*, 286.
77 *Essay on Man*, 86.

exclusion of nature and not pretend to evolve culture out of a continuum with nature; but Cassirer's attempt to relate culturing man and an original nature in a contradictory, polar union in which culture becomes the saving revelation of nature that becomes the source of life for culture[78] will not do either, because such a position confusingly reads cultivating man back into a cosmic, general nature and then antinomically reads that very nature out of man's culturing activity. From a biblical point of view, this world-bound position of Cassirer damns man to a restless, everlasting search for completion and final meaning that cannot help but be frustrated, because it's like the quest as an earthling for the holy grail—it would disappear as holy if you found and touched it.

Put briefly: Cassirer blindly misidentifies culture as creation and thus makes man God. His Neo-Idealistic Spirit affects modesty in not promising results, just the methods to work at results, and he is genuinely serious about redeeming man from barbarism for an abundant life. His philosophy does offer a loosening correction to much Positivistic dogma, as well as some protection against the technocratic death in Pragmatism and defeatism in Existentialism. Cassirer gives fruitful leads on the interrelational differences and order of formative/aesthetic/lingual/logical activities. But irremedially evil, centrally infecting all his analysis, is the fact that he turns the glorious *theatrum Dei* of creation into a *tohuwabohu* and mindlessly (ἐσκοτίσθη ἡ ἀσύνετος αὐτῶν καρδία, Romans 1:21) appropriates for human credit, in the Name of Cultural Task, the cosmic saving work of Jesus.[79]

Culture is a tremendously powerful idol because it corrupts something so close to the heart of us humans (Satan reserved it for the hardest temptation to Christ; Matthew 4:1–11). Cassirer's active Cultural Imperialism should put us on guard who mean to make earnest with a new-style Reformation, lest we be seduced by a twentieth-century impatience to covet and fight to get God's kingdom (methodologically) in the hand rather than in the bush. —I do not imply the biblical alternative is jump-

---

78 *Symbolic Forms*, 2:26; 3:189–90. "(Culture) is an organon of our self-knowledge . . ." (*Essay on Man*, 260).

79 "This spontaneity and productivity is the very center of all human activities. It is man's highest power and it designates at the same time the natural boundary of our human world. In language, in religion, in art, in science, man can do no more than to build up his own universe—a symbolic universe that enables him to understand and interpret, to articulate and organize, to synthesize and universalize his human experience" (*Essay on Man*, 278), "Cognition, language, myth and art: none of them is a mere mirror, simply reflecting images of inward or outward data; they are not indifferent media, but rather *the true sources of light, the prerequisite of vision*, and the wellsprings of all formation" (italics CGS) (*Symbolic Forms*, 1:93).

ing off a pinnacle of the temple to make your personal testimony of trust in the infallible Word of God, and let culture go at that! But it is still true: those who would save their life through cultural activity shall lose it, and whoever picks up one's inescapable gift of cultural activity *for Christ's sake* (in the spirit of 1 Corinthians 7:31, ὡς μὴ καταχρώμενοι)—able to let it go!—shall truly find life in their Covenanted, creaturely cultural task, and may expect with joy an obedient pilgrim-culture to be established by the Lord God self! who in Jesus Christ and through the workings of the Holy Spirit is specially faithful to the generations who stay close to the LORD God (Psalm 148:11–14).

Pedagogical Strengths of this Reformational Christian Methodology

One mark of normed teaching is simplification, and *sound simplification* characterizes the christian philosophical historiographic method I have illustrated. You face a student with a text and say, let's find out now, from the text, what the temper of the times were, and how did he think his world fit together, what did he recommend we live for, what's final in his book? You look inductively in the text for answers to your interview. Where are you, Cassirer, in the garden of our Lord God? ("Oh, walking up and down throughout the whole earth, very very busy studying civilization, a personal and universal view. . . .") What do you think of Jesus Christ, Machiavelli? ("I can't see him because the ruthlessly powerful Church obstructs my view. . . .") Meister Eckhart, what time is it historically? ("A time to throw stones and a time to pick up stones, a time to love and a time to hate. . . .") Who are your friends, Heraclitus, and who are your enemies? ("Much learning does not teach understanding, otherwise it would have taught Homer and Pythagoras, Xenophanes and Hectaeus. . . .")

That is, when you begin teaching the history of philosophy, of course you disguise your scientifically precise categories in a story-telling, narrative type of way. But the point is, you focus the student's attention in on the nub of the philosophical matter; you don't just let them wander down the primrose path strewn with stones, smelling the flowers. Beginning students who don't know precisely what to look out for get lost, or simply take down and scholastically mouth whatever the teacher tells them. With four or five interview questions, you can get them listening, looking, detecting themselves, as co-workers with the instructor, what counts for the philosophical text in front of them. And it is not mickey mouse or special pleading to find out whether a given thinker be Dualist or Monist. In his or her view of the human and the world, is the thinker a Universalist, Individualist, or something else? are you a Subjectivist, Objectivist, or Realist? Herschel Baker noted:

> The history of ideas, like the history of music, is astonishing for the virtually infinite variations and permutations of a few basic factors. That thousands of tunes have been written from the twelve tones of our scale is no more astonishing than that for about twenty centuries men have been working out combinations and developments of perhaps half a dozen basic ideas.[80]

That's right, and to be vague about the basic components of a philosophy—which is always formed by a certain constellation of leading ideas that constitute a committed perspective—serves no one in teaching the history of philosophy.

"Should you hammer away at the basic categories in the abstract and then apply them only when you know what they mean? or do you start reading Kant and then figure out whether and what categories make sense?" That is a question like whether one should learn declensions, conjugations, and the *der-die-das-die* paradigm first or should you begin sounding out *Vater unser*—which comes first, chicken or the egg? The answer is neither. The key to stop christian learning from becoming rote is to see the confessional depth to one's fundamental, working categories.

> I ran for cover once during a summer cloudburst in Florence to a tiny storefront doorway. Suddenly another figure raced there for refuge, a gaunt fellow with large, yellowed teeth and scraggily hair. Come to find out, he was an enthusiastic follower of Giordano Bruno, great Italian Renaissance philosopher (c. 1548–1600). The rain streamed down as he waxed eloquent in our cramped shelter on the truth of Bruno's philosophy. To counter my objections he began to shout, *Iddio è nel tutto. Poggi'! Poggi'!! Tutto è il Dio!* The smallest drop of rain is God! And as he shouted, hooked teeth close in to my face, gesticulating madly at the torrential, pounding rain, literally pouring down upon us, I understood what he meant. Since that day wet to the skin, Universalism, *understood christianly*, has never been for me a bookish term.

One should get an initial, skeleton understanding of the concepts and then see them grow flesh-and-blood meaning in the body of a philosopher's writing. It takes time to get a feel for these carefully circumscribed problems, and one does well not to start learning the history of philosophy by reading Cassirer or Kant or a complex modern thinker: but after years of experience you can almost sense the philosophical neighborhood you are likely in after reading only a few chapters attentively—

---

80 Herschel Baker, *The Image of Man: A study of the idea of human dignity in classical antiquity, the middle ages, and the renaissance* (Harper, 1961), 301.

Beginners would be helped to do disciplined christian analysis in the history of philosophy if they could be led to search, within a single text, for the thinker's answers to these basic questions, and reach tentative conclusions on the quite definite crucibles in which the answers seem to take shape. That's a simple way to start—not that every text has a worked out philosophical systematics! The more sure-footed a teacher is, the more representative or pivotal or influential a text the teacher will select for the communal investigation and research, knowing the students' abilities.

Another mark of normed teaching is opening up things provocatively. Next to its sound simplification—pointing precisely to the philosophical crux you must examine—the christian method of doing philosophical historiography I have illustrated has built-in for use in teaching a *panoramic sweep and relational pregnance*. Every time you approximate a given thinker's typological slant and *Zeitgeist*, immediately every other thinker you have ever met in that neighborhood, throughout the ages, comes to mind, and sparks of recognition, insight, and questions start to crowd the classroom; and everything you know about that certain period of history from its art and fashions, music, wars, and social conditions, becomes grist for filtering down to illuminate the Spirit gripping the text.

For example, in connection with the neighborhood of Geneticistic Contradictory Monism, this method spurs you to notice and ask: Would Hobbes be in the same ball park with Machiavelli, or would their neighborhoods just be close enough so they could talk over the backyard fence? Does this mean Hegel and Lenin are really bed-fellows, with essentially the same structure to their thought?—so people don't need to be mystified that Hegel got picked up by "dialectical materialism," and it's very true, obvious! what Peter Viereck mentioned in 1949 that fascism and (Soviet) communism are two sides of the same coin![81] And no wonder Cassirer spent half-a-book time parsing, of all people, Nicholas Cusanus.[82] It makes sense too that Cassirer, who gave the last word to Heraclitus,[83] could be so dispassionately positive toward Machiavelli

---

81 Peter Viereck, *Conservatism Revisited* (1949).

82 "Of all the philosophical movements and efforts of the Quattro-cento, only his doctrines fulfil Hegel's demand; only they represent a 'simple focal point' in which the most diverse rays are gathered. Cusanus is the only thinker of the period to look at all of the fundamental problems of his time from the point of view of one principle through which he masters them all" (*The Individual and the Cosmos*, 7).

83 "The dissonant is in harmony with itself; the contraries are not mutually exclusive, but interdependent: 'harmony in contrariety, as in the case of the bow and the lyre'" (*Essay on Man*, 286).

around Hitler's time[84] and not see that opportunism and imperialistic fascism is built-in to the thought-pattern of Hegel![85] And it's not unusual then, since Meister Eckhart attracted those rebelling against Scholastic Thomism, that Geneticistic Kierkegaard became a rallying point for those fed up with a Spiritualistic Lutheranism in the state of Denmark and the Scholastic Structuralism of so much stuffy, late nineteenth century Protestant orthodoxism? And so on.

The point is, this kind of opening-up, encyclopedic stimulation comes independent of whether the professor has a fascinating classroom personality or not (which is not, of course, to be discounted pedagogically). And the provocative stimulation is directed toward *philosophical* matters—a weak teacher of philosophy will often take refuge in general cultural history. (Also, when you are teaching the history of *philosophy*, the important *Zeitgeist* study must elucidate the *philosophical* position and not dissipate that focus.) Beginning students are not penalized because of their incomplete knowledge by this directed stimulation. Rather, if a student who has been analyzing Heraclitus carefully hears mentioned in the same neighborhood-breath thinkers like Cusanus, Eckhart, Machiavelli, Hegel, Kierkegaard, Lenin, and Cassirer, he makes a mental note of it, like receiving a fleeting handshake in a crowd, until he can go back and talk at length with Hegel. This method helps one slowly build up firsthand knowledge in the history of philosophy without being locked up, as it were, in a monographic room.

The strong panoramic sweep and relational pregnance is not forced. Similar type of philosophic position does not mean "influence" the way so may empiricistic Structuralistic thinkers would push it, on the model of physio-chemical, direct-effect causality (which, incidentally, only atomizes the historiography of philosophy into unrelated snapshot studies

---

84 *Myth of the State*, 153–154, 162. Cassirer believes one could extol the State but not thereby support a modern totalitarian system, so long as the State is kept from monitoring the culture (274–276).

85 "In this respect Hegelianism is one of the most paradoxical phenomena in modern cultural life. There is perhaps no better and more striking example of the dialectical character of history than the fate of Hegelianism itself. The principle defended by Hegel is suddenly converted into its opposite. Hegel's logic and philosophy seemed to be the triumph of the rational. The only thought which philosophy brings with it is the simple conception of Reason; that the history of the world presents us with a rational process. But it was the tragic fate of Hegel that he unconsciously unchained the most irrational powers that have ever appeared in man's social and political life. No other philosophical system has done so much for the preparation of fascism and imperialism as Hegel's doctrine of the state—this 'divine Idea as it exists on earth'" (*Myth of the State*, 273).

or the interminable "no doubt" evidence of so many Ph.D. theses).[86]
It just becomes an exhilarating, integrative experience for a student to
discover, at best by surprise, without being explicitly told, how similar
in makeup, for example, Heraclitus, Eckhart, Machiavelli, Hegel, and
Cassirer really are. Suddenly there comes a wholesome ordering principle into the unholy disarray of unrelated figures! And once one is able
to grasp that philosophic historical continuity is typological rather than
genetic, teleological, or nonexistent, and one begins to contrast philosophical neighborhoods,[87] the excitement increases, because then one is
empowered to expose the many false alternatives men and women have
stupidly accepted and reject the oversimplifications prevalent in traditional philosophical historiography, thanks to a largely common (unbiblical) myopia and astigmatic vision. Again, such provocative integration
is not dependent upon the learning and wisdom of a given teaching personality, but is a strength this particular method encourages and affords.

A key mark of normed teaching that would be a witness to christian
pedagogy is confrontation of the student with the Truth. *Structured confrontation with the Truth* is indeed an exceptional strength and blessing
of the philosophical historiographic method I have illustrated and recommend for teachers who are in earnest about christian historiography
of philosophy. You are faced by this method with the fact that there is
nothing new under the sun in philosophy if your stance on the crucial,
fundamental issues is at odds with the vision that the Biblical Scriptures
ask us to accept and obey. "Nothing new under the sun" does not just
mean your philosophy is unoriginal, repetitive, or dull. "Nothing new
under the sun" means, for example, that if your thought-pattern falls into
the contours of a Geneticistic Contradictory Monism, your philosophy is
filled with the Lie and is a philosophic Way of death!

You have compromised the open revelation of God in creation,
epitomized redemptively in God's Son, and made graciously known to
us fallen creatures again in the Bible, by confessing that the Source of
everything is hidden, whimsical, and uncertain. You have negated the
reality of sin by absorbing the matter of direction as well as structure into
an ongoing process that has no room for right and wrong, obedience and
disobedience against the law of the Lord, but only relative good responses
in contrary and contradictory tension, temporary failings that will come

---

86 See my comment on "Influence" in "Wisdom underneath Vollenhoven's Categories,"
    130 {see *AH*: 5}.

87 I had to omit this important feature from my illustration, like comparing Machiavelli
    with Francis Bacon or Cassirer with Croce, in order to keep a measure of brevity.

out in the wash. If you are a thinker caught in a Geneticistic Contradictory Monistic neighborhood of philosophy, you contrive to efface the
real struggle in history between the Rule of Jesus Christ and the godless
principalities of this eon by making-believe we should fight the good
fight of an elite race against the masses, gnostics against ritualists, the cultured against the unlettered, one nation against another earthly nation,
misleading and being misled. And you have smothered the possibility of
repentance and sanctified action among humans into a generally unat-
tached, deeply energetic, give-your-guts fervor of heroic activity. Such is
the particular dead-end character within the philosophical neighborhood
of Geneticistic Contradictory Monism.

This christian method of philosophical historiography makes clear
that there are a number of different, recurrent conceptual neighborhoods
(or, if you will, "families of ideas") that hold men and women captive,
and are attractive, thoughtful ways to go to hell. That has tremendous
pedagogical strength, because then teaching and learning the history of
philosophy is not some pointless archive work churned out by remote
specialists or like playing bridge well: it is a matter of life and death! So
it is, done christianly. Anyone whose mind is framed by a godless philosophical neighborhood—even a born-again Christian—is dead wrong,
and such a thought-perspective must be converted, subjected to Jesus
Christ, on pain of much evil and misery. And it is never a question of being fair or "doing justice" to a "dead thinker" as a christian teacher in the
history of philosophy. Instead, a christian teacher must make Machiavelli
or Kant or, say, Sartre, live as vividly as Proverbs 7 details the doings of
"the strange woman," so that students may indeed sense the seductive
pull of each earnest idolatry—idols are never straw men—the terrible,
suicidal vanity that makes you covet it yourself and simultaneously weep
bitterly at such wasted brilliance. The christian philosophical historiography I have illustrated sets up this kind of pedagogical confrontation
within biblically sure, christian categories that firmly lead one to discern
Truth clearly from the complicities of error.

Let no one think a christian philosophical historiographic methodology encourages students to hole away in their own little christian
neighborhood and close the doors and windows, since there is so much
contagious philosophical disease around. No Christian may be so self-
centered.

We who do have the Truth in philosophically earthen vessels[88] are

---

88 I have come to be unembarrassed by the fact that the Reformation, especially as
    captured in the perspective developed by John Calvin, was an important gift of God

called upon, if that is our professional ministry, to serve the philosophical neighborhoods of the world, devastated today by a plague of secular disbelief in Jesus Christ's Rule, serve them with critically christian, philosophical historiographic instruments and healing, before it is autopsy time. Not only to help protect the little ones of God's folk from stumbling, but also to be obedient in loving our neighbor, lest when the Lord returns he say, "And why did you not visit me (ἐνι . . . τῶν ἐλαχίστων) in the neighborhood of Geneticistic Contradictory Monism, and give me a cup of cold water and make me privy to your philosophical shalom?"[89]

I pray that this volume honoring Prof. J. A. L. Taljaard may encourage many of the younger generation of God's people to join in the work he has shared, studying and teaching redemptively the history of philosophy, so that the Lord may greet a host of obedient philosophical witnesses too, as faithful servants.

---

to Western civilization, already blessed with strains of faulty, christian cultural obedience. I adjudge the idea of a christian philosophy developed by Vollenhoven and Dooyeweerd out of that historic root to be not "under the sun" but enlightened by the Word of God enough—inceptionally—so that it does service in the order of Melchizadek. Its troubled cosmic contours cannot be charted, it seems to me, in any of the (distorted) philosophical neighborhoods Vollenhoven himself has unearthed.

89 Jaap Klapwijk's formula of "complete openness and total opposition" of the Christian to non-christian thinking is probably correct ("Calvin and Neo-Calvinism on Non-Christian Philosophy" in *The Idea of a Christian Philosophy*, 61); but it may give a better setting for our work to replace "ambiguity and ambivalence of non-christian thinking" with the terms Paul uses: ignorant (Acts 17:30) and perverse (Romans 1:18).

Section of Seerveld study, Toronto, Canada, 2000 AD

EARLY KANT AND A ROCOCO SPIRIT:
SETTING FOR *THE CRITIQUE OF JUDGMENT*

The Kant of Critical Pure Reason has been so etched upon generations of academic minds that popular scholarship acts as if Kant began to exist when he was almost sixty years old. (Kant was born 1724. His *Kritik der reinen Vernunft* was published 1781.) In a paper read on the bicentenary of Kant's birth, E. F. Carritt said:

> Kant's pre-critical treatise *Beobachtungen über das Gefühl des Schönen und Erhabenen* of 1764 is a very dull performance, which makes such classifications as that men are sublime and women beautiful, the English character sublime and the French beautiful. . . . The serious business begins in 1790 with *Die Kritik der Urteilskraft.*[1]

I should like to maintain the opposite in this paper: that Kant's observations on the feeling of the beautiful and sublime constitute a fascinating Aufklärung essay; and I should like to begin to demonstrate that if one takes Kant's *Observations* seriously, one gains important insight for understanding the *Critique of Judgment-power.* The fact that Kant's marginalia and interleaf notes made in his own copy of the *Observations* during the year(s) following its publication almost equal the length of the *Critique of Practical Reason* shows that at least Kant took the *Observations* seriously at the time (*KGS* 20:1–192),[2] even if many Kant scholars since have not. Now that the benign neglect of the third *Critique* is ending,[3]

---

1   E. F. Carritt, "The Sources and Effects in England of Kant's Philosophy of Beauty," in *Immanuel Kant,* Papers read at Northwestern University on the Bicentenary of Kant's Birth (Chicago: Open Court, 1925), 179–180.

2   All *KGS* designations refer to the edition of Kant's *Gesammelte Schriften* published by the Preussischen Akademie der Wissenschaften (Berlin, 1900–1955, 23 volumes), the volume: page-relevant/lines. Translations are my responsibility. I am happy to thank my colleague Albert Wolters for continually pulling my idiom back to literalness.

3   Cf. Hans-Georg Juchem, Die *Entwicklung des Begriffs des Schönen bei Kant* (Bonn, 1970), T. E. Uehling, Jr., *The Notion of Form in Kant's Critique of Aesthetic Judgment* (The Hague, 1971), Karel Kuypers, *Kants Kunsttheorie und die Einheit der Kritik der*

This essay was first published in *Philosophia Reformata* 43:3–4 (1978): 145–167.

we need as full a picture as possible of its setting, to help us understand the "argument."

There is one simple methodological principle integral to my analysis I wish to specify.

Two variables that define a thinker's position are (1) the basic conceptual pattern that structures his or her interrelating matters, and (2) *Zeitgeist*, an informing spirit of the times. The nexus of these two variable factors normally outline the historical position from which a thinker contributes knowledge or holds mistaken theses.

It is clarifying to note that thinkers with fundamentally different problematics may share the same spirit, and thinkers of a different age or driven by a different *Zeitgeist* may hold to a similarly structured, basic conceptual pattern of thought. Hume and Swedenbourg shared an Enlightenment spirit, but their ways of handling problems were as different as that of an urbane empiricist and a visionary theosophist. Both Hegel and Cusanus were committed to the Heraclitean orientation of *coincidentia oppositorum*. But the contours of Cusanus' thought breathed a transitional, fifteenth-century spirit of trying to recapture some kind of Patristic, synthetic christian humanism in the face of both Scholasticism and the Renaissance; Hegel's dialectic, on the other hand, was spirited by a surging, self-reliant Idealism that captivated many cultural formers of Europe moving into the nineteenth century.

This is not the place to argue for the reality of *Zeitgeist* or to document examples of illuminating combinations. I mention here these two co-ordinates of a thinker's position to clarify the heuristic device I use to analyze the development of a given man or woman's thought, a methodological principle that also helps one be more specific in delineating "influence."

Early Kant's moorings

As everyone knows, Immanuel grew up in one of the biggest seaports of East Prussia, solidly Lutheran Königsberg. His pious mother died when he was thirteen and had to be buried at poor-house costs, without the usual school children singing beside the coffin as it was carried to the

---

Urteilskraft (Amsterdam, 1972), Karl Neumann, *Gegenständlichkeit und Existenzbedeutung des Schönen* (Bonn, 1973), Donald W. Crawford, *Kant's Aesthetic Theory* (University of Wisconsin Press, 1974), Francis X. Coleman, *The Harmony of Reason: A study in Kant's aesthetics* (University of Pittsburg Press, 1974), a full day Symposium on Kant's Philosophy of Art, held at the 33rd annual meeting of the American Society for Aesthetics, in Baltimore, 31 October 1975, with papers by Ted Cohen, Coleman, Crawford, Ingrid Stadler.

graveyard.

> My mother often took me outside the city to make me notice the great works of God. She'd stand there in a quiet rapture talking aloud about the almighty wisdom and goodness of God. She engraved on my heart a deep reverence for the Creator of all things. I'll never forget my mother, for she planted and nourished the first seed of goodness in me; she opened up my heart to the myriad impressions of Nature. . . .[4]

Kant spent eight early years (1732–1740) at the pietist gymnasium Fridericianum, which was run by headmaster Franz Albert Schultz with a puritanic, spit and polish rigor worthy of its Prussian patron, Frederick Wilhelm I. Although Kant lodged at home, he underwent the full impact of Christian Wolff theology, drilled memorizing of the Latin poets, untold exercises in German versification, geography studies—part of the pietist reform in schooling—and a long, daily regimen of enforced prayers and quiet times. Fridericianum discipline drove out of Kant's mind any appreciation for christianity as a living faith, left him with an abiding passion for pedagogical reform, and stamped his habits and style for life.

At Königsberg University (1740–1746) he lived, of necessity, a frugal student life while specializing in mathematical and physical philosophy. Professor Martin Knutzen led Kant deep into Newton and Leibniz, so much so that after Kant finished his studies and spent eight years out in the farmland countryside away from Königsberg tutoring for his livelihood, first to the boys of a Reformed pastor and then to the sons of Major Bernhard Friedrich von Hülsen, when he returned to the city, what he published to achieve his *magister* degree, his *venia legendi* as *Privatdozent* at the university (*A New Clarification on the Principia of Metaphysical Knowledge*, 1755), and in his try for a professorship, which didn't materialize (*The Use of Metaphysics Joined with Geometry in Natural Philosophy, for example, a Physical Monadology*, 1756), all was basically Leibnizian. Kant made fine points to contrast and establish his position as his own, but he posited a universal system of corresponding substances whose mutual dependence of spirits in bodies and bodies in spirits was rigorously determined and masterminded by God (*KGS* 1:415–17/416–4); "freedom" is a name for spontaneous action governed by principles of internal, sufficient reason (*KGS* 1:402–12/20).

In a long anonymous publication Kant meant to be popular, written

---

4   Conversation with Kant transcribed by his trusted friend R. B. Jachmann, in *Immanuel Kant: sein Leben in Darstellungen von Zeitgenossen* (Darmstadt: Wissenschaftliche Buchgesellschaft, 1968, photographic reprint of the Felix Gross edition of 1912), 162–163.

in German, *General Cosmogony and Theory of the Heavens* (1755), spiced with half a dozen quotes from Pope's *Essay on Man*, along with the English Addison and the "most sublime," "philosophic" German poet, Albrecht von Haller, Kant presented a thoroughly secular hypothesis on the self-contained ("mechanical") genesis of our solar system. He corrected Newton who ascribed the order of planetary motion to "the immediate hand of God," by asserting that the original chaos of elementary stuff had in itself a natural aspiration to develop its more perfect formation, thanks to its being matter "that essentially follows the timeless pattern of Divine Intelligence" (*KGS* 1:262–63). Kant concluded the piece with a rhetorical speculation imagining one's immortal soul winging its way through the limitless expanse of the heavens, spending its endless future, "which the grave merely alters but cannot interrupt," getting an extra-terrestrial look at our own earth, viewing the satellites of Jupiter and other amazing things from close by; when you look at it that way,

> then the view of a starry firmament on a clear night affords a kind of cheerful pleasure that only noble souls can be sensitive to. Surrounded by the complete stillness of Nature and in the utter quietude of one's consciousness, the hidden knowing ability of your immortal spirit starts to speak unutterable speech and to proffer undisclosable thoughts, which you sense all right, but could never articulate. . . . (*KGS* 1:367–27/33)

After the terrible Lisbon earthquake of 1755 Kant took to the local newspapers to explain the *natural* causes and effects of earthquakes, and to challenge philosophically the "culpable forwardness" of the many sermonic interpretations of Lisbon that presumed earthquakes to be judgments of God upon wicked people. We don't know how God intends to rule the world, wrote Kant, but the moral is simply "that material goods can never afford satisfaction for the human drive to happiness." He practically quotes Pope's *Essay on Man* (i.60)—"Tis a part we see, and not a whole"—to curb man's temptation to think himself *all*-important. But just as Nature in her wisdom subordinates lower purposes in apparent violation of natural laws to achieve still higher purposes, argued Kant, so the human race must not act fated when faced with catastrophes (*KGS* 1:459–26/461–14) but "itself prescribe laws for the course of natural things"! So wrote Kant in journalistic awareness of the war breaking out among enlightened men of several European nations that spring, which was to last seven years.

The same steady optimism and excited curiosity for worldwide phenomena shows up in Kant's announcement for his lectures in Physical Geography (1757):

... I shall first lecture on [the animal, plant, and mineral kingdoms] in the natural order of classes, and shall finally treat all countries of the earth in a geographical survey so as to show the inclinations of men, which flow from the particular climate in which they live, and I shall examine the variety of human prejudices and ways of thinking, so far as it can serve to make Man better acquainted with himself. . . . (*KGS* 2:9–17/22)

Even the proper study of physical geography is man!

Kant's thoughts on matters "aesthetic" at this point were undeveloped, subordinate, and scholastically Baumgartian, something you treated briefly in a course on logic. When your lower sensitive powers click in an accord that yields pleasure, such a sense-judgment, for example, of a picturesque item in the descriptive passage of an epic poem, is called "taste," said Kant, and that kind of forthright sense knowledge is "aesthetic knowledge" (*KGS* 16:100–4/15 and 16:107–5/6). But early Kant's major concerns were in Nature science, bursting with an élan that later embarrassed him (for example, in an essay, *Some Considerations on Optimism*, 1759):

... I rejoice in realizing I am a citizen in a world that could not be better! . . . [although] I am a minor member, unworthy in myself, selected only for the sake of the Whole, I esteem my existence all the more because I have been elected to take a place in the best of plans. I call out to every creature that does not make itself unworthy to be called a creature: Blessed are we, because we exist! The Creator is well pleased with us! . . . I shall [continue to] look around me as far as I can . . . armed with the insight that has been granted my weak understanding, and learn to understand ever better that the Whole is the best, and for the sake of the Whole, whatever is, is right! (*KGS* 2: 34–32/359)

So the *weltanschaulich* and conceptual moorings of early Kant are clear: a reverence for visible Nature and respect for the feelings of deep awe that Nature can occasion; and commitment to a cosmos whose chain of being and parallel orders of substances is determined and moves in a calculation of mutual correspondences (similar to the *thought pattern* of philosopher Leibniz and deist poet Alexander Pope). Into his early thirties too, one could say, Kant explored this position in the confident spirit that was common to late seventeenth-century thinkers like Newton, Leibniz, Galileo, Descartes, and Spinoza: science—especially mathematical-physical science—will lead us on infallibly to the knowledge of reality and a satisfying order for life. This "scientialistic" *spirit*, which buoyed both Kant's academic and popular writings, was somewhat winsomely fresh and naive, I dare say, because of his having held the hand of a pious mother.

The gallant magister of Königsberg society

From the very start Master of Philosophy Kant gave a staggering number of lecture hours per week at the university, never less than sixteen and some semesters as many as twenty-eight. (His income depended upon the number of students he had, since only state-appointed professors received an annual salary.[5]) But Kant, who hated pedantry, did not become a drudge. Evidence of his sparkle is the attempt with J. C. Berens (in 1759) to reconvert Hamann back to deism after his London conversion to an evangelical christianity, by the ploy of asking Hamann to translate some of Diderot's *Encyclopédie* articles, for example, "Beau" and "l'Art" (*KGS* 10:7–16). *The False Subtlety of the Four Syllogistic Figures* was a written come-on by Kant to recruit students for his 1762 fall semester lectures on logic. The piece bristles with reform aimed at anyone who would mouth the traditional scholastic-aristotelian formulae without rethinking; it portends the shift in the wind blowing through Kant:

> All judgments, which stand immediately under the principles of agreement or contradiction, that is, judgments whose identity or opposition is understood not by some mediate characteristic . . . but immediately, are unprovable (*unerweisliche*) judgments. Human knowledge is replete with such unprovable judgments. . . . Those philosophers err who act as if there were no unprovable fundamental truths except one. Those are as much in error, [of course,] who without sufficient backup support are too generous in granting certain of their own propositions this privilege. (*KGS* 2:60–27/61–9)

Another publication finished in 1762, *The Only Possible Argument for a Demonstration of God's Existence*, has the same edge, maintaining that we have traditionally gone wrong by driving with a methodical madness onto the slippery ground of metaphysics as if it were a mathematical highway (*KGS* 2:71–22/32). And Kant's opening remark is more than a Socratic gambit:

> I don't have such an inflated opinion of the usefulness of my present effort as to suppose that the most important propositions of all our knowledge— that a God exists—is tottering dangerously without the aid of profound metaphysical investigations. Providence has not willed that the insights that are most essential for our blessedness should rest upon the subtlety of finely reasoned conclusions. Instead, Providence has delivered those insights immediately to natural common sense (*dem natürlichen gemeinen Verstand*), which never fails—unless one confuse it with deceitful skill—to lead us directly to what is true and useful, inasmuch as we are in great need

---

5   Cf. Karl Vorländer, *Immanuel Kant: der Mann und das Werk* (Leipzig: Felix Meiner, 1924), 1:84.

of the latter. (*KGS* 2:65–5/13)

Kant keeps the perfect, plenary ordered universe of his basic Leibnizian *thought pattern* as he argues for an "improved" physico-theological method that will be prepared to admit "supernatural occurrences" while it expects to find the unifying grounds of such events in necessary universal laws (*KGS* 2:136–23/31). Right there he quotes chapter and verse of Pope's *Essay on Man* again (ii.29–30), in the context of "presume not God to scan," as he goes on to argue for a natural, mechanical cosmogony that is compatible with knowledge "of a wise God" (*KGS* 2:148–7/13). The closing sentence is a masterpiece worthy of the best *Freigeister* of the age:

> It is certainly necessary that one be convinced of the existence of God, but it is not quite so necessary that it be demonstrated. (*KGS* 2:163–4/6)

A clue to what is going on in Kant here in 1762 is found in a footnote of the same *Demonstration*, which reports on the microscopic observations of an English Dr. Hill regarding a drop of water, teeming with "numerous beasts of a predatory nature, outfitted with weapons of destruction"—

> . . . when I consider the machination, violence, and revolution going on in a single drop of matter, and then raise my eyes up from that scene into the heights and see infinite space, swarming with worlds as with specks of dust! then no human speech can express the feeling such a thought excites. All subtle, metaphysical dissecting analysis pales to nothing before the sublimity and dignity intrinsic to such a view. (*KGS* 2:117–30/35)

Kant continues to stand amazed before Nature, struck dumb by its practically ineffable grandeur; every speck of visible Nature can flicker like a monadic mirror revealing worlds unknown, laden with supersensible quality. But Kant's vision of Nature now is losing its scientialistic drift. A *spirit* of being disenchanted with metaphysical subtleties and wary of trusting completely in mathematical science Q.E.D. seems to be opening Kant up to a different *Zeitgeist*, one happier with *le bon sens* or even akin to the spirit pulsing through Shaftesbury's Theocles as he makes his apostrophe to Nature in *The Moralists*:

> O glorious nature! supremely fair and sovereignly good! all-loving and all-lovely, all-divine! whose looks are so becoming and of such infinite grace; whose study brings such wisdom, and whose contemplation such delight; whose every single work affords an ampler scene, and is a nobler spectacle than all that ever art presented! O mighty Nature! wise substitute of Providence! empowered creatress . . .![6]

---

6   Anthony, Earl of Shaftesbury, *Characteristics of Men, Manners, Opinions, Times*, ed. J. M. Robertson (New York: Bobbs-Merrill, 1964), 2:98.

These are the days when young Herder is a student of Kant (Herder had to earn his bread by teaching at the Fridericianum; so Kant let Herder attend all Kant's university lectures free of charge), and after a particularly animated lecture by Kant on time and eternity, Herder was so captivated he spent the night putting the thoughts into poetry, handed it to Kant early the next morning who, taken with its brilliant verse, spontaneously declaimed the piece with gusto before the filled lecture hall. Kant was popular, and was moving in ways quite foreign to the scholarly tight spirit of endlessly argued Christian Wolff theology and schoolmen questions into which he had been earlier indoctrinated.

Things changed too in 1762 when the Russian occupation troops left Königsberg (Russian officers had paid Kant well for *privatissima*), and the Prussian military garrison returned in force to dominate polite society life of the city. General von Meyer, commandant of the Rohr dragoon regiment quartered in the city, frequently sent his carriage to pick up Kant for supper, who then stayed to lecture for the general and his staff on physical geography and ballistics. Lieutenant Friedrich Leopold Baron von Schroetter became close to Kant at these soirées; he later became the Provincial Minister of Prussia at the time when many of its basic laws were formulated. Kant also tippled wine, attended the theatre, and made short excursions with a circle of well-to-do English, Scottish, and German merchants of the seaport city—bank director W. L. Ruffmann gave him the portrait of Rousseau that hung in Kant's lodgings. Although Königsberg could not boast the glitter of Parisian salons nor sport the hot mineral springs of Bath where English gentry went to gossip and plan their portrait by Gainsborough, Königsberg did have a "Learned Society," composed of Privy Councilor Jacobi and wife, First Lieutenant von Lettow, Baroness von Thile, young Johann Göschen, a minister of the Königsberg mint, and Magister Kant. Select guests were invited from time to time to join this intimate group for dinner, conversation and light lectures.

Kant became a sought after figure in the fashionable life of Königsberg. So his *Observations* on temperaments, coquetry, and diverse nationalities are indeed based on observations. His comments on modesty, the fine line between what is waggish and what is obscene, what is prudery, for example, are incisive; and do what you will, says Kant,

> it is the sexual attraction that ultimately underlies all the other charms of a woman, and a woman is always the pleasant topic of a well-mannered conversation, as a woman. . . . (*KGS* 2:234–17/35)

Kant got to know the world of soldiery and the cultivated society of *politesse* with its foibles inside out. In fact he was an immediate witness to the local *scandale célèbre* of the '60s involving Jacobi's wife, Maria Charlotta née Schwinck, married at thirteen to the prominent Jacobi twenty-two years her senior, who served as the unofficial reigning belle and spoiled hostess of Königsberg's parties, balls, concerts, and festivities. There is an innocent note written by Frau Jacobi (1762) sending Kant a sweet spring kiss, inviting him to a garden visit (*KGS* 10:37). As a student Kant had played billiards, yes, but learn to ride horse, fence, or flirt with billet-doux, no! Yet Kant now in the later years was apparently gallant enough to feign willingness to accompany the lonely Frau Jacobi, in Berlin for a cure (1766), back to Königsberg (*KGS* 10:55), when in reality such a bone-shattering journey in the dead of winter would have been a physical disaster for the constitutionally frail man. As it happened, Maria Charlotta broke with her husband Jacobi, divorced, and married her lover, Kant's bosom friend, young Göschen of the "Learned Society"!

You wonder whether Kant's jottings on the inside cover of his copy of the *Observations*, made about the time the scandal became public, indicate his private musings on the affair:

> amazing and unusual   the strong one is kind   Jonathan Wild the courageous youth   temple at Ephesus   women are stronger because they are weak. . . love and respect   self revenge is sublime   certain wickednesses are sublime   assassination is cowardly and base   some don't have the courage to commit great wickednesses   sexual love presupposes a voluptuous love every time, in either sensation or fantasy this voluptuous love is either coarse or fine   tender love has a large mixture of respect in it   a female does not easily betray herself   that's why she is never drunk   because she is weak she is sly   in some marriage there is union without communion tender love is also something different than married love. (*KGS* 20:4–15/5–15)

At least the point is made: Kant was not locked up in the university, a meticulous, inhibited bachelor lost in abstract reasonings.

Kant's favorite reading is significant at this juncture because it discloses how integral his developing lifestyle and reflective outlook were. Alexander Pope in Hamburg poet Brockes' translation of 1740 and Pope's German counterpart, the edifying Albrecht von Haller, remained staples in Kant's literary diet. He valued the sublime Milton especially for *Paradise Lost*, where miserable ugliness of evil in hell is given "a hideous splendor" (*KGS* 2:208–27/28 and 15:331–1/2). Kant enjoyed the English *Spectator* and *Tatler* reportage on morals and mores (*KGS* 2:233–17/28) (available in German since 1745), and reveled in the "inimitable" polished naughtiness and "verve" of Christoph Wieland's elegant, rococo novels (*KGS* 10:488 and 15:357–13). Kant began to read Shakespeare, approving his genius,[7] in Wieland's translation (1762–1766). He read voraciously what his contemporaries read—Richardson, Lessing, Voltaire, Young, Winckelmann. Striking, however, is Kant's special appreciation for satire and the picaresque. With Hume he extolled Samuel Butler's *Hudibras*; Swift's *Tale of a Tub* (in German 1745) he esteemed highly, also the whimsical Sterne and Fielding's novels, especially *Tom Jones*.[8]

Paired with the English literature for Kant went the essays and enquiries of Shaftesbury (*The Moralists* and *An Inquiry Concerning Virtue and Merit* were in German by J. J. Spalding since 1745 and 1747), Hutcheson (a Lessing translation, 1756, and a new one of the *Inquiry* by J. H. Merck, 1762) and Hume (Sulzer German translation, 1755). What caught Kant's attention was their novel method, he said, for searching out the principia of morality (*KGS* 2:312–5/7) and their postulating "moral feeling" as a foundation for ethics—that is a beginning for some sound observations, wrote Kant at the end of his prize *Enquiry* submitted to the Berlin Royal Academy of Sciences in 1763 (*KGS* 2:300–23/25). Kant knew in 1762–63 that both practical and theoretical philosophy rested upon finally unprovable propositions, but how do you decide which judgments are unprovable and which unprovable judgments are sound, material (not just "formal") foundations? Could it be that parallel to *one's knowing* what is *true* immediately (cf. *False Subtlety* passage supra p. 322) one simply, unanalyzably *feels* the *good*? (Kant's underlinings, *KGS* 2:299–8/300–23)

Kant's struggle with the problem and delicate fusion of this English "moral feeling" with his own native sense (pietist-primed "conscience"?) of inner apriori shows up tentatively in another 1763 essay, *Introducing the Mathematical Concept of Negative Values into Practical Knowledge*. Aversion (*Unlust*) is not the mere absence of pleasure but a bona fide negative pleasure, says Kant, like tasting wormwood; inner feeling (*die innere Empfindung*) tells you that right away (*KGS* 2:180–10/24). Vice (*Untugend*) is not an empty negation but is a negative *virtus*,

> and takes place only in a creature where an inner law (either just conscience or consciousness of a positive law) has been countermanded. This inner law is a positive source of doing good . . . [An unreasoning animal is zero with respect to virtue, for] it has not been driven by an inner moral feeling

---

7 Relevant Notes taken from Kant's lectures by Stark are quoted in Paul Menzer, *Kants Asthetik in ihrer Entwicklung* (Berlin: Akademie Verlag, 1952), 12.

8 Cf. Karl Vorländer, *Immanuel Kant*, 1:376–77, 2:377.

to a good act and therefore its resulting omission is not determined by its having opposed such an inner law. . . . (*KGS* 2:182–30/183–20)

Because the gallant Magister of Königsberg society had shrewdly observed the irony of polite duplicity and the vagaries of civic virtue, he could easily say

. . . it's impossible for any man to determine with certainty the degree of somebody's virtuous disposition from seeing their external acts. The right to judge is reserved for only the one who can see into the innermost recesses of the heart. (*KGS* 2:200–19/22)

And with his own heart and mind full of Rousseau—in 1762 Kant read *Du Contrat Social*, which Königsberg bookseller Kanter brought back fresh from Holland, spending also a couple summer days and evenings in 1762 reading *Emile* when it appeared, totally absorbed—

Rousseau discovered for the first time the deeply hidden Nature of mankind underneath all the variety of human adopted disguises. . . . Rousseau discovered for the first time the concealed Law by which Providence is justified throughout man's observations. . . . God is justified by Rousseau as well as by Newton! Pope's doctrine is all the more true! (*KGS* 20:58–16/59–3)

Existentially Kant is wondering, how do we move with certainty in the realm of virtue and pleasure, society and taste, which doesn't seem to fit, it is quite different, parallel, you might say, to the arena of axiomatic mathematical knowledge. If rigorous science cannot plumb the coquette's heart and if morality is not swayed by syllogism, can we trust man's "simple," "inner" "moral feeling" or "sentiment" for direction there?

I think it makes eminent historical sense to say that Kant maintained his original conceptual pattern of different orders of reality that move in quite fixed, coordinated ways (fig. 1). And around 1762–64, in the overwhelming rush of Magister Kant's society life, along with his growing attraction to certain urbane, English essayists' way of marshalling observations on morals, impacted by the extraordinary eloquence of the "sensitive soul" Rousseau (*KGS* 20: 30–4/7 and 20:43–13/44–3), Kant began to think his systematic thoughts in a different spirit, one that could be characterized as a *rococo enlightenment spirit*. A spirit or mood that primes thought to playful niceties and popular relevance (*Weltweisheit*), breathing a sense of intimate elegance, when possible, a kind of cultivated negligence that displays intelligence, verve, and taste, upholding norms and getting at truth, of course, but not with prudish seriousness. What could be more natural a change for a scientialistic pietism becoming

Figure 1

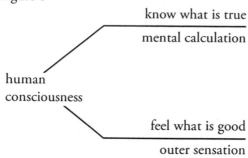

know what is true

mental calculation

human
consciousness

feel what is good

outer sensation

a microcosm of:

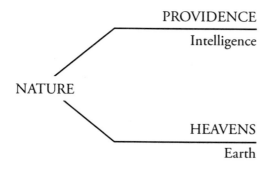

PROVIDENCE

Intelligence

NATURE

HEAVENS

Earth

secularly enlightened than to augment an earlier preference for didactic poetry and catechetical Alexandrines with a taste for satire, especially the picaresque variety—*Tom Jones*, Hogarth's engravings, Jonathan Wild indeed!—in which you can have your gallant, rococo cake and eat it somewhat playfully too.[9]

---

9   Kant ends chapter 1.3 of *Dreams of a Visionary, explained by Dreams of Metaphysics* (published 1766) with the first half of the following quote from Butler's *Hudibras* (*KGS* 2:348), which Adickes gives grounds for believing Kant read in the German translation made by the Swiss J. H. Waser, 1765 (*KGS* 15:201). The full quote captures (waggishly?) much of what Kant was expositing with great learning in the 1760's:

> What good of your design can come?
> As *wind* in th' *Hypocondries* pent
> Is but a blast if downward sent;
> But if it upwards chance to fly
> Becomes new *Light and Prophecy*:
> So when your Speculations tend
> Above their just and useful end,
> Although they promise strange and great
> Discoveries of things far set
> They are but idle *Dreams* and *Fancies*

There is extremely revealing support for this interpretation.

> By inclination I am a scientific investigator. I feel the total thirst for knowledge, the eager restlessness to get further in the exploration, and the contentment with each item of knowledge gained. There was a time when I believed this scientific investigation was the only thing that could add to the honor of mankind; and I despised hoi polloi who didn't know heads from tails. But Rousseau has brought me to the light. This mirage of privilege accruing to science is fading, I'm learning to honor people, and I would find myself more useless than an ordinary worker if I didn't believe that this view of things can bring worth to all the rest of society, to restore the rights of mankind. (*KGS* 20:44–8/16)

Kant made this Aufklärung confession to the blank, interleaved pages of his copy of the *Observations*, but similar evidence was forthcoming and public in the bulletin announcement of his university lectures for 1765–66. I am going to begin my lectures on Metaphysics, said Kant, with *empirical psychology*, "which is really the metaphysical experiential science of People" (*KGS* 2: 309–1/5). I am going to do this for those eager-beaver students whose zeal expires when the lectures get difficult and drop out; then they will at least have heard something

> . . . easy enough to be comprehensible, interesting enough to entertain, and with so many examples of applicability to life as to be useful. On the other hand, if I began with ontology [Science of God and World], a very difficult section of Metaphysics to understand, and would scare them off from continuing the course, whatever the student might have perhaps grasped can be of no further use to him at all. (*KGS* 2:309–29/310–5)

And I will teach the first half of Logic as a critical prolegomenon of *common sense*, that is, logical studies that will serve as a kind of

> . . . quarantine that the student must enter if he wishes to emigrate from the land of prejudice and error into the territory of more enlightened reason (*der aufgeklärteren Vernunft*) and science. (*KGS* 2:310–6/15)

Finally, Ethics, as we know, is a problem, because argued reason seems superfluous.

> . . . distinguishing between what is good and what is bad in acts, and our judgment on what is morally right can be easily and correctly known straightway by the human heart through what some call "sentiment," without the roundabout route of proofs. . . . For now I'm going to lecture on Universal Moral Philosophy and Ethics still using Baumgarten. Although the essays of Shaftesbury, Hutcheson, and Hume are incomplete

---

And savor strongly of the *Ganzas*.
II, canto 3:772–782.

and full of lacunae, they have still succeeded the furthest in penetrating to the principia of morality; my lectures will try to bring their thought the precision and completion they need. . . . I'll try to make clear with what method one should study Man. . . the Nature of Man, which remains constant, and his peculiar place in the creation order, so that one may come to know what excellencies are proper for man in a state of *rough* simplicity and what excellencies are proper in a state of *wise* simplicity, and further, what the guidelines for his behavior should be when he goes beyond both frontiers and tries to attain the highest level of physical or moral excellence but deviates more or less from both. . . . (*KGS* 2:311–10/312–4)

Kant's more *practice-oriented spirit* to which Rousseau waked him in 1762, while Kant held on to his own unified, layered anthropology, cosmogony, and apriori subject-oriented theory of knowledge out to a parallelist pattern,[10] is the existential setting in which Kant wrote his *Observations on the Feeling of what is Beautiful and Sublime* (written by October 1763, published 1764, Kant's own copy profusely annotated by himself most probably during 1765–1766).

Problematics and significant ideas of Kant's annotated observations
The *Observations* has a light touch, quite close in temper to the English *Spectator* and to Shaftesbury's *Characteristics*, that is neither philosophic fish nor literary fowl. I am sketching human feelings and foibles in all their "endless shadings," says Kant, as Hogarth draws and engraves them (*KGS* 2:214–22/25); I don't intend to present a detailed, argued classification of national character, but only want to portray a few prototypical features (much like Hume does in his essay "Of National Characters," which Kant quotes) (*KGS* 2:243–23/24 and 253–1/12). The cadences of the *Observations* are as balanced as Kant's memorized Latin poets, as playful and witty with feint and thrust as the most adept French *philosophe*, expertly fitted for the Königsberg salon of Frau Jacobi and her guests like the resplendently uniformed Hussar General D. F. von Lossow.

---

10 P. A. Schilpp's careful analysis and debate with Paul Menzer on whether the "unanalyzable feeling of what is good" that Kant distinguishes is identical to the "moral sense" of Hutcheson c.s. (*Kant's Pre-Critical Ethics* [Northwestern University Press, 2nd ed., 1960], 32–38, 42–45, 60–61) seems a bit forced to me because it is caught, I think, in a one-dimensional conception of influence. Kant's *conceptual pattern* is certainly not and never was to become "empiricist," like that of Hutcheson or early Hume. It can he shown, however, that Kant did use "sentiment" in the *enlightenment spirit* of the English thinkers, and Kant also did segregate "moral feeling," as one of the "finer feelings," from the ordinary five senses, but conceived it in the terms of his *own thought pattern*. My interpretation is reinforced by the judgment of Erdmanns and Vorländer, cf. Vorländer, *Immanuel Kant*, 1:152 n1.

But underneath a quasi "Rape of the Lock" banter and exquisitely refined, "instructive pleasantries" lies Kant's same *conceptual pattern* of a Providentially ordered chain of being, better, scale of feeling paired to understanding. The three basic sorts (*Gattungen*) of delicate feelings, which Providence has posited in mankind (fig. 2), tend to determine

Figure 2

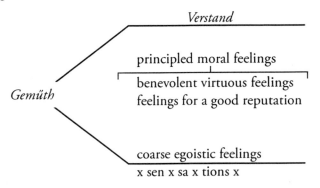

Verstand

principled moral feelings

benevolent virtuous feelings

feelings for a good reputation

Gemüth

coarse egoistic feelings

x sen x sa x tions x

corresponding temperaments and levels of moral character (*KGS* 2:218–34/219–10 and 222–9/11). All such "finer feelings"—including even the comparatively unfeeling, coarse and sensual, egoistic feelings (*um den Eigennutz*) that drive most people—form all together a stunning portrait of Human Nature as a whole. The most grotesque causes, if you can see it, rhyme nobly "with the design of Great Nature" (*KGS* 2:226–26/227–3). Egoistic feelings unintentionally serve the common good by their penchant for circumspect orderliness; the concern to maintain your reputation, which lurks in *all* human hearts (foolish if it dominates you, but extremely admirable as a subordinate desire), graces the whole setup with a delightful Beauty; benevolent instincts also enact the great Plan of Nature. There simply could not be a more harmonious, advantageous, purposeful unity amid the enormous multiplicity of feelings and temperaments than this over-all order, which exhibits and is rooted in a profound Universal feeling for the beauty and dignity of moral Human Nature (*KGS* 2:227–9/36 and 219–11/15). The section could easily have concluded with an epigraph from Pope's *Essay on Man* again (i. 289–290):

> All Nature is but Art unknown to thee;
> All chance, direction, which thou can not see.

Feelings toward non-moral things betray analogues of a man or woman's higher moral dispositional qualities. For example, if you are bored with light music, you will probably be immune to the bewitchments of love (*KGS* 2:225–2/8); and if one develops a sensitivity for expressive painting and music (not the ability to do it), it always entails some kind of linked connection with moral impulses (*KGS* 2:231–18/21). Further, it is so that what feeling senses is strictly a different affair from what understanding comprehends;

> at the same time, the faculties of the soul have such a unified connection that one can normally conclude from the feeling that shows up what the corresponding abilities of understanding are. Otherwise a person who has many strong points of *Verstand* would have been granted these abilities to no use if he did not simultaneously have strong sensitivity for the truly noble or beautiful, since the feeling for what is beautiful and noble is necessarily the mainspring for getting those mental gifts of understanding (*Gemüthsgaben*) into sound and regular use. (*KGS* 2:225–25/35)

Therefore it makes no sense to reason (*vernünfteln*) matters of fine taste with a man who lacks finer feelings for the beautiful and sublime, or with a man who is driven by egoistic feeling in the judgment, since orders of feeling and their parallel excellencies of *Verstand* are not all of one voice—although they all do carry out the great purposes of Nature (*Zwecke der Natur*) (*KGS* 2:224–25/29 and 226–7/17). And Kant assumes this basic conceptual problematics like a *basso continuo*, above which he weaves arabesques of sharp-eyed insights on myriad human characteristics, which are united and ordered in cosmic ladder fashion, with each different crease of the human heart showing both a feeling-side and an understanding-side.[11]

1. Kant distinguishes internal feeling from outward sensation, and differentiates the special, internal finer feeling for what is beautiful both from brute sense-pleasure (*Vergnügen*) and from sensitivity to what is needful or strictly moral (*KGS* 2:207–17/208–9 and 234–35/37; *KGS* 20:124–21/22). The finer feeling for what is beautiful has its identity in being delight at appearances only, amiable semblances.

> Agreeing closely with the nature of beauty is the art of shiningly seeming (*die Kunst zu scheinen*). . . . (*KGS* 20:61–10/15)

> The main reason for beauty continuing is semblance (*Schein*). Cosmetics. A kind of untruth more charming than truth. Correggio departed from Nature. . . . (*KGS* 20:71–1/3)

> The ability to experience delight or aversion in things that do not belong to

---

11 On the unity that Kant's Janus-faced intermediates give to all the parallel diversities, see Lambert Zuidervaart, *Kant's Critique of Beauty and Taste: Explorations into a philosophical aesthetics* (Toronto: Institute for Christian Studies thesis for M.Phil. degree, 1975), 69–71, 74,–76.

one's vital needs: taste. Taste is coarse the closer it is to the vital needs. Taste is fine, is true taste in that which is far removed from the vital needs. In so far as the soul's powers are not merely passive but are necessarily active and inventive, then taste may be called spirital or ideal taste (if the most distinguished feeling is not one stimulated by external sensation but is one stirred by what a man himself imagines in response to it) (*dazu dichtet*). (*KGS* 20:117–5/12)

Beauty is not a matter of utility, because utility denotes a pressing into service of something for another purpose, and consequently not a perfection complete in itself. So the more useful things are, the more angles they show, so to speak, as the means to adapt themselves to other connections sphericity is itself in itself finished. (*KGS* 20:133–10/14)

The illusionary appearance [of the beautiful] permitted is a sort of untruth that is still not a lie it is rather an inducement to an ideal pleasure whose object is not there in the things. (*KGS* 20:134–12/14)

While Kant sometimes uses the term *Gefühl* and *Empfindungen* interchangeably (for example, *KGS* 2:219–1/10), it is clear from the start that he is examining a special human feeling faculty in a context quite foreign to the stimulus-response conceptual pattern of an empiricist (*KGS* 2:207–4/7). Kant's *special, delicate feeling for the beautiful* assumes an active subject, immediate satisfaction (that does not wear itself out like amusement or a momentary irritation), and sustains a quality that may be thoughtful and open to moral suggestion but *has its own refined identity*, independent of objects. (*KGS* 2:208–10/15)

2. Kant affirms that this fine feeling for what is beautiful, and the still more refined variant of feeling respect for the sublime, together as taste, is given with humanity. There lives in every human breast, says Kant, a feeling for the beauty and dignity of human nature. This fundamental feeling is not an abstract precept and may not always shine brightly in every specimen of mankind; nevertheless, this feeling itself is the universal source of all one's action, the very final ground of our universal benevolent disposition (*der allgemeinen Wohlgewogenheit*) and our universal esteem for other humans, and it is for the highest perfection of the moral dimensions of this basic feeling that Providence has given us all manner of auxiliary drives (*KGS* 2:217–12/32, 219–11/13, 220–3/8, 221–13/15, 226–17/25).

Because mankind is innately prone to be good (*KGS* 20:18–10/11)—

Naturally we can't be holy; we lost that through original sin. But we can be morally good. (*KGS* 20:15–6/8)

I don't have any ambition to be an angel: my pride is simply that I am a man. (*KGS* 20:47–11/12)

—underneath the wide variety of geographic, national preferences and underlying the different orders of higher and lower feelings, says Kant, is this common sensitivity for the beauty and dignity of man. It is not just that all things work together for good, thanks to Providence; for example, the choleric man's artificial, reputation-conscious actions are almost as useful to the common good (*gemeinnützig*) as one who is really virtuous (*KGS* 2:223–33/224–1). But men everywhere, in matters of finer taste, as a matter of fact, judge rather uniformly on what womanly shape is pretty; opinions are not so diverse as is generally thought (*KGS* 2:237–27/31). All men everywhere live out of *this fundamental, unifying benevolent disposition*, which *affords the possibility of voicing agreement* if people can just get on the same feeling wave length (*KGS* 2:226–14/17).

> We must hold in honor the common understanding and the common taste. (*KGS* 20:167–14/17)

I do not mean the sympathetic tear of tenderhearted idlers, says Kant; but when this basic feeling for the well-being of your fellow humans has risen to its proper universality, has become sublime and somewhat colder, and taste has thus taken up its rightful place in your total human duty, then you have the optimum conditions for letting the beautiful order of Nature show through and of reaching concord on rightly understanding what it means to be a man (*KGS* 2:216–7/20 and 20:41–19/30).

3. Kant's idea of feeling what is sublime links that specially noble, principled feeling inextricably with morality. In fact, respect for the dignity of Man, "moral feeling" or "sentiment," acquires with Kant the status of "wise simplicity" and has the marks of a non-compulsory normativity that even rubs off authority proper and is peculiar to the fine feeling of (aesthetic) taste.

> The main point of Rousseau is that education be free and also make a man free. (*KGS* 20:167–3/4)

> Freedom in its proper sense . . . is the supreme principium of all virtue and also of all happiness. (*KGS* 20:31–10/12)

Now our feeling of delight and aversion that is freely an active, autonomous principium before good and evil is moral feeling (*KGS* 20:145–6/8):

> The certainty of moral judgments obtained by checking them out with moral feeling is as great a certainty as that which could be obtained by logical sensation; I will by analysis make a man just as certain that lying is hateful as I will by analysis make him certain that feeling by a thinking

substance is absurd. Deception happens with moral judgments just as it does with logical judgments—in fact, deception in logical judgments is more frequent. . . . (*KGS* 20:49–6/11)

And in *Dreams of a Visionary* (written 1765), practically contemporary with the annotations of the *Observations*, after comparing the problem to Newton's identifying the unifying cause of the universal attraction of material bodies as the law of gravitational force, Kant grounds this certifying, free moral feeling in

> . . . the private will's *felt dependence* upon the *volonté generale* . . . a consequence of the natural and universal interaction by which the immaterial world obtains its moral unity: the immaterial world forms itself into a system of spiritual perfection by the laws of this peculiar interconnection. (*KGS* 2:335–27/32)

When I talk about taste, says Kant,

> . . . I take my judgments myself in such a way that they be universally true according to the rule of taste (aesthetically), even if only some of them are valid according to the exact rule of formal reason (logically). (*KGS* 20:21–5/9) In all that which belongs to beautiful and sublime feeling, we do best when we let ourselves he led by the example (*Muster*) of the ancients. In sculpture, architecture, poetry, rhetoric, ancient morals, and the ancient conception of the state. . . . The ancients were closer to Nature; we have a lot of trifling, indulgent, or slavish corrupting influences between us and Nature. (*KGS* 20:71–16/21)

I do not mean the old times were simply better than now (*KGS* 20:119–22/24). I agree on this with Rousseau:

> The whole intention of Rousseau: to bring man by art to the point where he can unite all the advantages of culture with all the advantages of the natural condition. Rousseau doesn't want one to go back to an original state of Nature but to *see back* to [what is Natural]. . . . (*KGS* 15:890–3/7)

We do not need an ignorant simplicity but a rational and wise simplicity (*KGS* 20:180–16/17). A sublime disposition always discloses a sort of noble simplicity (*von edler Einfalt*) and naiveté (cf. *KGS* 2:235–1/8), which the Greeks and early Romans showed clear signs of (*KGS* 2:255–14/19); but such exemplary taste has been historically ruined by grotesque and adventuresome aberrations that "distort Nature, which is the archetype (*Urbild*) of all that is beautiful and noble" (*KGS* 2:245–1/3 and 255–19/31). While *moral feeling* in its natural freedom from logical prescriptions *is a paradigm for* how (*aesthetic*) *taste* is to use the ancients as models for *developing its own refined simplicity that is natural* and not artificial (*KGS* 2:224–8/9), reciprocally we must be aware that (aesthetic) taste is the basis for morals, science, and religion, and *as taste goes, so goes the nation* . . . in all matters of finer feelings (*KGS* 2:256–4/8).

A rococo enlightenment spirit in Kant's annotated *Observations*

It is notoriously difficult to specify a cluster of traits that will identify the spirit of Aufklärung permeating European culture throughout the middle generations of the eighteenth century. The main reason is probably this, that *Zeitgeist* does not walk around making tracks but blows where it lists. And once one makes allowances for national differences and honors the fact that a given man like Kant is busy responding to quite differently spirited, influential figures like Martin Knutzen and Winckelmann, Shaftesbury, Hume, and Rousseau, and is in flux himself, growing out of a training that breathed scientialism and wary of the Romantic *Schwärmerei* afoot among some of his students, one can easily lose any sense of a homogenous period and stay awash in idiosyncratic complexities. But if conceptual patterns are kept distinct from *Zeitgeist*, I think we can advance in detecting the rococo enlightenment spirit in Kant's *Observations* (see remarks begun above, pp. 325–28), which he shares for the time with the likes of Shaftesbury, Hume, Voltaire, Hogarth, his beloved Fielding, Wieland, and others.

Kant's *Observations* bubble with learning and literate references from Heraclitus and Terence to Milton and Richardson, but always lightly, with a composed artlessness. The piece is committedly popular and entertaining. While it exalts Kepler and his intellectual insights as exceedingly rare (*KGS* 2:208–16/22), Kant seems to feel quite at home with the less than noble sanguinary and choleric temperaments, faulting the poet Young for too sustained and belabored a sublime moral tone, that is no longer charming (*KGS* 2:211–30/34). Philosophy and science too are important, of course, but

> . . . the sciences are either good for show, e.g., mathematics, or good for stopping the evil that science itself has caused, or also good for a sort of modesty as side effect. (*KGS* 20: 7–14/15)

> A taste that is moral causes one to have a low opinion of science that fails to bring improvement. (*KGS* 20:7–14/15)

> Sciences inside your head are as useless to some people as the hair-powder on top of their head, and just as it would be very stupid to have flour on your tousled hair but none in the soup, so it's absurd to know superfluous arts and not value those crafts that make for the weal of life. (*KGS* 20:119–10/14)

There breathes throughout the *Observations* a concern for practice-oriented knowledge and an impatience with learning that is pedantically self-enclosed, science for the sake of doctrinaire science. Kant's critique of Swedenbourg's dogmas and theosophic problematics in *Dreams of a Visionary* testifies with the same spirit: it is sheer vanity for science to excuse its learning as important when it is really impossible and unnecessary!

> True wisdom alone is the companion of simplicity. Since the heart prescribes for the understanding in a simple person, such naiveté generally makes the great equipment of scholarly learning superfluous. . . . (*KGS* 2:372–19/22) *Moral faith* too is like [a sensitive, well-bred soul] whose simplicity can be spared so much of the subtlety of reasoning. Only moral faith is suitable for man in every circumstance, because it leads him without any runaround straight to his true purposes. So let's leave all noisy dogmas about such distant objects of speculation and concern to thinkers with time on their hands. (*KGS* 2:373–4/13)

Kant characteristically concludes the piece by paraphrasing Voltaire's *Candide* at the close of part I: "Very well, [all your debated, fine distinctions,] but let us take care of our happiness, go out and cultivate the garden" (*KGS* 2:373–26/27).

Coloring this practical, encyclopedist enlightenment spirit are all manner of rococo touches. There is humoring indulgence toward the gentler sex: for the female creature a little vanity is a delightful thing, so long as it does not become conceit (*KGS* 2:232–31/35). There is an erotic tickle in the *Observations* that hints every now and then at possible indiscretion:

> It's intolerable that one should not even once he able to do something wicked, if one actually wanted to, because then even neglecting to do it every time is only a very dubious virtue. (*KGS* 2:233–35/37).

The transparent elegance of Hume's essays, the digressive jumble of Shaftesbury's reflections that still seem somehow connected, and the witty puncturing of facades à la Hogarth, all meet in the style of the *Observations*. Describing the artful fellow in society who knows his way around, Kant writes:

> Sein Wohlwollen ist Höflichkeit, seine Achtung Zeremonie, seine Liebe Schmeichelei. (*KGS* 2:223–23/24)

There is writing with the kind of melancholic *Empfindsamkeit* that Dilthey judged earned Kant a place next to Winckelmann and Lessing among "the learned authors of our folk" (*KGS* 1:ix):

> Gemüthsarten, die ein Gefühl für das Erhabene besitzen, werden durch die ruhige Stille eines Sommerabenden, wenn das zitternde Licht der

Sterne durch die braune Schatten der Nacht hindurch bricht und der einsame Mond im Gesichtskreise steht, allmählich in hohe Empfindungen gezogen, von Freundschaft, von Verachtung der Welt, von Ewigkeit. Der glänzende Tag flößt geschäftigen Eifer und ein Gefühl von Lustigkeit ein. Das Erhabene rührt, das Schöne reizt. . . . (*KGS* 2:209–1/7)

And in the margins of many pages one finds an anticlerical comment picked up from Hume (*KGS* 20:179–4) or a tart exposé of good manners minus inner honesty as being merely so many ruffles over a dirty shirt (*KGS* 20:119–20/21), and later on there is an intimate reflection on why the zest for dancing wears out in married men (*KGS* 15:305–4/7): these kinds of insights, tone, and delicacy bespeak a rococo propensity.

The *Observations* dances with a spirit of rococo gallantry. To be sure, Kant rejects the vulgar *esprit des bagatelles* that likes to be cluttered with precious trifles (*KGS* 2:225–9/24) and would be satisfied with doggerel that parodies *Hudibras* (*KGS* 20:37–3). Kant pokes fun of Germans who travel to France to learn to become *galants*, when all they pick up is the appearance of cheeky, foppish lady-killers (*KGS* 20: 55–17/19). "I wouldn't use satire if I had the talent for it," says Kant so wistfully it belies his words, "because satire never makes things better" (*KGS* 20:106–6/7). But Kant was fascinated by "Gallantry—a new species of Moral Beauty—*politesse*" (*KGS* 20:133–15), wherein men and woman play playfully, engaging one another in delightful, respectful figures, you might say, of Watteauesque melancholia.

> A naughty amorous tendency (coquetry) in a refined intelligence, that is, an intentional attempt to captivate and charm [some one], is perhaps reproachable in an otherwise decorous person, but it is so beautiful, in fact, it is usually preferred to the respectable, earnest bearing. (*KGS* 2:212–36/213–2)

So the *Observations* approves flirtatious gallantry if it is honorable, and it is honorable when women and men are treated as different equals (2:229–20/33, 230–28/31, 240–32/34, 241–31/242–4). Kant believes, without discrimination, that "a conceited person of either sex always loves only himself—the opposite sex is then merely its play thing" (*KGS* 2:247–3/5), and such trifling with human creatures is deeply degrading. Kant's bow to (wild) Canadian women who preside over the councils of men (*KGS* 2:255–3/13) is balanced by his opinion that the complete woman will know the fashions and *divertissements* of modish life but will voluntarily choose the virtuous simplicity of family life (*KGS* 20: 185–8/12). When Kant approves domesticity as the greatest perfection (*KGS* 20:87–25), one senses a kinship with the quiet, wise (?) simplicity that fills Chardin's domestic scenes, and also catches a hint that magister Kant may be too serious a man to be buoyed indefinitely by a dallying, rococo enlightenment spirit. Either he will need to exchange the tentativity of gallantry for the rush and adventure of *Sturm und Drang*, or settle down with a more conservative idealism.

Results of the research this far, toward demonstrating the importance of the *Observations* as a setting for understanding the *Critique of Judgment-power*, can be briefly formulated in the following way:

A. The significant ideas distilled from Kant's annotated *Observations* (cf. above, pp. 330–333) are strikingly similar to key features of taste-judgment that Kant analyzes in his *Critique* of 1790.

That man has a special, autonomous feeling of delight for the beautiful (*Observations* 1.) is the brunt of Kant's exposition of the first moment of aesthetic judgment—a totally disinterested satisfaction (*Wohlgefallen ohne alles Interesse*) (*Critique*, §§1–5).

That mankind possesses a fundamental benevolent disposition, which affords the possibility of universal agreement, unargued but felt (*Observations* 2.) is crucial background for Kant's developed conception of a second moment of aesthetic judgment—its subjective claim to universal communicability (*Anspruch auf Allgemeingültigkeit . . . ohne Begriff*), grounded in *sensus communis* (*Critique*, §§6–9, 20–22, 40).

That taste, especially in its sublime dimension, has its own suasive quality and is a veritable propaedeutic for moral humanity (*Observations* 3.) sets up the idea of taste-judgment's free law-conformity (*freie Gesetzmässigkeit*) and exemplary necessity that Kant posits in connection with the certifying modality of taste-judgments (*Critique*, §18, Remark following §22); sublime taste also establishes already in 1764 the bond between (aesthetic) taste and moral humanity, which Kant ever continues to decipher, juxtapose, and interrelate (*Critique*, General Remark after §29, following the book on the sublime, also §59, and §60 on the method of taste—"*der Geschmack im Grunde ein Beurteilungsvermögen der Versinnlichung sittlichen Ideen*").

B. Kant's early conceptual problematics, derived from the awe for Nature instilled in him as a boy, codified via Leibnizian training and a deep attachment to Pope's poetry into an ordered universe of optimum harmony, which serves as the unquestioned pattern for his fine, parallel alignments obtaining in the *Observations* among feelings of the beautiful and sublime, argues for the fundamental priority and utter centrality of purposive system in Kant's reflection. This means, in the light of the *Observations*, that the two parts of the *Critique of Judgment-power* are not strangers to one another: taste (part I) and *Zweckmässigkeit der Natur* (part II) have been close companions in Kant's perspective at least since the 1760s when taste came to the fore in his concern.

Taste is a matter of feeling in the *Observations*. So when Kant came to think he was Copernicanly compelled to find an unconditioned ground for taste, he had to "deduce" a transcendental apriori for feeling. The fact that human judgment approving *die Zwecke der Natur* had statutory authority as it were for Kant, already in the *Observations*, made theological judgment (when it came to be formulated so) a natural, proximate context for a critical exposition of feeling-taste-judgments.

This orientation of the *Observations* I have detailed explains how Kant could rename his projected *Critique of Taste* (*KGS* 10:488) *Critique of Judgment-power* (*KGS* 11:40), by simply incorporating taste, with its own autonomy maintained, into the province of reflective judgment, as *Urteilskraft* itself began to assume larger dimensions, including the mediating task of linking *Verstand* and the scientific Nature-knowledge under its auspices with practical *Vernunft*, which witnesses especially to the dignity of Man (*KGS* 5:168–14/22). Kant had to develop his idea of "play," of "what is purposive without specific purpose" (*Zweckmässigkeit ohne Zweck . . . bloss kontemptativ*; see the third moment of taste-judgment in *Critique*, §§10–14), and had to come to understand taste as a "play" of one's cognitive powers before concept-less taste could be critically incorporated into the deeply rationally purposed framework of Kant's universe and unified make-up of man.[12]

---

12 This tentative reading of the development of Kant's aesthetics needs to be documented from the letters and handwritten reflections, which Paul Menzer has admirably and painstakingly begun to do in Kant's *Asthetik in ihrer Entwicklung*, and further tested to see whether it does not give a more complete account of how Kant soberly moved to his encyclopedic work.

Note: I do not deny a discontinuity in Kant's adopted *Zeitgeist* and even a change of conceptual pattern that occurs between the *Observations* and the *Critique of Judgment-power*. Kant's inaugural dissertation of 1770, *On the Forms and Principles of the Sensible and Intelligible World*, maintained his same original, parallelistic universe pattern of thought, but signaled a new spirit that breaks with the rococo enlightenment spirit as definitely, for example, as Mondrian suddenly adopted *De Stijl*. Rousseau shook up Kant in 1762. In the confessional of the margins of his *Observations* Kant wrote:

> Everything goes past us in a river-like-flow—the changing taste and the different fashions of men make the whole game uncertain and deceptive. Where do I find fixed points in Nature that man can never shift around? Where do I find fixed points in Nature that can give man the markers as to which riverbank he is supposed to hold onto. . . ? (*KGS* 20:46–11/15)

During the fifteen years, 1766–1781, of largely publishing silence, while Kant was

If the *Observations* is taken seriously as the historical setting for the *Critique of Judgment-power*, one may be spared reading the third *Critique* anachronistically under a Romantic prejudice that supposes Kant's aesthetics is basically (or should have been) a theory of fine art or genius. Kant's *Critique* is first of all a critique of taste before beautiful Nature. Even the highest beauty, ideal beauty (*Critique*, §§15–17) is exposited without reference to artistic production, not because of Kant's poverty in artistic experience, but because *schöne Künste* (examined at length in *Critique*, §§43–54) form only a subordinate part of his eighteenth-century understanding of the beautiful and sublime. Another little piece in the puzzle is the fact that it took until the second edition of the *Kritik der reinen Vernunft* (1787) for Kant to redefine "aesthetic" out of its Baumgartian sensational meaning so as to make "aesthetic judgment" a fit synonym for "taste judgment" (A21n/B35n), thus pioneering a modern conception of *aesthetics*.

C. The annotated *Observations* reveal magister Kant as a full-blooded Aufklärung man rather than as a disembodied mind. It remains to be shown from Kant's correspondence, the two introductions to the third *Critique*, and other documents, if Kant's lively concern for matters of taste and his changing view on "aesthetic" did not at least partly occasion his later (critical) method and philosophical position. At this point we may at least posit that if Kant remained at all true to the thrust and spirit of the *Observations*, then the *Critique of Judgment-power* must not be read as a German monument to architectonics by a failing sexagenarian or the subtle solution to a drawn-out argument. Rather, the third *Critique* is the linchpin in a cultural philosophy that presents a humanist manifesto of singular proportions.

> Fine art and sciences, which make man civilized, if not morally better, by a delight that is universally communicable and by a polish and refinement [made to order] for society, wrest us largely free from the tyranny of sense-drives and thus prepare man for a lordship in which reason alone shall have authority. Meanwhile, the evils that trouble us, due partly to Nature

---

searching for an Archimedean point in (human) Nature, trying to come to grips with the shock of Rousseau and Hume—

> The doubt I adopt is not a dogmatic one but a doubt of [methodical] delay . . . to search. . . . The method of doubting is useful in that it assists one's heart and mind to do things not speculatively but to act with common sense and sentiment. (*KGS* 20:175–13/19)

—Kant also modified his conceptual pattern, so that the *Critiques* disclose a somewhat more loosely unified and intricately complicated perspective than the *Observations*. However, the significant points, early problematics, and rococo enlightenment spirit of the *Observations* still hold as orientation for the deepening development.

and partly to the intolerable selfishness of men, simultaneously [serve to] summon, strengthen, and steel the soul's powers not to succumb to those evils, and so make us feel an aptitude for higher purposes that lies hidden within us. (KGS 5:433–30/434–3)

One gains a new appreciation for Kant's contribution when one notices that behind the critical idealist philosopher of the *Critique of Judgment-power* stands the rococo enlightenment *philosophe* of the *Observations*.

"Mythologizing Philosophy" as Historiographic Category

The specific matter I wish to broach for discussion is the nature of what may be called "mythologizing philosophy."[1] If we recognize mythologizing philosophy to be a recurrent stance various thinkers have adopted throughout the ages as a solution to the fundamental problem of cosmic order in conjunction with change, then our awareness of the basic options facing the disciplines philosophy of history and historiography, I contend, will be sharpened. I also think the so-called postmodern climate today, which purports to be fed up with Rationalist paradigms and has inherited the absence of tradition that a modernity composed of Renaissance and Enlightenment struggled to shuck: contemporary theory is fertile ground for "mythologizing philosophy" and its viruses.

Let me first try to give precision to the conception and delineate the problem in historiography and philosophy of history that mythologizing philosophy, I think, puts into question. Then I shall cite a few significant examples of latter-day mythologizing philosophy to show how its intriguing but fundamentally disquieting solution is important for our understanding the current scene of theory, artistic culture, political happenings, that is to say, human life on earth.

Myth, mythopoeia, mythology
Myths, shall we say, are age-old, mysterious stories believed to be true

---

1   D. H. Th. Vollenhoven introduced the term "mythologiseerende denken" in *Geschiedenis der Wijsbegeerte* (Franeker: Wever, 1950) to describe Pre-Socratic thinkers who valued the Greek heritage. Cf. also Vollenhoven, "De consequent probleem-historische methode," in *Philosophia Reformata* 26 (1961): 15; Translated by Robert Sweetman as "The Consequential Problem-Historical Method," in *The Problem-Historical Method and the History of Philosophy*, ed. K. A. Bril (Amstelveen: Haes, 2005), 110.

This essay was first published in *Myth and Interdisciplinary Studies*, eds. M. Clasquin, J. D. Ferreira-Ross, D. Marais, R. Sadowsky (Pretoria: The Myth Association at the University of South Africa, 1993), 28–48.

about origins, gods, Ur-catastrophes, and ultimate uncanny decisions.[2] A myth is received as an authoritative narrative holding hidden knowledge that legitimates and illuminates underlying structures of the present go-ing-ons.[3] Myths do not record discrete events with limiting consequences but like oracles present final, unquestionable tales that act as revelation of daemonic doings having eternality and necessity.[4] Whether the Egyptian myth of Osiris and the ancient Greek myth of Prometheus, for example, are garbled accounts of an oral proto-revelation on the beginnings of death and culture or more like ingenious human sacrifices for inexplica-ble powers and drives (as Feuerbach would claim explains any "religion"), it is so that myth harbors pronouncement on numinous matters beyond the borders of human ken—fertility, death, what is unearthly.

As I understand it, mythic accounts already mediate animistic hu-man life troubled by mana and tabu where the hit-or-miss contingency of magic lurks large: myth provides some kind of loosely connected, repeat-able handle for humans to defer the unknown reality that is to be taken seriously. **Mythopoeic** formulations like the Babylonian Enuma Elish and the Homeric *Iliad* and *Odyssey* develop myths into rambling con-geries of stories that seem woven together yet uncentered, overlapping, with subterranean echoes of each other that do not quite fit. Mythopoeic saga and legend ("epic") have an ill-defined relation to anything histori-cal, but their artistically heightened, ***weltanschaulich*** (world-and-life-viewic) literary quality—the oral becomes written—tends to soften the monstrous and brutal Nature forces assumed as axioms in myth. Myths are not anthropocentric;[5] but mythopoeic products like the cycle bearing Homer's name both humanize the superhuman powers and deities of myths into anthropomorphic deities and heroes and intimate a distanc-ing of humankind from living directly under the spell of myth.[6] If one

---

2 Cf. Henri Frankfort, *Before Philosophy* [1946] (Baltimore: Penguin Books, 1959), 14–15.

3 Hans Blumenberg, *Arbeit am Mythos* [1979], translated by Robert M. Wallace, *Work on Myth* (Cambridge: MIT Press, 1985), 113–114; Norman J. Girardot, "Behaving Cosmogonically in Early Taoism," in *Cosmogony and Ethical Order,* eds. Robin W. Lovin and Frank Reynolds (University of Chicago Press, 1985), 71.

4 Blumenberg, *Work on Myth*, 126–27.

5 Blumenberg, *Work on Myth*, 42, 121, 132.

6 "...de mythe ressorteert onder de producten van het streven naar een levens- en we-reldbeschouwing . . . neemt hij [Homerus] de betrokken goden reeds in de *Ilias* niet meer, gelijk de mythe doet, als ontzagwekkende, bovenmenschelijk machten, maar als, in vergelijking met de Grieksche helden . . . zelfs tot vrijwel decoratieve figuren verbleeken. Zoo werd Homèros de profeet van een niet mythologiseerende levens-houding." Vollenhoven, *Geschiedenis der Wijsbegeerte,* 1:44.

speaks carefully, "**mythology**" tends to press more non-contradictory identity and systematic pattern upon the unruly mix of divinities and deities abounding in mythopoeic accounts. Mythology bestows a quasi-analytic settlement of connection upon the many gods in play. Whether mythology be a synecdochic form of *magische Denken* (Cassirer)[7] or an unfinished hypostasis of continuing generations of procreative power (Jaeger),[8] mythologies are not scientific or theoretical constructs so much as conceptual hybrid, thinking together under the aegis of Names, around the matter of genesis, the originary progeny of all that inexplicably exists.

Hesiod's *Theogonia* exemplifies mythology as Western civilization has known it: an erotic Χάος fertile with Νύξ and Ὠκεανός bears Γαῖα and Οὐρανός that as primeval mother Earth and vengeful fatherly Heaven locked in hateful embrace issue a litter of monsters. Χρόνος in league with mother *Gaia* castrates father *Ouranos* whose curse then resounds that the savage deed of mutilation will repeat itself through all ensuing generations. Spectral Ἐρινύες spring up from Earth, and from the genitals of Heaven springs Ἀφροδίτη, a most ambiguous, seductive disturber of any peace.[9]

Hesiod's theogony—we don't need more details here—epitomizes the ordering thrust where mythology corrals any extant myths. Hesiod's text bears the stamp of the Olympian family of divided-power gods honored earlier by the Achaeans (c. 1400 BC), but there was room in Hesiod to accommodate the orgiastic Thracian cult of Dionysus,[10] especially the goddess Δίκη beloved by the conservative Boeotian farmers prone to respect the seasonal wheel of impartial regularity (with which almighty Zeus had little truck). There is only heterodoxy in mythology, not orthodoxy.

Nevertheless, the seething network of ancient Greek mythology (1) has an ominous cast when taken seriously, because a curse hovers over all that transpires, a primal scream that is perversely fecundive, a wound in reality that does not heal. I take it to be characteristic of mythology that (2) the processes it assumes evidence a fateful antagonism of constant subordination offset by chthonic forces forever undermining or tran-

---

7   Ernst Cassirer, „Sprache und Mythos: Ein Beitrag zum Problem der Götternamen," [1924] in *Wesen und Wirkung des Symbolbegriffs* (Darmstadt: Wissenschaftliche Buchgesellschaft, 1969), 151–54; translated, Susanne K. Langer, *Language and Myth* (New York: Dover, 1946), 92–95.

8   Werner Jaeger, *The Theology of the Early Greek Philosophers* (Oxford: Clarendon Press, 1947), 15–16.

9   Hesiod, *Theogonia*, 116–210.

10 *Theogonia*, 79–80.

scending every triumph. (3) There is never beginning or ending but only permanently an unbounded, interminable, inexorable becoming and be-going where the pluperfect, so to speak, or past perfect present fascinates, the originary. And mythology (4) has no place for human residents in a world except as semi-divine, daemonic offspring of gods.

Mythologizing philosophy

"Mythologizing philosophy" then is philosophical analysis, systematic reflection on the interrelated order, change, and meaning of things all together, whose analytic rigor as encyclopedic philosophical thinking is suffused with overlying mythological concerns and characteristics.

Testimonies of the Milesian Thales (fl. c. 585 BC) document his attempt to explain the structure and source of what is without recourse to theogony. Unlike Orphic texts, Musaios and Hesiod, Thales' philosophical analysis of φύσις is **without** a mythologizing coefficient. Even Thales' πάντα πλήρη θεῶν εἶναι, in connection with understanding magnetism (?), keeps the mysterious forces natural and does not theoretically divinize powers of Nature.[11] The fact that Plato introduces myths at conclusive places in his philosophical dialogues[12] does not make him a mythologizing philosopher either, because Plato uses the traditioned stories imaginatively to clinch arguments and to teach disciples eschatological theses that reinforce his ethics and anthropology with a trans-migratory soul that fits his increasingly Realist, utterly intellectualist ontology.[13] Late Plato is certainly a theoretical theist of sorts,[14] but Plato is never a theosophist.

Practitioners of mythologizing philosophy, however, tend to formulate philosophy with a theosophical aura and to be predominantly focused on the source(s) that generate and adjudicate praeternatural powers. Reality is taken to be at core an ever-recurring, quasi-sacred occurrence whose indeterminate re-source is secret but can become experientially known (γνῶσις) to initiates. Worldly things that emerge, pass away, and resurge in a repetitive process evidence an unearthly staying power; and poisonous snakes, healing plants, evil-eye precious stones,

---

11 Jaeger, *Theology of the Early Greek Philosophers*, 20–22.

12 For example, *Phaedo* 107d–114c, *Res Publica* 614b–621b, *Phaedrus* 243a–249c.

13 "En fait, le *Phédon* comme tant d'autres dialogues donne au mythe une fonction philosophique, et la place même du mythe, après des développements passionnants mais ardus et avant les ultimes exhortations, met en valeur œ fait." (Paris: Société d'édition "Les Belles Lettres," 1969), 22. Cf. also Josef Pieper, *Über die Platonischen Mythen* (München: Kösel Verlag, 1965), 22–26, 58–59, 73.

14 *Nomoi,* book 10.

and astral spirits intimate the absent presence of uncanny authority that is honored in the universe of mythologizing philosophy.

Anaximander's famous fragment on τό ἄπειρον (fl. c. 570 BC) is prototypical for mythologizing philosophy: an ungenerated and indestructible universal Reservoir of undefineable quality is the commanding ἀρχή from which all things issue and back to into which all determinate, conflicting contrasts necessarily in the course of time justifiedly dissolve and reissue, world without end.[15] The exacting parabola of genesis and destruction inhering Anaximander's *to apeiron* bodes a fateful mystery.

Early Taoism (c. 300 BC) is also a good example of mythologizing philosophy. Taoist texts that reflect on the constant generation and periodic returning creatures undergo take a philosophical position that foregrounds a protean spontaneous genesis (*tzu-jan*) out of primordial *hun-tun* with continual birthing resonances (*ying*) and reïngression of existences (*kan*). TAO is nameless, unfathomable, and *wu-tse* (nonlaw), but is everlasting One cosmogonic creative power and process whose polar duality of *yin* and *yang* supports the perpetual round of waxing/waning, becoming/decaying, like flow and ebb of coursing water, the gentle Way of the world. *Tao-te* (the self-empowering Way, "virtue") for humans is *wu-wei* (not taking purposive, decisive action), to acquiesce in the undulating TAO (*li*), like going with the grain of the jade, echoing whatever happens to be in play.[16]

Certain characteristics and basic tenets of early Taoist reflection could be highlighted: (1) Nothing is structurally constant but change. Temporal process is the just order of reality, and order is in change; but the change is regular, a generative, ever-changing, recurrent ectype of some hidden, underpinning archetype.

(2) Universal generative/degenerative flux has no ratiocinative rationale but is defined by an undefined quality of naturality that con-naturalizes humans into being fellow creatures with glorious trees, animals, lifegiving water, and even erases evil into a relative contrary of good—TAO is really before/beyond good and evil.

(3) Pursuit of knowledge is a mistaken move because nothing can be fixed conceptually, since both the other given knowable object or subject and the knowing subject will change circumstantially; therefore, returning to the silence of one's spirit-rootage in meditation (*ching-tsuo*, sitting

---

15 H. Diels-W. Kranz, *Die Fragmente der Vorsokratiker* (Berlin: Weidmansche Verlagsbuchhandlung, 1951), 1:89.

16 *Tao Te Ching*, translated and annotated by D.C. Lau (Hong Kong: The Chinese University Press, 1982); Alan Watts, *The Watercourse Way* (New York: Pantheon Books, 1975); also, Girardot, "Behaving cosmogonically in early Taoism," 79, 86–87.

peacefully [cf. herbal diet, breathing regimen]) one may tune in to TAO, divine, intuitively receive apathetic/ecstatic enlightenment as a sage.

(4) Since there is no end to the life-cycle at large, no telos that forces priorities or assigns causes and means, judgments and initiatives to alter the age-old round of genesis and nemesis seem to melt away into drifting and bearing whatever happens, as it happens.

The historical as ephapaxic eschatonic change

The specific problem to which mythologizing philosophy, as I have tentatively defined and historically exemplified it so far, presents a dubious but important resolution, is: what constitutes *history?* When is change *historically sound?* What, precisely, is a *historiographic* account called to trace?

I shall not try to give a taxonomy of the basic, incompatible philosophical positions taken on this problem throughout the centuries.[17] I want to zero in on how mythologizing philosophy presents a viable alternative to the dominant answers of (a) teleological schematicism, and (b) evolutionary/dialectical geneticism. Schematicist philosophers of history like Vico, Ranke, Burckhardt, Windelband, Croce, and Jaspers tend to view changes as discrete items whose sum will fill out the structural possibilities and typical patterns of what is a blueprinted order, a master meta-narrative or schema impervious itself to change—there is nothing really new under the sun. Geneticist philosophers of history like Hegel, Herder, Comte, Dilthey, and Marx read order in terms of an ongoing melioristic or dialectically incorporative progressive flow of genuine, irreversible development—that leaves past fixed accomplishments blowing in the mediated wind.

Rather than adumbrate my own position that tries to track the (diachronic) continuous trail of fecundive or wasteful change in a given dated/located entity or cultural inheritance against the backdrop of discontinuous (synchronic) periods, amid perennial types of (perchronic) larger-than-individual positioned traditions,[18] let me indicate how myth-

---

17 Cf. Karl Löwith, *Meaning in History* (University of Chicago Press, 1949); D. H. Th. Vollenhoven, *Kort Overzicht van de Geschiedenis der Wijsbegeerte voor den Cursus Paedagogiek M.O.A.* [1956], in *De Probleem-historische Methode en de Geschiedenis van de Wijsbegeerte*, ed. K. A. Bril (Amstelveen: Haes, 2005), translated by John de Lievit as "Short Survey of the History of Philosophy," in *The Problem-Historical Method and the History of Philosophy*, ed. K. A. Bril (Amstelveen: Haes, 2005), and "De consequent problem-historische methode," *Philosophia Reformata* 26 (1961): 1–34; H. R. Smart, *Philosophy and its History* (La Salle: Open Court, 1962).

18 C. Seerveld, "Towards a Cartographic Methodology for Art History," *Journal of Aesthetics and Art Criticism* 39:2 (1980): 143–54 {see *AH*: 61–78} and "Footprints in the Snow," *Philosophia Reformata* 38 (1991): 16–19 {supra pp. 254–257}.

ological philosophy actually puts history, historical, and historiographic activity into question.

By conflating **structural** order for norming change with the very **durational** matrix making change possible, mythologizing philosophy, as I understand it, gives order a **genetic finality** and conceives genetic duration as the everlasting, over-arching **repetitive order**.[19] Mythologizing philosophy virtually holds process and order-for-process together indistinguishably, fused rather than enmeshed; so there is no cosmic theatre for operation where indelible unique events can take place with irreversible sequences, so much as an amorphous screen where flit tentative, ephemeral images bespeaking, perhaps, eternal verities.

If you conceive history, as I do, to be concerned with significant change within a universe defined by temporality, whose ἐφάπαξ (once only) nature is due to its ἔσχατον (towards something last) orientation, then mythologizing philosophy fails to pick up the gauntlet of recording **definitive** acts and events once upon a time somewhere, because mythologizing philosophy is rather indifferent toward passage of time, and views present occurrences, as it were, as réprise of earlier happenings. Also, because it breathes so directly its pretheoretical vision and native-storied faith commitments on praeternatural powers, content to leave ἀρχή undefined and *Archimedean point* logically unanswerable, resting with a troubled world that still fascinates, mythologizing philosophy has a very literary cast to its reflective analysis, a suggestive imprecision, and normally redirects exacting historiographic accounting toward imaginating more utopian prospects.

Mythologizing philosophy, which denies the ephapaxic eschatonic temper of change, correctly avoids any theodicy and resists foisting rationalistic frameworks upon the bloody, accident-strewn exploits throughout time of especially human creatures in the world.[20] But mythologizing philosophy, by discounting the unrepeatable singularity of temporal events and the unifying effect an *eschaton* has upon the course of things, does augur closure upon interpreting events and in deciding "What now is to be done?" a stifling ontological closure most contemporary variants of mythologizing philosophy profess to avoid.

A legacy
The overall thrust and approach of mythologizing philosophy has had ad-

---

19 C. Seerveld, "Biblical Wisdom underneath Vollenhoven's Categories for Philosophical Historiography," *Philosophical Reformata* 38 (1973): 137–38 {see *AH*: 14}.

20 Blumenberg, *Work on Myth*, 32, 100.

herents in many periods of human culture because the ontic problem of history, historical action, and historiographic accounting demands that systematic thinkers like philosophers and reflective cultural leaders take a stand on what is at stake.

Already in the Hellenistic period a figure like Valentinos of Alexandria who went to Rome (c. 140 AD) developed a syncretist Egyptian-Jewish version of Hesiod within Christian circles that radically disqualified the earth-world as inherently fallen and lauded shadowy heavenly creatures like Σοφία, also πνεῦμα sent out by the eternal mother *Sigé* to rapture those purified-in-the-know (πνευματικοὶ) from the rat race of history, and so to reverse the process of estrangement that occurred in the ineffable, transcendent πλήρωμα of the godhead.[21] The chiliastic Montanist movement in Phrygia indicted the Roman church as lusting for earthly political power, and proposed instead a spiritual regimen that included castration, xenophagic routines that induced trances for glossolaliac prophecies that updated written revelation, and thus played havoc with the Bible, all canonic institutional authority, and fixed societal order. The Babylonian faith of Mani recognized Evil as an independent primal principle of Darkness opposed to the Good, the Light, forever; and the Manichaean mythologizing cosmogony seemed to assume dispensations where revelation touched down in India through Buddha, Persia through Zoroaster, the West through Jesus, and now finally worldwide through the Paraclete Mani.

All such varied gnostic reflections—Valentinos, Montanus, Mani—deny in common the cosmic goodness of creatures, and therefore were perceived as deeply anti-Christian by Christian thinkers, not the least because of the ecstatic rejection of a provident world order where evil is a surd because of sin once upon a time and shall be historically overcome, rather than an ontic negative permanently given.[22] The best way to deal with history, says gnostic doctrine, is to leave it.

There are philosophers in the so-called Renaissance days of Europe whose categorial frameworks of thought carry traits similar to the gnostics, heavily indebted to the Jewish Cabala tradition, thoroughly divested of any biblically Christian historicality. While Luther was writing in the language of the people, "Ein feste Burg ist unser Gott . . . aus aller Not

---

21 Gerald Hanratty, "Hegel and the Gnostic Tradition," in *Philosophical Studies* 30 (Spring 1984): 25–26.

22 Cf. Steven Runciman, *The Medieval Manichee* (Cambridge University Press, 1947), 5–25; Richard H. Popkin, "Manicheanism in the Enlightenment," in *The Critical Spirit,* Essays in honor of Herbert Marcuse, ed. Kurt H. Wolff and B. Moore, Jr. (Boston: Beacon Press, 1967), 51–54.

der uns itzt hat getroffen," Johann Reuchlin was writing *De Arte Cabbalistica* (1517) and Agrippa von Nettesheim, *De Occulta Philosophia* (1510) where human magic assumes a mediatorial role between an unknown transcendent God and the three worlds of spirits, heavenly bodies, and earthly elements. Skeptical of the worth of scholastic theology and dubious of reasoning's ability to probe the secrets of praeternatural and supernatural powers, such thinkers gravitated toward the occult, to alchemical fascination with transmutability of matter and the possibility of elixirs to forestall death. Paracelsus held that decay signals generation, corruption leads to creation, the universe is homogenous, bisexual, and hylozoic, and time is cyclical. Autodidact Jacob Böhme epitomizes a mind-boggling, convoluted theosophical mix where an Ur-*Ungrund, ein ewig Nichts,* which Evil and Good both inhere, engenders a modal trinitarian process of divine conflictual willing that spawns unruly war in heaven and on earth. Human life is like a hinge on the mysterious turning wheel of black and white magic, where one's continual withdrawal from the ongoing influxes of astral spirit, Lucifer *Vernunftgeist* constitutes the crucible of travail for becoming a God-child.[23]

That is, a strain of thinkers has persisted for whom evil seems essential to reality, so the decision on succession to ordinary human deeds loses significance, and those-in-the-know turn to revelations tuned into a secret, omni-divine spiritual network of machinations that surpass any ratiocinative calculation.

Such thinkers, however, have not been mainline. Philosophers like Swedenborg (1688–1727) and poet-artist, mythographer William Blake (1757–1827) were looked at askance by their Rationalist opponents. The Kantian anthroposophist Rudolph Steiner (1861–1925), whose strong anti-materialist position supports concepts of astral body and reincarnation, an extensive angel-demonology reinforced by apocalyptic meditations, is normally considered curiously speculative, if not obscurantic. The Russian theosophist Solovyov (1853–1900), who appeals to the Romantic philosopher Schelling's *intellektuelle Anschauung* as well as to the Cabala and gnostic texts, and even Berdyaev (1874–1948), have largely remained peripheral to Western secularized reflection, disqualified as arcane and "mystical." Only the mythologizing philosophical psychology of late Freud, and the quite different, penetrating treatises by Jung on archetypes, which like a mandala hold the key of knowledge to the

---

23 *Sex Puncta Mystica* (1620), 2:7, 13; *Mysterium Pansophicum* (1620) 9:1–2. Cf. Jacob Böhme, *Six Theosophic Points,* translated by John R. Earle (University of Michigan: Ann Arbor Paperback, 1958), 120–21, 161.

Universal *Unbewusste* of us middling human consciousnesses, have been treated as kosher by expressly analytic philosophy, approved by "science."

Yet it is precisely this legacy of mythologizing philosophy, which evidences by and large certain conceptual, structural similarities throughout the generations, that I dare suggest is the peculiar pedigree if you will, the orienting context to achieve a proper understanding of figures like Nietzsche, late Heidegger, Foucault, and others.

Glints of latter-day mythologizing philosophy

Die ewige Wiederkunft is central to Nietzsche's philosophy[24] and crystalizes his early rejection of the progress ideal foisted upon history by his Hegelian and Darwinian positivistic contemporaries—which has neutered our German historical sense, said Nietzsche, with factitious trivia.[25] *Der letzte Mensch*, small-minded and petty as the flea, craving tiny moderate pleasures, will never muster the will to overcome the gospel of linear history and superterrestial hopes, to become *Übermensch*, the bridging human *Übergang und Untergang*, who affirms the eternal recurrence of every good and evil detail.[26] But once the interminable fated sameness of real life is affirmed, the frightful, ironic seriousness of one's every deed comes alive: you are walking over the abyss on a tightrope heartily laughing—history with no end![27] You have learned from Zarathustra's animals that the world and your self are Dionysian.[28]

No wonder the good historian (Plutarch, Goethe, Burckhardt), according to early Nietzsche, needs the artistic imagination to recast the past into a comprehensive symbol that will stir us on now to become self-reliantly *große Männer*, like the ancient Greeks—Wagner's music is the rebirth of Greek antiquity,[29] which will create a new and improved

---

24 *Frölich Wissenschaft* (1882), par. 341.

25 "Von Nutzen und Nachteil der Historie für das Leben," *Unzeitmässige Betrachtungen* II [1874] in *Nietzsche Werke*, eds. G. Colli and M. Montinari (Berlin: Walter de Gruyter, 1972), 268–69, 275–80, 285.

26 *Alzo Sprach Zarathustra* (1883–85), part 3, "Der Genesende."

27 *Alzo Sprach Zarathustra*, part 4, "Vom höheren Menschen"; cf. also Prologue to *Alzo Sprach Zarathustra*, 6, 9–10.

28 "...sich selber bejahend noch in dieser Gleichheit seiner Bahnen und Jahre, sich selber segnend als das, was ewig wiederkommen muß, als ein Werden, das kein Sattwerden, keinen Überdruß, keine Müdigkeit kennt—: diese meine dionysische Welt des Ewig-sich-selber-Schaffens, des Ewig-sich-selber-Zerstörens, diese Geheimniswelt der doppelten Wollüste, dies mein 'Jenseits von Gut und Böse' ohne Ziel. . ." Nietzsche, *Wille zur Macht*, par. 696.

29 *Die Geburt der Tragödie aus dem Geiste der Musik* (1872), par. 19.

natural human race.[30]

When Heidegger turned from Husserlian analysis of *sein zum Tode* to Hölderlin and poetry *in dürftige Zeit* of no-more runaway gods and the not-yet god-coming, as a more apophatic open-ended Way to encounter *Sein*, so that the unconcealment of Truth might covertly occur, language became, as it were, sacred to Heidegger, the "Open Sesame" of human *Dasein*. *Worte* (sayings) and *Gespräch* (bespokenness) intimate that earthlings become free as they dwell in poeting, coming to stand in the presence of gods, near the essence of things—poet as Delphic oracle of Agnosto Theo.[31] *Sprache* (speaking), as performative calling (*Ruf*), prays for closer presence of what is while letting be, honoring the *difference* and necessary rift within intimacy.[32]

Late Heidegger totally rejects any semblance of macho-ratio: *Das Denken jedoch ist Dichten*.[33] And poeting authenticates humanity by imagining, that is, sighting the wholly alien invisible Other in the familiar.[34] The whiling spell of poetry is a history-making event for Heidegger—no record to speak of—as art that lets truth originate is historical,[35] since uncanny poetic epiphanies that skirt the abyss of meaninglessness like a prayer or a rising phoenix leave hardly a trace.

Foucault in the text *Les mots el les choses* (1966) wants to excavate below the constrictive scientific modern project of instrumental language and to dig back underneath the classical grid of metaphysical representation and discourse, to espy in the Macro-microcosmic Renaissance episteme the network of similitudes and hidden resemblances their *erudition*

---

30 Neitzsche, "Von Nutzen und Nachteil der Historie fur das Leben," 288–90. Also: "Dies ist ein Gleichnis für jeden Einzelnen von uns: er muss das Chaos in sich organisieren. . . . So entschleiert sich ihm der griechische Begriff der Cultur als einer neuen und verbesserten Physis. . ." 329–30.

31 *Hölderlin und das Wesen der Dichtung* [1936], translated by Douglas Scott, in Martin Heidegger, *Existence and Being* (Chicago: Henry Regnery, 1949), 279–84, 286, 288–91.

32 "Die Sprache," in *Unterwegs zur Sprache* [1950], translated by Albert Hofstadter, in Martin Heidegger, *Poetry, Language, Thought* (San Fransisco: Harper Colophon, 1971), 198–200, 202–8.

33 "Der Spruch des Anaximander" [1946] in *Holzwege* (Frankfurt: Vittorio Klostermann, 1957), 303.

34 ". . . dichterisch wohnet der Mensch" [1951] in Heidegger, *Vorträge und Aufersätze* (Pfullingen: Günther Neske, 1954), 200–02.

35 "Geschichte ist die Entrückung eines Volkes in seine Aufgegebenes als Einrückung in sein Mitgegebenes . . . die Kunst in ihrem Wesen ein Ursprung und nichts anderes ist: eine ausgezeichnete Weise die Wahrheit seiend und du geschichtlich wird." Heidegger, *Der Ursprung der Kunstwerk* [1935–35] in *Holzwege*, 64–65.

and *divinatio* thrived on to penetrate through to the primal *écriture* of things, the secrets behind/of the mute stigmata of Nature.[36] Foucault is intent upon following up the questioning experiences of Mallarmé, Nietzsche, Hölderlin, and Heidegger, he says, to plumb "ce non-connu à partir duquel l'homme est sans cesse appelé à la connaissance de soi." Human self-knowledge is a ceaseless, constantly checkmated, unfinishable task for thinking because being human undeniably reaches back to an unconscious, unthought-unthinkable abyssal opening of murmuring darkness, the unfathomable Other, which inevitably keeps silently receding as one approaches *le vide de l'origine, la déchirure*.[37] While human studies, but especially counter-sciences like psychoanalysis, ethnology, and hermeneutics are transcendental attempts today to honor the endless oscillation of the ever-elusive, originless origin behind that inscrutable fold (*ce pli*) where one enters life, labor, and language, we need, says Foucault, a mode of thinking hitherto unknown, so radically pure it may come down to "un rire Philosophique—c'est à dire, pour une certain part, silencieux."[38]

Foucault's praxis of genealogy demonstrates his belief that perhaps something new may be dawning: the return of the Same, the new, same gods already foaming up on the mythic Ocean of the future, while the construct of autonomous, cogitative man begins to be erased "comme à la limite de la mer un visage de sable."[39] Foucault would disrupt all teleological, historical narrative into an archaeological diagnostic that makes no pretense at imposing a comprehensive continuity upon the development, meaning, and value of any thing—such order is a tranquilizing, demagogic sham:[40] genealogy strictly documents details of descent and emergence in their isolated, singular, random eventuality.[41] Historical sense, for Foucault, comes not by remembering and patiently retracing past reality but by shunning the violence of would-be objective knowledge and by sporting a carnival counter-memory to parody the past.[42]

---

36 *Les mots et les choses: Une archéologie des sciences humaines* (Paris: Gallimard, 1966), 40–57.

37 *Les mots et les choses*, 334–39, 343–45.

38 *Les mots et les choses*, 431, 347, 349, 353–54.

39 *Les mots et les choses*, 396–398.

40 Michel Foucault, *L'Archéologie du Savoir* [1969], translated by A.M. Sheridan Smith (New York: Pantheon Books, 1972), 14.

41 "Foucault, Nietzsche, genealogy, history" [1971] in *Language, Counter-Memory, Practice*, ed. Donald Bouchard, translated by D.F. Bouchard and S. Simon (Ithaca: Cornell University Press, 1977), 139–40, 145–48, 152–57.

42 "Nietzsche, genealogy, history," 161–64.

Landmarks and premonitions

Time fails for me to tell of others in the cloud of witnesses for mythologizing philosophy. Walter Benjamin's aphoristic theses on the philosophy of history deny any progressive or cumulative history through time but treasure Messianic eruptions of truth (*Jetztzeit*). And Benjamin tried to save baroque German *Trauerspiele* posthumously by delineating their *acedia* (in 1924–25) as an opening through which the Messiah might enter.[43]

Since every text is a pretext for Jacques Derrida, the formidable, interminable commentaries under his name disseminate originally strategic deconstructions of any and every logocentric set-up,[44] but also, for example, breathe backhanded support for Artaud's *théâtre de cruauté* (a kind of organized Dionysian anarchy where dreams are on a par with life awake). The alchemy of Artaud's gestural, primal scream theatre, not pacified by the word, according to the Derrida text, is its awakening a non-transcendental, sacred experience of divine cruelty that attends the origination of life.[45]

Jean Baudrillard identifies the aim of his cultural theory on the hyperreality of media simulation, where referents actually disappear, as a certain kind of Manichaeism.[46]

Given the presence of a post-Rationalist, skeptical spirit of brilliant gamesmanship in Western academic circles, and a cultural dynamic for annihilating not only the idols of security Francis Bacon targeted in the 1600s AD, but the very fabric of a universe, an integral order for things, a grounded meaning for human nature after Auschwitz and Hiroshima, the unity of history mediated by Jesus Christ; and given the incredible on-going vaporization and trivialization of urban societal life under the technocratic wile of functionaries in the institutionalized media, along with a concomitant worldwide, unnerving surge of marginalized peoples like women, nonwhites, and the poor who are driven, if not greedy, to hold power: one may expect the attempted remytholigization of our thoroughly secularized age.[47] An agnostic culture loses direction and mo-

---

43 Walter Benjamin, "Theses on the philosophy of history" [1940/1950], translated by Harry Zohn, in *Illuminations* (New York: Schocken, 1969), Theses xiv, xviii, A, B.

44 Jacques Derrida, "Interview" in *Diacritica* 3 (Winter, 1972): 36–7, 39–41.

45 Derrida, "The theatre of cruelty and the closure of representation" [1966] in *Writing and Difference,* translated by Alan Bass (University of Chicago Press, 1978), 239–43, 248–50, 332–33 n15.

46 Baudrillard, *The Evil Demon of Images* [1984] (University of Sydney: Power Institute Publications, 1988), 43–46, 50–51.

47 "No period since the early Renaissance has been more concerned with, has addressed

tivation: myths give humans orientation, and therefore empower a person to act (we must not forget that ideologies couch or serve as secular myths.).[48]

Mythologizing philosophy is marked by (1) an undisguised admission of the human transcendental need to be related to an *Arché* other than one's human positivities. Anaximander, the Gnostics, Heidegger, or Foucault assume an ontogenetic setting and try to affirm the sovereign Origin not with a rational metaphysical specificity so much as by an imaginative gesture. Theosophy, not theology, reigns. Mythologizing philosophy is also always marked by (2) a vivid recognition of implacable evil. Hesiod, Marcion, Böhme, or Baudrillard know reality lies under a curse and inhuman powers struggle for domination. Although the biblical conception of sin has been evacuated, because the dimension of personal responsible disobedience is missing, there remains the conviction of violation, victimization, destruction, and ruin, as if somehow constitutive of reality there is no theodicy; in fact, God and godly cohorts are likely to be blamed for the perennial misery of our World.

Mythologizing philosophy is marked by (3) the aura of oracle. A founding prophet, like Zarathustra, and a penchant for orality are usually present and conjure up the temper of enigmatic, hidden truths with transformative powers. Whether it is the ardent Pythagorean cult and number magic, the Manichaean fellowship, Paracelsus, Johann Georg Hamann, or Derrida, oral speech is taken to be pivotal; disciples receiving the spoken word from the lips of the master or guru bathe the tenets and mode of reflection in a holy stillness. Adherents become a lodge, a kind of close-knit secret society. Mythologizing philosophy, finally, is marked by (4) the impress of believing in the overwhelming reality of change as following a cyclical process, the periodic circle of genesis, expiration, and regeneration. The cosmogony of eternal return of the Same that is found in Taoism, Nietzsche, and Foucault leaves their thought curiously floating, drifting away from the dated/located nature of his-

---

itself more insistently to, the nature of the mythical than our own. Remythologization in a time which has found agnostic secularism more or less unendurable may, in future, be seen as defining the spirit of the age." George Steiner, *Real Presences* (University of Chicago Pres, 1989), 221.

48 "...dat het mythologiseerende denken tot de vroegst phase der philsophie beperkt bleef, is m.i. niet houdbaar: eer dergelijke struisvogelpolitiek stelt den betrokkene telkens voor ongedachte situaties—men denke aan de bevreemding van menigeen bij de doorbraak der nationaal-socialistische ideologie..." Vollenhoven, *Geschiedenis der Wijsbegeerte* 1:45.

torical succession.[49] If you think in the circularity of the eternal return, life receives an enchantment of sorts—your life is charmed—and while today may be the end of art, the end of theory, the end of history, the end of the world, it is simultaneously the new age.

To complete the characterization of mythologizing philosophy I have given, I would need to enter caveats as one rightly notices individual peculiarities and emphases in specific thinkers. But let me conclude with a couple of provocative judgments on why I think a move in the coming generation of thinkers to mythologizing philosophy would entail philosophical closure, historical regression, and not be good.

(1) While the Rationalistic pieties of Western theo-teleo-ontological culture are basically worn out and discredited, theosophical pieties remain disconcertingly uncertain. To receive oracles from *das Ganz Andere* or its chosen emissaries closes off critical reflection and stymies gritty analysis for shaping cultural life, because authoritative riddles, like *koans*, admit of no solution—they are meant to mystify, to disciple you, to initiate you into *esoteria*, not direct you on how to order your priorities. Just because human reason has betrayed our confidence does not mean human imagination deserves unquestioning trust.

(2) To gloss over evil as *privation boni* has been an unconscionable intellectualist legerdemain, but to give evil an ontic foothold in reality is to invite the demonic to take up residence in the world. The wonderful goodness of creaturehood—the amazing miracle of tidal waters, earthworms, rock crystals, thumbs, a friend, forgiveness—creaturely marvels have been deeply disturbed historically, often perverted, but the presence of evil remains a surd, or one jeopardizes sanity.

(3) To make a success story out of the rise and fall of civilization would indeed be a fairy tale, even if you believe it. But to profess the discontinuous recurrence of random events and the absurdity of historical conjunctions one can build on, and the advent of a final judgment, beckons one into a labyrinth of monsters and forfeiture of humanity because without the funded underground of traditions carried over into the present, one generation's task toward posterity is neither limited nor able to be held and accountable, and inhumanity is at the door.[50]

---

49 "This eternal return reveals ontology uncontaminated by time and becoming." Mircea Eliade, *The Myth of the Eternal Return* [1949], translated by Willard R. Trask (Princeton University Press, 1974), 89.

50 "Darum stellt Tradition heute vor einen unauflöslichen Widerspruch. Keine ist gegenwärtig, und zu beschwören; ist aber eine jegliche ausgelöscht, so beginnt der Einmarsch in die Unmenschlichkeit." Theodor Adorno, "Über Tradition" [1966] in *Ohne Leitbild. Parva Aesthetica* (Frankfurt: Suhrkamp, 1979), 35.

The cure for the ills of Humanism is not inhumanity any more than a good antidote for Rationalism is skepsis or nihilism. As the Beast slouches toward Bethlehem, Toronto, or Pretoria, to quote Yeats, the fact that mythologizing philosophers are busy, like the legendary Penelope, unraveling nights what was skillfully woven and knotted during the day, is not much comfort, even if carried on with Sisyphean pluck. In its attempt to reinvest secular thinking with a post-Christian spirituality, mythologizing philosophy cannot help but be syncretistic, atavistic, somehow too late, and therefore conservatistically ruthless in its singleminded attempt to exorcise falsity and invoke meaning, because "spirituality" that lacks the biblically revealed ingredients of grace is, I believe, not winsome but as harsh as the pagan "sacred."

If we love our neighbor as we respect ourselves, we do well to understand the terrible attraction and plight of mythologizing philosophy in our day, and then we find an alternative for our bankrupt culture of colliding wills and brutal acts, an alternative that will offer wisdom of self-sacrificing mercy, also in our thinking.

Revisiting Stonehenge while lecturing for a week-long "Faith and Learning Seminar" of Seventh-Day Adventist professors from around the world, organized by Umberto Rasi, at Newbold College, Berkshire, England, 1994

The William Hogarth image on page 190 is in the public domain.

The graphics on pages 192, 286, 292, 296, and 305 were done by Ana Feliciano; the one on page 4 by Willem Hart.

Index

aesthetics, christian philosophical 17, 19, 188

aesthetics, theological 17-9, 114, 124

aesthetic taste-judgment 243, 321, 332-6, 339-41

allusivity 19, 188

amnesia, cultural 68, 71, 74, 184, 265, 267-8

apologetics 18, 123, 176, 211, 225, 231-4, 274

Aristotle 31-4, 138, 178, 184-6, 205-6, 213, 219, 288

artistry 18-9, 53-4, 118, 188-9

atheist, wanted: 179

authority 6, 17, 34, 91, 122, 137, 156, 166-7, 185, 200, 214, 216, 221, 246, 251, 263, 289; see tradition(s)

Babel 132-3, 138, 141-2, 144; 175

Babylon(ian) 52, 60-1, 133, 143, 163, 169-71, 287, 307, 344, 350

the beautiful and sublime, (Kant:) feeling for 317, 330, 332-5, 339, 341

beauty 19, 114, 237, 331-3, 338, 341

Calvin, J. 4-9, 13, 22-3, 29, 49, 87-8, 97, 113, 120, 145, 184, 187, 200, 315

Carvill, B. 133, 145, 147, 196

Cassirer, E. 201, 217, 301-13

change 51, 89, 111, 231, 286, 293, 343, 346-9

  significant 47, 222, 226-7, 254-6, 259-64, 281, 349

christian education 86, 88-90, 93-5, 99-100, 110

  college 1-2, 9-13, 17, 20-2, 140, 175, 177-8

  university 38, 42-3, 50, 53-4, 92, 96, 98-102, 193-4, 197

christian philosophy 3-4, 9, 13-7, 19-20, 23, 27, 43-6, 48, 50, 121, 123-4, 174-8, 180-1, 196, 199, 208-9, 211, 225, 231-2, 244, 315

Christ, body of 2, 5-6, 13, 18, 64-5, 118, 134, 203-4, 211, 213, 224-5, 228, 233, 255; i.e., the faithful people of God

church 6, 15-6, 66, 119, 124, 154, 162, 166, 186, 189, 193, 250; see Christ, body of

  Reformed 10, 88, 187, 194,

  denomination(al) 11, 36, 88, 176

  institutional 98, 225, 243

  Roman (Catholic) 34, 89, 97, 185, 249, 252, 288-9, 292, 295, 350

CLAC (Christian Labour Association of Canada) 154-71

clay jars 184, 191-2

college 20-1, 27; see christian education

conceptual pattern 318, 330-1, 333, 336, 340-1

consciousness-setting 10, 51, 63, 65-6, 86, 90, 99-100, 112, 117, 119

cosmonomic idea(s) 200, 202, 204, 206, 208

cultural dynamics 46, 115, 117, 140, 355

Cusanus, N. 311, 318

Derrida, J. 265-6, 355

devil(s) 6, 75, 100, 110, 163, 235, 239

dialogue 209, 231, 237, 252, 258

differentiation 29, 55, 66, 89, 94-6,174, 191, 214-22, 225-9, 231, 274

  undifferentiated society 216-7

direction, spirited 109-10, 115-7, 254, 260

distinctions, making 90, 174, 215, 245

diversity 42, 45-6, 56, 229

  creatural 41, 44, 133-4, 142, 144-5

  cultural 226, 230

dogma 16, 218, 288, 299, 308, , 337

dogmatic theology 15-6, 45-6, 108, 176, 225

Dooyeweerd, H. 3-4, 13-4, 94-7, 114, 176, 191, 194, 199-209, 211, 213-31, 242, 274-5, 280, 315

doxological acts 54, 147-8

Eckhart, Meister 250, 288-94, 309, 312-13

faith 5, 18, 36, 41, 74, 92, 167,-8 186-7, 225, 307

  christian 4, 6, 10, 39, 45, 100, 113-